Assessing the Quality of Democracy

A *Journal of Democracy* Book

•

Published under the auspices of
the International Forum for Democratic Studies

Assessing the Quality of Democracy

Edited by *Larry Diamond and Leonardo Morlino*

The Johns Hopkins University Press

Baltimore

9 8 7 6 5 4 3 2 1

Chapters 1–6 in this volume appeared in the October 2004 issue of the *Journal of Democracy*. For all reproduction rights, please contact the Johns Hopkins University Press.

The Johns Hopkins University Press
2715 North Charles Street
Baltimore, Maryland 21218-4363
www.press.jhu.edu

Library of Congress Cataloging-in-Publication Data

Assessing the quality of democracy / edited by Larry Diamond and Leonardo Morlino.
    p. cm. — (Journal of democracy book)
"Began with a conference at Stanford University in October of 2003, and many of the papers were subsequently presented at two different panels at the 2004 Annual Meeting of the American Political Science Association"—Ack.
Includes bibliographical references and index.
    ISBN 0-8018-8286-9 (hardcover : alk. paper) — ISBN 0-8018-8287-7 (pbk. : alk. paper)
    1. Democracy—Congresses. 2. Comparative government—Congresses.
I. Diamond, Larry Jay. II. Morlino, Leonardo, 1947– III. American Political Science Association. Meeting (2004 : Chicago, Ill.) IV. Series.

    JC423.A793 2005
    321.8—dc22

                           2005019365

A catalog record for this book is available from the British Library.

CONTENTS

ACKNOWLEDGMENTS

Assessing the Quality of Democracy is the seventeenth *Journal of Democracy* book published by the Johns Hopkins University Press. While most of our early books focused on the problems of emerging and less-developed democracies (such as nationalism and ethnic conflict, economic reform, and civil-military relations), this book (like our recent volumes on horizontal accountability, globalization, and political parties) reflects the growing interest of the *Journal of Democracy* in the challenges and problems confronting both the advanced democracies and those of the developing and postcommunist worlds. Perhaps more than any of our previous works, this book sets forth an analytic framework that is meant to apply to all the world's democracies. Furthermore, it presents paired case-study comparisons from every major region of the world where democracies can be found: Western Europe (representing all the advanced democracies), Eastern Europe, Latin America, South Asia, East Asia, and sub-Saharan Africa.

This book began with a conference at Stanford University in October of 2003, and many of the papers were subsequently presented at two different panels at the 2004 Annual Meeting of the American Political Science Association. We are grateful to Stanford's Center on Democracy, Development, and the Rule of Law for hosting the original conference. We owe a particularly large debt to Leonardo Morlino, coeditor of this volume, who first proposed the idea of a *Journal of Democracy* book on this subject, crafted the original conceptual and comparative framework for the conference, and organized it together with Larry Diamond. We want also to thank the first two directors of the Center, Coit D. Blacker and Stephen Krasner, for their support of the conference and the project.

The production of this book involved demanding tasks of editing, production, and design. We pay special tribute here to the outgoing managing editor of the *Journal of Democracy,* Maureen Malone Wellman, who coordinated the production and design, set the text, tables, and figures for the chapters, and kept the project on schedule with extraordinary efficiency, precision, grace, and good humor. This was

Maureen's last major project as *Journal* managing editor and we will miss her skill and dedication. As with the chapters in all of our previous books, the ones here have benefited from the outstanding work of a very talented group of *Journal* editors—Phil Costopoulos, Anja Håvedal, Sumi Shane, and Zerxes Spencer—and of two former *Journal* editors, Jordan Branch and Annette Theuring, who were temporarily "recalled to duty" to assist with the editing of some of the comparative case studies. Jordan Branch had also earlier helped with the editing of the originally very long essay of Guillermo O'Donnell. We're especially grateful to Zerxes Spencer and Joseph Tucker for stepping in at a late stage to produce a first-rate index.

Each one of the *Journal* books has owed a debt to a number of people and institutions that have supported the *Journal* since its inception in 1990. We want to extend again our heartfelt thanks to the Lynde and Harry Bradley Foundation for its continuing financial support, and to our parent organization, the National Endowment for Democracy (NED), its Board of Directors, and our dear friend and colleague Carl Gershman, the longtime president of NED and one of the most enthusiastic readers and promoters of the *Journal*.

Finally, we are deeply gratified to have had the opportunity to work over the past sixteen years with the Johns Hopkins University Press, the fine team in its journals division, and a splendid executive editor in its book division, Henry Tom, whose creativity, judgment, and consummate professionalism have had much to do with the remarkable success of our book series.

–Marc F. Plattner and Larry Diamond

INTRODUCTION

Larry Diamond and Leonardo Morlino

As democracy has spread over the past three decades to a majority of the world's states, analytic attention has turned increasingly from explaining regime transitions to evaluating and explaining the character of democratic regimes. Much of the democracy literature of the 1990s was concerned with the consolidation of democratic regimes.[1] In recent years, social scientists as well as democracy practitioners and aid agencies have sought to develop means of framing and assessing the quality of democracy. This stream of theory, methodological innovation, and empirical research has three broad motives: First, that deepening democracy is a moral good, if not an imperative; second, that reforms to improve democratic quality are essential if democracy is to achieve the broad and durable legitimacy that marks consolidation;[2] and third, that long-established democracies must also reform if they are to attend to their own gathering problems of public dissatisfaction and even disillusionment.

In fact, these latter trends—the broad decline of public confidence in governmental and political institutions, the growing citizen alienation from political parties in particular, and the widespread perceptions that democratic governments and politicians are increasingly corrupt, self-interested and unresponsive—are common to many democracies, new and old, and have even led prominent scholars to speak of a "crisis of democracy."[3] Touching as it does on basic questions of norms and legitimacy, the quality of democracy is a value-laden and hence controversial subject. Who is to define what constitutes a "good" democracy, and to what extent is a universal conception of democratic quality possible? How can the effort to address deficiencies of democracy avoid becoming paternalistic exercises in which the established democracies take themselves for granted as models and so escape scrutiny? How can assessments of democratic quality go beyond mere analytics and be useful to political reformers, civil society activists, international donors, and others who seek to improve the quality of democracy? These are only some of the questions that pervade and motivate this growing subfield of study.

The five thematic essays that make up the first section of this book are part of a collaborative effort, launched at a conference at Stanford University, to elaborate and refine the concept of democratic quality. The section's concluding essay, by Marc F. Plattner, develops critical comments he offered at that conference. The authors of the five thematic essays were each asked to define and articulate a particular dimension of the quality of democracy, to explain how it relates to other dimensions in our framework, to suggest possible indicators for measuring the dimension, to identify ways in which this element of democratic quality is subverted in the real world (and how these subversions can be empirically detected), and to offer (where possible) policy recommendations for reform and improvement of democratic quality. As we explain below, we do not assert that these five conceptual dimensions—rule of law, vertical accountability, responsiveness, freedom, and equality—fully constitute the quality of democracy. The framework we outline below in fact has eight dimensions, including as well participation, competition, and horizontal accountability. Others could be identified as well, transparency and the effectiveness of representation, for example. The different aspects of democratic quality overlap, however, and we choose to treat these latter two as elements of our principal dimensions. In fact, the more we enumerate distinct dimensions, the denser and more complex the overlaps become.

We attempt here to identify some of the ways in which the different elements of democracy not only overlap but also depend upon one another. In identifying these different linkages, we suggest that democratic quality can be thought of as a system, in which improvement in one dimension can have diffuse benefits for others (and vice versa). At the same time, however, there are sometimes tradeoffs between the different dimensions of democratic quality, and it is impossible to achieve each of them to the maximum degree. This is one respect in which each democratic state must make an inherently value-laden choice about what *kind* of democracy it wishes to be.

We begin by offering brief definitions of the terms "democracy" and "quality," and we then suggest how these two concepts can be integrated into a multidimensional conception of democratic quality. In the main body of the paper, we define and analyze eight different dimensions of democratic quality. We then reflect further on the linkages and interactions among them. Finally, we review how the six case studies employ and illuminate our analytic framework.

"Democracy" and "Quality"

To analyze the quality of democracy, and to identify what is "good" democracy, we must first define what democracy is. At a minimum, democracy requires: 1) universal adult suffrage; 2) recurring, free, competitive, and fair elections; 3) more than one serious political party; and 4) alternative sources of information.[4] If elections are to be truly meaningful, free, and fair, there must be some degree of civil and political freedom beyond the electoral arena, permitting citizens to articulate and organize around their political beliefs and interests.[5] In addition, formal democratic institutions should be sovereign—that is, they should not be constrained by elites or external powers that are not directly or indirectly accountable to the people.[6] Once a regime meets these basic conditions, further empirical analysis can assess how well it achieves the three main goals of an ideal democracy—political and civil freedom, popular sovereignty (control over public policies and the officials who make them), and political equality (in these rights and powers)—as well as broader standards of good governance, such as transparency, legality, and responsible rule.[7]

Thus, the analysis of a good democracy should exclude hybrid or "electoral authoritarian" regimes, which by failing to conduct free and fair elections fall short of an essential requirement for democracy.[8] By definition, we will find the quality of democracy quite low in *defective democracies,* which are "exclusive" in offering only limited guarantees for political rights, or "dominated" in allowing powerful groups to condition and limit the autonomy of elected leaders, or "illiberal" in the inadequacy of their protections for civil rights and the rule of law.[9] We can also expect the quality of democracy to be quite deficient in *delegative democracies,* which have electoral competitiveness and relative civil and political freedom, but whose officials, once elected, are only minimally responsive to citizen preferences, constrained by other agencies of government, and respectful of the rule of law.[10]

A second step in evaluating democratic quality requires a clear definition of "quality." A survey of the use of the term in the industrial and marketing sectors suggests three different meanings of quality, each with different implications for empirical research:

• *Procedure:* A "quality" product is the result of an exact, controlled process carried out according to precise, recurring methods and timing;

• *Content:* Quality inheres in the structural characteristics of a product, such as its design, materials, or functioning; and

• *Result:* The quality of a product or service is indirectly indicated by the degree of customer satisfaction with it, regardless of how it is produced or its actual content.

What Is a "Quality" Democracy?

Starting from the definitions above, we consider a quality democracy to be one that provides its citizens a high degree of freedom, political equality, and popular control over public policies and policy makers through the legitimate and lawful functioning of stable institutions. A good democracy is thus first a broadly legitimated regime that satisfies citizen expectations of governance (quality in terms of *result*). Second, a good democracy is one in which its citizens, associations, and communities enjoy extensive liberty and political equality (quality in terms of *content*). Third, in a good democracy the citizens themselves have the sovereign power to evaluate whether the government provides liberty and equality according to the rule of law. Citizens and their organizations and parties participate and compete to hold elected officials accountable for their policies and actions. They monitor the efficiency and fairness of the application of the laws, the efficacy of government decisions, and the political responsibility and responsiveness of elected officials. Governmental institutions also hold one another accountable before the law and the constitution (quality in terms of *procedure*).

With the above in mind, we identify eight dimensions on which democracies vary in quality. The first five are procedural dimensions: the rule of law, participation, competition, and accountability, both vertical and horizontal. Though also quite relevant to the content, these dimensions mainly concern the rules and practices.[11] The next two dimensions of variation are substantive in nature: respect for civil and political freedoms and the progressive implementation of greater political (and underlying it, social and economic) equality. Our last dimension, responsiveness, links the procedural dimensions to the substantive ones by measuring the extent to which public policies (including laws, institutions, and expenditures) correspond to citizen demands and preferences, as aggregated through the political process. These eight dimensions are elaborated below.[12] Each may vary in the specific form of its institutional expression, and in its degree of development. Capturing and explaining this variation requires indicators that reveal how and to what degree each dimension is present in different countries, and in different models of a good democracy. The resulting empirical data will also make it possible to track trends in the quality of democracy in individual countries over time, including the effectiveness of institutional reforms.[13]

The multidimensional nature of our framework, and of the growing number of democracy assessments being conducted in individual countries, implies a pluralist notion of democratic quality. As we note below, there are not only dense linkages, but also tradeoffs and tensions among the various dimensions of democratic quality, and democracies will differ in the normative weights they place on the various dimensions of democratic quality (for example, freedom versus responsiveness). There is no objective way of identifying a single framework for measuring democratic quality, one that would be right and true for all societies.

The analytical framework proposed here partially differs somewhat from other studies on the quality of democracy, such as that of David

Altman and Aníbal Pérez-Liñán and that of Arend Lijphart.[14] While both of these studies develop a quantitative comparative strategy for empirical analysis, we emphasize the virtuous combination of qualitative and quantitative measures. Some difference also emerges in our definition of a good democracy and consequently in the dimensions and the related indicators. Altman and Pérez-Liñán refer to three aspects of quality—civil rights, participation, and competition—drawing on Dahl's concept of polyarchy. Lijphart includes indicators such as female representation, electoral participation, satisfaction with democracy, and corruption; these indicators can be associated with four of our dimensions—equality, participation, responsiveness, and rule of law, respectively.

The institutions and mechanisms of representative democracy are the main objects of the analysis of democratic quality. This is not to ignore direct democracy as perhaps the purest expression of democratic quality, but to acknowledge the actual experience of representative democracies and their real potential for improvement. As the analysis has to be focused on representative democracies, (vertical) accountability becomes a truly central dimension in so much as it grants individual citizens and organized civil society actors means of control over politicians and political institutions. In a good democracy, this feature attenuates the difficulties that emerge out of the shift from direct to representative democracy.

Vertical accountability is implicitly based on two assumptions from the liberal tradition that highlight the interconnectedness of all of the dimensions explained above. The first assumption is that if citizens are genuinely given the opportunity to evaluate the government's performance, they are in fact capable of doing so, possessing above all a relatively accurate perception of their own needs and preferences. The second assumption is that citizens, either alone or as part of a group, are the only possible judges of their own interests and needs. Generally, we accept these assumptions, though they are debatable; as Dietrich Rueschemeyer notes in his essay on equality, those actors with more wealth and cultural capital have disproportionate influence over citizen policy preferences.

Freedom and equality, however they are understood, are necessarily linked to accountability and responsiveness. Indeed, provision of freedom and equality is one standard by which citizens may assess the performance of their political leaders and representative institutions. In addition, an effective rule of law is also indispensable for a good democracy, in part because it guarantees—at least through the mechanism of a politically neutral and independent judiciary—the defense of citizens' rights and equal status before the law and in the political arena. As the next section will explain, freedom, equality, and even accountability are unobtainable if respect for law is ineffective or if the elected government cannot govern authoritatively. These are the fundamental presuppositions necessary for identifying and implementing reforms to improve the quality of democracy.

Procedural Dimensions of Democratic Quality

We are now ready to explore more concretely our eight dimensions of democratic quality. For each of them, we provide an empirical definition, explore the conditions under it develops and thrives, and the means by which it is commonly subverted. We begin in this section with the five procedural dimensions.

The Rule of Law. As Guillermo O'Donnell explains, the rule of law means that all citizens are equal before the law, and that the laws themselves are clear, publicly known, universal, stable, non-retroactive, and fairly and consistently applied to all citizens by an independent judiciary. These characteristics are fundamental for any civil order and a basic requirement for democratic consolidation, along with other cognate features of a constitutional order—such as civilian control over the military and the intelligence services, and an elaborate network of other agencies of horizontal accountability complementing the judiciary.

We do not consider here a basic or "thin" notion of rule of the law, that is, a rule of law characterized by civil order maintained by governmental actors with a monopoly on violence. In the democratic context, the "thick" notion is more relevant: Thus, a "good" (or in essence, a liberal) democracy has a strong, vigorous, diffuse, and self-sustaining rule of law in the following respects:

• The law is equally enforced toward everyone, including state officials; no one is above the law;

• The legal state is supreme throughout the country, leaving no areas dominated by organized crime, local oligarchs, or political bosses who are above the law;

• Corruption is minimized, detected, and punished, in the political, administrative, and judicial branches of the state;

• At all levels, the state bureaucracy applies the laws competently, efficiently, and universally, and assumes responsibility in the event of an error;

• The police force is professional, efficient, and respectful of individuals' legally guaranteed rights and freedoms, including rights of due process;

• Citizens have equal and unhindered access to the courts to defend their rights and to contest lawsuits between private citizens or between private citizens and public institutions;

• Criminal cases and civil and administrative lawsuits are heard and resolved expeditiously;

- The judiciary at all levels is neutral and independent from any political influence;
- Rulings of the courts are respected and enforced by other agencies of the state; and
- The constitution is supreme, and is interpreted and defended by a constitutional court.

What further distinguishes and completes a democratic rule of law, O'Donnell argues, is that the legal system defends the democratic procedures, upholds citizens' civil and political rights, and reinforces the authority of other agencies of horizontal accountability.

It may seem odd to begin elucidating democratic quality with the rule of law, as the existence of several dozen illiberal democracies in the world attests to the possibility for competitive elections and popular participation to coexist with considerable lawlessness and abuse of power.[15] Nevertheless, the rule of law is the base upon which every other dimension of democratic quality rests. When the rule of law is weak, participation of the poor and marginalized is suppressed; individual freedoms are tenuous and fleeting; civic groups may be unable to organize and advocate; the resourceful and well connected have vastly more access to justice and power; corruption and abuse of power run rampant as agencies of horizontal accountability are unable to function properly; political competition is distorted and unfair; voters have a hard time holding rulers to account; and thus, linkages vital to securing democratic responsiveness are disrupted and severed.

The above aspects concern in large measure the impartial and efficient application of the law and the fair resolution of disputes within the legal system. Each of these aspects can be gauged by means of various indicators, and the relevant data can be analyzed on a case-by-case basis using both qualitative and quantitative techniques. Of course, a detailed assessment of judicial fairness and efficiency would be extremely expensive and difficult to apply to a high number of cases. Nonetheless, one can examine across many cases the degree to which public officials are responsible before the law, or enjoy relative impunity; the extent of official corruption, as measured (quite roughly and imprecisely, to be sure) by indices of perceptions of corruption and market distortions; the extent of civil-liberty violations; the access of citizens to the court system; and the average duration of legal proceedings.

The ways in which the rule of law may be subverted in a democracy are myriad. For example, politicians may use the law as a "political weapon" against their political and civic adversaries;[16] and democratically elected leaders may attempt to pack the judiciary (particularly the constitutional court) with political loyalists. Moreover, there is a growing tendency among individual citizens or economic interest groups to use the courts to assert their own interests (as opposed to strictly defending against illegal actions). The political culture also plays an important role in sustaining or undermining the rule of law: A democratic rule of law is diminished in many countries by the diffuse cultural attitude that views the law merely as an impediment to realizing one's own interests, a nuisance to be circumvented in any way possible. In many countries, this attitude extends widely from the popular to the entrepreneurial classes and is captured by the Italian saying, *fatta la legge, trovato l'inganno* (fraud goes hand in hand with law).

Research suggests that the fundamental conditions aiding the development of the rule of law are the diffusion of liberal and democratic values among both the people and, especially, the elite; strong bureaucratic traditions of competence and impartiality; and the institutional and economic means for fully implementing a rule of law. These conditions are not all that common, however, and they are very difficult to create from scratch—hence, the weakness of the rule of law in many recently established democracies (and in a number of older ones, as well).

The literature on rule-of-law development is sobering. The best approach is probably to proceed incrementally to build up the independence, capacity, and authority of the entire judicial system. No amount of training and financial resources (including generous external assistance) will suffice unless democratic leaders exhibit both political will and self-restraint. This in turn requires a mobilized and aware civil society, and efficient democratic instruments of competition so that voters can remove public officials who obstruct rule-of-law reforms.

Participation. No regime can be a democracy unless it grants all of its adult citizens formal rights of political participation, including the right to vote. But a *good* democracy must ensure that all citizens are in fact able to make use of these formal rights by allowing them to vote, organize, assemble, protest, lobby for their interests, and otherwise influence the decision-making process. With regard to the dimension of participation, democratic quality is high when citizens participate in the political process not only by voting, but by joining political parties and civil society organizations, partaking in the discussion of public-policy issues, communicating with and demanding accountability from elected representatives, monitoring the conduct of public office-holders, and engaging in public issues at the local community level.

Participation in these respects is intimately related to political equality, because even if formal rights of participation are upheld for all, inequalities in political resources can make it much more difficult for lower-status individuals to exercise their democratic rights of participation. Thus a fundamental condition for widespread participation is broad diffusion of basic education and literacy, and with it political knowledge of the system of government, its procedures, rules, issues, parties, and leaders. Important again, as a supporting condition, is the political culture, which should value participation and the equal worth and dignity of all citizens. The latter implies tolerance of political and social differences, and thus acceptance on the part of all individuals and organized groups of the right of others (including their adversaries) to participate equally, so long as they obey the law. Finally, extensive participation also requires a rule of law that will defend the right and ability of weaker social groups to participate fully.

Participation is subverted and constrained in a variety of subtle and overt ways in democracies around the world. A common subversion comes through the apathy of a citizenry that doubts the efficacy of democratic mechanisms or has become alienated from the democratic process as a result of the low quality of democracy in other respects (for example, corruption, abuse of power, and a lack of competitiveness). Of course, such systemic flaws can, under the right conditions of popular outrage and effective civic mobilization, generate *increases* in participation, but in the absence of viable reform alternatives, they induce civic withdrawal. Participation may be constrained by conditions of lawlessness and violence that make it risky for citizens to organize, assemble, or even to vote. To preserve their own entrenched privileges, powerful groups may, by means of intimidation and victimization, suppress the political influence of the poor, the landless, as well as ethnic, regional, and religious minorities. Participation is most commonly measured by voter turnout rates, but this captures only one aspect of democratic participation. No less important are the extent of membership and active participation in political parties, social movements, and nongovernmental organizations; the frequency of communication with elected representatives and other office-holders; and the extent to which citizens express themselves on public issues.

Competition. In order to be a democracy at all, a political system must have regular, free, and fair electoral competition between different political parties. But democracies vary in their degree of competitiveness—in the openness of access to the electoral arena by new political forces, in the ease with which incumbents can be defeated, and in the equality of access to the mass media and campaign funding on the part of competing political parties. Depending on the type of electoral system, democracies may also allow for more or less decisive alternation of power. Here we confront a tradeoff within the overall goal of competition: Electoral systems based on proportional representation score well on one element of competitiveness—ease of access to the electoral arena and parliament on the part of multiple political parties—but at the expense of another element of competitiveness—the ease of alternation of power (or the efficiency of the electoral process). The latter is true because the presence of multiple parties with relatively defined shares of the vote tends to produce a succession of coalition governments that gain considerable continuity in party composition over time.[17] There is no objective, *a priori* way to determine from this respect alone which electoral system produces a higher quality democracy, though Lijphart argues that proportional representation (PR) does a better job of fulfilling other dimensions of democratic quality, such as the more equal representation of women and minorities.

One condition for vigorous competition is the legal and constitutional order. In contemporary democracies, political-party and campaign finance is such an important foundation of electoral viability that it is difficult for challenging parties and candidates to compete effectively without some fair minimum in this regard. While there is considerable skepticism about the efficacy of laws that limit campaign spending, in part because of the ease with which they are evaded in new and old democracies alike, some floor of public funding for significant parties and robust requirements for the reporting of all contributions to parties and campaigns do seem to promote greater electoral fairness and competitiveness.[18] In first-past-the-post systems, the means by which electoral districts are drawn also heavily shape competitiveness. Where partisan bodies are able to draw electoral districts to their own advantage (as in the United States, where such gerrymandering is performed every decade by state legislatures, with the aid of increasingly sophisticated computer programs), they are likely to do so in ways that will promote partisan and incumbency advantage. As a result, elections to the U.S. House of Representatives have seen the rate of defeat of incumbents steadily decline, and less than 10 percent of House seats are now competitive. Of course, electoral competitiveness also depends on fairness in access to the mass media, pluralism in media ownership (and viewpoints), some dispersion of economic resources in society, and the enforcement of political rights by an independent judiciary. There is also an important linkage with horizontal accountability, because the most important institutional guarantee of freedom and fairness (and hence competitiveness) in elections is an independent and authoritative electoral commission.[19]

Competition can be constrained or subverted through partisan control of the electoral administration, not just the drawing of electoral-district boundaries but the design and enforcement of rules regarding the conduct and financing of campaigns and the administration of the actual vote. Competitiveness can also be diminished by the actions of parties and other nonstate forces that suppress the freedom of different groups and parties to contest for office, or that commit outright electoral fraud. If these subversions become so extensive that the declared electoral outcomes do not represent the will of the people, or if it proves all but impossible to replace the ruling party through elections, the system falls beneath the threshold of democracy into some form of electoral authoritarian rule. But some regimes straddle ambiguously the boundary between low-quality democracy and semi-democracy.

Competition is one dimension of democratic quality that is relatively amenable to quantitative measurement—though no quantitative measure can fully capture the extent of it. Altman and Pérez-Liñán propose an indicator of the "balanced presence of opposition in parliament," which has a negative value when the governing party dominates the legislature in terms of seats or when the opposition is so strong that it poses problems for the decisional efficacy of the government.[20]

Vertical Accountability. Accountability is the obligation of elected political leaders to answer for their political decisions when asked by citizen-electors or other constitutional bodies. Schedler suggests that accountability has three main features: information, justification, and punishment or compensation.[21] Information on the political actions of politicians or branches of government is indispensable for holding them accountable; justification refers to the reasons furnished by the governing leaders for their actions; and punishment or compensation is the consequence imposed by the elector or some other authoritative body following an evaluation of the information, justification, and other aspects and interests behind the political action.

Accountability can be either vertical or horizontal. Vertical accountability is that which citizens as electors can demand from their officials in the course of campaigns and elections, and which political and civil society actors can exercise at moments of political controversy. As Philippe C. Schmitter explains, in modern democracies, elected representatives play a crucial mediating role in the accountability relations between citizens and rulers. This is especially true in parliamentary systems, where elected representatives can bring down the government. But in all democracies, representatives help to share and structure citizen preferences and expectations.

The electoral form of vertical accountability has a periodic nature and is dependent on the various local and national election dates. Ideally, the performance of the incumbent is reviewed and evaluated, policy alternatives are debated, and the voters either reward the incumbents by voting for them, or punish them by voting for an opposition party or abstaining from the vote. As Schmitter notes, the outcome of accountability may just as likely be reward (reelection) as punishment (defeat), for the most accountable leaders are really those whose conduct and decisions conform to citizen expectations as well as to the law. The dynamics of vertical accountability extend beyond elections and the interplay between voters and their elected representatives, encompassing also the efforts of civic associations, NGOs, social movements, think tanks, and the mass media to hold government accountable in between elections. Catalina Smulovitz and Enrique Peruzotti refer to this as "societal accountability."[22]

Political competition and participation are crucial conditions for vertical accountability. If voters are to be able to hold their public officials and ruling parties accountable periodically through elections, they must be engaged, knowledgeable about the issues and the performance of those in power, and they must turn out to vote in large numbers. At the same time, vertical accountability requires genuinely competitive elections, in which institutionally strong parties are able to offer programmatic alternatives to the voters, and in which voters are able to "punish" incumbents for poor performance or unwanted policies. In short, political competition and the distribution of power must be fair and robust enough to allow for genuine alternatives at the various levels of government, and to produce some electoral alternation over time, so that incumbents face a credible threat of electoral punishment. The vertical process of monitoring, questioning, and demanding justification through the work of nongovernmental organizations, think tanks, the mass media, professional associations, interest groups, opposition parties, and other civil society actors requires freedom for these groups to function and a rule of law that protects them from intimidation and retribution.

In both electoral and nonelectoral respects, vertical accountability therefore requires a strong system of horizontal accountability to sustain the rule of law and thus the integrity of these vertical processes. At the same time, it also depends upon strong and well-established intermediary structures; a responsible, vigilant political opposition; independent and pluralistic mass media that are conscious of their civil function; and a well-developed, vigorous, and vigilant democratic civil society.

Vertical accountability is subverted when office holders take advantage of their incumbency to handicap the political opposition, or when they extend control over the media and other actors in civil society to the point that the latter fear to question the incumbents' conduct in office. In the modern era, where mass media in general and television in particular are so vital to political influence and debate, efforts to subdue or eliminate independent, critical media outlets are a common means by which incumbents try to vitiate both the electoral and the civic instruments of vertical accountability.

Beyond these rather blatant and deliberate subversions lie more subtle, intrinsic, and pervasive difficulties in securing political accountability from below. Given the opacity and complexity of government, politicians have ample opportunity to absolve themselves of any concrete responsibility. Thus, accountability frequently becomes a catchphrase more connected to the image of a politician than to decisions made or results achieved. Office-holders often justify negative outcomes by blaming unforeseen events, or by taking advantage of a favorable press to influence public opinion. At the same time, real progress and good results achieved by means of wise and prudent leadership sometimes comes at the cost of temporary sacrifices by those governed; this might lead to office-holders being punished in the next election as a reaction against those sacrifices.

The often ideological and instrumental way that parties and other opposition actors, or even of powerful media actors, operate highlights the difficulty of achieving accountability. The lack of clear distinctions between incumbent leaders and party leaders means that parties, be they of the opposition or of the majority, are hindered in carrying out their role as watchdogs for their constituents. At the parliamentary level, party discipline is considered more important than accountability to the voters and, in most democracies, the parliamentary majority (where it exists) supports the government without really controlling it. If accountability is to be achieved, there needs to be a clear distinction between the responsible leader, either of the government or of the opposition, and the intermediate layers of party actors that range from activists to sympathizers. There needs to be a bottom-up process that gives direction for how parties should control the government or organize their opposition. Yet recent research on party organization in a few advanced democracies shows a trend toward strong, oligarchic leaders who collude—rather than compete—with other parties.[23]

For European citizens, the supranational architecture of the European Union generates additional difficulties in holding national rulers accountable, enabling leaders to blame the EU for unpopular decisions even if they concern clear-cut issues such as streamlining national administrations or reorganizing state finances to address large national deficits. Governments and politicians justify unpopular actions by claiming that their hands were forced by opposing coalitions in the EU Council of Ministers or in the European Council of prime ministers and chiefs of state, or by votes in the European Parliament. A similar tactic is often used—not without justification—by elected governments in developing countries in relation to economic policy constraints imposed by international financial institutions and the World Trade Organization.

Horizontal Accountability. Democratic quality also requires that office-holders are answerable to other institutional actors that have the expertise and legal authority to control and sanction their behavior. In contrast to vertical accountability, the actors are, more or less, political equals. Horizontal accountability is usually manifest in the monitoring, investigating, and enforcement activities of a number of independent government agencies: the opposition in parliament; parliamentary investigative committees; the various tiers of the court system, including, crucially, the constitutional court; audit agencies; counter-corruption commissions; the central bank; an independent electoral administration, the ombudsman, and other bodies that scrutinize and limit the power of those who govern.[24]

The counter-corruption commission is a particularly crucial agency of horizontal accountability in contemporary democracies. To be effective, this body must be charged not only with receiving but also monitoring and verifying the assets declarations of the president or prime minister, cabinet ministers, members of parliament, state or provincial governors, high-level bureaucrats, major military and police officers, and other elected and appointed public officials. A truly comprehensive effort in a large country will also provide for the commission to have branch offices at the provincial level to monitor provincial and local government officials and legislators. The commission must then have the staff to investigate annually on a random basis some significant percentage of these assets declarations, and systematically the declarations of the country's highest officials.

Scrutiny must be comprehensive if it is to be effective, and if the threat of detection is to be credible. This requires a lot of resources: accountants, investigators, and lawyers trained in the ways that wealth is moved, accumulated, and hidden, along with computer specialists and other support staff to back them up. Not only does a counter-corruption commission need a lot of well-trained staff, it needs to pay them enough to deter temptation and establish a high *esprit de corps*.

Scrutiny is not enough, however. If credible evidence of wrongdoing emerges, there must be the institutional means to try the suspected offender and impose punishment on the guilty. The single most common and crippling flaw in systems of corruption control is an inability to enforce this function free from interference by the government. The counter-corruption commission should have the ability to prosecute officials who have allegedly violated ethics laws. One of the most important changes introduced by Thailand's 1997 democratic constitution was to grant the National Counter Corruption Commission independent prosecutorial authority, even if it means overruling the attorney general.[25]

The ombudsman's office (which may go under many names, including, in South Africa, the office of the public protector) receives and investigates public complaints of abuses of office. Members of the public or the press should have a right to—indeed be encouraged to—bring evidence to the counter-corruption commission if they believe a public official has misrepresented his or her assets or abused their office. But democracies need a supplementary channel of public access to remedial government authority if the counter-corruption commission does not pursue its mission, or if it determines that some abuse of power to lie outside its scope of authority. Even if the system is working well, the ombudsman may occasionally come upon evidence that the counter-corruption commission does not have, or that reinforces investigations the commission has already opened. Agencies of horizontal accountability work best when they may be held accountable by one another for failure to do their job.

The powers and functions of the office of the ombudsman vary widely across countries. In some countries, it is simply a mechanism to receive and investigate citizen complaints. The Philippine constitution, however, gives the ombudsman an explicit mandate to fight corruption through public assistance, prevention, investigation, and prosecution of suspect public officials. It can order "any government official or employee remiss in his duties to do his job, or stop, prevent and remedy improper and abusive acts." In the Philippines, this office need not wait for citizens to come forward, and it can act on anonymous complaints. Moreover, it can choose either to refer charges (against lower-ranking officials) to the courts or to prosecute directly.[26] Thus the office combines the more limited functions of an ombudsman with many of those of a counter-corruption commission or even a supreme audit agency.

Independent, systematic audits of public accounts form another crucial link in the web of accountability. Clearly, it is not enough simply to monitor the personal accounts of public officials. A dense, overlapping system of accountability requires that all major government bureaus, agencies, and ministries have their accounts regularly audited, and that they be open to inspection and evaluation of their performance more generally. To conduct these checks, each major government agency or bureau should have its own auditing office and inspector-general. But periodic external audits are also essential. The government should have an office of the auditor-general with the authority to conduct external audits on a periodic or random basis, and audit any agency at any time when there is evidence of wrongdoing. One model is the General Accounting Office of the United States, which is the investigative arm of, and is responsible to, the U.S. Congress—thus giving it substantial autonomy from executive-branch agencies.

Horizontal accountability is most effective when it is comprehensive, that is, when the agencies that comprise it interlock and partially overlap in a systemic fashion. Overlapping authority ensures that if one institutional actor fails to perform its duty to expose, question, and punish—and ultimately deter—corrupt behavior, another institution may initiate the accountability process. Interlocking authority means that the different institutions relate to one another in a way that is complementary and reinforcing, so that, for example, an audit agency can uncover fraud, a counter-corruption commission can impose civil penalties for it, and the judicial process can function on its own to press for criminal penalties, while an ombudsman may stand by to investigate and report if other institutions do not work or to assist and stimulate their work. Guillermo O'Donnell, who is in some ways the intellectual founder of the term and the field of horizontal accountability, argues that "Effective horizontal accountability is not the product of isolated agencies but of networks of agencies that include at their top—because that is where a constitutional legal system 'closes' by means of ultimate decisions—courts (including the highest ones) committed to such accountability."[27]

The vitality of horizontal accountability hinges most of all on a legal system that, as mentioned above, provides for the exertion of checks and balances by public entities that are independent of the government, and not competing as an alternative to it. Such a system begins with the body of law itself (including the constitution), which must provide for strong authority for various governmental institutions to check and monitor one another, while protecting their independence through tenure in office and means of appointment that rise above patronage or partisanship. If the agencies of horizontal accountability—beginning with the courts—are to work, they must have institutional capacity, training, and leadership that is at once capable, vigorous, and responsible. Like the law itself, the agencies of horizontal accountability can be used as a weapon against political opponents, undermining the credibility of the entire institutional network.

One particularly important type of law regards freedom of information. Malfeasance thrives in secrecy and obscurity. The more transparent and visible the government's transactions and operations, the more feasible it is to expose, deter, and contain corruption. For this reason, citizens must have the legal right to request and receive information on all functions and decisions of government that are not a matter of national security or that do not infringe on individual rights of privacy. In the fight against corruption, the public availability of information on government finance, procurement, and contracting is particularly important; ideally, such information should be posted on the Internet. In particular, all government procurement above a certain (modest) level should be done through competitive bidding that is advertised on government Web sites.

Particularly in political systems with a tradition of corruption and abuse of power, where democratic norms are not deeply rooted, agencies of horizontal accountability, like the electoral administration, need constitutional autonomy. There are a number of possible models for this. In Costa Rica, the Supreme Electoral Tribunal is virtually a fourth branch of government, whose members are elected to staggered six-year terms by a two-thirds vote of the Supreme Court. In India, the electoral commission's independence is protected by explicit constitutional mandate, and by a powerful chairman, who is appointed by the nonpartisan president. In some other countries, such independence is attained through supervision by a judicial body or by making agencies accountable to parliament rather than to the executive branch.[28]

Subversion of the institutions of horizontal accountability comes most frequently in the appointment process. If the government is able to appoint politically pliable individuals to head these agencies, their potential to scrutinize, question, challenge, and punish may be largely neutralized from the beginning. Executive actors also attempt to undermine horizontal accountability by limiting the legal authority of these agencies, or making them completely dependent for funding on the budget requests of the executive, or preventing them from pursuing any legal action (including criminal prosecution) save through a ministry of justice that is controlled by a political loyalist.

The Substantive Dimensions: Freedom and Equality

Freedom. Freedom can be seen to consist of three types of rights: political, civil, and social or socioeconomic.[29] Political rights include the rights to vote, to stand for office, to campaign, and to organize political parties. These rights make possible vigorous political participation and competition, hence vertical accountability. But they are not as simple as they seem. As David Beetham explains, a good democracy must ensure that voters can cast their ballots in secret, without coercion or fear, and "with effective choice between candidates and parties" that are able to contest on a level playing field. An even richer version of this right is achieved when citizens can choose the candidates of political parties, through intraparty (primary) elections.

Essential civil rights include personal liberty, security, and privacy; freedom of thought, expression, and information; freedom of religion; freedom of assembly, association, and organization, including the right to form and join trade unions and political parties; freedom of movement and residence; and the right to legal defense and due process. There are also a number of what could be called "civil economic rights," including not only the rights to private property and entrepreneurship, but also the rights associated with employment, the right to fair pay and time off, and the right to collective bargaining.

As the overwhelming majority of democratic legal systems have established this collection of civil rights, there are two primary dimensions that appear to be important for a good democracy. The first pertains to the capacity to enrich the legacy of rights and freedoms enjoyed by citizens without limiting or damaging others. The second concerns the actual procedures by which these rights are granted to all residents in a certain area. This latter takes us back to the issues of efficiency that were raised in the discussion on the rule of law. For example, the right to a legal defense entails the right to due process, to a speedy trial, and to legal assistance regardless of one's economic means. Although the overlapping of such rights appears messy and less-than-elegant from a theoretical point of view, it is inevitable if one wishes to demonstrate how rights and freedoms are the "content" of democracy, that are important in their own right.

One condition for ensuring the provision of these rights is clarity in the law. As Beetham notes, many human rights documents, including the International Covenant on Civil and Political Rights and the European Convention, authorize exceptions and qualifications for preventing dis-

order and protecting public "health and morals." Unless the courts have
clear and final authority to adjudicate on these exceptions and to protect
rights, any government can contrive an excuse to suppress these rights.
Freedom is more secure to the extent that these exceptions are absent
from the law entirely.[30] Secure freedom also requires clear constitutional
and legal provisions establishing civilian supremacy over the military
and intelligence services, to ensure that they do not become unaccount-
able violators of citizens' rights. Except in circumstances of true national
emergency bordering on civil war, the military should be prohibited from
engaging in domestic security or surveillance operations.

Assuring political and civil rights requires many of the institutional
conditions of fairness and horizontal accountability discussed above
with respect to participation, competition, and vertical accountability.
First and foremost among these institutions is an independent, capable,
and constitutionally authoritative judiciary, along with a broader legal
system and legal culture that ensures the rule of law. Other important
instruments of horizontal accountability—what Beetham calls "agencies of protection"—are an independent electoral commission, an
ombudsman and human rights commission, and local police commissions.[31] Finally, if as Benjamin Franklin said, "vigilance is the eternal
price of liberty," then an indispensable condition for sustaining political and civil freedom is an active and well-organized civil society that
monitors and defends civil liberties and the integrity of the electoral
process. This includes independent and vigorous mass media that are
able not just to report but to investigate, question, and expose abuses of
power that violate rights.

From these conditions, we can infer the more common sources of
subversion of rights. These include executives who manipulate perceptions or fears of national security to enlarge their powers, curb criticism
and dissent, and silence particularly troublesome opposition; judicial
systems that are either too incompetent or too politically partial to
defend citizens' rights, or that themselves abuse these rights in their
prosecutorial zeal; police who abuse the rights of the accused and detained, or who target groups for purely political reasons; and military
and intelligence actors that intimidate and crush political opposition
under the guise of fighting terrorism or defending national security.

Equality. Many of the previous dimensions imply or require, and the
very word democracy commonly symbolizes, the formal political equality of all citizens. Thus, such phrases as "equal rights under the law"
and "one person one vote" are bedrock elements of democracy. The
principle of equality can be grounded on more or less radical socialist
or communist doctrines. It may derive from the Catholic tenet of solidarity or from the well known principle of "brotherhood" made popular
by the French Revolution. It may succinctly take the meaning of "re-

ductions of differences." However, a good democracy ensures that every citizen and group has the same rights and legal protections, and also meaningful and reasonably prompt access to justice and power. This also entails the prohibition of discrimination on the basis of gender, race, ethnicity, religion, political orientation, or other extraneous conditions. It is fairly safe to state that a substantial degree of political equality, that is a specific kind of equality, is needed for advance in other dimensions, especially accountability, participation, and freedom.

Even more so than some of our other themes, equality is an ideal that is never perfectly achieved, even in strictly political terms. As Dietrich Rueschemeyer observes, individuals and groups with better education, more information, and more resources will inevitably have more power to shape public debate and preferences and to determine the choice of leaders and policies. We come then to a fundamental dilemma: Democracy as a political system does not in itself require a certain set of social or economic policies; rather, the democratic process is precisely about the struggle to determine those policies, and to shape the distribution of benefits across groups and even across generations. To enjoy political equality, however, citizens must also have some measure of equality in income, wealth, and status. The more extreme are social and economic inequalities, the more disproportionate will be the power of those who control vast concentrations of wealth and hence their ability to make leaders respond to their wishes and interests. This is especially true in rural sectors polarized into a small class of wealthy landowners and a mass of landless and dependent peasants, generating semifeudalistic relations and cumulative grievances that breed radical politics and various forms of repression in response.

Where, as in the Andean region of Latin America, such class polarities overlap with regional and ethnic cleavages, democratic politics becomes even more polarized and unstable. Whether rural or urban, to the extent that extreme inequality is associated with widespread poverty—as it is in much of Latin America, the Philippines, and South Africa, for example—this generates enormous policy challenges (including intense pressures for redistribution, high rates of crime, and lawlessness) and formidable barriers to the effective exercise of citizenship rights.[32] These barriers are not only structural—in that the desperately poor lack the knowledge and resources necessary to use and defend their rights—but also cultural, as massive status inequalities, reproduced across generations, lead the rich to view the poor as inferior, irresponsible, and incapable of self-governance.[33]

In the countries mentioned above, a lot of poor are led to accept their situation as given and "natural." Such cultural views lead to extremely paternalistic treatment of the poor at best, and often justify raw exploitation. It also inhibits the self-organization of the disadvantaged. Yet, democracy with anything approaching comprehensive suffrage would not have come about if these inhibitions had been effective under all conditions. Mobilization by the poor can attenuate this impact: In India, the poor and lower castes actually vote in higher percentages than the wealthy. So can rules and institutions (such as party- and campaign-finance laws) that mitigate the capacity of the wealthy to convert financial resources into political ones, or that put a minimum floor of political resources under the feet of all major parties. To some degree, however, the problem confronts all democracies.

Even if we conceive of the equality dimension in narrow political terms, we cannot ignore its economic and social correlates. According to widespread conceptions of democratic politics, democracy must be judged by the extent to which over time it achieves greater social rights: the right to mental and physical health, the right to assistance and social security, the right to work and to strike, the right to education, the right to a healthy and clean environment, and the right to housing. Constitutions vary in the extent to which they formally acknowledge and guarantee these rights, but newer democratic constitutions are increasingly explicit about them, as in, for example, the last Constitutional Treaty of the European Union.

Unlike "first generation" political and civil rights, which, as Reinhard Bendix would put it,[34] were usually conquered by the mobilization of lower classes and can mainly be secured by the correct legal functioning of the state, social and economic rights place a burden on the state for positive action and are thus more difficult and much more financially costly to uphold. Consequently, there have been attempts to redesign policies to achieve social rights in a way that diminishes or better distributes the economic burden on society.

The main prerequisites for the achievement of social rights are sufficient affluence to fund social policies and wise strategies to achieve egalitarian policy goals with the greatest efficiency and lowest drag on economic prosperity. Efficiency requires that the available resources go as much as possible toward investments in physical infrastructure and especially human capital (public health and education) that will raise the productivity of the poor over time. This in turn necessitates the control of corruption, and hence strong institutions of horizontal accountability.

There is a circular nature to the quest for greater equality, or at least for the steady reduction of absolute poverty. If it requires wise and progressive policies, where are these to come from if the leaders elected through the disproportionate power of the privileged are not enlightened enough to reach beyond immediate political self-interest? Historically, the answer has lain heavily, as Rueschemeyer notes, in the collective mobilization of autonomous groups and parties representing lower class and status groups. In particular, unified and strong trade unions have played an important role in winning the extension of many economic and social rights.[35] But it is also vital that the legal system protect the political and civic rights of subordinate and vulnerable groups to organize, assemble, protest, lobby, campaign, and vote.

The Results Dimension: Responsiveness

Finally, we can analyze democratic quality by what it achieves in terms of government responsiveness to the expectations, interests, needs, and demands of citizens. This dimension is closely related to vertical accountability, and hence to participation and competition. In turn, it also influences how well citizens will be satisfied with the performance of democracy, and to what extent they will view it as the best form of government for their country.

As G. Bingham Powell, Jr., explains, democratic governments are responsive when the democratic process induces them "to make and implement policies that the citizens want." As Powell portrays it, the democratic process that produces responsiveness takes place in a chain of three linkages. First, choices are structured in a way that distills citizens' diverse, multidimensional policy preferences into more coherent national policy choices offered by competing political parties. Second, citizens' electoral preferences are aggregated, by different institutional means in different types of democracies, into a government of policymakers. And third, elected officials and their appointees then translate policy stances and commitments into actual policy outcomes. The products of responsiveness also include government services, the distribution of material benefits to constituents, and the extension of symbolic goods.[36]

The empirical study of responsiveness, however, is more complicated. In fact, the idea that even educated, informed, and politically engaged citizens always know their own interests and desires in relation to specific policies is an assumption (we mentioned this earlier) especially tenuous in situations where citizens might need specialized knowledge to accurately identify and evaluate what will work to their benefit. A dilemma also occurs, Powell notes, when policymakers have to weigh the tradeoff between responsiveness to short-term citizen preferences and longer-term citizen interests. Different institutional forms also present different problems for responsiveness. Majoritarian systems make it possible for voters to bring in a new government with a decisively different policy course, but they may fail to be responsive to the needs and demands of different minorities. Consensual systems, based on proportional representation, are more broadly responsive in the latter respect but less so in their ability to mandate and empower a sharply different policy course. Powell notes a host of other conceptual and practical problems. When the issues fall on multiple dimensions and partisan orientations do not neatly sort between them, it becomes difficult to infer an electoral policy mandate to which a new government owes responsiveness. The responsiveness chain also fails from the start when competing parties and candidates do not clearly structure policy choices for the voters, or when no party offers the policy citizens want.

The contextual conditions that favor responsiveness are similar to those that support vertical accountability. They include a well-established, independent, informed, and engaged civil society, and a stable, coherent party system that is capable of defining clear national policy choices for the electorate and then translating those policy programs into agendas for legislative and executive action. It is fairly obvious why these factors are essential. Effective political parties and civil society institutions of all kinds are essential for articulating and aggregating citizen interests and demands. But the government must then be capable of translating those preferences into policies and programs. This requires, as Powell notes, a government bureaucracy that is not only capable and professional but also honest and transparent. Thus, strong horizontal accountability, to limit corruption and misrule, is important for securing this final linkage in the chain of responsiveness.

There are at least three objective limits on responsiveness. First, democratically elected leaders do not always seek to understand and respond to the concerns, preferences, and demands of citizens. Often they instead work to maximize their own autonomy and take advantage of the complexity of problems as well as the political shifts over the course of an electoral term. When demagogic leaders seek to divert attention from, or manipulate public sentiment about, public policy issues in order to aggrandize their power and wealth, we move from the phenomenon of constraint to active subversion.

Government responsiveness to citizen demands is also constrained by limited resources and budget deficits, even in the wealthiest countries. For example, if an aging population demands higher pensions and better health care and other benefits with no increase in the retirement age or other offsets, a government burdened with budgetary limitations may simply be unable to meet their expectations in a sustainable way. Likewise, the persistent problems posed by unemployment and immigration further illustrate the near impossibility of finding generally satisfactory, legitimate, and responsive solutions in contemporary democracies. No government can afford for long to be fully responsive to all the different demands of major constituencies for services, benefits, and other program expenditures. Governing responsibly—as opposed to purely responsively—involves setting priorities and making difficult choices. One of the most important aspects of responsiveness in a democracy is to infer from the cacophony of policy commitments, election results, and interest group demands precisely what "the electorate's" priorities are. Inevitably, some groups will be disappointed.

The third limit on government responsiveness derives from the di-

minishing control that national governments have over their own economies in an era of globalization, as we have mentioned above with respect
to vertical accountability. Of course, responsiveness may be constrained,
undermined, or subverted in other ways as well: for example, when
political parties are organized along ethnic or identity rather than programmatic lines; when electoral systems yield severely disproportional
outcomes that penalize minorities and prevent the real distribution of
preferences from being reflected in the legislature; or when the process
of policy formation and implementation becomes distorted by blatant
corruption and the disproportionate lobbying power of wealthy interest
groups that contribute heavily to political parties.

These constraints and subversions, combined with the pure intracta-
bility of policy problems such as entrenched poverty and inequality,
demographic shifts, and the staggering short-term costs of structural
economic reforms, breed discontent, dissatisfaction, and malaise in many
contemporary democracies, even long-established ones. Such conditions, particularly when combined with the reality or perception of
extensive political corruption, erode the legitimacy of democratic systems and encourage populist and irresponsible alternatives.

One way to measure responsiveness is directly: to simply ask citizens, in surveys, to what extent they believe government is responsive
to their needs and concerns. Another way is to infer responsiveness from
citizen satisfaction with the way democracy works. Empirical measures
of citizen satisfaction can be found in the surveys that have been regularly conducted for many years, especially in the United States and
Western Europe, but also increasingly in Latin America, Central and
Eastern Europe, Africa, and Asia.[37] Some scholars have also indirectly
obtained a second indicator of responsiveness by measuring the distance between the governors and the governed on certain policies, and
not just in terms of left-right divisions.[38]

The System of Democratic Qualities

We have presented here eight different dimensions of democratic
quality, and noted how other dimensions could be isolated from within
these as well. In one sense, we can speak of different "qualities" of
democracy, and assess the level of development of each one individually. But as we have emphasized throughout, these different dimensions
densely interact and reinforce one another, ultimately converging into
a system. Although it is possible to identify different types of lower-
quality democracy, which are deficient in different qualities, the various
dimensions are closely linked and tend to move together, either toward
democratic improvement and deepening or toward decay. Where we
find democracies very weak on some dimensions, such as freedom and
the rule of law, they tend to be noticeably deficient on others as well.[39]

The linkages among the different elements of democracy are so densely interactive and overlapping that it is sometimes difficult to know where one dimension ends and another begins. Without extensive protection for and facilitation of civil and political rights, many citizens will not have the ability to participate in the political process, both in the electoral arena and outside it. Unless there is fair and unimpeded access to the electoral arena, vertical accountability may be greatly diminished. This requires not only the prevention of electoral fraud, and of violence and intimidation against voters, candidates, and parties, but also—as Beetham argues—the prevention of more subtle denigrations of electoral rights, including rights to some measure of equality in access to political finance and to the mass media. If because of the accumulated unfair advantages that the ruling party enjoys voters are not able to convert their dissatisfaction with the incumbents into electoral support for the opposition, or if any party, ruling or not, overwhelms its opponents and drowns out their messages with vastly superior funding and media access, the electoral dimension of vertical accountability may be vitiated. If voters cannot effectively hold their rulers accountable at the polls—and put in office an opposition whose policy promises they prefer—then a crucial linkage in the chain of accountability as defined by Powell breaks down.

Civil and political rights are thus critical to the vigorous participation and competition of parties, interests, and organizations that make for vertical accountability and responsiveness. They are necessary as well for horizontal accountability, in that agencies of horizontal accountability in the state become more active and effective when they are reinforced, beseeched, and informed by agents of vertical accountability, particularly the mass media, nongovernmental organizations, and other civil society actors.

But none of this is possible without the rule of law, wherein an independent and impartial judiciary affirms rights and penalizes and prohibits violations of the institutional safeguards for vertical and horizontal accountability. Neither can a rule of law be sustained and the abuse of power preempted and contained without strong institutions of horizontal accountability, which also ensure that the electoral instruments of competition and vertical accountability will not be abused. At the same time, participatory citizens, voting at the polls and acting in various organized ways in civil society, are the last line of defense against potential executive efforts to subvert rule-of-law and good-governance institutions.

To be sure, all good things do not go together smoothly. A government highly responsive to majority wishes may trample on the rights of minorities. Maximizing the procedural dimensions of popular sovereignty—participation, competition, and vertical accountability—can under certain circumstances come at the expense of freedom and equality. A high-quality democracy thus is not infinitely high in every democratic quality. Rather, it represents a balance between virtues that lie in tension. As Guillermo O'Donnell has suggested, polyarchies (or by implication, good and robust democracies) "are the complex synthesis of three historical currents or traditions: democracy, liberalism, and republicanism."[40] Seen in this way, citizens and their organizations participate and compete to choose and replace their leaders and obtain responsiveness from them. That is the democratic element. The liberal element protects the rights of all individuals and groups under the law while the republican element, through unelected instruments of horizontal accountability, enforces the law and ensures that public officials serve the public interest. Good democracies balance and integrate these three distinct traditions. Yet they do so with distinctive mixes and institutional designs, reminding us that democratic quality is a flexible and pluralistic concept, shaped by the normative choices of society.

There remains a vexing philosophical as well as empirical set of questions: Will a quality democracy necessarily produce quality results and citizen satisfaction? Will improvements in quality relieve the apparent growing disaffection of democratic citizens in many countries? A government may score generally quite highly on our eight dimensions of quality, including responsiveness, yet many citizens may still be dissatisfied. This may be true for several reasons. First, as we suggested earlier, citizens do not always know what policies will produce the outcomes they seek, such as broad economic prosperity and stability. Second, we live in an era when news and information reach citizens with unprecedented speed, and when competition among the mass media tends to generate a tendency toward sensationalism and negative exposure. This makes the failings of democracy appear more scandalous and more frequent than they would have in a previous era. Third, as we have noted, responsiveness in a democracy is intrinsically complex and multidimensional. With so many different interests in society capable of aggregating in so many different ways, it is impossible for governments to be responsive to all interests and concerns. Democracy is about competition and choice, and losers are bound to be dissatisfied—at least temporarily.

Nevertheless, we think that part of the present disenchantment with democracy does concern procedures and institutions, and stems not only from more information about the failings of government, but also higher citizen expectations of what democracy can deliver both procedurally and substantively in terms of results. We do not believe it is wrong for increasingly informed and aware democratic citizens to want more scope for participation; greater accountability, transparency, and competitiveness; a stronger rule of law; more freedom and equality; and more responsive—or at least reasonably responsive—government. In fact, we think that the long historical evolution of democracy suggests that if citizens mobilize effectively, these aspirations for a higher quality of democracy can gradually, if still imperfectly, be achieved.

Lessons from the Case Studies

The empirical chapters of this book cover all areas of the world affected by democratization processes during the twentieth century: Western Europe, Central and Eastern Europe, Latin America, South Asia, East Asia, and Africa. Within each of these regions, some choice was necessary for obvious reasons, including the difficulty of dealing effectively with a higher number of cases. Thus, we favored a series of binary comparisons, each between two countries that are from the same region. Each pair of countries shares some cultural and historical commonalities but differ in some crucial aspects, most especially in their features and qualities of democracy and often in such structural factors as population, size of territory, and economic development.

We asked each author to assess comparatively the quality of democracy in the two countries along the key dimensions sketched out in the first part of this introduction, namely, the rule of law; participation, competition, and vertical accountability; horizontal accountability; responsiveness; freedom; and equality. We left each case-study author some latitude to structure the analysis in a manner that seemed most appropriate to the particular comparison of cases, and to select specific indicators for each of the individual dimensions. Consequently, some authors have relied heavily on quantitative indicators, such as data from public-opinion surveys, while others have leaned more toward qualitative indicators (in India and Bangladesh for example, little relevant, comparative public-opinion data was available). We expected each author to develop a systematic comparison of the two countries and to explain why each country has the level and characteristics of the quality of democracy described in the first part. In conclusion, each comparative case study was to identify the dimensions and related aspects most important to the quality of democracy in the analyzed cases, and the authors were also free to recommend policies that could enhance democratic quality in each country.

The comparative case studies provide some illuminating answers, or at least hints of answers, to five key empirical questions in the comparative analysis of democratic quality:

1. Do our different dimensions provide a fairly exhaustive portrait of the quality of democracy in each country, or would a more parsimonious—even one-dimensional—approach to quality be more efficient and revealing?

2. Does the empirical analysis of each pair of cases show a consistency among the different dimensions, or is there a clear tradeoff between a particular dimension and some other one? Going further, do beliefs in

some value make the related dimension or dimensions more relevant than others?

3. Is there a dimension of democratic quality that is easier to achieve at a high level, and, in addition to equality, is there a dimension that is consistently across the cases more difficult to achieve?

4. Looking at these cases only, can different models of high-quality democracy be detected? Do we also find particular models of low-quality democracy?

5. Finally, would analysis of the subversion of different dimensions of democratic quality be a more effective or complementary research strategy to assess the quality of democracy?

To begin with the first question, we think that the case studies affirm the value of our conceptual framework. On the whole, the country chapters of this book give a revealing overall picture of these democracies and their qualities or lack of quality. Even more, the analysis of the various dimensions brings to light several aspects of political life that often extend beyond macropolitics and concern the everyday life of citizens. Of course, there is inevitably the problem that a comparative case study of two countries assessing several different dimensions in the limited space of one book chapter cannot offer a truly in-depth of analysis of any one of them. Would a one-dimensional analysis be more successful in explaining the trajectories of these democracies? If, as we can safely assume, democracies are complex and multidimensional phenomena, and if, as stated at the beginning of this introduction, there are at least three different notions of quality (procedure, content, and result), then the multidimensional strategy is the only possible one. Indeed, we think this approach finds strong support in all the empirical chapters. A one-dimensional analysis would only give a very limited, partial picture of how citizens experience democracy. We can safely say that there are democratic "qualities" and that all of them are relevant.

What about the empirical consistency of the different dimensions of democratic quality? As expected, equality—and even just political equality—has a different position vis-à-vis all other dimensions, and is only reasonably achieved (and even then, only in relative terms) in the more advanced and wealthy countries. Across the cases, the rule of law, horizontal accountability, vertical accountability, and freedom all appear very much related; achievements in one of these four dimensions are generally matched by the other ones. Competition and participation, which tend to vary together, emerge as key causal aspects in the performances of other dimensions. This point is particularly supported by the analyses of Poland and Romania by Alina Mungiu-Pippidi and of Brazil and Chile by Frances Hagopian.

Responsiveness is often consistent with the other dimensions. Empirically, this is an important result. In fact, in most of the case studies this dimension has been analyzed through public-opinion data, which at least measure the extent of "perceived" responsiveness. This perceived responsiveness appears related to other dimensions, such as competition and participation, empirically as well as logically.

As expected, in some of the democracies examined, the rule of law appears weaker than other dimensions and develops somewhat independently of them over time. This is especially evident from Doh Chull Shin and Yun-han Chu's analysis regarding citizens' perceptions of different dimensions of democratic quality in South Korea and Taiwan. In both countries, the indicators of perceived rule of law are much lower than those of freedom and fairly lower than those of the other dimensions. Problems of corruption, abuses of power by elected executives and bureaucrats, and inadequate independence of the judicial system are more than enough to explain that perception.

With regard to possible tradeoffs between different dimensions, the empirical analysis does not suggest any relevant conclusion. Of course, this is not to say that within each case study's pair of countries, one democracy consistently ranks higher in quality than the other. That may be the case, as Sumit Ganguly shows in his comparison of the imperfect and yet deepening and impressively institutionalized Indian democracy, and the illiberal and unstable democracy in Bangladesh. Hagopian's comparison of Chile and Brazil, however, does not connote as much of an overall contrast in democratic quality between the countries. Chilean democracy has been more effective at ensuring rights and the rule of law, while Brazilian democracy has achieved greater accountability and responsiveness to citizens—but this does not necessarily mean that the two clusters of qualities are in tension, so much as it shows the weight of history (including the differing authoritarian legacies and modes of transition to democracy), political culture, and social structure. Tradeoffs, however, can exist among various policies to reduce inequality and to remove the most extreme poverty, or even within specific policies, such as education or health care. But these are aspects that the essays had no real possibility to address.

The cases reveal in part the importance of the cultural dimension, namely, what a society most values in its political system. If a democracy with strong liberal values is preferred, then the rule of law and freedom are the two dimensions on which to focus; if an equalitarian democracy is preferred, then forms of equality are the main policies to implement; if efficiency and governance are the only goals, then rule and law and accountability should be pursued. But if there is some consistency among the different dimensions, then the true problem is one of priorities only. That is to say, there are dimensions and related indicators that can be made to come first, but eventually all other dimensions are salient as well. This means that within the different possible ways to detect the democratic quality, there is a limited range of variation but no large differences; the indicators are always the same and the problem is in deciding which to prioritize.

We do not find among the cases the basis for firm generalizations about whether some dimensions of democratic quality are easier to achieve than others. To the extent that political freedom can be improved simply by the state refraining from certain types of repressive practices, then it would logically seem that freedom may be easier to achieve. The objective and subjective data from Korea and Taiwan and from Ghana and South Africa suggest exactly this, given the rapid progress that each country made after its authoritarian transition in providing (and being seen by its citizens to provide) significantly greater freedom. Yet as virtually all of the six case studies show, corruption persists as a much more tenacious problem, precisely because effectively controlling and punishing it so often requires institutional reforms and legal actions that can be blocked by those who hold political power and who do not have a strong desire to be held accountable. In their comparative analysis of Italy and Spain, Leonardo Morlino and Rafael López-Pintor offer a rather striking portrait of two democracies that are quite advanced, liberal, and highly institutionalized, yet are still plagued with abuses and scandals that diminish the rule of law and leave quite a number of their citizens dissatisfied with the way democracy works.

When we search for explanations for the differing levels of democratic qualities, almost all the case studies point to similar factors, such as some socioeconomic condition, the legacy of the past, institutional design, and the modes of transition for countries that became democratic more recently. At the same time, the participation of organized civil society and the role of political competition, when not pushed to radical extremes, are the two key factors that emerge from almost all essays to explain the existing level of quality. Given this, then one particular type of democracy seems better fit for a higher democratic quality: namely one that generates and facilitates high levels of participation and competition and therefore vigorous vertical accountability and at least some degree of system responsiveness. Thus the key question becomes how to bring about those results: Is it enough to financially support representative channels, such as parties, and have a constitutional design and an electoral system that allow for participation and competition? Or do we need new and more creative recipes?

Indirectly, this finding at least partially contradicts the conclusion by Arend Lijphart that consensus democracies are better suited than majoritarian democracies to achieving democratic quality.[41] At a minimum, his hypothesis should be reformulated: It is not whether a democracy is consensual or majoritarian that matters for democratic quality so much as whether democracy—consensual or majoritarian—provides incentives and opportunities for participation.

Last but not least, we cannot affirm that a strategy analyzing subversions of democracy, as mentioned in the first theoretical part of this chapter, would better evaluate democratic quality than the simple analysis of the different dimensions we have presented here. Such a strategy would mean empirically analyzing the subversion of:

• the rule of law, by executives and other political and bureaucratic actors who use the law as a political weapon, as a tool to advance certain economic interests, or a set of rules to circumvent, characterized by limits in implementation;

• accountability, carried out by a strongly majoritarian institutional design (with low competition), weak parties or party discipline in oligarchical parties, and the shifting of blame to supranational levels of authority;

• responsiveness, characterized by elite manipulation of information, corruption, and the complexity of actual problems;

• freedom, by incumbents who seek to stifle opposition and dissent through the use of their formal and informal powers, or by elements of the state security apparatus (the military, intelligence, or police) that have not been brought fully under civilian, democratic control; and

• equality, either by elevating the institutional power and influence of a particular group or by marginalizing from the political process some segment of the citizenry.

The instruments, strategies, and dynamics of subversions of democracy are complex and often subtle. They reveal themselves more easily in the case of a country that has seen a dramatic decline in the quality of democracy (or even a reversion from democracy to authoritarianism, as in Russia) than in our cases here, which for the most part have seen gradual if uneven improvements in democratic quality over time as they move toward becoming more liberal and consolidated democracies. (The exception among our 12 cases in this regard is Bangladesh, which, as Ganguly shows, has failed to make any significant progress in deepening and consolidating democracy). Active subversion of democratic quality is an important topic for future research, but will clearly require a different research design and probably a rather different selection of cases.

For Want of a Conclusion

The theoretical analysis in this chapter and in the five thematic chapters that follow suggest the richness and promise of this field of research, but the promise can only be realized through empirical analysis along two different lines. First, we think that a comparative strategy combining both qualitative and quantitative methods and looking in depth at a manageably small number of cases is likely to be more fruitful than a purely quantitative strategy that analyzes a few set variables over a large number of cases. Only such a "small n" research design, built essentially on case studies, can allow us to examine how democratic institutions actually work in each country and how this democratic functioning (and change) affects the way citizens view democracy. Such a "small n" set of comparisons can also enable us to control better for different alternative explanations of democratic quality, and even to suggest policies to deepen quality or some dimension of it. Of course, we can gain some important insights from "large n" quantitative studies by seeing to what extent some general, measurable factors—such as institutional designs, age of democracy, region, or level of economic development—may account for differences in some of the dimensions of democratic quality that have been measured cross-nationally—such as freedom, corruption, and other aspects of governance.

Second, even a "small n" comparative strategy needs to be systematic and select a set of qualitative or quantitative indicators that are mostly relevant for each dimension. For example, with regard to the rule of law, we could concentrate on the set of indicators related to the independence of the judiciary, civilian control of the military and the police, and lack of corruption; for competition and participation, we could focus on the electoral and party indicators; for accountability, on indicators related to the role of parties, the mass media, and the agencies of horizontal accountability at the top constitutional level; for responsiveness, on survey results for such items as satisfaction with the way democracy works; for freedom, on the actual guarantee of civil and political rights, as well as citizens' perceptions of freedom; and for equality, on social rights, broadly conceived. The case studies basically followed these guidelines and achieved a good picture of the dimensions of quality, but they were limited by the unavailability of data. Even when data from public-opinion surveys were available for each of the countries being compared, the surveys did not always employ precisely the same questions to measure the underlying concept. Needless to say, comparative assessment of the quality of democracy will be greatly enhanced by standardization in the collection of both objective and subjective data on democratic quality. In the meantime, our cases show that these methodological discrepancies can at least be managed or attenuated by utilizing different, but related indicators for the same concept.

The various chapters in this volume also underscore the inescapable point that democracy is intrinsically about making choices, and sometimes managing difficult tradeoffs. There is no one sequence of reforms to improve the quality of democracy that would be right for all countries. As we see from our cases, there is simply too much variation among the cases in their strengths and weaknesses, and in their historical inheritances. However, any democracy has limited resources—both financially and in terms of the political capital for reform that its leaders can expend at any one time. It follows that democracies may have to make choices about whether at a certain moment to invest more in building a highly effective rule of law, in reforming the financing of political parties and campaigns, or in the implementation of responsive policies and the extent of guarantee of different rights. Moreover, as we see from the Indian case, deepening democracy in some respects (such as the incorporation of new groups into the political process) may for a time coincide with deterioration in others (such as the rule of law, control of violence, and protection of minority rights). Because the different dimensions of democratic quality do not always move together, or in the same direction, and because change in quality may entail tradeoffs, a democracy may be perceived as high-quality by some and as low-quality by others.

Perhaps the most important general finding that emerges from the case studies is that competition and participation are engines of democratic quality. These, however, are typically qualities of democracy that benefit stronger, better-organized, and more resourceful social groups, and much less so weak and marginalized segments of society. For those who lack effective political skills and resources—be it because of poverty, illiteracy, discrimination, or other forms of marginalization—democracy is always liable to be seen as lacking quality. Leveling such inequalities, giving voice to the voiceless, and bringing all citizens more fully into the arenas of civic participation and political competition remain the most enduring and difficult challenges for the deepening of democracy.

NOTES

We would like to thank all participants in the conference, held at the Center on Democracy, Development, and the Rule of Law of the Stanford Institute for International Studies on 10–11 October 2003, for their very helpful comments and reactions to a first draft of this introduction. We would also like thank Dietrich Rueschemeyer for his detailed and insightful comments on a subsequent draft.

1. See for example, Juan J. Linz and Alfred Stepan, *Problems of Democratic Transition and Consolidation: Southern Europe, Latin America, and Post-Communist Europe* (Baltimore: Johns Hopkins University Press, 1996); Leonardo Morlino, *Democracy Between Consolidation and Crisis: Parties, Groups and Citizens in Southern Europe* (Oxford: Oxford University Press, 1998); and Larry Diamond, *Developing Democracy: Toward Consolidation* (Baltimore: Johns Hopkins University Press, 1999).

2. From the perspective advanced by Philippe C. Schmitter in this collection, and in his other writings on democratic consolidation, however, democracy may become consolidated at any level of quality, so long as citizens and politicians come to accept the rules of democratic competition.

3. Max Kaase and Kenneth Newton, *Beliefs in Government* (Oxford: Oxford University Press, 1995). The recent classic work on this subject is Susan J. Pharr and Robert D. Putnam, eds., *Disaffected Democracies: What's Troubling the Trilateral Countries* (Princeton: Princeton University Press, 2000).

4. See for example, among a myriad of possible sources, Robert Dahl, *Polyarchy: Participation and Opposition* (New Haven: Yale University Press, 1971).

5. See "Preface," in Larry Diamond, Juan J. Linz, and Seymour Martin Lipset, eds., *Democracy in Developing Countries: Africa* (Boulder, Colo.: Lynne Rienner, 1988), xvi.

6. Philippe C. Schmitter and Terry Lynn Karl, "What Democracy is . . . and is not," in Larry Diamond and Marc F. Plattner, eds., *The Global Resurgence of Democracy* (Baltimore: Johns Hopkins University Press, 1993), 45–46.

7. For a related approach, see David Beetham, "Towards a Universal Framework for Democracy Assessment," *Democratization* 11 (April 2004): 1–17.

8. Larry Diamond, "Elections without Democracy: Thinking About Hybrid Regimes," and Andreas Schedler, "Elections without Democracy: The Menu of Manipulation," in *Journal of Democracy* 13 (April 2002): 21–35 and 36–50.

9. Wolfgang Merkel and Aurel Croissant, "Formal Institutions and Informal Rules of Defective Democracies," *Central European Political Science Review* 2 (December 2000): 31–47.

10. Guillermo O'Donnell, "Delegative Democracy," *Journal of Democracy* 5 (January 1994): 60–62.

11. Herbert Kitschelt and his coauthors also consider accountability to be a "procedural" dimension. See Herbert Kitschelt et al., eds., *Post-communist Party Systems: Competition, Representation and Inter-party Cooperation* (Cambridge: Cambridge University Press, 1999).

12. Our original framework, which guided the case studies, did not delineate participation and competition as distinct dimensions of democratic quality, nor did it separate horizontal and vertical accountability. While most of the case studies do treat vertical and horizontal accountability as distinct dimensions, they analyze participation and competition more implicitly as contributing factors to vertical accountability or responsiveness.

13. These are among the purposes of a formal democracy assessment, for which International IDEA has recently published a guide. See *International IDEA Guide to Democracy Assessment* (New York: Kluwer Law International, 2001), available at *www.idea.int/ideas_work/14_political_state.htm.*

14. David Altman and Aníbal Pérez-Liñán, "Assessing the Quality of Democracy: Freedom, Competitiveness and Participation in 18 Latin American Countries," Kellogg Institute working paper, Notre Dame University, 2001; Arend Lijphart, *Patterns of Democracy: Government Forms and Performance in Thirty-Six Countries* (New Haven: Yale University Press, 1999).

15. One empirical way to classify a regime as an "illiberal democracy" is if it meets the test of an electoral democracy: It has regular, free, fair, and competitive elections to fill the principal positions of power in the country, but it does not qualify as Free in Freedom House's annual ratings of civil liberties and political rights. By this measure, there were 33 such regimes at the end of 2002. The Freedom House surveys are available at *www.freedomhouse.org.*

16. José María Maravall, "The Rule of Law as a Political Weapon," in José María Maravall and Adam Przeworski, eds., *Democracy and the Rule of Law* (Cambridge: Cambridge University Press, 2003).

17. See the debate among Arend Lijphart, Guy Larderet, and Quentin L. Quade

in Larry Diamond and Marc F. Plattner, eds., *The Global Resurgence of Democracy* (Baltimore: Johns Hopkins University Press, 1993), 146–77; and also Arend Lijphart, *Patterns of Democracy.*

18. Michael Pinto-Duschinsky, "Financing Politics: A Global View," *Journal of Democracy* 13 (October 2002): 69–86; U.S. Agency for International Development's Office of Democracy and Governance, *Money and Politics: A Guide to Increasing Transparency in Emerging Democracies* (November 2003), available at *www.usaid.gov.*

19. Robert Pastor, "A Brief History of Electoral Commissions," in Andreas Schedler, Larry Diamond, and Marc F. Plattner, *The Self-Restraining State: Power and Accountability in New Democracies* (Boulder, Colo.: Lynne Rienner, 1999), 75–82.

20. David Altman and Aníbal Pérez-Liñán, "Assessing the Quality of Democracy."

21. Andreas Schedler, "Conceptualizing Accountability," in Andreas Schedler, Larry Diamond, and Marc F. Plattner, *The Self-Restraining State,* 17.

22. Catalina Smulovitz and Enrique Peruzotti, "Societal Accountability in Latin America," *Journal of Democracy* 11 (October 2000): 147–58.

23. The most extreme hypothesis related to this phenomenon is that parties, supported by public financing, in fact constitute a kind of political "cartel." See Richard S. Katz and Peter Mair, "Changing Modes of Party Organization and Party Democracy: The Emergence of the Cartel Party," in *Party Politics* 1 (January 1995): 5–28.

24. Andreas Schedler, Larry Diamond, and Marc F. Plattner, *The Self-Restraining State.*

25. James R. Klein, "The Constitution of the Kingdom of Thailand, 1997: A Blueprint for Participatory Democracy," Asia Foundation Working Paper Series, March 1998, 29.

26. Sheila S. Coronel and Lorna Kalaw-Tirol, eds., *Investigating Corruption: A Do-It-Yourself Guide* (Manila: Philippine Center for Investigative Journalism, 2002), 257–264, quote from 259.

27. Guillermo O'Donnell, "Horizontal Accountability in New Democracies," in Andreas Schedler, Larry Diamond, and Marc F. Plattner, *The Self-Restraining State,* 39.

28. Robert Pastor, "A Brief History of Electoral Commissions," 78–79.

29. See for example Robert Dahl, *Polyarchy*; and T. H. Marshall, *Sociology at the Crossroad* (London: Heinemann, 1963).

30. For example, this is what motivated the drafters of the Iraqi interim constitution, the Transitional Administrative Law adopted on 8 March 2004, to exclude all such qualifications and limitations from the Iraqi bill of rights, in chapter two of that document.

31. Prison complaint boards provide a more specific line of defense and accountability against one of the most pervasive forms of abuse of rights.

32. On the implications for democracy in Latin America, see Larry Diamond, Jonathan Hartlyn, and Juan J. Linz, "Introduction: Politics, Society, and Democracy in Latin America," in Larry Diamond, Jonathan Hartlyn, Juan J. Linz, and

Seymour Martin Lipset, eds., *Democracy in Developing Countries: Latin America* (Boulder, Colo.: Lynne Rienner, 1999): 48–53.

33. This is an important reason why Seymour Martin Lipset asserted that economic development makes democracy more sustainable, because it generates a "diamond-shaped" distribution of wealth, with a large middle class, thereby narrowing status differences in society. See his classic essay, "Economic Development and Democracy," in Seymour Martin Lipset, *Political Man: The Social Bases of Politics* (Baltimore: Johns Hopkins University Press, 1981), 27–63.

34. Reinhard Bendix, *Nation Building and Citizenship: Studies of Our Changing Social Order* (New York and London: Wiley and Sons, 1964).

35. Dietrich Rueschemeyer, Evelyne H. Stephens, and John D. Stephens, *Capitalist Development and Democracy* (Chicago: University of Chicago Press, 1992). However, these authors also stress that the organized working class was too weak to achieve political rights without allies even where it was strongest.

36. Heinz Eulau and Paul D. Karps, "The Puzzle of Representation: Specifying Components of Responsiveness," *Legislative Studies Quarterly* 3 (August 1977): 233–54.

37. A common question, for example, is "How satisfied are you with the way in which democracy functions in your country?" See Leonardo Morlino, *Democracy Between Consolidation and Crisis,* ch. 7.

38. See, for example, Arend Lijphart, *Patterns of Democracy*, 286–88. There are a number of quantitative studies that analyze this theme, including Heinz Eulau and Kenneth Prewitt, *Labyrinths of Democracy* (New York: Bobbs-Merrill, 1973); Heinz Eulau and Paul D. Karps, "The Puzzle of Representation"; Sidney Verba and Norman Nie, *Participation and Political Equality: A Seven-nation Comparison* (London: Cambridge University Press, 1978), and more recently, Gary King "Electoral Responsiveness and Partisan Bias in Multiparty Democracies," in *Legislative Studies Quarterly* 15 (May 1990); and John D. Huber and G. Bingham Powell, Jr., "Congruence Between Citizens and Policy Makers in Two Visions of Liberal Democracy," *World Politics* 46 (April 1994): 291–326.

39. This is why we observe a strong correlation, for example, between the Freedom House country ratings on civil liberties and those on political rights. See the annual surveys at *www.freedomhouse.org.*

40. Guillermo O'Donnell, "Horizontal Accountability in New Democracies," in Andreas Schedler, Larry Diamond, and Marc F. Plattner, *The Self-Restraining State,* 31.

41. See Arend Lijphart, *Patterns of Democracy,* ch. 16, where women's representation, electoral participation, satisfaction with democracy, and some other indicators are analyzed in connection with consensus democracy.

I

Dimensions of Democratic Quality

1

WHY THE RULE OF LAW
MATTERS

Guillermo O'Donnell

Guillermo O'Donnell *is Helen Kellogg Professor of Government and International Studies at the University of Notre Dame. This essay combines new material with a reorganized version of some of the author's other writings on this subject, especially* The Quality of Democracy: Theory and Applications *(2004) and "Polyarchies and the (Un)Rule of Law in Latin America" in Juan Mendez, Guillermo O'Donnell, and Paul Sérgio Pinheiro, eds.,* The Rule of Law and the Underprivileged in Latin America *(1999), both published by the University of Notre Dame Press. The essay originally appeared in the October 2004 issue of the* Journal of Democracy.

The rule of law is among the essential pillars upon which any high-quality democracy rests. But this kind of democracy requires not simply a rule of law in the minimal, historical sense that I will shortly explain. What is needed, rather, is a truly *democratic* rule of law that ensures political rights, civil liberties, and mechanisms of accountability which in turn affirm the political equality of all citizens and constrain potential abuses of state power. Seen thus, the rule of law works intimately with other dimensions of the quality of democracy. Without a vigorous rule of law, defended by an independent judiciary, rights are not safe and the equality and dignity of all citizens are at risk. Only under a democratic rule of law will the various agencies of electoral, societal, and horizontal accountability function effectively, without obstruction and intimidation from powerful state actors. And only when the rule of law bolsters these democratic dimensions of rights, equality, and accountability will the responsiveness of government to the interests and needs of the greatest number of citizens be achieved.

Although in some of my previous writings readers may find partial attempts at the theoretical and normative justification of a democratic rule of law, here I make only passing reference to these matters. My intention is to contribute to a discussion concerning if and how something called the rule of law, or the democratic rule of law, may be conceptualized and, insofar as possible, empirically gauged. To this end, the concluding section of this essay proposes a set of variables for the exploration of this dimension. Please note that what follows has been formulated with contemporary Latin America centrally in mind; it is of course an open question how well it might apply outside this region.

The "rule of law" (like partially concurrent expressions such as *Rechsstaat, état de droit,* or *estado de derecho*) is a disputed term. For the time being, let me assert that its minimal (and historically original) meaning is that whatever law exists is written down and publicly promulgated by an appropriate authority before the events meant to be regulated by it, and is fairly applied by relevant state institutions including the judiciary (though other state institutions can be involved as well). By "fairly applied" I mean that the administrative application or judicial adjudication of legal rules is consistent across equivalent cases; is made without taking into consideration the class, status, or relative amounts of power held by the parties in such cases; and applies procedures that are preestablished, knowable, and allow a fair chance for the views and interests at stake in each case to be properly voiced. The following is a minimal but significant criterion: If A is attributed the same generic rights (and, at least implicitly, the same legal personhood and agency) as the more powerful B with whom A enters into a crop-sharing arrangement, employment contract, or marriage, then it stands to reason that A has the right to expect equal treatment from the state institutions that have, or may acquire, jurisdiction over such acts.

This implies formal equality, in two senses. First, it is established in and by legal rules that are valid (at least[1]) in that they have been sanctioned following previously and carefully dictated procedures, often ultimately regulated by constitutional rules. Second, the rights and obligations specified are universal, in that they attach to each individual considered as a legal person, irrespective of social position, with the sole requirement that the individual in question has reached competent legal adulthood and has not been proven to suffer from some (narrowly defined and legally prescribed) disqualification. These rights support the claim of equal treatment in the legally defined situations that underlie and may ensue from the kind of acts above exemplified. "Equality [of all] before the law" is the expectation tendentially inscribed in this kind of equality.

There is another important point: The rights and obligations attached to political citizenship by a democratic regime are a subset of the more general civil rights and obligations attached to a legal person as a member of a given society. In addition to the well-known participatory rights to vote and run for office in fair elections, I am thinking of the freedoms (of expression, association, movement, and the like) that are usually considered necessary to the existence of a democratic regime. In many highly developed countries, these and similar freedoms became legally sanctioned civil rights well before becoming political freedoms.

On the other hand, strictly speaking there is no "rule of law," or "rule by laws, not men." All there is, sometimes, is individuals in various capacities interpreting rules which, according to some preestablished criteria, meet the condition of being generally considered law. Such a situation is clearly superior to a Hobbesian state of nature or the creation and application of rules at the whim of a despot. Yet it is not enough that certain actions, whether of public or private actors, are *secundum legem,* that is, in (interpreted) conformity with what a given law prescribes. For as I illustrate below, an act that is formally according to law may nonetheless entail the application of a rule that is invidiously discriminatory or violates basic rights. Or such an act may involve the selective use of a law against some, even as privileged sectors are enjoying arbitrary exemptions. The first possibility entails the violation of moral standards that most countries write into their constitutions and that nowadays, usually under the rubric of human rights, countries have the internationally acquired obligation to respect. The second possibility entails the violation of a crucial principle of fairness—that like cases be treated alike. Still another possibility is that in a given case the law is applied properly, but by an authority that does not feel obligated to proceed in the same manner on future equivalent occasions.

These cases may be construed as being "ruled by law," but they do not meet the criteria we normally have in mind when using the term "rule of law." Rather, these possibilities indicate the absence, or at least serious breaches, of a reasonable application of what the rule of law is supposed to be.

Toward a Positive Definition

Advancing toward a positive definition of the rule of law is no easy matter. A first complication is that the concepts of the rule of law and of *estado de derecho* (or *Rechsstaat,* or *état de droit,* or equivalents in other languages of countries belonging to the Roman-originated civil-law tradition) are not synonymous[2]—a topic to which I will return. Furthermore, each of these terms is subject to various definitional and normative disputations. Therefore, I will limit myself to some basic observations. First, in both the civil-law and common-law traditions, most definitions have at their core the view that under the rule of law, the legal system is a hierarchical one (usually crowned by constitutional norms) that aims at yet never fully achieves completeness. This means that the relationships among legal rules are themselves legally ruled, and that there is no moment in which the whim of a given actor may justifiably cancel or suspend the rules that govern his or her actions. No one, including the most highly placed official, is above the law. In contrast, the hallmark of all forms of authoritarian rule, even those that are highly institutionalized and legally formalized, is that at their apex sits some person or entity (a king, a junta, a party committee) that is sovereign in the classic sense of being able to make decisions unconstrained by law when the sovereign judges that there is a need to do so.

Second, to say that "the government shall be ruled by law and subject to it" and that "the creation of law . . . is itself legally regulated"[3] is to imply that the legal system is an aspect of the overall social order that in principle "brings definition, specificity, clarity, and thus predictability into human interactions."[4] Achieving this situation, though not necessarily an unmixed blessing, is a great public good. A necessary condition for this is that the laws have certain characteristics. Many lists of such characteristics are available. Here I adopt one that legal scholar Joseph Raz espouses:

> 1. All laws should be prospective, open, and clear; 2. Laws should be relatively stable; 3. The making of particular laws . . . must be guided by open, stable, clear, and general rules; 4. The independence of the judiciary must be guaranteed; 5. The principles of natural justice must be observed (i.e., open and fair hearing and absence of bias); 6. The courts should have review powers . . . to ensure conformity to the rule of law; 7. The courts should be easily accessible; and 8. The discretion of crime preventing agencies should not be allowed to pervert the law.[5]

The first three points refer to general characteristics of the laws themselves. Each point pertains to the proper enactment and content of the laws, as well as to a fact that Raz and others stress: The laws must be possible to follow, and should not place unreasonable cognitive or behavioral demands on the addressees. The other points of Raz's listing refer to the courts and only indirectly to other state agencies. Point four requires specification: The value of independent courts (itself a murky idea) is shown, *a contrario,* by the often-servile behavior of the judiciary in relation to authoritarian rulers. But this independence may be misused—and has been misused with some frequency in democratized Latin America—to foster the sectoral privileges of judicial personnel or to allow unchallenged, arbitrary interpretations of the law. Consequently, it also seems required "that those charged with interpreting and enforcing the laws [must] take them with primary seriousness."[6]

To this I would add that the stewards of the law must hold themselves ready to support and expand that very democracy which, in contrast to the old authoritarian order, confers upon them such independence.[7] This is a tall order everywhere, and not least in Latin America, where a long roll of institutional innovations has shown scant success in striking a proper balance between judicial subjection and excessive judicial independence. In this region another difficult accomplishment is implied by point six, especially with respect to overseeing the legality of acts performed by presidents who feel themselves electorally empowered to do whatever they think best while in office. I will illustrate below the denial of redress to many of the poor and the vulnerable (points five and seven). The same goes for the eighth point, particularly as regards the impunity enjoyed by police and other (so-called) security agencies, as well as violence perpetrated by private agents who often take advantage of police forces and courts that are culpably indifferent toward or even complicit in such unjust acts.

Aspects of the Rule of Law

At this point we should notice that, unlike *estado de derecho* and equivalent terms, the English-language phrase "rule of law," defined as above, does not refer directly to any state agencies other than courts. This is not surprising given various countries' respective traditions, including the particularly strong role that the courts have played in the political history of the United States. Nevertheless, the whole state apparatus and its agents are supposed to submit to the rule of law.

Furthermore, if the legal system is supposed to texture, stabilize, and order manifold social relations, then when state agents or even private actors violate the law with impunity, the rule of law is truncated. Whether state agents perpetrate unlawful acts on their own or give private actors de facto license to do so does not make much difference, either to the victims of such actions or to the (in)effectiveness of the rule of law.

The corollary of these reflections is that, when discussed in relation to the theory of democracy, the rule of law—or *estado de derecho*—should be conceived not only as a generic characteristic of the legal system and the performance of the courts, but also, and mostly, as the legally based rule of a democratic state. This entails that there exists a legal system that is itself democratic, in three senses: 1) It upholds the political rights, freedoms, and guarantees of a democratic regime; 2) it upholds the civil rights of the whole population; and 3) it establishes networks of responsibility and accountability which entail that all public and private agents, including the highest state officials, are subject to appropriate, legally established controls on the lawfulness of their acts.[8] As long as it fulfills these three conditions, such a state is not just a state ruled by law or a state that enacts the rule of law; it is a state that enacts a democratic rule of law, or an *estado democrático de derecho*.

In addition to the legal system itself, there are a number of state institutions that are directly related to a democratic regime. Thus the legal system is not just a set of rules but a system properly so called, which interlaces legal rules with legally regulated state institutions. In turn, a democratic legal system is a species of this genus, with two main features: It enacts and backs the rights attached to a democratic regime; and it holds all officials and institutions in the state (and indeed in society) at large answerable to the law—no one is *de legibus solutus*. In an *estado democrático de derecho,* everyone is subject to the legal authority of one or more institutions—the legal system closes, in the sense that no one is supposed to be above or beyond its rules. In turn, this characteristic is intimately related (as the tradition of liberal constitutionalism recognized early) to the protection of political and other rights. Absent the safeguard of universal answerability to the law, there would exist some ultimately uncontrollable power or powers that could unilaterally curtail or simply take rights away.

In a democracy, rulers are supposed to submit to three kinds of accountability. One, vertical electoral accountability, results from fair and institutionalized elections, through which citizens may change the party and officers in government. Another kind of vertical accountability, of a societal kind,[9] is exercised by groups and even individuals who seek to mobilize the legal system to place demands on the state and the government aimed at preventing, redressing, or punishing presumably illegal actions (or inactions) perpetrated by public officials. Still a third kind of accountability, which I have labelled horizontal, results when some properly authorized state institutions act to prevent, redress, or punish the presumably illegal actions (or inactions) of public officials.[10]

Note, however, that these types of accountability differ in an important way. Vertical or electoral accountability must by definition exist in a democracy. The degree and effectiveness of societal and horizontal accountability, by contrast, vary across cases and time periods. These variations are relevant to attempts to assess democratic quality. The lack of a vigorous and self-assertive society, for instance, or the incapacity or unwillingness of certain state institutions to exercise their prescribed authority over other state institutions (especially elected officials) is a telltale sign of low-quality democracy.

Another important measure is the effectiveness of the legal system at actually bringing a beneficial degree of order to social relations. This is a function of the interactions among the elements that compose this system. At one level, which we might call "interinstitutional," the authority of a judge dealing with a criminal case would be nil were it not joined, at several stages, by that of police officers, prosecutors, defense attorneys, and so on, as well as by, eventually, higher courts and prisons. Horizontally, in a democratic legal system no state institutions or officers are supposed to escape from legal controls regarding the lawfulness of their actions. In a third, territorial, dimension, the legal system is supposed to extend homogenously across the space delimited by the state—there must be no places where the law's writ does not run. In a fourth dimension—that of social stratification—the legal system must treat like cases alike irrespective of the class, gender, ethnicity, or other attributes of the respective actors. In all these dimensions, the legal system presupposes what Juan J. Linz and Alfred Stepan call an "effective state.''[11] In my terms, it is not just a matter of appropriate legislation but also of a network of state institutions that converge to ensure the effectiveness of a legal system that is itself democratic. The weakness of this kind of state is one of the most disturbing characteristics of most countries in Latin America.

Regarding the relationship between democracy and the state, it is important to note that by assigning various political rights to citizens, democracy construes them as agents. In addition, the citizens are carriers of subjective rights that are legally assigned on a boundedly universalistic basis. Now I add that this legal system, beginning with its highest (that is to say, constitutional) rules, establishes that the citizens, as they make their voting decisions in fair elections, are the source of the authority exercised over them by the state and the government. Citizens are not only the carriers of certain rights; they are the source and the justification of the very claim to rule upon which a democratic polity relies when making collectively binding decisions. Contemporary democracy hardly is *by* the people; but it certainly is *of* the people and, because of this, it should also be *for* the people.

That they derive their authority from the citizenry is quite obviously true in respect to holders of elected governmental positions. It is also true of all other state officials insofar as, in a democracy, they derive their authority from the highest—elected—powers of the country. Furthermore, the jurisdiction and obligations of those state officials are determined by the same legal system that subjects all public officials, elected and not, to horizontal accountability. Finally, everyone, including those who are not political citizens (nonadults and foreigners), is construed as an agent by the legal rules that regulate civil and social relationships.

It follows that an individual is not, and should never be seen as, a subject, a supplicant of the good will of the government or the state. This individual—an agent and carrier of a bundle of civil and eventually also social rights, whether she is or is not a political citizen—has a legally grounded claim to be treated with full consideration and respect, and on an equal basis with everyone else. Furthermore, this treatment must be based on the application of laws and regulations that are clear, knowable by the citizens, and enacted in ways that accord with democratic procedures.

Insofar as state institutions effectively recognize these rights, these institutions may be deemed democratic, or at least as behaving consistently with the duties that democracy imposes upon them. Indeed, this is arguably the most difficult aspect of democracy. When it comes to fair elections and the exercise of political rights, citizens normally find themselves placed on a level of generic equality. In dealing with state institutions, however, individuals (whether citizens or not) often find themselves placed in situations of sharp de facto inequality. They may face bureaucracies that act on the basis of formal and informal rules which are seldom transparent or easily understandable, and that make decisions (and omissions) which often have important consequences for their "subjects." It is a sad law of human nature that, when individuals are placed on the upper side of sharply unequal relationships, they tend to forget that their right to exercise authority derives from those "below," who are carriers of rights and should be treated with full consideration and respect. This is a problem everywhere. It is more serious and systematic when the subject of these relationships is one of those afflicted by severe and extended poverty and inequality. These ills breed a social authoritarianism that is sadly reflected in the way that too many state institutions treat too many citizens. This is, to my mind, another crucial dimension of the quality of democracy. In Latin America, with its deep and persistent inequalities, this dimension is one where contemporary democracies fall most gravely short.

The rights of political and civil citizenship are formal, in the double sense that they are supposed to be universal and that they are sanctioned through procedures established by the rules of authority and representation inherent in a democratic regime. The political citizen of democracy is homologous to the civil citizen of the universalist aspects of the legal system: The rights of associating, expressing opinions, moving freely, entering into contracts, not suffering violence, and expecting fair treatment from state agencies are all premised on individuals who share the autonomy and responsibility that make them, as both civil and political citizens, legal persons and agents of their own actions. This is a universal premise of equality that appears in innumerable facets of a democratic legal system. It underlies the enormous normative appeal that democratic aspirations have evinced, even if often vaguely and inconsistently expressed, under varied historical and cultural conditions.

Flaws in the Rule of Law

Yet even in countries where aspirations for democracy have been satisfied by the inauguration of democratic regimes, the rule of law may be compromised. Indeed, most contemporary Latin American countries, like new democracies in other parts of the world, are cases where national-level democratic regimes coexist with undemocratic subnational regimes and severe gaps in the effectiveness of basic civil rights. Major ways in which the rule of law may be hindered in Latin America include:

Flaws in the existing law. In spite of progress recently made, there still exist laws, judicial criteria, and administrative regulations that discriminate against women, members of indigenous peoples, and various other minorities, and which often force defendants, detainees, and prison inmates to endure conditions that are repugnant to any sense of fair process.

Flaws in the application of the law. "For my friends, everything; for my enemies, the law." This sentence, attributed to Brazil's President Getúlio Vargas (1930–45, 1950–54), expresses an attitude typical of dictatorships. The discretionary, and often exactingly severe, use of the law against the political enemy or the vulnerable can be an efficient means of oppression. The other side of this is the manifold ways in which, even in a democracy, the privileged manage to exempt themselves from the law. There is an old Latin American tradition of ignoring or twisting the law in order to favor the strong and repress the weak. When a shady businessman said in Argentina, "To be powerful is to have [legal] impunity,"[12] he expressed a presumably widespread feeling that to follow the law voluntarily is something that only morons do and that to be subject to the law is not to be the carrier of enforceable rights but rather a sure signal of social weakness. This is particularly true—and dangerous—in encounters that may unleash the violence of the state or powerful private agents, but an attentive eye can also detect it in the stubborn refusal of the privileged to submit themselves to regular administrative procedures, to say nothing of the legal impunity that they too often obtain.

Flaws in the relations between state agencies and ordinary citizens. This defect is related to the preceding. Perhaps nothing underlines better the deprivation of rights of the poor and vulnerable than when they interact with the bureaucracies from which they must obtain work, or a work permit, or retirement benefits, or simply (but sometimes tragically) when they have to go to a hospital or police station. For the privileged, this is the far side of the moon, a place they deploy elaborate strategies to avoid. For those who cannot escape this ugly face of the state, there is not only the immense difficulty of obtaining what nominally is their right. There is also the indifferent, if not disdainful, manner in which they are treated, as well as the obvious injustice entailed when the privileged escape these hardships. The distance between this kind of world and a truly democratic ethos of respect for equal human dignity may be gauged by observing the grievous difficulties that usually ensue for anyone who, lacking the "right" social status or connections, nonetheless dares to approach these bureaucracies not as a supplicant begging for favors, but as the bearer of a right.

Flaws in access to the judiciary and to fair process. Given my previous comments, I will not provide further details on this topic, which has proved quite vexing even in highly developed countries.[13] Across most of Latin America, the judiciary is too distant, cumbersome, expensive, and slow for the poor and vulnerable even to attempt to access it.[14] And if they do manage to obtain judicial access, the available evidence often points to severe and systematic discrimination. Criminal procedures in particular often tend to disregard the rights of the accused before, during, and after trial.

Flaws due to sheer lawlessness. This is the issue that I emphasize
more in my previous work, where I argue that it is a mistake to conflate
the state with its bureaucratic apparatus.[15] Insofar as most of the formally
enacted law existing in a territory is issued and backed by the state, and
as the state institutions themselves are supposed to act according to
legal rules, we should recognize that the legal system is a constitutive
part of the state. As such, what I call "the legal state" (that is, the part of
the state that is embodied in a legal system) penetrates and textures
society, furnishing a basic element of stability to social relations. In
many countries of Latin America, however, the reach of the legal state is
limited. In many regions, not only those geographically distant from the
political centers but also the peripheries of large cities, the bureaucratic
state may be present in the form of buildings and officials paid out of
public budgets, but the legal state is absent: Whatever formally sanctioned law exists is applied intermittently, if at all. More importantly,
this intermittent law is encompassed by the informal law enacted by the
privatized—patrimonial, sultanistic, or simply gangsterlike—powers that
actually rule those places. This leads to complex situations involving a
continuous renegotiation of the boundaries between formal and informal legalities, situations in which it is vital to understand the interplay
between both kinds of law and the uneven power relations that develop.
The resulting informal legal system, punctuated by temporary reintro-
ductions of the formal one, supports a world of extreme violence, as
abundant data from both rural and urban regions show. These "brown
areas" are subnational systems of power that have a territorial basis and
an informal but quite effective legal system, yet they coexist with a
regime that, at least at the national political center, is democratic.

The problems that I have summarized indicate a severe incompleteness of the state, especially its legal dimension. Sadly, in many cases in
Latin America and elsewhere, this incompleteness has increased during
democratization, thanks to economic crises and the sternly antistatist
economic policies that have prevailed over the past two decades. There
is evidence, too, that this deficiency has been fostered by the desire of
national politicians to shape winning electoral coalitions by including
candidates from the perversely privatized areas to which I have referred.
These local politicians use the votes they command and the institutional positions they attain at the center in order to reproduce the systems
of privatized power they represent. Not incidentally, in Argentina and
Brazil, legislators from these "brown" areas have shown a keen interest
(with frequent success) in dominating the legislative committees that
appoint federal judges in those same regions—surely an effective way
of removing their fiefs from the reach of the legal state.

Thus we see that in many new (and not so new) democracies, in Latin
America and in other regions, there exist numerous points of rupture in
formal legal systems. To the extent that this is true, the rule of law has

only intermittent existence. In addition, this observation at the level of
the legal state is mirrored by numerous violations of the law at the
social level, which jointly amount to a truncated, or low-intensity, citizenship. In these countries, many individuals are citizens with respect
to political rights but not in terms of civil rights. Indeed, they are as
poor legally as they are materially.

At present, many international and domestic agencies support the
expansion of the rule of law as they conceive it, and legions of experts
are busy with various aspects of this task. In principle this is not bad
news, but there is a danger due to the strong orientation of the resulting
legal and judicial reforms toward the perceived interests of the dominant sectors. Typical areas of reform include domestic and international
commercial law, some aspects of civil law, and the more purely repressive aspects of criminal law. This may be useful for attracting investment,
but it tends to produce a "dualistic development of the justice system,"
centered on those aspects

> that concern the modernizing sectors of the economic elite in matters of an
> economic, business, or financial nature . . . [while] other areas of litigation
> and access to justice remain untouched, corrupted, and persistently lacking
> in infrastructure and resources.[16]

For societies that are profoundly unequal, these trends may reinforce
the exclusion of many from the rule of law, while further exaggerating
the advantages that the privileged enjoy by means of laws and courts
favoring their interests.

Dimensions of a Democratic Rule of Law

As the preceding discussion implies, the relevant question concerning the rule of law and democracy should address the various dimensions
and degrees along which the attributes of a democratic rule of law, or
estado democrático de derecho, are present or absent in a given case.
This requires convenient analytical disaggregations of the various aspects that the rule of law in general, and the democratic rule of law in
particular, include. The next step is to identify the empirical indicators
(variables or standards) that may allow a mapping of levels and variations along the various dimensions that have been defined. These tasks,
of course, are fraught with difficulties. I believe, however, that it is
possible to achieve some reasonable approximations of at least some of
the dimensions of interest, a task that I address below.

As I have defined it, a full democratic rule of law has not been reached
in any country—and arguably it might be undesirable to do so. Furthermore, against the somewhat positivistic inclinations of earlier legal
views, today practically all theories about law—despite their differ-

ences in other respects—hold that, like any other rule, the actual meaning or intent of the laws are defined by the dominant or authorized interpretations.[17] The "proper" interpretation of laws and, indeed, constitutions is one of the great topics around which political battles are fought. Contrary to technocratic and positivistic views, we should never forget that the law, in its content and application, is largely (like the state of which it is a part) a dynamic condensation of power relations, not just a rationalized technique for the ordering of social relations. Societal change, as well as unending struggles for the acquisition of new rights and the reinterpretation of old ones, makes the rule of law, especially the democratic rule of law, a moving horizon.

For these reasons I believe that, in assessing the rule of law and its linkages with democracy and democratic quality, one should begin by defining a point below which, though there may be some rule *by* law, there is no rule *of* law. Having established more or less approximately such a cutting point, what lies above it is a multidimensional continuum showing the degrees (or levels) to which, along the various dimensions into which the concept has been disaggregated, it may be said that the rule of law exists, especially in its incarnation as a democratic rule of law.

The dimensions discussed below are a preliminary attempt to disaggregate relevant dimensions that may be, at least in principle and with various degrees of approximation, empirically mapped. Furthermore, you may notice that this listing reflects the various aspects of the (democratic) rule of law that I discuss above.

The suggestions that follow come from a larger work in which we try to assess the finality of democracy, a theme of which, indeed, the rule of law is an important component. For reasons of space, I must refer to this work for details.[18]

The dimensions of a democratic rule of law as suggested here are as follows:

In relation to the legal system. First, we may look at the degree to which the legal system extends homogeneously across the entire territory of the state—the "brown" areas discussed above in reference to Latin America are clear signs of gaps. In addition, there is the degree to which the legal system behaves uniformly relative to various classes, economic sectors, and other societal groupings. Also, the rule of law entails the enactment and application of rules that prohibit and eventually punish discrimination against the poor, women, foreigners, and various minorities. Especially of concern in many Latin American countries is the degree to which the legal system deals in a respectful and considerate manner with indigenous communities and their legal systems and cultures. Finally, there should be generalized recognition of the supremacy of the constitution, and a supreme or constitutional court that effectively interprets and protects it.

In relation to the state and the government. First, we must examine the extent to which there exists a state that exercises effective and law-bound control over its whole territory. Second, there should exist adequately authorized and empowered state institutions for the exercise of horizontal accountability, including in relation to cases of presumed illegal actions (or inactions) by elected officials. Finally, state institutions should treat all individuals with due consideration and respect, and there must be adequate mechanisms for the prevention and redress of situations that ignore this requirement.

In relation to the courts and their auxiliary institutions. The judiciary must be free of undue influences from executive, legislative, and private interests, and if this is the case, the judiciary must not abuse its autonomy for the pursuit of narrowly defined corporate interests. There should be reasonably fair and expeditious access to courts, differentiating by kind of courts. We should also examine the degree to which courts recognize, and to what extent and in what kind of cases, international covenants and treaties, including those on human, gender, childhood, economic, social, and cultural rights. A democratic rule of law should also entail reasonably effective arrangements for ensuring that the poor, the illiterate, and otherwise deprived persons and groups have access to courts and to competent legal counsel. The police and other security forces must respect the rights of all individuals, and individuals should not be held in prison or subject to other ills in violation of basic rules of procedural fairness. Finally, the prisons should be in conditions adequate to the human dignity of the inmates.

In relation to state institutions in general. A democratic rule of law requires that all state institutions beyond merely the courts treat everyone with fairness, consideration, and respect. The rules that regulate state institutions should be clear, publicly available, and properly enacted. Finally, prompt and effective mechanisms must be in place to prevent, stop, or redress state violations of citizens' rights.

In relation to the social context. Beyond the right to associate in directly political organizations, the right of participation must exist, with at least the civil rights (and eventually the labor rights) of members being upheld. Furthermore, adequate rights and guarantees must exist for the functioning of diverse social organizations and for the exercise of vertical societal accountability.

In relation to civil and human rights. In terms of assessing the extent to which rights are violated, one should investigate the numbers, social position, gender, age, and geographical location of individuals who are victimized by physical violence, including domestic and police-perpetrated violence. Furthermore, data could be collected on the number and geographical locations of various crimes, especially homicides, armed robberies, and sexual and family violence. Finally, foreigners should be assigned the same civil rights as citizens, should be allowed at least at the local level to participate in political affairs, and should be treated by state agents and citizens with due consideration and respect.

Much has been said and written lately concerning the rule of law. To this large amount of discourse I would like to add the regretful observation that at times the rule of law (or at any rate, the rhetoric of the rule of law) has been employed in the service of authoritarian ideologies. In earlier times, in countries riven by severe inequality as so many in Latin America have been (and too often still are), practices associated with the law were not used in the service of fairness, but rather to entrench sharp inequalities and the manifold social ills associated with them.

Here I have tried to specify the proper sense and context within which the rule of law may be truly said to be consistent with democracy. In doing so, I have also tried to indicate some dimensions of law-based rule that can help us understand what makes it effective and how it relates to other aspects of the performance of countries that include a democratic regime among their institutional set. Of course, much more remains to be done, in theory and in practice. That much is sure.

NOTES

1. With this parenthetical expression I am sidestepping some complex issues of legal theory that I do not need to deal with here.

2. For a flavor of these differences in relation to common-law countries, see Ian Shapiro, ed., *The Rule of Law* (New York: New York University Press, 1994). In relation to civil-law countries see Michel Troper, "Le Concept de l'Etat de Droit," *Droits: Revue Française de Theórie Juridique* 15 (1992): 51–63; and Leó Hamon, "L'Etat de Droit et Son Essence," *Revue Française de Droit Constitutionnel* 4 (1990): 699–712.

3. Joseph Raz, "The Rule of Law and Its Virtue," *The Law Quarterly Review* 93 (1977): 196; Herbert L.A. Hart, *The Concept of Law* (Oxford: Oxford University Press, 1961), 197.

4. John Finnis, *Natural Law and Natural Rights* (Oxford: Oxford University Press, 1980), 61.

5. Joseph Raz, "The Rule of Law and Its Virtue," 198–201. For another influential listing that is similar to Raz's but disagrees on some theoretical matters that need not detain us here, see Lon Fuller, *The Morality of Law,* rev. ed. (New Haven: Yale University Press, 1969).

6. Lon Fuller, *The Morality of Law,* 162.

7. For a cogent analysis of this and related matters, with a focus on Latin America, see Ernesto Garzón Valdés, "Derecho y Democracia en América Latina," *Anales de la Cátedra Francisco Suárez* 33 (1999): 133–57; and Ernesto Garzón Valdés, "El Papel del Poder Judicial en la Transición a la Democracia," *Isonomía* 18 (2003): 27–46.

8. This is another topic upon which I do not need to elaborate here; see Andreas Schedler, Larry Diamond, and Marc F. Plattner, eds., *The Self-Restraining State: Power and Accountability in New Democracies* (Boulder, Colo.: Lynne Rienner, 1998).

9. Catalina Smulovitz and Enrique Peruzzotti, "Social Accountability in Latin America," *Journal of Democracy* 11 (October 2000): 147–58.

10. For discussion of horizontal accountability, I refer to my chapters in Andreas Schedler, Larry Diamond, and Marc F. Plattner, eds., *The Self-Restraining State,* and in Scott Mainwaring and Christopher Welna, eds., *Democratic Accountability in Latin America* (New York: Oxford University Press, 2003).

11. Juan J. Linz and Alfred Stepan, *Problems of Democratic Transition and Consolidation: Southern Europe, South America, and Post-Communist Europe* (Baltimore: Johns Hopkins University Press, 1996), 37.

12. *Clarín* (Buenos Aires), 10 May 1997, 8.

13. In relation to the United States, see Marc Galanter, "Why the 'Haves' Come Out Ahead: Speculations on the Limits of Legal Change," *Law & Society Review* 9 (1974): 95–160; and Joel Grossman, Herbert Kritzer, and Stewart Macaulay, "Do the 'Haves' Still Come Ahead?" *Law & Society Review* 33 (1999): 803–10.

14. It bears mentioning that in a December 1992 survey that I did in the metropolitan area of São Paulo (n=800), an overwhelming 93 percent responded "no" to a question asking if the law was applied equally in Brazil, and 6 percent did not know or did not answer. In a similar vein, in a survey taken in 1997 by Guzmán Heredia y Asociados in the metropolitan area of Buenos Aires (n=1,400), 89 percent of respondents indicated various degrees of lack of confidence in the courts, 9 percent expressed they had some confidence, and only 1 percent said they had a lot of confidence.

15. Guillermo O'Donnell, "On the State, Democratization and Some Conceptual Problems: A Latin American View with Glances at Some Postcommunist Countries," *World Development* 21 (1993): 1355–69.

16. Pilar Domingo, "Judicial Independence and Judicial Reform in Latin America," in Andreas Schedler, Larry Diamond, and Marc F. Plattner, eds., *The Self-Restraining State,* 169.

17. Apposite reflections on this matter in Fred Dallmayr, "Hermeneutics and the Rule of Law," in Gregory Leyh, ed., *Legal Hermeneutics: History, Theory, and Practice* (Berkeley: University of California Press, 1992).

18. See Guillermo O'Donnell, Jorge Vargas Cullell, and Osvaldo M. Iazzetta, eds., *The Quality of Democracy: Theory and Applications* (Notre Dame: University of Notre Dame Press, 2004). This book comments on the valuable and pioneering "Audit on the Quality of Democracy" in Costa Rica, reported in the chapter by Vargas Cullell.

2

THE AMBIGUOUS VIRTUES OF ACCOUNTABILITY

Philippe C. Schmitter

Philippe C. Schmitter is professor emeritus of political science at Stanford University, professorial fellow in the department of political and social sciences at the European University Institute in Florence, and recurring visiting professor at the Central European University in Budapest .

When Terry Karl and I hit upon the concept of accountability as the key to the broadest and most widely applicable definition of "modern representative political democracy," our effort in 1991 met with a surprising amount of indifference or even hostility.[1] In the last ten years, however, there has been a veritable explosion of scholarly concern with the notion of political accountability, not to mention such cognate concepts as "corporate social accountability," "communitarian responsiveness," and "individual moral responsibility."

Generically speaking, political accountability is a relationship between two sets of persons or (more often) organizations in which the former agree to keep the latter informed, to offer them explanations for decisions made, and to submit to any predetermined sanctions that they may impose. The latter, meanwhile, are subject to the command of the former, must provide required information, explain obedience or disobedience to the commands thereof, and accept the consequences for things done or left undone. Accountability, in short, implies an exchange of responsibilities and potential sanctions between rulers and citizens, made all the more complicated by the fact that a varied and competitive set of representatives typically interposes between the two. Needless to say, there are many caveats, loose linkages, and role reversals in this relationship, so that its product is almost always contested. Information can be selective and skewed; explanations can be deflected to other actors; sanctions are rarely applied and can be simply ignored.

All stable political regimes probably have some predictable form of accountability to some type of constituency. Sultanistic autocracies have their coteries and cadres. Military dictatorships have their juntas and deals among the different armed services. Even absolute monarchs are supposed to be accountable to God—not to mention more earthly dynastic and marital concerns. What democracy has that these do not is *citizens*—a constituency covering the entire country and populated (these days) by virtually all adults minus resident foreigners. Moreover, in terms of political accountability, each citizen has the same rights and obligations, that is, to be informed (with limited exceptions) about official actions, to hear justifications for them, to judge how well or poorly they are carried out, and to act accordingly—electorally or otherwise.

What makes the role of citizens increasingly complex is that they have had to rely more heavily than ever on specialized *representatives*, that is, on agents who in turn act as principals when it comes to ensuring that elected or appointed rulers are held accountable. As if this were not complex enough, these very same agents-cum-principals may have ruled in the past and probably aspire to rule again in the future. Meanwhile, citizens go from being principals to being agents when they are obliged to conform to official decisions that they may have opposed or did not even know about.

However complex it may be, political accountability must be institutionalized if it is to work effectively. This means that it has to be embedded in a mutually understood and preestablished set of rules. Some of these may be formalized in constitutions, legal codes, or sworn oaths, but political accountability is not the same as legal, financial, or ethical accountability. Rulers can be investigated and held to account for actions that did not break the law or result in illicit personal enrichment or violate common mores. They may have simply made bad political choices that failed to produce their intended effect or cost vastly more than initially announced. And rulers can even be held accountable for acts of omission as well as commission in somewhat the same way citizens can, provided that the rules were made by previously established consent.

Finally, it should be noted that the process of political accountability still goes on even when incumbents win, as most often they do. The exchanges of information, justification, and judgment that make up the ordinary cycle of accountability are less obtrusive than the "big bang" of "throwing the rascals out," but no less real and significant for all that. Thus it would be wrong to think that only an electoral turnover, the loss of a confidence vote in parliament, a presidential impeachment, or a premier's resignation demonstrate that political accountability is working. In all likelihood, the most accountable rulers are those who never face the immediate threat of such measures. These leaders make it a practice to take citizens' expectations on board, to explain to citizens what the leaders are doing and why, and, therefore, have nothing to fear from accountability. Indeed, such rulers may even find that the degree to which

TABLE 1—THE SEVEN ITEMS OF THE QUALITY-OF-DEMOCRACY SCALE

Q-1	Agreements on the partial regimes and constitution itself are effectively applied to all groups and territories.
Q-2	Conditions of effective political competition are equal for most citizens and groups.
Q-3	Effective participatory equality produces greater substantive (income) equality for most citizens and groups.
Q-4	Voter turnout decreases or increases significantly, or remains the same over three successive national elections.
Q-5	Membership in associations and movements increases and extends its coverage to a wide range of interests.
Q-6	Individuals show an increasing tendency to regard themselves as "politically efficacious."
Q-7	Gender equality improves.

they hold themselves plainly answerable to citizens gives them greater legitimacy when they have to act against immediate popular opinion.

Measuring That Which Eludes Measurement

My first, failed attempt to measure accountability's impact on the quality of democracy rested on induction. Using the burgeoning literature on the alleged defects of new democracies, I came up with the seven items listed in Table 1. None defines democracy in the "accountable" sense that I have proposed, but one or more authors found each of these conditions to be a likely and desirable product of well-functioning democratic institutions.

Finding a reliable way to gauge these items proved difficult. Converting them into cardinal or even ordinal measures was virtually impossible. Moreover, the items may be connected to one another—either causally or functionally—which implies that they should scale. To give one example, survey research indicates that increases in a person's sense of "political efficacy" (item 6) are related to an increase in the likelihood of voting (item 4). While much evidence on this and other relationships at the individual level has been gathered and analyzed, we still do not know how they cluster at the level of whole polities.

Judging the extent to which the constitution and other major rules are evenly applied across a nation's physical and social landscape is obviously hard. Guillermo O'Donnell speaks of "brown areas"—often outside major cities and presumably outside dominant ethnic, class, or social circles as well—where democratic guarantees and legal norms are routinely violated or ignored. This too is widely attested yet not easily measurable, either in extent or significance. Counting legal challenges involving the misapplication of laws would likely be in vain since "brown areas" where the rule of law fails to apply are not likely to be places where the weak and marginalized would dare to take their cases to court. To gauge how great a real-world effect the formal extension of the rights to vote and to associate is having, one might look at indicators such as margins of electoral victory, with smaller margins likely bespeaking greater competitiveness. Or one might look for the presence of stable sets of competing class-based organizations as a sign that free associational life has become politically significant.

Changes in income and gender equality can be measured fairly readily in both comparative and historical terms within and across many polities. Not so data on things like whether or not people feel a "sense of personal political efficacy." Changes in voter turnout are easy to chart, but hard to interpret. Nearly every neodemocracy has seen an early "orgy" of civic participation associated with founding elections followed by declines in turnout. Does this indicate relative citizen satisfaction and rational "free-riding," or growing disenchantment with the new system and the politicians that it has produced? Data on the diversity of purposes and membership of individuals in civil society organizations are notoriously hard to come by and easily distorted. Seizing on one type of organization for which there exist data—whether it is trade unions or bowling societies—can be quite unrepresentative of collective actions that are occurring elsewhere in society.

My hunch about the flaws in my quality-of-democracy research is that I chose the right items, but fell short when it came to figuring out a rigorous method for reliably scoring these qualities or conditions. Let me add that my first hunch could be wrong: I may have chosen the wrong items. Yet this too is hard to say, for the simple reason that the entire discussion regarding democratic quality has been beset by fallacies.

The first is the unquestioned assumption that *all or most neodemocracies are inferior in quality,* whether considered absolutely or in relation to older democratic regimes. This assumption is mistaken on both counts: Not only are most recently established democracies doing far better than anyone had the right to expect, but most older democracies are performing less well than this assumption implies and less well than they used to.

One could examine any established Western democracy one or even two decades after it started democratizing and find a decidedly mixed picture. What was Britain like in the late 1830s? How would 1860s Denmark or 1890s France measure up? Were any of them doing as well as East European or Latin American countries today? In those earlier democratizing societies would you really find less in the way of public corruption, vote-buying, legislative malapportionment, favoritism for the privileged, and disregard of the oppressed—not to mention the denial of voting rights to women, illiterates, and the poor? I doubt it.

Of course, this comparison is unfair. Political history has accelerated and expectations have changed. Modern democracy has different rules and benchmarks. Today's fledgling democracies are supposed to be better than yesterday's, and the equal of contemporary established democracies as well. The century or more it took the latter to reach their current levels of public transparency, electoral fairness, effective rights guarantees, equal access, and citizen accountability somehow drops out of sight.

To avoid this fallacy of anachronism, the criteria we use to judge democratic quality must be temporally appropriate. This implies that: 1) We must avoid holding neodemocracies to the sorts of elevated performance standards that took previous democracies decades or more to reach; and 2) we must refrain from blaming older democracies for failing to do things (like, say, giving women the vote or abolishing rotten boroughs) that virtually no one would have expected them to do at the time. Clearly, the post-1974 and post-1989 democracies must be evaluated according to a "normal" range of variation drawn from the experience of the modern West. This means holding them to standards higher than their predecessor democracies. But it does not mean assessing them according to "best practices" rather than "normal benchmarks." The goal posts, in other words, must shift to reflect the historical reality of the current moment in the evolution of democracy. But they cannot be set so high or far that only top Western competitors can reach them, or moved again just to discredit the game's latest entrants.

The second potential fallacy is *idealism,* or the holding of all actual democracies to unrealistic standards. Any democratic regime is going to suffer from some degree of unfairness, citizen apathy, politically salient inequality, self-serving behavior by public officials, and so on. But democracy, unavoidably, is not just a descriptive term for a regime characterized by significant if imperfect equality, citizen participation, transparency, and so on. It is also a term used to denote a normative goal that can be approached but never in practice fully attained. Thus we are stuck with a word that has both empirical and normative connotations. Unless we recognize that much of democratic theory is hortatory—aimed at encouraging us to do better in the future than we have done in the past—we will be unable to make fair and "realistic" assessments about what neodemocracies have or have not accomplished.

The third fallacy is *partisanship.* It is very tempting to assume that the neodemocracy one is studying should be doing what one would like it to do substantively. Not infrequently, at least among North American and West European observers, this is not unrelated to what they would like their own preferred party of reference to accomplish at home. Social democrats castigate neodemocracies for not making incomes more equal, free-market liberals complain about the slow pace of privatization, traditional conservatives bewail the decline of old ways or old elites, and so on. To limit the sway of partisanship, the trick is to focus on such widely endorsed goals as respect for human and civic rights, decline in poverty, holding rulers accountable, protecting national identity, and so forth. When applying less generic standards—such as gender equality or agricultural subsidies—it is wise to be sensitive to the observable preferences of the citizens in the specific polity one is dealing with.

Behind all three of these potential fallacies lies the prospect that *consolidating a democracy in no way guarantees its quality*. Consolidation, as I understand it, means getting people to compete and cooperate according to rules and within institutions that citizens, representatives, and rulers alike find mutually acceptable. The rules and institutions thus consolidated may produce a democracy of low, medium, or high quality. In the first two events, one hopes that citizens will demand improvements, but nothing is certain and the process can take a long time. One of the main hypotheses of democracy advocates is that even a low-grade, purely procedural democracy is more likely to improve these conditions eventually than is a high-quality autocracy—if such a thing exists. Democracy cannot ensure improvements in the short run, but does offer the possibility of making them in the future. Hence, any democracy is better than no democracy.

Indeed, it may even prove counterproductive to aim for too high-quality a democracy during the transition. To insist on the radical changes that this would require may be to invite a backlash from groups that feel threatened but which might have gone along with a slower, more disarmingly procedural approach. And such patience should be easier under democracy, since there is always supposed to be another free and fair election around the corner. Democracy is unique among generic regime types in that it can lawfully and consensually change its own rules and make itself into a different type of democracy.

Can Proximate Measures Work?

Can an indirect approach to measuring the quality of democracy succeed where my direct one failed? Can we observe how well or poorly neodemocracies build in accountability during the consolidation process, and then see if this correlates positively with economic growth, social and gender equality, a more evenly distributed rule of law, better rights protection, and the like? Since we have no reason to believe that the mere consolidation of democracy will bring all these benefits right away, perhaps the missing link to a better future lies in the various mechanisms that connect citizens to rulers via representatives.

The spatial metaphor that political scientists have traditionally used when discussing political accountability stresses "vertical" power relations between citizens, representatives, and rulers. Various kinds of information, justifications, and sanctions or threats of sanctions move up and down the chain in an ongoing exchange. To this vertical dimension, advocates of the "liberal" aspect of democracy and scholars of democratization have added a "horizontal" one.

Horizontal accountability is a matter of interactions, not between rulers and ruled, but between arms or branches of the regime and state acting according to preset constitutional or legal rules. Such regular "checks and balances" are supposed to ensure greater accountability— and in some accounts even to trump the vertical connection with citizens—as, for example, when a constitutional court strikes down a law that most citizens support or when a central bank ignores a popular government's request to cut interest rates for the sake of keeping up employment levels.

While I have my doubts about whether this type of accountability actually works very well or is truly democratic,[2] there is no gainsaying either the extraordinary efforts that have gone into creating new institutions of horizontal accountability in older democracies or the energy with which such institutions have been urged upon newer democracies. Some horizontal-accountability mainstays are juridical in nature, such as high courts to deal with constitutional issues or more specialized courts to deal with matters concerning human rights, race and labor relations, or the conduct of elections. Others intervene in executive-legislative-judicial relations to provide "outside" accountability. These "guardian" agencies (to use Robert A. Dahl's term) can include auditing offices, inspectorate generals, and offices of the ombudsman as well as a plethora of independent regulatory agencies.

How useful is it to apply these spatial metaphors—to which one might add the idea of "oblique" accountability to various civil society groups—to our thinking about democratic political accountability and the methods or mechanisms through which it might work? Here I am ambivalent. There must be something significant behind the proliferation of these institutions and the persistence with which Western democracies demand that newcomers try to adopt them, but is this not about the need for stable property rights and secure elite interlocutors rather than the quality of democracy per se?[3]

For this reason, I have chosen to use the dimension not of space but of time, as illustrated first in Table 2 below. Democracy has a set of rhythms. Elections, popular mobilizations, policy cycles, public attention spans, and even the popularity of politicians follow more or less predictable patterns over time in any consolidated democratic polity— even if their coincidences occasionally produce exciting moments of *fortuna* or improvised acts of *virtú*. Broadly speaking, there are three movements to the dance: The *overture,* labeled "before" in Table 2, is a relatively lengthy period of proposing, discussing, and agenda setting. The *intermezzo* is more compressed. Labeled "during" in Table 2, it is the period when a decision is made via interest alliances, interagency bargaining, and executive-legislative transactions until eventual ratification is achieved. The *finale,* often drawn out, sees the proposal— now having taken on the form of a law or regulation—undergo

TABLE 2—THE GENERIC PROPERTIES OF SUCCESSFUL ACCOUNTABILITY:
TIME X ACTORS

	BEFORE	DURING	AFTER
CITIZENS	Participation	Attention	Obligation
REPRESENTATIVES	Mobilization (for and against)	Competition	Compliance
RULERS	Accessibility	Deliberation	Responsiveness

implementation, produce its intended and unintended effects, and possibly be subjected to court review or become a topic for wider political debate.

The hunch behind this emphasis on time rather than space—on "when" rather than "where" as the decisive factor in the process of mutual accountability—is admittedly not something that one can prove. But one can try to build upon it and see if it turns out to be more fruitful than the usual spatial metaphors in explaining the benevolence or malevolence of outcomes.[4]

In Table 2, I have cross-tabulated the temporal aspect of the decision-making process with the type of actor whose behavior is being evaluated. This generates nine criteria for evaluating a successful accountability sequence. The most "classic" is probably the one in the upper left-hand corner: *participation*. It has long been presumed that the more citizens participate actively in the "decision to make a decision" (that is, in the discussion about whether a decision should be made, what should be on the agenda, and who should be involved in making the decision), the more *attention* they will pay to the subsequent process and the more likely they will feel *obligated* to conform to whatever is decided—even if they opposed the decision itself.

Representatives in the broad sense (elected or otherwise) will presumably play a key *mobilization* role in the "before" phase by telling their "constituents" (who may be but need not be formally grouped into territorial units) what is at stake, and by canvassing their opinion. During the making of a decision, these representatives *compete* under preestablished rules against rival sets of representatives to influence its substance. Should they fail, it is understood they will nonetheless *comply* with the result and try to persuade their supporters to accept it as well.

Following a similar logic, the more that rulers provide *accessibility* to the greatest number and widest variety of individual citizens or organizations from civil society, the higher will be the level of information that they will carry into their more restricted *deliberations* and the greater will be the likelihood that the decisions they eventually take will be *responsive* to the interests and passions of citizens and their representatives.

TABLE 3—THE GENERIC PROPERTIES OF FAILED ACCOUNTABILITY:
TIME X ACTORS

	BEFORE	DURING	AFTER
CITIZENS	Absention	Indifference	Resentment
REPRESENTATIVES	Mobilization (against)	Obstruction	Resistance
RULERS	Exclusion	Collusion	Imposition

Note that these criteria are not functionally or necessarily interrelated. Rulers can gain access to relatively passive and disorganized citizens (for example, via informal soundings, survey research, or focus groups) and active and well-organized citizens can participate in "unconventional" ways that do not involve being granted formal access (for example, by demonstrating against their lack of access). The active participation of individuals in the initial phase may not be a guarantee of their subsequent interest in a particular issue, and they may feel no obligation to conform once the decision has been made and is being implemented. Representatives can find themselves in a particularly ambiguous position. On the one hand, they must mobilize their followers in order to have a chance of influencing the decision. On the other hand, once the decision is made the rulers will expect them to deliver the compliance of these same people—even if their influence has been marginal. Failure to deliver compliance could lead to the representatives' being labeled disloyal and excluded from future decisions.

Table 3 simply inverts the previous matrix in an effort to capture what qualities might emerge if the process of political accountability were to go wrong. There is no reason to provide any detail about these negative criteria. They are merely intended to capture the reverse of those discussed above. Their theoretical importance will become more evident as we turn to the thorny issue of measurement, for accountability seems to be one of those political concepts, like legitimacy, that usually becomes apparent only when it is defective or absent. When the accountability process is working well not much seems to be happening, and one could reach the false conclusion that it makes no contribution to improving the various qualities that a democracy should display.

Measuring Accountability

Before turning to measurement issues in detail, we should be sure that we are not fine-tuning indicators without first having asked ourselves if the mode of scoring or aggregating them is consistent with the very notion of accountability itself. A great deal of the recent empirical work on democratization suffers from precisely this defect, especially from the urge to collapse a sizeable range of data into a single number or name. As a result, two cases that receive the same score or fall into the same box can reveal, on closer inspection, radically different overall "profiles." Only after one has coded the more discretely equivalent variables and then tested them for scalability does it make sense to use the aggregate result and to compare countries according to their relative approximation to such complex phenomena as liberalization, democratization, or accountability.[5]

Accountability is not only hard to measure directly, as we have seen, but also has a rather "tricky" conceptual structure. For one thing, some of its "positive properties" may be incompatible with each other, or at least may involve complex tradeoffs. High levels of individual participation may not be so benevolently linked to subsequent attention and sense of obligation. Citizens may become passionate advocates only to tire quickly or blame their representatives unfairly for making necessary compromises. Rulers may be highly accessible, but may not have the time to take what they hear seriously because they have to deliberate with each other under a deadline.

Even more commonly, persons in positions of authority—whether elected or selected—may honestly be convinced that they have done their best to be responsive to citizen preferences, only to discover that citizens did not really want what they said they wanted or have changed their minds in the meantime. Democratic and accountable politicians very frequently have to take risks of this sort and follow courses of action that are not immediately popular, making the calculation that once the effects are experienced the citizenry will have learned to accept them. I infer from this that the scores on the variables are highly unlikely to produce a single scale of accountability. The most one should expect are distinctive clusters of scores that will generate accountability profiles which might be equally effective or defective in different social, cultural, institutional, or historical contexts.

One should also expect that the relation of many of these variables to accountability will be anything but linear and incremental. Officials may be so accessible that they do not make a decision in time to solve the problem. Representatives may mobilize their followers and, thereby, raise expectations to unrealistic heights. Or some representatives may stalemate other representatives of major interests so effectively that the intervention of a tiny minority determines the outcome—undermining both citizen responsiveness and compliance. Thus, when trying to fit the nominal scores generated above into a single scheme of evaluation, one should attend to the likelihood that there will be curvilinear or perhaps parabolic relationships with the quality of democracy. There may even be bizarre "kinks" due to peculiar sequences or unique combinations.

Finally, the operationalization of these variables will be almost inevitably contaminated by prior knowledge about the longevity, stability, or reputation of the regime being scored. It will be difficult not to conclude that, say, Norway, Switzerland, and the United States must have more accountable practices than, say, Germany, Japan, and Italy simply because liberal democracy has been around for so much longer in the former countries. Needless to say, all the neodemocracies (except perhaps Uruguay) will automatically be suspected of "defects" in their accountability mechanisms. The scientific answer to this problem would be to deprive the data of their national identity and code it anonymously, but this would be simply impossible to do. If somehow one could invent a way of decontaminating the data-gathering process, counterintuitive scores might emerge. For example, Norway, Switzerland, and the United States—each with its long democratic history and (relatively) satisfied body of citizens—might turn out not to have more-accountable rules and practices, in which case we would have falsified not only the hypothesis that "high accountability" improves the quality of democracy (at least, as assessed by citizens), but also the hypothesis that it is causally related to the survivability of such a regime.

My approach to measurement would be to come up with simple yes-or-no questions (with the possibility of a "fuzzy" intermediate score) for each variable and only then to try to see if they produce a single scale or cluster into nominal categories. The questions should be multiple for each variable and they may well prove uncorrelated with one another. They should be capable of capturing both the positive and negative aspects in the cells of Tables 2 and 3. And they should be composed of a mix of generic and specific issues—although the latter will be difficult since not all polities have had to deal with the same policy issues within the same timeframe and with the same intensity. Since I have only just begun thinking conceptually about accountability, I have not yet come up with operational suggestions for all of the requisite questions. But let us begin with the easiest, which is *participation* (or *abstention*) by individual citizens:

> 1) Has turnout over the past three elections for the national legislature increased significantly (1), remained about the same (0.5), or decreased significantly (0)?
> 2) [Pick a salient issue area of contemporary politics, say, environmental protection.] Have individuals over the past five years tended to join and support parties focusing particularly on this issue much more than other parties (1), about the same (0.5), or much less than other parties (0)?
> 3) Have individuals responding to public opinion polls over the past five years expressed a greater interest in politics (1), about the same interest (0.5), or less interest (0)?

Note that the first and last questions touch on generic matters, while the middle question deals with a more specific topic. Note also that they involve different techniques of gathering data. This is deliberate: While it may be tempting to rely on easily available survey data to assess the perceived degree of accountability, it would be a mistake to do so exclusively, especially for comparative purposes. Responses to opinion polls are difficult to interpret across languages and cultures; are "costless" when they are uttered; and may reflect immediate circumstances rather than deeply held values or judgments. (On a related note, the evaluation should be made over a period long enough to screen out momentary fluctuations.) The subjective data collected by opinion pollsters have a place in research on accountability, but only when surrounded by more-objective measures of actual behavior.

A somewhat more challenging task would be to formulate questions on the topic of how *responsive* (or imposing) rulers are seen to be:

1) [Presume that most citizens would benefit from the enhanced competitiveness of their respective national economies.] According to the best available indicators of economic competitiveness, has [country X] improved (1), sustained (0.5), or diminished (0) its relative position over the past five years?

2) Has the national legislature over the past five years tended to approve the annual government budget within the prescribed time limit (1), with a slight delay (0.5), or with a considerable delay (0)?

3) When polled over the past five years, have citizens reported that they believe that their leaders pay more attention to persons such as themselves (1), about the same amount (0.5), or less (0)?

Finally, let us focus on representatives and the perceived degree to which they *compete* (or *collude*) for control over (or obstruct) the decision-making process:

1) In the past five years or so, have there been major incidents in which significant parties, associations, or movements have refused to participate in hearings or discussions of important legislation (0), minor incidents (0.5), no noticeable incidents (1)?

2) Is it the general practice of executive decision makers to invite spokespersons from competing parties, interest groups, or social movements to discuss the drafting of major laws before they are submitted to the legislature (1), more or less while parliamentary debate is taking place (0.5), or only after a formal decision has been made (0)?

3) Have there been frequent incidents over the past five years in which significant parties, associations, or movements have urged their supporters to boycott or resist the implementation of government decisions they deem to have been improperly taken (1), a few incidents (0.5), or no noticeable incidents (0)?

Coming up with a full repertoire of such tripartite question sets should be feasible. Some will no doubt be more difficult to formulate than others, especially when it comes to so-called objective indicators. But as long as one avoids excessive dependence on one source or method of observation, triangulation should allow one reasonable confidence about prospects for coming up with a valid score. As I said above, it is highly unlikely that these scores will produce a single reproducible scale of political accountability. I would be quite satisfied if the effort ended with a nominal typology of different "profiles" that might produce more or less the same quality of democracy (and of legitimacy) in societies of different composition and historical trajectory.

After all, if we have learned one thing from the recent study of transitions from autocracy and consolidations of democracy, it is "equifinality." Many countries having left from different points of departure and chosen different modes of transition have been ending up, not with the same type of democracy, but with similarly stable and consolidated institutions. Why should there not be multiple ways of exercising political accountability and translating that accountability into improvements along the various measures of quality according to which democracy can be assessed?

NOTES

1. Philippe C. Schmitter and Terry Lynn Karl, "What Democracy Is . . . and Is Not," *Journal of Democracy* 2 (Summer 1991): 75–88. Our definition, offered at page 76, holds that democracy is "a regime or system of governance in which rulers are held accountable for their actions in the public domain by citizens acting indirectly through the competition and cooperation of their elected representatives." If we had it to do over again, we would change two particulars. First, we would replace the word "governance" with "government" after critical engagement with the vast literature on "governance" and its too-common tendency to use the term to justify the introduction of less-than-democratic practices. Second, we would delete the word "elected" that an overzealous editor inserted in front of "representatives," since our concept of representation was and is far broader than the kind that is putatively secured through elections.

2. Philippe C. Schmitter, "The Limits of Horizontal Accountability," in Andreas Schedler, Larry Diamond, and Marc F. Plattner, eds., *The Self-Restraining State: Power and Accountability in New Democracies* (Boulder, Colo.: Lynne Rienner, 1999), 59–63. There I worry that "servants of the state" will often be tempted to collude and protect their shared privileges, and I note that the architects of the U.S. constitutional order saw checks and balances as "auxiliary precautions" meant precisely to place limits on potentially unjust or unwise majority desires.

3. It is worth noting that whatever a country's other democratic credentials, if it refuses to adopt horizontal-accountability institutions—including a technocratically run central bank—it will never have a chance of gaining admission into the European Union. Yet many a well-established democracy has managed to survive quite well without this element of horizontal accountability. France, Austria, the Netherlands, and the Scandinavian countries all have had centralized government structures, less independent central banks and relatively few regulatory agencies. There is no firm empirical evidence that autonomous central banks boost the stability or quality of democracy. Moreover, even their ostensible goal of controlling inflation may not be a democratic objective.

4. An associated hypothesis would be that there has been a tendency—accelerating in recent years—on the part of rulers to convince citizens to rest content with *ex post facto* accountability only, and especially that offered by elections. The usual reason given is that the increased scale and scope of governing, combined with the rising importance of technology, makes the average citizen less capable of evaluating the costs and benefits of a given course of action before the fact. Technocrats and other specialists should do the forecasting, the argument goes, and voters can rule on it all when next they visit the polls. One way to keep citizens from getting into the vertical-accountability game "too early" is to shift ever more decision-making power to "horizontal"—and to citizens, inaccessible—agencies such as autonomous central banks, independent regulatory commissions, and the like. With parties in many countries coming to adopt platforms that resemble each other's fairly closely, citizens seem to feel increasingly dissatisfied with electoral accountability, and ask whether they even have real choices. In neodemocracies, especially, the response to growing technocracy and unsatisfying elections seems to be stratospheric levels of electoral volatility and frequent turnovers of power. And yet even in these countries citizens do not seem to feel any evident sense of satisfaction at having exercised so successfully their capacity to hold rulers accountable. Basic policy orientations change little; the old rulers later return to power; and disenchantment with democracy encounters no adequate response.

5. Terry Lynn Karl and Philippe C. Schmitter, "Concepts, Assumptions, and Hypotheses About Democratization: Reflections on 'Stretching' from South to East," and Philippe C. Schmitter and Carsten Q. Schneider, "The Liberalization of Autocracy, Mode of Transition and Consolidation of Democracy: Data on Central and Eastern Europe, Middle East and North Africa, Southern Europe, South America, Central America, and the Republics of the Former Soviet Union." Both papers were presented at a workshop on "Regime Transitions: Transitions from Communist Rule in Comparative Perspective," sponsored by the Center for Democracy, Development, and the Rule of Law at the Institute for International Studies, Stanford University, 15–16 November 2002.

3

FREEDOM AS THE FOUNDATION

David Beetham

David Beetham *is professor emeritus at the University of Leeds and fellow of the Human Rights Centre at the University of Essex. As associate director of the U.K. Democratic Audit, he has contributed to developing methodologies for democracy assessment of both established and transitional democracies. His latest book is* Democracy: A Beginner's Guide *(forthcoming, 2005).*

When I began studying political science it was common to talk of "liberal" democracy as a particular type of democracy, to be contrasted with participatory democracy, single-party democracy, or Marxist democracy.[1] Remnants of that thinking persist, though a moment's reflection will show that this typology is based on a conceptual confusion, for without liberty there can be no democracy. If people are to have any influence or control over public decision making and decision makers, they must be free to communicate and associate with one another, to receive accurate information and express divergent opinions, to enjoy freedom of movement, and to be free from arbitrary arrest and imprisonment.

This essay begins with some further elaboration of the relations between freedom, rights, and democracy, and then briefly summarizes the connections between these and other elements of democratic quality addressed by other contributors to this volume. It subsequently sets out a procedure for assessing the quality of a country's democracy in four successive steps: first, defining the appropriate democratic "goods"; second, identifying standards of best practice as a benchmark of attainment for each of these goods; third, analyzing the typical modes of subversion which may prevent their attainment; and fourth, exploring possible agencies of protection against these subversions.

The integral connection between freedom and democracy was already well understood in ancient Athens. In Pericles's famous Funeral Oration (circa 430 B.C.E.), recorded and probably rewritten by Thucydides, the

Athenian leader celebrates the values of freedom and openness, along-side equality, as the distinctive attributes of Athenian democracy in contrast to the militaristic Spartan regime. Aristotle considered freedom to be the *telos,* or goal, which democracy was designed to foster. Plato caricatured democracy for "bursting with the spirit of freedom," and imagined that in such a system, even the donkeys would bump you aside as you walked down the street.[2] In his definitive book on rhetoric in ancient Athens, Josiah Ober demonstrates how public communication and freedom of speech were essential to argument and debate in both assembly and law courts, and how this freedom presupposed the validity of individual freedom of thought.[3]

The idea that such freedoms are distinctively modern stems from a misreading of Benjamin Constant's distinction between the liberty of the ancients and that of the moderns. Writing in the first quarter of the nineteenth century, Constant contrasted the idea of liberty as direct participation in public affairs with notions of liberty that viewed it as having mainly to do with the protection of essentially private pursuits and interests. In Constant's contrast we can recognize an early version of Isaiah Berlin's distinction between positive liberty and the negative principle of noninterference.[4] To be sure, the public culture of Athenian democracy expected citizen participation and looked askance at those who were too bound up in their private affairs. This is an important difference. Yet, for the public activity of direct deliberative democracy to take place, there clearly had to be freedom to hold and express differences of opinion and to discuss these openly with others. And a broader freedom of inquiry was a necessary condition for the achievements of classical philosophy and science.

So democracy without freedom is a contradiction in terms. What is distinctively modern is the idea that the freedoms necessary to democracy cannot be preserved in practice unless they are guaranteed as a set of individual rights in a constitutionally protected bill of rights. Such documents now typically conform to the UN-sponsored International Covenant on Civil and Political Rights, which first went into force in 1976. National bills or charters of rights typically include the physical liberty and security of the person and the guarantee of due legal process as necessary conditions if the democratic freedoms of expression, association, and assembly are to be realized in practice. That these freedoms are guaranteed as *individual* rights, however, should not be allowed to obscure their essentially *collective* context and purpose: taking part with others in expressing opinions, seeking to persuade, mobilizing support, demonstrating, and all those other activities intrinsic to the democratic process as one of public rather than private decision making.

Democracy in the United Kingdom survived longer than in any other country on the idea that these freedoms could be realized simply by the law's silence, while British politicians and lawyers believed, somewhat

patronizingly, that bills of rights were only necessary for countries that
did not enjoy the inbuilt British "culture of freedom." Yet the successive erosions of liberty at the hands of parliaments dominated by the
executive eventually convinced the political class that formal incorporation of the European Convention on Human Rights into British law
was necessary, though this was disingenuously called "bringing rights
back home," as if they were a peculiarly British invention in the first
place.[5]

The idea of a "culture of liberty" is not, however, irrelevant to the
quality of democracy. The freedom of expression may be constitutionally guaranteed, but there may still be little diversity of opinion or few
sources of public information, and the media may be dominated by
trivia. Freedom of association may be guaranteed, but there may still be
little self-organization of civil society, or readiness to challenge an
elected government. How far freedoms are actually used may be difficult
to assess, but there is a long tradition of political analysis which holds
that this makes a key difference to a democracy's quality.

Rights, Equality, and Democracy

If the freedoms necessary to democracy require protection in a bill of
rights, then that protection is secure only to the degree that the courts
charged with upholding such a charter are independent of the executive
and the legislature. At this point, there is of course considerable overlap
with the idea of the "rule of law," which could be regarded as the foundation of any civilized existence, let alone democratic government.
Experience has also shown that effective rights protection requires two
further conditions: One is the right of individual appeal to the courts in
the event of infringement or violation of one's rights, with the realistic
prospect of remedy or restitution; the other is the power of the courts to
determine whether the conditions allowing a right to be restricted or
even derogated from have been met.

This latter issue merits further discussion, as it is a point where subversion of rights frequently occurs in practice. Most bills of rights (the
first ten amendments to the U.S. Constitution form an exception) are
hedged about with qualifications, limitations, and exceptions. The classic example is Article 10 of the European Convention (though similar
examples can be found in the corresponding International Covenant).
This article boldly asserts that everyone has the right to freedom of
expression, but it then adds that this right may be subject to such
formalities, conditions, restrictions, or penalties as are prescribed by
law and are necessary in a democratic society, in the interests of national
security, territorial integrity, or public safety, for the prevention of
disorder or crime, for the protection of health or morals, for the protection
of the reputation or rights of others, for preventing the disclosure of

information received in confidence, or for maintaining the authority and impartiality of the judiciary.[6]

It may seem that this right is worthless. But the key point is whether the courts have the power to decide if all the conditions justifying a particular limitation have been met. If they do not have that power, or are simply subservient to the executive, then the latter can suppress rights at will and claim the mantle of constitutionality for doing so. Of course it is up to governments to take the initiative in balancing freedoms with security or public order; but it is up to the courts, if appealed to, to judge whether any such limitation is justified, and to demand the evidence necessary to make that judgment, not just to take the government's say-so. Here the procedure and substance of rights protection go hand-in-hand.

Many people still insist that it is undemocratic for the courts to restrict or frustrate the will of a popularly elected government. But democracy is only secure if the conditions for the exercise of the popular will are guaranteed on an ongoing basis, through a protected set of basic freedom rights. Democracy cannot be equated with any particular measure of an elected government. In any case, since bills of rights have typically been endorsed in popular referendums, the limits they impose on legislative as well as executive discretion should be seen as a form of democratic self-limitation, which the courts are properly upholding.[7]

In any exercise of the kind we are undertaking there is bound to be considerable overlap between the different subject areas. Two points are worth making here about the close relation between rights and equality. First, rights entail equality, since all rights are in principle guaranteed to all equally. Most rights conventions are either prefaced or concluded by a strong antidiscrimination clause, and the way many rights are denied in practice is through intended or unintended preferential treatment of particular groups. Subversion of rights in a democracy is typically patterned, rather than wholesale or across the board.

To declare that all rights are in principle guaranteed to all equally, however, requires some specification of the relevant community within which such a declaration holds good. As long as democracies are confined to the territory of the individual state, then such political rights as the right to vote and stand for elective office will typically exclude those who are not citizens of the state in question. In such cases, equality will mean equality among citizens, rather than among all residents. Yet the key civil rights, as basic human rights, apply not only to citizens but to all residents. That is why the denial of due process rights to aliens under the U.S. Patriot Act and the U.K. Anti-terrorism, Crime, and Security Act of 2001—both of which permit the indefinite detention of noncitizens without charge—is such a cause for concern.

Moreover, it is increasingly insisted on in human rights circles that civil and political rights should not be separated from economic and social rights. The logic is the same as that appealed to by philosophers in discussions about the concept of freedom. If freedom is a good only because of the value that lies in exercising it, then those who lack the capacity or resources to exercise a given freedom are being denied the enjoyment of it, even though they may not formally be obstructed from it. In a similar vein, we could say that exercising or taking advantage of one's civil and political rights may be conditional upon one's education and resources. To ensure equality of civil and political rights, however, does not require equality of economic and social conditions. What is needed is a floor below which no one is allowed to fall, plus specific resources such as legal aid; at the top end, there should be regulations to limit the advantages of the wealthy in access to public office, and to prevent their undue influence over officeholders and channels of public information.

The guarantee of civil and political rights provides an essential foundation for all the other dimensions of democracy. If we consider political participation, then citizens will be deterred from becoming politically active, or even involving themselves in the associational life of civil society, if their freedom to communicate and associate with others is obstructed, or compromised through government surveillance. Without such freedom, the development of an attentive and critical public opinion will also be impaired. If we consider the vertical accountability of government, to which the electoral process is central, then this requires the right of candidates and parties to a fully open and fair arena of electoral competition, through independent and effective administration of elections as well as mechanisms that ensure more equal access to political finance and the mass media. If we consider government responsiveness to public needs, then again this requires the independent articulation of citizen interests and opinions such as only a strong rights framework can secure. And as G. Bingham Powell, Jr., argues, a crucial link in the chain of responsiveness is ruptured if the integrity of vertical accountability through elections is not ensured. Draw out any strand of the complex web of democracy, and you will find it leads to some specific civil or political right, without whose security the fabric will start to unravel.

Four Steps in Assessing Democracy

In making an assessment of the quality of a country's democracy, we could specify four steps to be taken in order. The first is to itemize the content of the "goods" that a democracy should deliver: in this case, the specific rights needed to realize democratic freedoms. A list of these rights forms the starting point of any assessment.

Second, we need to identify the relevant international standards of best practice for realizing each of these rights. Because democracy is not an all-or-nothing matter, but rather a question of degree, we need an appropriate and concrete benchmark to tell us what should count as a "good" level of attainment in each area for any given country. Good sources for such "best practices" standards could include relevant international codes and conventions, or individual country codes that experts in this field generally regard as exemplary. Certainly, it may be unrealistic to expect all standards to be realized together in any one country; democracy in practice often requires tradeoffs between different "goods." Yet only an assessment against an example of best practice will enable us to identify where such tradeoffs are actually taking place.

The third step is to list the typical modes of subversion that can prevent these democratic standards from being realized in practice. Assessing the quality of democracy is not just a matter of evaluating the relevant legal codes, but of investigating how effectively they are actually applied. Understanding the different ways in which practice may fall short of a legally prescribed standard is an important aid to such investigation. It may be that the term "subversion" is too restrictive a term here, as it implies intentionality, whereas democracy can also be undermined by unintended inadequacies in institutions, procedures, or personnel.

The fourth and final step is to specify typical agencies of protection that have proved effective against these subversions, and to assess how successful they are in practice.

In the following analysis, I deal with civil rights and political rights separately: first civil rights, which cover the main freedoms necessary to democracy, and then political rights, which cover access to political office and elections. For each of these, I follow the four steps outlined above.

Let us first review civil rights. The following are the main rights that a democracy should secure: life and security of the person; liberty and freedom of movement; freedom of thought and expression; freedom of assembly and association (including trade unions and political parties); freedom of information; protection against discrimination; rights of vulnerable and disadvantaged groups; and due process rights.

For purposes of investigating the quality of democracy, these items could be framed as a series of comparative questions. For example: How free are all people from physical violation of their person and from fear of it? A list of such questions covering all the main aspects of democracy can be found in the *International IDEA Handbook on Democracy Assessment*.[8]

For all the above, except freedom of information, standards of best practice are to be found in the main international human rights conventions and their jurisprudence, including cases of general significance from regional and national jurisdictions. These standards cover both the formulation of the right in question (including legitimate exceptions) and the procedures for implementation, such as the powers and independence of the relevant courts and the right of individual appeal and redress.[9] Human rights lawyers are often best placed to assess these aspects of a country's democracy. Standards of best practice for freedom of information can be derived from those national jurisdictions that are generally recognized as exemplary in this area—such as the United States and Sweden.[10]

It is rare for the subversion of rights to be caused by inadequacies in the formulation of a national charter or bill of rights, since it is easy to get these looking good "on paper." Nevertheless, comparison with international definitions should always form the starting point of an assessment. Of *generic* modes of subversion, the following are among the most typical:

• inadequacies in the judicial process of rights protection, such as insufficient competence or independence of the courts, or systematic obstacles to individual appeal and redress;

• arbitrary or oppressive policing, including intimidation of protesters, detention without charge, maltreatment in detention, discriminatory treatment of particular groups, collusion with paramilitary forces;

• use of emergency powers or antiterror legislation, often against opposition groups, to bypass normal judicial safeguards; and

• systematic exclusion of certain groups from rights protection—for example, unpopular or vulnerable minorities, immigrants and asylum seekers, or those defined as enemies or opponents of the government outside the national territory.

Subversions of *specific* rights include:

• life and security of the person: incidence of physical assault and murder by other civilians such as to make the public space an unsafe area, whether generally or for specific groups;[11]

• unacceptable levels of physical abuse and deaths in custody, whether from poor prison conditions, self-harming, or at the hands of fellow inmates or prison wardens (Winston Churchill's second-most famous statement about democracy is worth noting here—how prisoners are treated is a good litmus test of democracy's quality);

• freedom of expression: inadequate pluralism in media ownership, views, and public information, whether through state or private oligopoly; defamation laws and the cost of defending them being used to restrict legitimate comment on public officials or private corporations; incidence of official and unofficial harassment of journalists;

• freedom of association and assembly: exclusionary rules on registration of voluntary associations, trade unions, or political parties; discriminatory application of registration requirements; loss of independence of voluntary associations through government cooptation or contracts; undue obstacles to public assembly, such as unrealistic timescales for notification, inappropriate locations, police harassment of protesters; and

• freedom of information (supposing there is such a legal right in the first place): unduly restrictive "official secrets" legislation, including absence of public-interest defense for "whistleblowers"; excessive costs of gaining access to legally permitted information.

Different types of data will be needed to identify the incidence and seriousness of these various possible subversions. These include quantitative data on the incidence of abuses; the qualitative analysis of key cases; public opinion surveys for subjective assessments of access to justice and rights protection; and quantitative data on media ownership as well as content analysis for pluralism of viewpoints.

In some areas it is possible to find quantitative indicators that are symptomatic of serious problems: for example, in the justice field, the average length of time taken to bring cases to court, the proportion of prison inmates on remand, or the ratio between the actual prison population and the official prison capacity. These are all significant indicators of the state of the justice system. But even in such cases it is important to complement quantitative indicators with qualitative analysis, because it is a common misconception that the quality of democracy can be assessed simply by a checklist of quantitative indicators.

States typically have a number of agencies, including but not confined to law courts, whose official mission is to guard against these subversions. Indeed, where courts are not doing their job, nonjudicial agencies may be key. All these protective agencies should be seen as essential features of a "good" democracy in the area of civil rights protection. Such agencies include:

• an ombudsman (or in South Africa, the office of Public Protector) which receives and investigates citizens' complaints about abuses of power by state authorities. In many countries people find offices of this type more accessible and trustworthy than the formal courts, but a lot depends on having a good geographical presence across the country;

• a national human rights commission, with the power to initiate investigations on its own account and to have its reports debated in the legislature;

• active public "watchdogs" ready to investigate and publicize abuses—for example, organizations dedicated to the protection of investigative media and civil liberties or human rights—or to support cases through the courts;

• independent complaints and inspection processes for all law-enforcement agencies, including the prison service; and

• supranational human rights courts with enforcement powers and the right of individual appeal, such as the European Court of Human Rights.

Political Rights

The three main political rights that a democracy should secure are: 1) the right to campaign for elective public office in an unimpeded manner and on a level playing field; 2) the right to elect the main political offices at each territorial level of government by universal and equal suffrage, at regular intervals, by secret ballot, and with effective choice between candidates and parties; and 3) the right to vote directly in a referendum on substantial changes to the constitution affecting the rights of electors or the reach and powers of national elective office.

International codes of conduct now exist to set best-practice standards for most aspects of the electoral process.[12] These cover the following: impartial registration of candidates and parties, according to clearly defined criteria; guaranteed security and freedom of movement and communication for candidates and parties; equality of access to state and public-service media, and nonpartisan coverage by these; inclusiveness and simplicity of registration of electors; accessibility to polling stations for all voters and clarity and security of voting procedures; security of ballot boxes and impartiality of the count; transparency and impartiality of procedures for resolving electoral disputes; and supervision of the electoral process by independent election officials, preferably by an independent and fulltime electoral commission.[13]

But these international codes for the conduct of elections exclude four major issues that all have an important bearing on the reach and fairness of the electoral process. The first issue has to do with the scope of elected offices. There are regimes wherein the major elected office-holders are deliberately denied substantive power, perhaps by being subordinated to the military or to religious bodies, as in Iran. This may seem self-evident, but even the most perfect electoral system loses its purpose if major offices are excluded, or if those who are elected do not enjoy effective political control. This is a problem for countries within the European Union, whose citizens are subject to laws and policies initiated or approved by bodies that are not directly elected. Although there may be considerable international agreement as to what offices should be subject to election at the national level, there is much less agreement on the principles appropriate for quasi-states such as the European Union, or on the balance between supranational and inter-governmental arrangements for electoral accountability.

The second problem concerns the nature of the electoral system. Such systems are overwhelmingly national affairs, governed by unique traditions and circumstances and subject to few or no internationally agreed-upon standards to help distinguish better from worse when it comes to a country's choices regarding electoral rules and institutions. That said, it still stands to reason that there must be a level at which an electoral system becomes so skewed and unequal, whether to voters or to parties other than the favored one, that basic principles of fairness and justice have been compromised and democracy diminished, perhaps gravely. At a procedural level, changes in the electoral system should be made by interparty agreement, rather than by the decree of the governing party or coalition.

The third problem concerns party and election financing. As the cost of elections rises and party memberships decline, candidates have become increasingly dependent on business sponsorship, with the danger that government policy comes to be determined more by the need to satisfy sponsors than by the views of ordinary citizens. A standard of best practice is emerging in this area, which combines tough limits on election expenditure with rules requiring transparency in party funding, including limits on the size of individual donations and the exclusion of foreign donors.[14]

Fourth is the problem of unevenness in the electoral playing field that occurs before the election period. This can include obstacles placed in the way of the political opposition by governing parties or their supporters, and the ongoing advantages that accrue to governing parties from their control over official information and other state resources. While it may be possible to draw a formal distinction between party and government, in practice this is difficult to maintain outside of the election period itself.

The ways in which political rights can be deliberately or accidentally subverted are as diverse as the different aspects of the electoral process itemized above. I shall omit here the most obvious infringements such as physical violence, intimidation, and obstruction—whether by the state, political-party militias, or other nonstate actors—and other rights violations that have already been included in the section on civil rights (such as the freedoms of movement, expression, and assembly). Of the other typical modes of subversion, intentional or unintentional, the following are worth noting: government discretion over the timing and duration of elections; preferential use of official state resources by the governing party during the election campaign; an electoral system or constituency boundaries that systematically advantage some parties and candidates over others; lack of regulation on political finance, which allows grossly unequal access to resources for parties or candidates or distorts electoral programs; markedly unequal access to elective public office for particular social groups; systematic exclusions or disadvantages for particular groups of citizens in registration, access to polling stations, or exercise of the ballot; electoral fraud, whether in voting, handling of ballot boxes, or at the count; inadequate independence of election officials from the government or governing party; and the loss of public confidence in the electoral process as a means to influence the personnel or policy of the government. Quantitative data, including election results and survey data, will obviously be important for identifying these inadequacies. Yet such data need to be complemented by legal and case-study analysis.

The main agencies of protection against these abuses or subversions, besides those mentioned under civil rights, are twofold. First is an inde-

pendent, properly staffed, and well-funded election commission, responsible for supervising every aspect of the election process, and granted
the authority to enforce its decisions.[15] In some countries the impartiality
of elections has been secured only by additional means, as in Bangladesh
by the establishment of a caretaker government for the ninety days
between the dissolution of parliament and the election. Second is the
existence of election monitors—both national, drawn from independent
NGOs and the political parties, and international, from organizations
that carry local credibility for their track record of thorough and
independent monitoring. Other abovementioned subversions are
products of unfair rules or inadequate regulation, and can only be put
right by the domestic mobilization of reform coalitions. Such
mobilization can be greatly aided by the wide dissemination of the
results of a democracy assessment, in which national arrangements are
tested against international standards of best practice.

Assessing a Country's Democracy

The model utilized above to assess the quality of democracy has four
stages: first, *identifying* for empirical investigation and analysis the relevant
items that together comprise a "good" democracy; second, *comparing*
those items against international standards of best practice; third, *checking*
the items for typical subversions, combined with an appraisal of how their
practice is perceived by citizens themselves; and fourth, *analyzing* how
well the protective agencies guard against these typical subversions. These
four stages are not necessarily separate in practice, but rather form part of
an iterative or reflexive process. Separating them analytically is useful,
however, as a guide to a procedure of assessment. This four-step procedure
was utilized in the 2002 democratic audit of the United Kingdom.[16]

A summary of this audit's conclusions (for the areas covered by this
article) are included in the Appendix below; it exemplifies what the
results of a quality-of-democracy assessment can look like.

The model of setting out a list of citizen rights and investigating in a
systematic way how far they are guaranteed in practice reaches far in
assessing the quality of a country's democracy. Yet it is not quite enough
on its own. There are other, complementary aspects of a "good" democracy to consider; the other contributors to this collection do exactly
that. This article's goal has been to make it clear that rights entail responsibilities. In all human rights jurisdictions there is a notable
asymmetry in the distribution of rights and responsibilities. Rights belong to individuals; the duties to protect them reside with states—the
signatories to the relevant international conventions. What this legal
framework obscures is that states are only effective in rights protection
to the extent that citizens themselves are prepared to acknowledge the
rights of others. In a democracy, this entails, above all, respect for the

rights of others when they differ from yourself, and a readiness to accept the result when others win out in a fair competition for votes.

A key issue for democratic quality is the character of the citizen body itself—a quality that is different from, but connected to, the quality of political institutions. In the cultivation of public virtues—a central feature of Athenian democracy—modern democracies need at least the following: a readiness to exercise one's civil rights and to stand up for them when threatened, a tolerance of difference, and an acknowledgement of reciprocity between winners and losers in a fair competition for political power. The criteria by which we may identify the presence of these qualities are not straightforward, but identifying them may be among the most important tasks in assessing the quality of a country's democracy. Defects in political institutions are unlikely to undergo remedy unless enough people demand it. Such defects may therefore prove less significant than the less tangible "capacity for self-renewal" upon which any society that aspires to true democracy must rely as one of its most prized and distinctive features.

Appendix

Some qualifications should be borne in mind when reading the summary results of our latest audit of democracy in the United Kingdom. First, only two out of 14 sections are included here—those that concern civil and political rights. These two sections do not cover all the items mentioned in this essay, though those missing are covered elsewhere in the audit. Second, these bullet-point summaries are backed up by a great wealth of empirical evidence, which is to be found in the main body of the audit.[17] Third, the audit was completed before the new post-9/11 anti-terrorist legislation was introduced, with its implications for civil liberties.

Section 3: Are civil and political rights guaranteed equally for all?
• The Human Rights Act, 1998, which incorporates the European Convention on Human Rights into British law, has gone a long way to remedying the systematic inadequacies of civil and political rights protection identified in our first audit. The inclusion of a human rights component in the new compulsory citizenship education program reflects an emerging rights culture in the United Kingdom.
• In Northern Ireland, the shift away from organized violence coupled with the accompanying reduction in state-security operations and reform of the police service have contributed to a safer society. However, the level of sectarian violence and intimidation remains unacceptably high.
• The high incidence of deaths in prisons and police custody, including suicide, reveals an inadequacy in the duty of care towards detainees. The United Kingdom has the highest imprisonment rate in the European Union after Portugal with severe overcrowding, unsanitary conditions, and curtailed rehabilitation programs as a consequence.
• Freedom of expression is curtailed by the nine-decade-old Official Secrets Act and ancient common laws against defamation, blasphemy, and sedition. Defamation in particular enables the wealthy and powerful to protect themselves from adverse criticism, and there is inadequate protection for "whistleblowers."
• Under antiterror legislation passed since 1997, protesters risk being branded as terrorists where serious damage to property occurs or is even threatened.

• The Human Rights Act has transformed the law on privacy, which hitherto was not recognized as a general right. At the same time privacy is also threatened by the actions of the state's covert surveillance agencies and the accumulation by public bodies of personal information obtained from private institutions and service providers.

• The government has passed a Freedom of Information Act, establishing a general "right to know" on the part of the public. The large number of class exemptions from disclosure, however, plus the executive's power to override the decisions of the independent Information Commissioner, indicate that the traditional habit of secrecy on issues that the government considers sensitive will continue.

Section 5: Do elections give the people control over the government and their policies?

• The composition of the lower chamber of Parliament, and thereby the selection of the governing party, is determined by periodic secret ballot. Despite attempts at reform, the upper chamber remains wholly unelected, and thus eludes popular accountability.

• The Representation of the People Act makes procedures for registration and voting easier and more inclusive, though electoral turnout remains comparatively low by European standards.

• Supervision of ballot registration and voting is independent of government and party control, and the establishment of the Electoral Commission should ensure that future changes to constituency boundaries are fully independent.

• Opportunities for free broadcasting and mailing by political parties at election time help create a more level playing field between them. However, the governing party still enjoys an unfair advantage through prior use of official government advertising, and the prime minister's customary power to decide on the timing of a general election (subject only to the proviso that one must be held at least once every five years).

• The Labour government's readiness to introduce more-proportional election rules for the devolved assemblies in Scotland and Wales plus the European Parliament has not been matched by change in the first-past-the-post rule used to fill seats in the House of Commons at Westminster. The Westminster system continues to produce excessively disproportionate results between the national vote for parties and their share of parliamentary seats, and to safeguard the dominance of Labour and the Conservatives at Westminster. Since 1979, there has only been one change in the governing party at Westminster.

• The House of Commons is socially unrepresentative of the population, being dominated by white, middle-aged, middle-class men. The efforts of the Labour Party produced a dramatic improvement in the number of women elected in 1997, but their proportion (18 percent) is still low by European standards. Ethnic representation is also low.

• Given the decline in their membership, and in support from trade unions and corporate sponsors, the two main parties increasingly rely on donations from wealthy individuals to meet their expensive election costs. This dependency fuels the suspicion that large donors exercise an improper influence over policy, or gain other advantages for themselves.

NOTES

1. See, for example, Crawford B. MacPherson, *The Real World of Democracy* (Oxford: Clarendon, 1966).

2. *Republic* 563c.

3. Thucydides, *The Peloponnesian War* (Harmondsworth, U.K.: Penguin, 1954), 117–18; Josiah Ober, *Mass and Elite in Democratic Athens* (Princeton: Princeton University Press, 1989).

4. Benjamin Constant, *Political Writings* (Cambridge: Cambridge University Press, 1988), 316–18.

5. See Ronald Dworkin, *A Bill of Rights for Britain* (London: Chatto and Windus, 1990); John Wadham and Helen Mountfield, *Human Rights Act 1998* (London: Blackstone, 1999).

6. The text of the European Convention for the Protection of Human Rights and Fundamental Freedoms can be found in Ian Brownlie and Guy Goodwin-Gill, eds., *Basic Documents on Human Rights,* 4th ed. (Oxford: Oxford University Press, 2002), 398–420.

7. I develop this argument further in "Human Rights and Democracy," in Roland Axtmann, ed., *Understanding Democratic Politics* (London: Sage, 2003), 22–30.

8. David Beetham, Sarah Bracking, Iain Kearton, and Stuart Weir, *International IDEA Handbook on Democracy Assessment* (The Hague: Kluwer Law International, 2002).

9. See Ian Brownlie and Guy Goodwin-Gill, *Basic Documents on Human Rights,* Part 2; Francesca Klug, Keir Starmer, and Stuart Weir, *The Three Pillars of Liberty* (London: Routledge, 1996), ch. 2.

10. Patrick Burkinshaw, *Freedom of Information: the Law, the Practice and the Ideal* (London: Butterworths, 2001). A comprehensive listing of standards of best practice across all the areas of democratic life is to be found in Part 3 of the *International IDEA Handbook on Democracy Assessment,* cited in note 8 above.

11. It is important to note that protection from threats to life and security from within civil society is as relevant to the quality of democracy as protection from abuse by state personnel. A government that fumbles the job of protecting people from the savagery of "run-of-the-mill" street crime, for instance, is failing at a basic duty. The same goes for a government that tolerates organized subnational groups, such as paramilitary militias, that violate rights.

12. See Guy Goodwin-Gill, *Free and Fair Elections: International Law and Practice* (Geneva: Inter-Parliamentary Union, 1994); Guy Goodwin-Gill, *Codes of Conduct for Elections* (Geneva: Inter-Parliamentary Union, 1998).

13. See Rafael López-Pintor, *Electoral Management Bodies as Institutions of Governance* (New York: UNDP, 2000), Jørgen Elklit and Palle Svensson, "The Rise of Election Monitoring: What Makes Elections Free and Fair?" *Journal of Democracy* 8 (July 1997): 32–46.

14. See Reginald Austin and Maja Tjernström, eds., *Funding of Political Parties and Election Campaigns* (Stockholm: International IDEA, 2003).

15. Robert Pastor, "A Brief History of Electoral Commissions," in Andreas Schedler, Larry Diamond, and Marc F. Plattner, eds., *The Self-Restraining State: Power and Accountability in New Democracies* (Boulder, Colo.: Lynne Rienner, 1999), 75–82.

16. David Beetham, Iain Byrne, Pauline Ngan, and Stuart Weir, *Democracy*

under Blair (London: Methuen and Politico's, 2003).

17. Reginald Austin and Maja Tjernström, eds., *Funding of Political Parties and Election Campaigns.*

4

ADDRESSING INEQUALITY

Dietrich Rueschemeyer

Dietrich Rueschemeyer is professor of sociology and Charles C. Tillinghast, Jr., Professor of International Studies Emeritus at Brown University.

Equality points to one of the critical dimensions along which the quality of democracy varies. What is at stake is political equality, not equality in all areas of social life. Yet the structures of social and economic inequality are intertwined with political equality, and shape it in profound ways both directly and indirectly. Dominant groups can use their social and economic power resources more or less directly in the political sphere. And they can use their status and influence over education, cultural productions, and mass communications—their "cultural hegemony," in short—to shape in a less direct way the views, values, and preferences of subordinate groups. If these effects of social and economic inequality are not substantially contained, political equality will be extremely limited.

Even in its minimal and most formal varieties, democracy creates a measure of political equality by giving every adult an equal vote. Yet the democratic ideal demands much more. As Robert A. Dahl says, it requires "the continuing responsiveness of the government to the preferences of its citizens, considered as political equals."[1] This ideal stands in tension with the inevitable embeddedness of political decision making in social structures of power and influence. The distance between the ideal and the reality of democratic equality has varied greatly over time and continues to vary widely from one country to another. In each instance, this "equality gap" represents a compromise between dominant groups and "the many." We know in outline which factors shape such compromises. The list includes the power balance within society, the relations between the state and civil society, international power constellations, the organization and degree of cultural autonomy that subordinate groups enjoy, and the extent to which dominant groups see democratization as a threat to their interests.[2]

Even the most elementary forms of democracy require a certain zone of autonomy within which political decision making can take place. Politics must be "differentiated" from the overall structure of power and the system of social inequality as a whole. A democratic polity is conventionally defined by freedoms of expression and association, regular elections with comprehensive suffrage, and the government's responsibility to those elected as the people's representatives. Such a regime could never subsist under feudalism nor under communism, each of which in its own way fuses political authority with control over labor and the means of production. Critics have deprecated the conventional definition of democracy as merely "formal" because it works to even out advantages only within a circumscribed political sphere (by safeguarding competition and the rights to free expression and association), while overlooking broader and subtler ways in which social inequality shapes politics.

Two important distinctions emerge from these initial observations. The first separates structures and processes that advance or diminish political equality within the relatively autonomous political sphere from those that limit or foster "spillovers" which begin with inequalities in other areas of life and then flow into the political sphere. The central questions here are: Can one restrain the conversion of wealth or status into political advantage and, if so, how? A second distinction divides measures dealing with spillovers of social inequality into the political sphere from policies that tackle social and economic inequality directly as it affects the degree and scope of political equality.

Advancing political equality is clearly not an uncontested goal. It is at odds with major interests, and it may involve the sacrifice of competing values. Opposition to greater political equality, whether based on interest or principle, is likely to vary depending on whether the topic is the political realm narrowly conceived, the conversion of socioeconomic into political advantage, or the overall impact of social inequality on the political sphere.

Normative Questions and Competing Values

Does increasing political equality constitute an unqualified good? Or does it involve sacrificing important other values? If there are tradeoffs, how do we judge different outcomes? This essay will not resolve these normative issues. But given the intertwining of normative and empirical claims that marks discussions about equality, it seems reasonable to sketch some of the major issues to be evaluated and to indicate my views of them.

Even if we stay purely within the political realm, there are two major objections to advancing political equality as much as possible. The first is that "the many" are not competent to choose reasonable policies. The

second is that increasing the number of participants can worsen coordination problems to the point of system overload and ungovernability.
The conventional form of democratic rule, representative democracy,
answers most of these objections by interposing a professional state
apparatus (answerable to elected officials) between voters and collec-
tive-action outcomes.[3] Once we take representative democracy for
granted, the issues of voter competence and coordination problems vary
widely across countries and historical situations. This variation may be
decisive in assessing any particular case.

Both the objection from competence and the objection from numbers raise issues of reduced efficiency and its costs. While these costs
may sometimes be bothersome in practice, they seem outweighed in
principle by three considerations of a different sort. First, "efficiency"
takes on substantive meaning only in light of the aims being pursued,
and these in turn depend on material and immaterial interests on which
people are often divided. Second, a reasonable principle holds that all
members of a political community whose interests are affected by collective decisions should have a say in them, even if not all members are
learned in the subjects at hand. Affected interests trump limited competence. Finally, political equality is an acknowledgement of the
decisively similar dignity of all citizens as human beings who are entitled to the rule of reciprocity.

None of this means that trying to cut costs in efficiency is a bad idea.
Indeed, it might even be an especially good idea because some efficiency boosters—among them high-quality general education, multiple
sources of information and analysis, and trustworthy organizations to
represent and aggregate interests that are otherwise at a disadvantage—
also enhance, as we will see, political equality.

Limiting the conversion of assets from other spheres into political
advantages is far more controversial. And objections mount even further against policy proposals to level differential assets outside the
sphere of politics because spillover effects are too difficult to contain.

The most prominent discussion swirls around the political uses of
economic assets. The U.S. Supreme Court has ruled, much to the outrage
of some, that spending money in campaigns for political office enjoys
the protection of the First Amendment much like speech. The decision
sees this broadened freedom of expression as overriding the concern for
democratic equality. The Court, in effect, dealt with economic inequality as if it was irrelevant to the integrity of the democratic political
process, and refused to allow the use of direct proscription to limit the
conversion of economic advantage into political gain. Alternative ways
to erect such limits might include public campaign financing made
contingent on candidates' acceptance of caps on private contributions
as well as the offer of free television time (by far the biggest source of
expense in modern campaigning) to all qualified candidates. But mea-

sures such as these face different political obstacles, and none is likely
to shut off the flow of money into politics completely, as interested
parties will find ways to circumvent legal obstacles.

Economic inequality has consequences for political equality that
go far beyond the issues of a level playing field in electoral campaigns. The wealthy can disproportionately influence how policies
are made and implemented. Monopolistic and oligopolistic market
power in particular can easily be turned into political bargaining advantage. Different levels of government are dependent on investment
decisions of large corporations. This applies also to national governments as the mobility of capital across international borders continues
to increase. In addition, the majority of the population depends for its
economic security on employment. The threat of unemployment is
taken for granted in capitalist societies, but it has a major impact on
the political dynamics of Western countries. It not only undergirds
work discipline but also aligns the interests of workers with those of
corporations.

All advanced capitalist countries have legislation that seeks to constrain the creation and use of monopolistic economic power. But such
measures have at best slowed the trend toward concentration in corporate ownership structures, and have focused on constraining such power
asymmetries in strictly economic settings rather than on blunting their
impact on politics. Employment security through legal constraints on
firing is somewhat stronger in some countries than in others. These measures, currently under attack as "labor-market rigidities," have largely a
delaying and, in the long run, possibly even an exacerbating effect on
unemployment. More important are macroeconomic policies, provisions
for training and retraining, and differences in income-replacement policies meant to help tide workers over periods of joblessness. The
significance of some degree of income security becomes clear if one
compares the political impact of high unemployment in the 1930s, when
the jobless of the Great Depression often had virtually nothing to fall
back on, with that of similar rates in postcommunist Eastern Europe and
parts of Western Europe in the early 1990s, when higher living standards and public supports provided a buffer.

Attempts to go further in limiting the conversion of economic power
into political gain are subject to fundamental ideological objections
and, perhaps more importantly, to pragmatic arguments that the pursuit
of equality will harm economic growth. While the value of economic
freedom for entrepreneurs and capital owners is in principle hardly a
match for the value of increased political equality, claims that measures
compromising the functioning of markets will impair growth have persuasive power in all Western countries. The more comprehensive welfare
states in advanced capitalist countries insist, however, that this protection of the market mechanism has to be combined with relatively

generous compensatory measures, which make the functioning of the market socially sustainable.

Wealth Distribution and Cultural Hegemony

If measures to limit the conversion of economic advantage into political power have only a partial effect, does the pursuit of political equality warrant measures that reduce inequalities of income and wealth more directly? There can be little doubt that differences in the distribution of income and wealth across countries and over time within countries make for significant variations in political equality.

Competing value claims dominate the discussion of policies meant to change the distribution of income and wealth. It is on the issue of direct political action to reduce income and wealth differentials that the claims of an inherent contradiction between equality and freedom have concentrated. These claims are plausible when we think of sudden policies of increased taxation and expropriation aimed at leveling incomes and wealth. Such policies would be fought by the privileged with all means at their disposal, and breaking this opposition could indeed lead to ruthless dictatorship. Quite clearly, greatly reduced levels of economic inequality would then coincide with the destruction of democratic equality. On the other hand, we know of examples—the Scandinavian countries are the most prominent—where popular policy orientations pursued over decades have resulted in significant reductions of after-tax and after-transfer income inequalities. Yet political freedom remained unimpaired, while the scope and quality of political participation in these countries indicate higher levels of democratic equality. As for efficiency considerations, it is worth noting that no long-run drop in economic growth has accompanied these policies.

The other major issues beset by value controversies have to do with cultural hegemony. There is little question that the views of the better educated and of people in high-status occupations have a disproportionate influence on the production of culture as well as on its diffusion through education and mass communications. To list a few other major sources of disproportionate influence on popular and high culture, including corporate funding, tax-supported private charities, institutions of higher education, and religious groups, is to realize that in most advanced capitalist countries the groups with disproportionate cultural influence are quite heterogeneous in character.

The pattern of cultural influence, then, is pluralistic, but it is unequal nevertheless. And unequal cultural influence creates substantial political inequality. If the material and immaterial interests of the more influential groups have a strong if varied influence on the production and communication of culture and entertainment (an influence that may include promoting distractions from social and political problems), many citizens will have a harder time identifying and advancing their own best interests in society, the economy, and political life.

Cultural hegemony represents inequality of a peculiar kind: Its effects remain largely invisible to those whose views, values, and preferences it shapes, and they are taken for granted by those whose material and immaterial interests find expression under the hegemonic status quo. Many regard arguments about cultural hegemony as spurious expressions of Marxist ideology—the claims of "false consciousness" in a new guise. Yet even though its effects may be hard to pin down empirically in a given time and place, each ingredient of the pattern seems beyond doubt in principle. People's values and knowledge of society do not simply reflect social and economic interests, but are shaped by education, mass communication, and social networks structured by status differences. Those in positions of influence find it easier to take their own situations for granted and be relatively unruffled by others' deprivations. Sponsors of news, entertainment, and the production of high culture may defer to norms and traditions of autonomy of journalism and scholarship, but are often not above seeking to attach influence to their money where this can be done without directly violating such standards. In turn, the standards themselves impose a nonpartisanship on news journalism, teaching, and research that is informally defined in terms of "mainstream" notions that may be widely acclaimed yet still far from universal. Finally, there is something unreal about a model of politics which assumes that citizens are even roughly equal when it comes to identifying and pursuing their respective interests. This model rejects claims of hegemonic inequality as unpersuasive by simply *assuming* an essential autonomy and equality of all participants.[4]

Policy responses to issues of cultural hegemony and normative arguments about actual and potential policies are complex. Most rich democracies have policies hindering if not obstructing the trend toward concentrated ownership of newspapers, broadcasting networks, publishing firms, and mass-entertainment companies. Most such countries also support public broadcasting systems with a special degree of autonomy, though the generosity of support and the degree of autonomy vary. The standards of news journalism and of academic freedom and analytic universalism constitute an important protection against conversions of wealth and political influence into control over news and research.

At the same time, measures that would go beyond these broadly accepted policies of insulating certain cultural institutions and spheres against direct partisan influence are not much discussed. The reasons seem clear. Most people who care about undue influence in cultural production and diffusion are part of the dominant, though internally heterogeneous, mainstream. Efforts to curtail such influence, furthermore, quickly run up against two important and commonly accepted injunctions: 1) Do not limit freedom of expression; and 2) respect the autonomy of different cultural spheres such as art, news reporting, or academic research. Since some existing protections against the conversion of economic and political clout into cultural influence rely precisely on these principles, it seems doubtful whether more far-reaching policies at odds with these principles could be reasonable or even have a chance of success.

To cap these brief reflections on political inequality and some of the value conflicts that emerge when relevant policies are considered, we should stress that the normative assessment of equality and competing values is analytically distinct from factual assertions about what advances or undermines political equality. Many arguments on the subject tend to mingle normative and factual assertions without being clear on the difference between the two types of claims, which is all the more reason to be clear about it. If competing values argue against trying to rein in processes that have inegalitarian implications, the effects of these processes are not thereby rendered any less real or consequential.

Differential Power Resources

How do disparities in various power resources between "the few" and "the many" affect their respective pursuit of such political activities as voting, lobbying government between elections, influencing the opinions of others, and participating in political organizations? *Coercive power* is a fundamental resource that is inherently distributed unequally. Most states strive to monopolize coercion, albeit with uneven success. Of course, force or threats of force can easily compromise democratic rule. If the state succeeds in monopolizing coercive power, democratic equality is protected only if the use of that power is regulated by law and if equality before the law is sufficiently realized to rule out political advantage from differential intimidation. While this can roughly be taken for granted in most rich democracies today, pockets of private coercive power, sometimes tolerated by the state, and gross imperfections in equality before the law are major factors subverting political equality in many countries belonging to the developing and postcommunist worlds.

The *state administrative apparatus* represents another power resource of great reach, combining expertise, tax-based funding, ready-made organizational capacity, and ultimate recourse to coercion. In liberal political theory, the state looms large as the great adversary of society in the process of democratization. The civil servants in modern states, by contrast, see themselves as neutral executors of the political directives that in a democracy are defined by elected political representatives, though this self-conception antedates the rise of democracy. Valuable as such views may be in a well-run civil service, the realistic tradition of political theory from Locke to Marx and Weber has always maintained that civil servants not only tend to take care of their own interests un-less constrained by effective injunctions, but also are likely to look with more favor on the interests of people whose social and economic standing resembles their own. Imperfectly steered by small political elites and wielding various relatively subtle means of influence, the complex administrative organizations of modern states preempt a good deal of decision making and can create substantial imbalances in politi-cal equality. While the classic barrier to democracy in the nineteenth century was limitation of the franchise, more recent impediments tend to take the form of unequal rules for safeguarding the freedoms of speech and association as well as reductions both formal and informal in the administrative state's responsiveness to its putative elected masters.

Economic class is, as already indicated, a major obstacle standing in the way of realistic political equality. Until well into the nineteenth century, there was a general consensus among political thinkers that only those with property could be voting members of the political com-munity. Only slowly did the idea of a democratic community inclusive of men from all classes become common, and equal rights for women came to be accepted even later.

Capital ownership carries power over marketing, investment, and employment unless competition reduces ownership decisions to an au-tomatic function of the market, a textbook claim that applies to pure models as well as—in a rough way—to small owners in competitive markets, but not to major concentrations of capital. This economic power appears in the political sphere as direct bargaining power and more indirectly as persuasive influence. Since control over financial capi-tal—homeowning and small shareholding aside—is highly concentrated in even the richest capitalist countries, both direct bargaining power and indirect influence rest in the hands of a handful of decision makers who often have no political competition or supervision to restrain them. Aside from legislative and administrative attempts to curb growing cor-porate concentration, encouraging political competition may be the most promising antidote.

In developed countries, income distribution tends to be much more even than the distribution of property and capital ownership. At the same time, income distributions vary greatly from one country or re-gion to another, as well as across time periods. The two ends of the distribution have the greatest significance for democratic equality. Pov-erty means not only a lack of economic resources but also a loss of standing in the community, and those who fall below a certain level of income and status tend to lose political voice as well. The poor are never as powerful a political constituency as their formal voting poten-tial would indicate. In turn, people who earn incomes that exceed average earnings by factors in the hundreds rather than the teens will have dis-proportionate political clout despite the best measures seeking to stem the influence of money in politics. It bears repeating that much more is at stake here than the role of money in electoral campaigns. The wealthy have a tremendous influence on all phases of policy making and policy implementation even if direct corruption is effectively under control, which of course it is not in many countries.

Socioeconomic inequality has powerful direct and indirect effects on the quality of democratic governance. This is perhaps most evident in Latin America where class inequality is particularly pronounced. In an essay on the long-term divergence of political development in North and South America, Terry Karl speaks of a "pathology of inequality" in Latin America.[5]

We misunderstand *social status* if we think of it simply in terms of prestige. Rather than representing just a point on a scale of esteem, it involves social attachments and aversions. Social status shapes interaction patterns, offering entrance to, and imposing exclusion from, different social circles. Politically most important, it defines the chance to be heard and to be trusted; it increases or diminishes one's political "voice."[6]

The importance of status differentials varies considerably across countries, but both their salience and the steepness of the status hierarchy tend to persist over time. However, some major correlates of status, including economic position and level of education, are not policy-independent, and these can override even persistent differences grounded in ethnic, racial, and gender status. Broadening access to secondary and tertiary education and flattening the distribution of post-tax and post-transfer incomes are likely to reduce both the inequality and the salience of social status in the long run.

The change in women's status in the most advanced industrial countries over the past century and a half provides ample evidence of change and persistence as well as of the mechanisms of change. Recent comparative work on the election of women to political office offers an interesting glimpse. Women have better chances in systems of proportional representation than in winner-take-all, single-member–district arrangements. This suggests that it is easier for women to get elected as members of a party list, whose composition is determined by activist organizations and party members, than in the direct confrontation between individual candidates often chosen in broad-based preliminary voting. Changes in gender status in the wider population seem to lag behind politically more active organizations, even as they are influenced by them.[7]

The *unequal influence on the production and diffusion of culture* exerted by varied but small cultural, religious, and economic elites constitutes, as noted, a major problem for political equality. It is a problem easily underestimated because what is influenced are the values, views, and preference structures of people, factors whose variation tends to be neglected by simple rationalist individualism.

Perhaps it is useful to explore these problems of inequality in regard

to the specific issue of politically relevant *knowledge*. Political knowledge is surely a major power resource and its distribution is profoundly
unequal. This is true most obviously in the simple sense of information.
Those who are favored by education and their position in the networks
of information have clear advantages over those less favored. Furthermore, the claim of unequal distribution of knowledge holds also for the
background knowledge necessary for judging and absorbing the flow
of information and for the ability to resist spin. This is largely a function of education and repeated use of such background knowledge.[8]

Beyond these forms of knowledge, however, there is another, more
basic kind—the knowledge that is generated by systematic inquiry.
And here the question is not only and not so much how this newly
generated knowledge is diffused, but rather whether the problem formu-
lations and specific questions asked in research are shaped by concerns
and presuppositions as well as by blind spots that correspond to the
concerns and blind spots of select groups while neglecting the interests
and perspectives of others more or less completely. An example may
make the point more specific.

Talcott Parsons reflected faithfully the consensus of family sociology in the 1940s and 1950s when he claimed that the gender division of
labor of the American middle-class family with a single breadwinner
had a strong functional fit with the prevailing structures of advanced
industrial societies and that on a more abstract level it reflected in fact
near-universal patterns of sexual division of labor across cultures. It
was only after the famous attack on these claims by Betty Friedan that
research on the gender division of labor in modern societies came to
quite different empirically based results.[9] It would be easy to multiply
similar if perhaps more subtle examples dealing with working-class issues or matters of race.

That feminists and African-Americans have succeeded in establishing scholarly niches staffed exclusively by women and blacks,
respectively, may go against norms of scholarly universalism, but it
certainly is an indication that for a long time these norms had rather
disappointing results. Here it may be useful to note the obvious fact
that an underrepresentation of the problems of subordinate classes in
scholarly research cannot be tackled in the same way as an
underrepresentation of the interests and concerns of ascriptive status
groups. Researchers from a lower-class background acquire in the process of their training and career a new social and economic status, and
they have better career chances if they stay within established theoretical frameworks of basic assumptions and problem formulation.

That the orientation of research is of great importance for long-term
political gains is also reflected in the proliferation of privately financed (though tax-supported) think tanks in the United States, the
majority of which have—to put it modestly—a right-of-center out-

look. In many other Western countries, the orientation of similar centers is less weighted toward one side and often balanced by publicly supported institutions. German universities, for instance, have for generations sustained professorships and institutes devoted to welfare-state policies. Cumulative effects of public policy shape to some extent orientations in the academic world. Thus it seems a reasonable guess that the long political dominance of Roosevelt's New Deal was one of the factors accounting for the prevalence of liberalism in American higher education before the "L-word" became a fighting word in conservative counterattacks.

Organization for collective action in voluntary associations, unions, and parties is the most promising power resource of "the many." It is here that there are possibilities of compensation for the impact of social and economic inequality on democratic politics. Collective organization can mobilize voters and campaigners; it can raise substantial funds if membership and small contributions are numerous enough; it can represent otherwise dispersed interests between elections; and it can compensate to some extent for the cultural hegemony of the most influential groups and institutions, advancing its own views and symbols and shielding followers against the dominant influences.

This compensation for the impact of social and economic inequality requires, however, that these organizations be relatively autonomous from dominant groups and responsive to their constituencies. Responsiveness may be endangered by oligarchic tendencies that are hard to control. Furthermore, dominant interests quite often seek to protect themselves by sponsoring sympathetic organizations and parties with broad appeal. Many voluntary associations rely on private (though, again, often tax-supported) funding from a relatively small number of wealthy patrons. A simple measure of participation in civil society, then, is not sufficient to gauge the compensatory potential of collective organization. What is decisive is that relatively autonomous organizations protect otherwise disadvantaged interests.

The importance of autonomous collective organization in parties and politically relevant voluntary associations for leveling political inequality can hardly be exaggerated. If the economic and political power of concentrated wealth, the cultural hegemony of a limited set of elites, and the decision-making power of an imperfectly controlled state apparatus are the most important factors underlying political inequality, strong and autonomous organization of subordinate interests is the most important counterbalancing factor. It offers political competition to the influence of wealth and high status and limits the relative autonomy of the state vis-à-vis subordinate interests. It gives subordinate groups some protection against hegemonic influence by offering alternative views and orientations. And it can strengthen the universalistic norms of academic social and political analysis as well as of news reporting by sponsoring research informed by the concerns and interests of subordinate groups.

Among the conditions favoring or hindering the development of such forms of collective organization are mutually reinforcing processes in the political sphere. Generally, the prospect of political success stimulates political participation while its absence stifles it; this seems to be a major reason why in many countries politically oriented participation is more prevalent among the middle classes than the working class or the dependent poor.[10] Gaining or losing political influence on decisions about legislation and implementation can in turn favor or hinder collective organization. Thus, it seems reasonable to argue that the growing influence of environmental concerns in many Western countries has had a positive feedback on their green parties. It is well known that the long dominance of the Social Democrats in Swedish politics is one reason for the extraordinary strength of labor unions in Sweden. And the strength of public-employee unions in different U.S. states is partly explained by how much state politics favors or discourages unionization, while unionization of workers and employees in private industry has declined since 1960 due to structural changes in employment as well as adverse national political developments.

In countries whose institutional setting has been shaped by strong unions, strong parties of the left, and significant participation of these parties in government, class and status differences in social and political participation are much reduced or eliminated. This claim has empirical support, and on simple reflection it makes good theoretical sense. It is no real surprise that the sustained impact of successful self-organization of subordinate interests and of the representation of these interests in the governance of societies diminishes the social, economic, and cultural factors maintaining political inequality and leads to a leveling in the social and political participation of different socioeconomic strata. By contrast, the disappointing performance of recently democratized political systems in Latin America seems largely due to a renewed weakness in the organized representation of subordinate interests.

These interactions between collective organization and political success can create stable paths of advance or decline of equality in a political system, once critical turning points are passed. Therefore, the chances of a political self-organization of subordinate interests and its potential effects on political equality may well be dependent on historical conditions that are not easily changed.

Comparing Inequalities: Indicators and Metrics

To compare political inequality internationally is difficult since the weight of its different manifestations and determinants varies across countries and historical periods. However, some measures may yield a first approximation. A crude picture emerges from participation rates in politics and in politically relevant associations, broken down by class, race or ethnicity, and gender. This can be complemented by qualitative information on the strength, autonomy, and effectiveness of organizations devoted to advancing the interests of subordinate groups.

Another avenue of assessment is to look for results. The incidence of poverty and of social exclusion as well as of decidedly substandard education can be gauges of political inequality. This follows from the assumption that the economic and knowledge resources required for meaningful participation in society are almost universally valued and that their absence indicates a drastically unequal political position of the groups so disadvantaged, at least if we focus on the long run.

Both kinds of indicators will gain in credibility if they are embedded in an analysis of the main conditions and policies that, according to the best estimates, enhance or undercut political equality. I have offered a number of such estimates in this essay, though these may have to be adapted to different kinds of conditions by looking separately, for instance, at rich and well-established democracies, newly established ones in poorer countries, and countries in the early phases of democratization.

Democratic equality is a critical dimension of the quality of any system of democratic rule. It stands in tension with the structure of social, economic, and cultural inequality. Even democracy as minimally conceived is only possible if political decisions are to some extent separated from the system of class, status, and power. But since structured inequality can never be entirely eradicated and political decision making can never be fully emancipated from the inequality in power resources, democratic equality is a goal that can only be approximated at a considerable distance. At the same time, democratic equality is a value that is not just ceremonially acknowledged but that is grounded in many practices and commitments common in modern societies. The principle of an equal vote is only one but not the least among these.

The tension between democratic equality and the impact of differential economic, cultural, and social power is not a constant across modern democracies. There exists a great deal of variation, which ranges from democracies that remain extremely shallow in their egalitarian substance to realistic, if still limited approximations to democratic equality that are built on a significant empowerment of socially, economically, and culturally subordinate groups.

Even formal democracy is more than what its critics denigrate, because it is an opening for greater democratic equality. To deepen democracy in the direction of greater political equality requires systematic and strong policies promoting social and economic equality. The quality of democracy, then, depends on social democracy, on long-sustained policies of social protection and solidarity.

NOTES

The author wishes to thank Miguel Glatzer, Patrick Heller, Charlie Kurzman, and Jim Mahoney for helpful comments on an earlier draft. This article has benefited from the discussion at the Stanford University conference on the quality of democracy and from continuing conversations with Ed Broadbent, member of the Canadian Parliament.

1. Robert A. Dahl, *Polyarchy: Participation and Opposition* (New Haven: Yale University Press, 1971), 1.

2. See Dietrich Rueschemeyer, Evelyne H. Stephens, and John D. Stephens, *Capitalist Development and Democracy* (Cambridge: Polity, 1992); as well as Evelyne Huber, Dietrich Rueschemeyer, and John D. Stephens, "The Paradoxes of Contemporary Democracy: Formal, Participatory, and Social Dimensions," *Comparative Politics* 29 (April 1997): 323–42; and Gerard Alexander, *The Sources of Democratic Consolidation* (Ithaca, N.Y.: Cornell University Press, 2002).

3. This is of course itself a major limitation of political equality. On electoral control under modern-day "big government," see Paul Pierson, "The Prospects of Democratic Control in an Age of Big Government," in Arthur M. Meltzer, Jerry Weinberger, and M. Richard Zinman, eds., *Politics at the Turn of the Century* (Lanham, Md.: Rowman & Littlefield, 2001), 140–61.

4. The conception of cultural hegemony just sketched does not presuppose the idea of "false consciousness." Rather than claiming superior knowledge of people's "objective interests," it merely argues that elite views and interests tend to shape the views and preferences of subordinate groups more than vice versa.

5. Terry Lynn Karl, "Economic Inequality and Democratic Instability," *Journal of Democracy* 11 (January 2000): 149–56. See also the comments in the introduction to Larry Diamond, Jonathan Hartlyn, Juan J. Linz, and Seymour Martin Lipset, *Democracy in Developing Countries: Latin America,* 2nd ed. (Boulder, Colo.: Lynne Rienner, 1999), 48–53. Evelyne Huber, Dietrich Rueschemeyer, and John D. Stephens see recent developments of formal democracy in Latin America as stunted by the persistence of drastically unequal class power; see their "Paradoxes of Contemporary Democracy."

6. See Albert O. Hirschman, *Exit, Voice, and Loyalty: Responses to Decline in Firm, Organizations, and States* (Cambridge: Harvard University Press, 1970).

7. On the effect of electoral systems, see Pippa Norris, "Women: Representation and Electoral Systems," in Richard Rose, ed., *The International Encyclopedia of Elections* (Washington, D.C.: Congressional Quarterly, 2000): 348–51; Pippa Norris and Ronald Inglehart, "Cultural Barriers to Women's Leadership: A Worldwide Comparison," paper presented at the 2000 Congress of the International Political Science Association in Quebec City, Canada, on 1–5 August 2000, offers extensive cross-national evidence; the situation in Eastern Europe after the fall of communism is the subject of Richard E. Matland and Kathleen A. Montgomery, eds., *Women's Access to Political Power in Post-Communist Europe* (Oxford: Oxford University Press, 2003).

8. Paul Pierson, "The Prospects of Democratic Control," emphasizes issues of information and cognitive capacity of the electorate in his review of the chances of democratic control of big government. Recognizing that simple techniques such as taking one's cue from trusted others and the collective superiority of aggregates of people who are individually only moderately informed curb the impact of ignorance and lack of judgment on the part of most voters, he remains skeptical that these mechanisms are sufficient to ensure electoral control of government based on at least rough equality.

9. See Talcott Parsons, "The Kinship System of the Contemporary United States," *American Anthropologist* 45 (March 1943): 96–114; and Talcott Parsons with Robert F. Bales, James Olds, Morris Zelditch, and Philip E. Slater, *Family, Socialization, and Interaction Process* (New York: Free Press, 1955). See also Betty Friedan, *The Feminine Mystique* (New York: Dell, 1963). For a study of dual-career marriages of professionals in three countries, see Marilyn Rueschemeyer, *Professional Work and Marriage: An East-West Comparison* (London: Macmillan, 1981).

10. See for instance Dietrich Rueschemeyer, Marilyn Rueschemeyer, and Björn Wittrock, "Conclusion: Contrasting Patterns of Participation and Democracy," in Dietrich Rueschemeyer, Marilyn Rueschemeyer, and Björn Wittrock, eds., *Participation and Democracy East and West: Comparisons and Interpretations* (Armonk, N.Y.: M.E. Sharpe, 1998): 266–84.

5

THE CHAIN OF RESPONSIVENESS

G. Bingham Powell, Jr.

G. Bingham Powell, Jr., is the Marie C. Wilson and Joseph C. Wilson Professor of Political Science at the University of Rochester. His recent publications include Elections as Instruments of Democracy: Majoritarian and Proportional Visions *(2000) and the coedited text* Comparative Politics Today *(2004). He is a former editor of the* American Political Science Review.

Let me begin by defining terms. For present purposes, "democracy" is identified by the institutional features of universal adult suffrage, free and competitive elections to choose policy makers, multiple information sources, multiple political parties, and civil and political rights. "Democratic responsiveness" is what occurs when the democratic process induces the government to form and implement policies that the citizens want. When the process induces such policies consistently, we consider democracy to be of higher quality. Indeed, responsiveness in this sense is one of the justifications for democracy itself.[1]

Responsiveness is not the only measure of democratic quality. Freedom, equality, vertical and horizontal accountability, and the rule of law contribute directly to the quality of democracy. These features also facilitate democratic responsiveness, as we shall see.

Democratic responsiveness is a complex process, somewhat like a chain whose links are causally connected (see the figure below). It begins with the policy preferences held by citizens, and moves link by causal link through such stages as voting, election outcomes, the formation of policy-making coalitions, the process of policy making between elections, and public policies themselves. The process is ongoing and dynamic: The policies that are actually adopted and the consequences that flow from them affect the future preferences of citizens. Connections, whether actual or at least anticipated, must exist between each of the stages. The severing of any of the major linkages—in the figure

FIGURE—DEMOCRATIC RESPONSIVENESS: STAGES AND LINKAGES

LINKAGE I	LINKAGE II	LINKAGE III
Structuring	Institutional	Policy Making
Choices	Aggregation	

STAGE 1 ———→ STAGE 2 ———→ STAGE 3 ———→ STAGE 4

Citizens'	Citizens'	Selecting	Public Policies
Preferences	Voting	Policy Makers	and Outcomes
	Behavior	*(election outcomes,*	
		government formation)	

labeled "Structuring Choices," "Institutional Aggregation," and "Policy Making"[2]—can cause failures of responsiveness.

A correspondence between the policies that citizens desire and the outcomes that government produces does not necessarily indicate democratic responsiveness. Good luck or advantageous circumstances are not the same thing as systematic responsiveness. In a democracy, moreover, responsiveness cannot depend solely on the good will of policy makers. Responsiveness implies that institutionalized arrangements, and above all elections, reliably connect citizens to those who make policy in their name.[3]

High-quality democracy is sustained when institutional arrangements provide incentives supporting each of the major linkages of responsiveness. Such inducements might flow from: 1) the systematic eviction of unresponsive or inept policy makers, encouraging their successors to anticipate and realize citizens' desires more carefully; 2) the direct election of powerful, promise-keeping governments that are publicly committed to policies the citizens want; and 3) the election of multiple, representative parties that are committed to negotiating as agents on behalf of the respective policies favored by the various subgroups of citizens who elected them. Different theorists and commentators on democratic processes have varying opinions as to the relative likelihood that one or another of these connections will be effective.[4] In addition to these incentives deriving from competitive national elections, other facilitating conditions must be present.

Conceptual Difficulties and Theoretical Disputes

It is difficult to evaluate and compare democratic responsiveness over time and from one country to another. The last half-century of theoretical and empirical research by political scientists has taught us that such key concepts as citizens' preferences, election outcomes, political influence, and policy consequences pose exquisitely complex analytical challenges. Moreover, the connections that can break down or be subverted are manifold, and may vary widely from case to case.

Finally, theories differ as to which causes and consequences affect each connection at each stage of the political process.

Linkage I in the figure connects the preferences of citizens to their behavior in elections. This connection involves both the citizens and the alternatives presented to them at the time of elections. The conceptual difficulties here are large. To begin with, how can one know "what citizens want"? We have defined as democracies only those systems with multiple information sources and multiple parties. We can assume away one conceptual difficulty, that of a citizenry possessing "enlightened understanding,"[5] by supposing that the larger numbers of information sources and parties supply such understanding. But this supposition is empirically shaky. The relative ignorance of even educated populations regarding the basic alternatives and processes of public policy is well known, and a general problem for democracy. At a minimum, an educated citizenry should be a facilitating condition for enlightened understanding.

Even more challenging is the problem that arises from the complexity of citizens' preferences. Social-choice theorists have spent a great deal of time studying whether and how the varied preferences of multiple individuals can be coherently aggregated into a single choice. The Nobel Prize–winning economist Kenneth Arrow got a famous paradox named after himself by showing how preferences among three or more alternatives may often be distributed among a group of citizens in such a way that no single alternative commands unequivocal majority support over and against each of the other possible choices.[6] Indeed, the sole circumstance in which "Arrow's impossibility theorem" definitely does not imply uncertainly about what citizens might want collectively is when all preferences can be summarized on a single dimension. Under that condition, the position of the median voter will defeat any other position (assuming that citizens always favor the position closer to them).

The problem that Arrow identified has led even as convinced a democrat as political scientist William Riker to conclude that since "the outcomes of voting are, or may be, inaccurate or meaningless amalgamations, what the people want cannot be known."[7] Riker argues instead for a purely procedural assessment of democracy, in which a majority of citizens can collectively remove an incumbent government, but no policy implications can be inferred: "The kind of democracy that thus survives is not, however, popular rule, but rather an intermittent, sometimes random, even perverse, popular veto."[8]

Assuming, despite Riker's reservations, that citizens' preferences are coherent enough to allow one to speak in a meaningful way of "what they want" and to evaluate responsiveness accordingly, we should bear in mind the party-choice side of the structuring problem. In brief, the party system must make it possible for citizens to express their preferences. If none of the party choices are related to what citizens want, then the chain of democratic responsiveness is broken at its first link. There must be at least one party or candidate that offers the alternative the citizens most desire. (When preferences can be arrayed along a single dimension, this will be the median position, which can defeat any other position in a head-to-head vote.)

While theorists split over the question of whether there must be a party for each major opinion configuration in a given society, they generally agree on three points. First, candidates must be linked into some kind of coherent national policy offerings, ordinarily through nationally organized political parties or coalitions.[9] Second, there needs to be some degree of stability in the party offerings and levels of support, in order for voters to vote rationally in using elections to support their policy preferences.[10] Third, to encourage the Stage III linkage in responsive policy making there must be reasonable alternatives of some kind, at least between incumbents and credible opponents, to enable voters to exercise retrospective "vertical" accountability by punishing incumbents who fail to keep their promises.

Linkage II as shown in the figure indicates a bond between election outcomes and the selection of policy makers committed to doing what the citizens want. Here, political scientists and other students of responsiveness have debated two large issues. The first issue concerns the relative merits of a majoritarian as opposed to a proportional (or consensual) vision of which institutions best connect election-endorsed alternatives with policy-maker selection. The majoritarian goal is directly to convert citizens' expressed voting preferences into governments with exclusive policy-making power. Proportionalists, by contrast, favor institutions that first channel into the legislature the various major configurations of citizen preferences—weighted, of course, according to the respective sizes of the groups holding those preferences. Then, the proportional vision seeks policy-making institutions shaped proportionally by the preferences of these representatives.

In part, the majoritarian-versus-proportional debate reflects differing norms about whether policies should respond to majorities or to "as many people as possible," including those not in the majority.[11] Also in play are differing empirically based theories about the "mechanical" difficulties of single-stage aggregation (by which votes are converted directly into governments) versus the "agency" difficulties of allowing elites to negotiate policies by bargaining among themselves (elite-level "horse trading" after elections is a staple of many parliamentary regimes).[12]

The second major issue in the area of institutional aggregation has generated a large body of writing by scholars of comparative government. This is the debate over parliamentarism versus presidentialism. In play are a number of questions related conceptually to the issue of whether concentrated or dispersed policy making is best—this should sound familiar from the majoritarian-proportionalist dispute—and institutionally to issues of this or that specific power and whether a parliament, a cabinet, or a head of state is the best repository for it. The interlocutors in this debate have been primarily concerned with the durability of democracy itself, which is, of course, a precondition of democratic responsiveness. But they have also argued about the identifiability and responsiveness of policy makers under the alternative institutional forms.[13] Perhaps there is no answer to the institutional issue that works best under all conditions, especially given the difficulty of assessing the costs of deadlock and the status quo. But a growing weight of evidence suggests reasons to be wary of highly concentrated political power, whether it reposes in the hands of a presidential or a parliamentary (that is, prime-ministerial) executive.[14]

The figure's Linkage III connects the policy makers, who are at least publicly committed to doing what the citizens want, to the public policies that get implemented and to their various outcomes. At least three issues seem to need attention. First, the complex, multidimensional nature of policy alternatives can make the strength or even existence of this linkage hard to discern. Within a single policy realm alone—take that of economics, for instance—it can be difficult to say whether unemployment, growth, inflation, health policy, tax policy, and their respective instruments and trade-offs are linked consistently to "what citizens want?" More broadly, can citizens' preferences on abortion policy, crime, or foreign-policy and national-security issues be reliably identified as parts of a majority package linked to policy choices?

Then too, the status quo looms large whenever one tries to trace how preferences translate into policies. The context in which citizens are living inevitably shapes their perception of the importance and the content of the policies they desire. Questions about national health policy in the United States and Britain, for example, begin from quite different starting points since the policies now in place in each country are so distinct from those that are in place in the other. Levels of income inequality and welfare transfers differ sharply across countries. So do levels of inflation and current government expenditures. It is difficult to get at citizen preferences apart from these contexts.

The second problem is the impact of exogenous, uncontrollable conditions. Such conditions can weigh heavily indeed when we attempt to assess the preference-to-policy linkage. There are many relevant conditions that policy makers cannot control, especially in the short run. These may include economic development and productivity, human and natural resource endowments, social demographics, degree of dependence on international trade and aid, short-term economic fluctuations caused by factors far beyond a country's borders, bureaucratic capacity, and so forth. Variations in such conditions will affect what even the most responsively inclined policy makers can do about reducing poverty, providing for the elderly, increasing literacy, retraining the unemployed, supporting agriculture, or whatever else citizens may want to see when it comes to public policy.

To know whether and to what degree citizens determine public policy, we need direct or indirect measures of citizens' preferences, and we must apply them within a larger analytical design that also takes into account the effect of all the types of shifting and hard- or even impossible-to-control conditions outlined above. (Distinguishing between truly uncontrollable conditions and those that national policy makers can alter, and within what time frame, is part of the challenge.)

We must not assume that a rich country which spends twice as much per capita on welfare or education as a poor country is ipso facto more responsive, even if both citizenries say that they want equivalent welfare or education policies. Indeed, when one allows for varying governmental capacities, the poorer country might well turn out to the more responsive of the two.

For this reason, simple cross-national comparisons of policy outcomes are extremely dubious as indicators of the quality of democratic responsiveness, even if we could assume that all citizens everywhere straightforwardly favor a goal such as economic growth. If we wanted to follow such a route to analyzing responsiveness, we would need to draw on sophisticated public-policy studies that incorporate measures of the extent and intensity of citizen support for various political parties, use multivariate modeling techniques, and control for conditions beyond policymakers' control.[15]

A third issue is that of short-term citizen preferences versus longer-term citizen interests. Susan Stokes has raised this matter forcefully in her discussion of voter "mandates" for economic policy in Latin America in the 1980s.[16] A number of successful presidential candidates in that region made campaign promises to eschew promarket reforms and harsh economic adjustments, only to switch rather swiftly once in office to the very sort of "neoliberal" economic and fiscal policies that they had rejected while on the hustings. Stokes suggests that these switches might be justified as actions taken to serve the true interests of the citizenry, and that under some conditions voters could offer approval or disapproval at the next election. While I fear that such "bait-and-switch" tactics diminish the quality of democratic responsiveness in the short run, Stokes's analysis reminds us both that responsiveness is not the only public virtue and that one election may be an insufficient basis for judgment.

Subversions of Each Linkage

Having sketched some of the principal conceptual difficulties and theoretical disputes, together with some tentative answers, we can now

TABLE—PRINCIPAL SUBVERSIONS AND FACILITATING CONDITIONS FOR EACH LINKAGE IN DEMOCRATIC RESPONSIVENESS

	STRUCTURING CHOICES	INSTITUTIONAL AGGREGATION	POLICY MAKING
SUBVERSIONS	Information control Choice limitations Party incoherence	Vote-seat distortion Vote-executive distortion Condorcet winners lose Party switching Deadlocks/Decree-power use	Bait and switch Constraints Corruption
FACILITATING CONDITIONS	Education, media Stable party competition National discourse	Parliamentary PR Party coherence Inclusive policy making	Partisan accountability Horizontal accountability Bureaucratic capacity

consider directly what conditions and behaviors are likely to break each of the succeeding linkages. These are summarized briefly as "subversions" in the top half of the table.

Structuring Choices. Three principal types of subversions threaten the structuring of citizens' electoral choices in working democracies. These subversions are: 1) defects in the willingness or ability of citizens to gather and process accurate information; 2) parties that are incoherent when it comes to national policies; and 3) limitations on alternatives. It is clear that even with opportunities for collecting information, citizens may not take advantage of such opportunities (especially if education or literacy levels are low), or the sources may be biased by state control or by the predominance of groups or persons with strong class, regional, or ethnic leanings.

Political parties can be associated with at least two different types of subversions. First, parties may be slow to develop nationally coherent policy agendas, remaining mere collections of local elites. The personalities of local candidates may overwhelm weak and poorly organized national parties, limiting the degree to which elections can produce consequences that are structured enough to join citizen preferences to institutional aggregation in a reliable fashion. A volatile political landscape of rapidly splitting and fusing parties can leave citizens confused. At the same time, or perhaps separately, a strong president or demagogic party leader may overshadow the choice process strongly enough to obscure the issue preferences that are at stake. In such an environment, the vote shares of various parties may fluctuate wildly. As observers of Latin American and postcommunist states have noted, this may be a sign that citizens are finding it difficult to transmit their preferences through their votes. None of these is a decisive indicator on its own, but theory and empirical work suggest that these conditions can threaten to break the chain of democratic responsiveness and are "red flags" that the structuring of choices may be undergoing subversion.

Institutional Aggregation. Various institutional arrangements are susceptible to somewhat different subversions. In majoritarian systems (whether parliamentary or presidential), where political power is normally concentrated in a strong government chosen via a single-stage election, the subversive force is often a mathematical distortion of the vote-to-outcome relationship. Sometimes the interaction of geographic distributions with election rules causes this, whether by chance or through deliberate "gerrymandering." In other instances, the problem may lie in a "coordination failure,"[17] meaning that too many parties or candidates work similar electoral turf in search of the same offices. Traditional measures of vote-seat disproportionality (a governing party that gains 65 percent of the seats in parliament on the strength of a 40 percent popular-vote share would be a glaring example) may hint of problems, as may victories for plurality losers, although neither of these necessarily implies winners far from the median.

If we can map the policy positions of the parties (or electoral coalitions) relative to one another and to the citizen median, we can see if median parties as defined by voting have nonetheless found themselves stopped by vote seat distortion from becoming legislative medians. We might also see asymmetric coordination failure if a plethora of parties vie for the same voters and thereby clear the way for the election of a government that is farther from the citizen median, but which has profited electorally from the splintering of the potential majority that might otherwise cluster around that position. "Condorcet winners" among the candidates or parties—meaning those who could beat any rival in a head-to-head matchup—can lose, while as Joseph Colomer points out, Condorcet losers can win.[18]

Proportional as distinguished from majoritarian systems typically feature more parties as well as multistage methods of aggregating votes into governing power. Postelection bargaining among parties and institutions is a proportionalist hallmark. Electoral coordination is less demanding than it tends to be under the majoritarian rule of "first-past-the-post," but can still be a problem if a number of parties are competing and the popular-vote threshold that must be met in order to win seats in parliament is high enough, as was the case with many of the votes held soon after communism fell in Eastern Europe. The combination of proportional outcomes and relatively concentrated policy-making power usually means that under this system the elite level is where the subversion threats live. Elites may coordinate with one another in ways that voters and theorists alike find troubling and unexpected. The spectacle of newly elected officeholders switching parties can undermine voter confidence and the links that ensure democratic responsiveness.

Elite coalitions can form surprisingly far from the legislative median. In other cases, paralyzing elite deadlock and cabinet instability can set in. Diffused policy-making power may not preclude such problems so much as shift them to the arena of conflict among institutions: The legislative-executive struggles common to some presidential systems are an example. A president exasperated with such wrangling may try to rule by decree; legislators fed up with the president may try impeachment. In either case, the implications for democratic responsiveness can be dubious.[19] Again, none of these conditions by itself proves that responsiveness is being subverted, but they are cause for concern.

Policy Making. In addition to the "bait-and-switch" campaign tactics discussed previously, simple corruption can obstruct policy implementation: It is hard to keep a promise to build roads if the funds to pay for them have been stolen. A similar but perhaps more ambiguous phenomenon is that of excessive special-interest influence or lobbying. Officeholders who do things for lobbies are in a sense being "responsive," of course, but rent-seeking and other instances of special interests gone too far are widely decried problems in more than a few working democracies. Finally, constraints that the larger policy-making setting can impose on even the most sincere officeholders may also impede responsiveness. Inadequately developed bureaucratic and security organizations may create serious limitations domestically, and international factors such as global economic conditions or pressures from external actors may also force changes in promised policies or result in outcomes different than those sought.

While there may from time to time be legitimate justifications for promises unkept, in general these should be taken—along with high levels of observed corruption and rent-seeking—as "red-flag" indicators that policy makers are engaged in subverting responsiveness. Direct policy outcomes that fail to achieve goals that citizens desire are harder to assess, but comparison with selected nations in similar economic circumstances may provide warning benchmarks in a given case.

Strengthening the Chain

Generally speaking, the other dimensions of democratic quality—freedom, equality, vertical and horizontal accountability, and the rule of law—are also qualities that facilitate democratic responsiveness. In addition to these, however, there are other conditions that can reinforce a responsive connection at each link along the way. The lower half of the table lists these helpful conditions.

An active and independent mass media, educated citizens, and parties wedded to national-scale discourse promote an informed public whose preferences are sufficiently coherent to make responsiveness meaningful. While we do not know much about how such a responsiveness-friendly political landscape takes shape, it seems plain that party competition is part of the picture. So are electoral rules that do not encourage competitive party decentralization and localism. Fairly low barriers to the entry of new parties should help to keep the party system attentive to what citizens want. At the same time, a relatively stable voting pattern (not in itself a circumstance friendly to new parties) can play a role in enhancing citizens' grasp of the available alternatives and ability to coordinate their electoral choices.

Rules and institutions that encourage fairly drawn electoral boundaries are generally helpful to responsive institutional aggregation. The number of substantial competing parties should not exceed the number of representatives per district plus one. Proportional representation with a moderately low threshold seems to be conducive to fair, undistorted representation. (Different social conditions may interact with the rules in unexpected ways, however, as we can see from the mixed systems of Eastern and Central Europe.) A balanced, nationally oriented party system with a fairly small number of parties that win roughly consistent vote shares from one contest to the next provides information helpful in bargaining and hence aids responsiveness. So do parties that accept democratic rules and national boundaries. Parliamentary systems with fairly inclusive policy-making rules (strong committees and minority rights) seem to encourage representative involvement in the policy process.

Institutions that foster vertical and horizontal accountability also promote responsive policy making. Legal provisions to ensure fairer or even minimally guaranteed mass-media access to all major candidates and parties can be helpful, as can campaign finance reforms to ensure a more even playing field. Competition among a relatively small number of parties or coalitions makes vertical accountability (that is, elected officials answering to voters) easier. We must observe the irony, however, that precisely such conditions are often associated with governments which sit relatively far from the citizen median, due, perhaps, to the selective effects and influences of party activists.[20]

Horizontal accountability (when one part of the government answers to another) derives strength from the dispersion of power, at least to monitor whether the canons of due process are being observed in the process of policy making. Independent monitoring institutions, including courts and election commissions, can themselves be more easily sustained by somewhat dispersed substantive policy-making power (for example, a bicameral legislature in which each house is elected on a different basis). Institutional deadlocks and standoffs are a danger here, of course. Finally, an autonomous, well-organized, and skilled corps of public servants able to implement policies effectively and with minimal corruption can be a powerful bureaucratic buttress to the edifice of responsiveness. Such capacity on the part of the "permanent government" seems in turn easier to build and maintain in more educated, complex, and economically developed societies.

Measuring Democratic Responsiveness

Putting a yardstick to the sometimes-elusive quality of responsiveness in a democracy is a daunting task. The complexity of many of the concepts; the need to establish a chain of causal mechanisms; the lack of comparative empirical studies of citizen attitudes, party coherence, and legislative policymaking; and the normative and theoretical disputes that come into play all contribute to the magnitude of the problem. The dearth of large comparative studies focusing on democratic responsiveness is no accident. Yet simplifications of various kinds can open the way for cross-national analyses. Not only will these make it possible to say something about comparative democratic responsiveness, but as we develop the ability to examine alternative measures, we shall gain confidence in our inferences from any one approach.

The ideal study of democratic responsiveness would trace the full causal chain outlined in our figure, from citizen preferences through elections and policy-maker selection to policy making, using measures that are comparable across countries. At the moment, the lack of appropriate units for comparing preferences in a commensurate fashion across societies is a serious obstacle, especially given the diversity of needs and preferences in different countries. The best cross-national approximations have thus far appeared for the developed democracies, especially those of Western Europe, where the availability of a generally accepted left-right discourse has greatly facilitated comparison.

An initial effort at comparative responsiveness analysis might be possible using the above suggestions about the "red flag" subversion markers that can pop up at each link along the chain. Yet such suspicions would only alert the analyst to the need for deeper investigation into particular cases.

A more ambitious but still feasible enterprise would be to create an index for each of the principal "subversions" listed in the table. Some of these, such as information control and corruption, are already available in some form. Others, such as vote-seat distortions, plurality losers, and party switching, could be fairly easily obtained. Yet other subversions, such as losing Condorcet winners and bait-and-switch policy making, would be more difficult and probably involve at least new expert surveys. But existing studies show in principle how these could be done. Once the study had indices, these could be aggregated in various ways into a combined measure of putative responsiveness failures.

Another variant would be to commission expert surveys that would ask explicitly about a list of breaks in the causal chain.

An approach involving more radical simplifying assumptions could take for granted that all citizens want certain policy outcomes and examine whether national performances correspond with these. Beyond freedom, equality, and the rule of law, we could assume that all democratic citizens want certain kinds of economic performance. Obviously, the needs and the constraints vary with initial economic conditions, as well as international ones, so simple general comparisons of economic growth, for example, are too simplistic and likely to give very misleading results. But could we not create reference groups of countries with fairly similar demographic and economic profiles—countries that one may fairly assume will face much the same repertoire of needs and constraints—and examine policy performance on key indicators relative to other group members? The danger in this approach, of course, is that citizens in different countries might have different preferences regarding trade-offs, say, between health care and jobs or equality and growth. There is also the danger that our profiles—or, in a more complex version, our economic models of policy performance—might not capture the constraints adequately.

A simple and promising entrée to the study of responsiveness might be to use citizens' own assessments of their democracy as a measuring rod. At best, we could design survey questions asking citizens whether they thought that policy makers were pursuing policies that commanded majority support. (It would be crucial to draw up questions that would avoid eliciting answers focused on the individual respondent's sense of personal efficacy.) Even well-educated citizens of highly developed countries will often not have mastered all the intricacies of their nation's political process, and are almost certainly not walking around with the equivalent of our responsiveness figure in their heads. Some of them may generalize from inappropriate evidence or offer assessments filtered through partisan eyes. Yet none of this may be terribly damaging: If we are looking for gross differences in democratic quality, then probably only egregious breaks in the responsiveness chain will be of interest. Regarding these—one thinks of glaring vote-seat distortions, numerous broken campaign promises, rampant corruption, parties that have nothing coherent to say about national policy, and so on—citizens will in all likelihood have a fairly reliable sense, at least in outline, of where the links of responsiveness have become strained or have even snapped altogether.

A closely related approach, which could be undertaken more or less immediately and without the need to design and carry out new mass-opinion surveys, is to use the widely available questions about how well people think democracy is "working" in their own countries. The fair assumption here is that citizens will respond negatively to breaks in

the responsiveness chain. There have been many empirical studies using this measure and various versions related to it. Analyses of these
studies do suggest that citizens' responses reflect their impressions of
how various institutions are doing, and not the value that people place
on democracy itself.[21]

Yet we cannot know if citizens are making assessments that are consistent with our theoretical conception of democratic responsiveness. It might
be acceptable, even desirable, for citizens in different countries to react
in varying ways to different kinds of problems that threaten to undermine
responsiveness. But there is a danger that people may actually be assessing the quality of democracy not according to "responsiveness" at all,
but rather according to the rule of law, accountability, equality, or some
other measure. Or they may be aware of responsiveness as an issue, but
may find it massively less relevant and immediate than concerns such as
personal security or well-being.

It is disconcerting to find that a concept so close to the essence of
democracy and its justifications as responsiveness is so difficult to analyze and compare. Suppose for a moment that we consider two approaches
employing even more radical simplifications.

First, we could focus just on the processes of democratic linkage,
without worrying about substantive policy content. We could simply
look at how voting results match up with election outcomes, for instance. Do plurality winners gain office? Are losing incumbents
evicted?[22] The ready availability of voting and officeholding data makes
these questions easier to investigate and provides a comparable metric
for comparison. Research on these issues is appropriate and useful, but
insufficient. The difficulty is that just focusing on procedure misses
critical issues that lie near the heart of democratic responsiveness. Suppose that because of the ways the vote is split the plurality winners
promise radical transformation of the society against the wishes of a
substantial majority of citizens. Or suppose the properly elected government forgets its election promises and proceeds, legally, to loot the
treasury. Doing what the citizens want—not just following procedures—
is the essence of democratic responsiveness.

Second, we could merely search for some positive connections, without trying to examine the total picture across linkages and across issues.
Perhaps we have posed unrealistic standards and we should be satisfied
with some successes, rather than looking for subversion. But the problem with ignoring linkages is that a serious break at any point in the
chain really does vitiate responsiveness—good vote-seat connections
mean little if some issues are suppressed in the campaigns, or if the new
rulers let thugs run wild. The problem with focusing on a single issue
may not be quite as severe (hence the temptation to stress economic
performance alone). Yet it can allow policy makers to pick and choose
on the basis of their own preferences, not their promises to citizens.

For these reasons, then, I suggest a more complex research agenda, involving multiple, context-sensitive measures of procedure, substantive content, and citizen evaluation. Impatience with so ambitious an agenda is understandable, but overlooks the rich dividends that such research could yield, not only for our ability to describe and compare this dimension of democratic quality in and across new democracies, but also for our understanding of the possibilities and limits that reside within the nature of democracy itself.

NOTES

The author wishes to thank Leonardo Morlino and Andreas Schedler for commenting on an earlier version of this essay, and also extends his appreciation to the other participants at the conference where it was first presented.

1. Robert A. Dahl, *Democracy and Its Critics* (New Haven: Yale University Press, 1989), 95.

2. "Structuring choices" denotes the connection between citizens' preferences and their electoral choices; "institutional aggregation" refers to the connection between citizens' electoral choices and the selection of policymakers; and "policy making" is the link between the selection of policy makers and the policies that are chosen and implemented. I am indebted to the discussion of the "chain of democratic choice" in Andreas Schedler, "Democracy Without Elections: The Menu of Manipulation," *Journal of Democracy* 13 (April 2002): 36–50.

3. See Hanna F. Pitkin, *The Concept of Representation* (Berkeley: University of California Press, 1967), esp. 232–34.

4. See the review and discussion in G. Bingham Powell, Jr., *Elections as Instruments of Democracy: Majoritarian and Proportional Visions* (New Haven: Yale University Press, 2000), ch. 1.

5. Robert A. Dahl, *Democracy and Its Critics,* 112.

6. Kenneth J. Arrow, *Social Choice and Individual Values* (New York: Wiley, 1951).

7. William H. Riker, *Liberalism Against Populism: A Primer* (San Francisco: W. H. Freeman, 1982), xviii.

8. William H. Riker, *Liberalism Against Populism,* 244.

9. See, for instance, James Bryce *Modern Democracies* (New York: Macmillan, 1921), 119; V. O. Key, *Southern Politics in State and Nation* (New York: Vintage, 1949); E. E. Schattschneider, *Party Government* (New York: Holt, Rinehart & Winston, 1942).

10. Anthony Downs, *An Economic Theory of Democracy* (New York: Harper & Row, 1957), 80; William H. Riker and Peter C. Ordeshook, *An Introduction to Positive Political Theory* (Englewood Cliffs, N.J.: Prentice-Hall, 1973); Eleanor N. Powell, "The Development of Party Systems in Post-Communist Democracies," unpublished manuscript, 2004.

11. Arend Lijphart, *Democracies: Patterns of Majoritarian and Consensus Government in Twenty-One Countries* (New Haven: Yale University Press, 1984), 4–5.

12. G. Bingham Powell, Jr., *Elections as Instruments of Democracy,* ch. 1.

13. Matthew S. Shugart and John M. Carey, *Presidents and Assemblies* (New York: Cambridge University Press, 1992).

14. See, for example, Adam Przeworski, et al., *Democracy and Development* (New York: Cambridge University Press, 2000), ch. 2.

15. For an example of such a sophisticated study, see Robert Franzese, *Macroeconomic Policies of Developed Democracies* (New York: Cambridge University Press, 2002). An additional factor complicating such studies is the likelihood that conditions which are truly beyond the control of policy makers will vary across a range of policy areas and general societal characteristics.

16. Susan C. Stokes, *Mandates and Democracy: Neoliberalism by Surprise in Latin America* (New York: Cambridge University Press, 2001).

17. Gary Cox, *Making Votes Count* (New York: Cambridge University Press, 1997).

18. Josep M. Colomer, "Electoral Rules and Governance," paper presented at the Annual Meeting of the American Political Science Association, Philadelphia, 27 August–1 September 2003.

19. John Carey and Matthew Shugart, eds., *Executive Decree Authority* (Cambridge: Cambridge University Press, 1998); Gary W. Cox and Scott Morgenstern, "Epilogue: Latin America's Reactive Assemblies and Proactive Presidents" in Scott Morgenstern and Benito Nacif, eds., *Legislative Politics in Latin America* (New York: Cambridge University Press, 2001), 446–68.

20. G. Bingham Powell, Jr., *Elections as Instruments of Democracy,* ch. 8.

21. See Damarys Canache, Jeffrey J. Mondak, and Mitchell A. Seligson, "Meaning and Measurement in Cross-National Research on Satisfaction with Democracy," *Public Opinion Quarterly* 65 (Winter 2001): 506–28; Robert Mattes and Michael Bratton, "Learning about Democracy in Africa," Afrobarometer Working Paper 31, 2003; Christopher Anderson and Yuliya V. Tverdova, "Corruption, Political Allegiances, and Attitudes Toward Government in Contemporary Democracies," *American Journal of Political Science* 47 (January 2003): 91–109.

22. G. Bingham Powell, Jr., *Elections as Instruments of Democracy,* chs. 3 and 4.

6

A SKEPTICAL PERSPECTIVE

Marc F. Plattner

Marc F. Plattner *is coeditor of the* Journal of Democracy *and codirector of the International Forum for Democratic Studies. The holder of a Ph.D. in government from Cornell University, where he concentrated in political philosophy, he is the author of* Rousseau's State of Nature *(1979).*

The motives that have led scholars of comparative politics to turn their attention to the quality of democracy are both noble and sensible. With the progress of the third wave of democratization, political scientists were inevitably led to shift their focus from democratic transitions to democratic consolidation—from the ways in which democratic regimes come into being to the ways in which they can be rendered stable and secure. But eventually even the focus on the consolidation of new democracies was bound to seem too confining. In the first place, some of the third wave cohort can now reasonably be considered to have consolidated their democracies, yet that hardly means that they are no longer a worthy object of study. Second, no matter how rigorously one tries to restrict the meaning of consolidation solely to forestalling regression toward authoritarianism, it is hard to escape the common sense notion that democracies have a better chance to survive if they function well. Hence the new focus on the quality of democracy, which seems to offer both a common standard against which to measure newer and more established democracies and a way of thinking about how democracy can be improved and strengthened.

But what does it mean to speak of the quality of democracy? The word quality simply refers to the character of something, whether good or bad. Thus we speak of something as being of high quality or of low or poor quality. A high-quality democracy, then, is one that has the good characteristics appropriate to a democracy. But what are these? The answer depends on what sort of thing we understand democracy to be.

These kinds of questions, which soon lead us to the deepest regions of political philosophy, are not easily resolvable within the boundaries of empirical political science. I do not worry about preserving some pristine notion of a value-free and hence purely scientific study of democracy. The whole field of democratization studies is animated by a "normative" preference for democracy—and properly so, in my view. In fact, the dangers that I fear arise precisely from taking too seriously the scientific pretensions of what Larry Diamond and Leonardo Morlino call the "growing subfield" of studies of democratic quality. Those dangers are, first, a tendency to reduce the complexity of the questions at issue in order to come up with measurable "indicators," and, second, a tendency to enshrine the particular political preferences of scholars as objective standards of quality.

It is true that all the articles in this section acknowledge in one way or another the complexity of the phenomena that they seek to assess. Diamond and Morlino, in particular, call attention to the "trade-offs and tensions among the various dimensions of democratic quality," and warn that "all good things do not go together smoothly." Yet I do not believe that any of them fully confront the tensions at the heart of democracy itself, and the difficulties that these present for any effort to identify noncontroversial criteria of democratic quality. Broadly speaking, I see two basic complications: 1) Modern liberal democracy has a composite nature, consisting of often conflicting aspects; and 2) democracy is a *form of government* that must not only be democratic but also effectively govern.

Contrary to David Beetham's assertion at the opening of his essay, I believe that it is essential to distinguish *liberal* democracy—which we usually have in mind when we speak of democracy today—from other (mostly older) forms of popular rule. After all, the word "democracy" was invented by the ancient Greeks, and it would hardly be fair to deny that label to Greek cities ruled by the *demos*. Yet, again contrary to Beetham, even Athens by no means provided the protection for individual rights that we today consider a hallmark of democracy. It is not only Benjamin Constant who emphasized the disjunction between ancient and modern notions of liberty and rights. Both Montesquieu and the *Federalist* highlighted the insecurity of individual rights in the ancient city, and the new liberal political institutions they recommended were intended precisely to remedy this crucial defect, even at the cost of limiting the power of the people.

Modern liberal democracy seeks to make the people sovereign but, in order to protect the rights of individuals and minorities, it also places significant constraints on what government can do. There is always a tension, almost a kind of schizophrenia, within liberal democracy, as it simultaneously tries to affirm and to limit popular rule. The eight "dimensions" of democratic quality discussed by Diamond and Morlino may be divided into these two aspects. Equality, participation, competition, vertical accountability, and responsiveness all aim at strengthening the influence of the popular will over government. Rights or freedoms, the rule of law, and horizontal accountability all aim at restricting government, even when it reflects the will of the people, and minimizing the damage that it can do to individual citizens.

Most citizens eventually become habituated to the dualistic character of liberal democracy, which restrains popular rule through institutions and provisions that protect the rights of individuals and minorities. Virtually everyone now accepts that certain basic rights should not be vulnerable to legislative majorities, but the difficult question is where the line should be drawn between issues to be decided by the people and those to be settled by the courts. The disputed realm includes some of the most contentious "social issues" of our time: abortion, capital punishment, gay marriage, and the like. Would it be more democratic to adopt a specific policy on these questions or to allow them to be decided by popular majorities? Which approach would be the mark of a higher-quality democracy? Can different countries (or the same countries at different times) deal with these issues in different ways without enhancing or diminishing the quality of their democracy?

Democracy and Governance

An even more troublesome obstacle to evaluating the quality of democracy stems from democracy being not simply a goal in itself but also a form of government. Whatever other criteria it must satisfy, it also has to be able to deliver the benefits that any form of government is expected to provide, ranging from economic growth to education to personal and national security. But the extent to which a democracy can deliver these benefits is not necessarily related to how democratic it is, nor will improving its specifically democratic features always make it better governed. Even if it is generally true that democracy favors good governance, it would be hard to deny that some nondemocracies have been better governed in many respects than some democracies.

But how is the quality of governance to be reflected in appraisals of the quality of democracy? Here we face a dilemma. If we include governance when measuring the quality of democracy, we wind up judging democracy partly on the basis of performance criteria that often have little or nothing to do with "democraticness" (whether understood in terms of individual rights or popular control). Poor economic growth, for example, may be the result of counterproductive economic policies that reflect popular choices in a way that is exemplary from a democratic perspective. Can we say that this indicates a lower quality of democracy than if unelected technocrats fashion policies opposed by the majority?

It is tempting, then, to exclude government effectiveness altogether from evaluations of democratic quality. Yet this leaves us with an even more curious result. For, at least in principle, one might then give the highest rating for democratic quality to a government that utterly fails to promote economic growth, curtail crime and corruption, or provide a decent education to its people. Of course, one might say that such a democracy would fail to merit a high score in terms of what Diamond and Morlino call "quality of results," as measured by the degree of "customer satisfaction." But this is merely a way of restating the problem. History is filled with examples of democracies that lost popular support because of their failure to satisfy their citizens. The complaint against them, however, has typically not been that they were insufficiently democratic, but rather that they were weak or feckless or inefficient. So it still seems to me that we are dealing with, and often confusing, two different notions of quality: one understood in terms of democraticness and the other understood in terms of effective governance.

Another way to try to get around this problem is by stretching the concept of responsiveness. If we presume that virtually all citizens want, say, high economic growth and low crime rates, but their elected government fails to deliver these goods, then there must be a deficiency in democratic responsiveness. At one point in his extremely careful and nuanced analysis, G. Bingham Powell, Jr., briefly offers a suggestion along these lines, but I think it is unpromising for reasons beyond those he adduces. For if we measure responsiveness according to the goals that citizens seek rather than their preferences for particular policies, we in effect give government *carte blanche* to pursue whatever policies it chooses in pursuit of these goals. Thus even if an electorate clearly favored curbs on free trade, a government could claim to be acting in a democratically responsive manner by following precisely the opposite policy, on the grounds that this would better serve the citizenry's desire for economic growth.

It would seem more accurate and sensible simply to say that popular majorities can be wrong about matters of policy (as, to be sure, can insulated technocrats as well). Thus perfect responsiveness on the part of government might sometimes lead to terrible policies. Countries with the finest democratic institutions and procedures may commit policy blunders, but this does not diminish the quality of their democracy as such. Indeed, there are some specialized policy areas where virtually everyone agrees that expertise is essential, and hence democratic decision making (though not oversight) must be forgone. Moreover, in all policy areas constraints must be put on the length and inclusiveness of democratic deliberation for the sake of efficiency. So just as there is a tension between the liberal and the populist (or majoritarian) aspects of democracy, there is also an inevitable tension in some respects between democracy and government effectiveness.

The ambiguity besetting the quality of democracy can be taken to still a deeper level by raising the question of the relationship between democracy and the quality of a society as a whole. This is suggested by a couple of passages in David Beetham's essay. At one point he asserts, "The idea of a 'culture of liberty' is not . . . irrelevant to the quality of democracy," noting that even constitutionally protected free media may be "dominated by trivia." Elsewhere he stresses that a "key issue for democratic quality is the character of the citizen body itself." These observations remind us that the purposes of a political order may not be exhausted by the provision of liberty, security, and prosperity to its citizens. One can imagine a country with an impeccably democratic and efficient government where the culture is tawdry, families are in disarray, and the people are selfish and shallow. Can we fully evaluate the quality of a democratic regime without considering its quality of life in this sense?

On a more practical level, the problems inherent in measuring the quality of democracy become apparent in so-called democracy audits or assessments. These seek to evaluate democratic quality in particular countries on the basis of standards devised by some combination of international and local experts. But both the choice of which features to measure and the standards selected tend to reflect the intellectual or political preferences of those experts. Take, for example, the issue of electoral systems, which on several occasions has been hotly debated in the pages of the *Journal of Democracy*. In their essay in this volume, Diamond and Morlino note the respective advantages of first-past-the-post and proportional systems and conclude that there is no objective way to determine which promotes a higher quality of democracy. Yet in the summary of the results of the 2002 audit of the United Kingdom included in the appendix to Beetham's essay, Britain's Westminster system is faulted for its lack of proportionality, and the government is chastised for not acting to change it. Some sense of the political cast of the U.K. audit, which features on its cover page the face of Tony "Blairapart" imposed on a classic Jacques-Louis David portrait of Napoleon on horseback (available at *www.democraticaudit.com/download/Findings6LR.pdf*).

Democracy audits are no doubt a useful innovation that can aid citizens in evaluating their own democracies, but they are also easily subject to distortion. In particular, they inevitably tend to reflect the outlook of experts, even though it may often be at odds with the outlook of electorates. For example, Beetham asserts that "human rights lawyers are often best placed to assess" a country's performance with respect to civil rights. Yet there is every reason to expect that when there are tensions between civil rights and security, for example, human rights lawyers are much more likely than most other citizens to come down on the side of civil rights. And it is questionable whether their views should carry greater weight in assessing the quality of democracy.

So let us vigorously debate the quality of democracy and try to evaluate the democratic performance of particular countries—but let us never lose sight of the complexity of the issue or the danger that biases of various kinds may distort our assessments.

II

Comparative Case Studies

7

ITALY AND SPAIN

Rafael López-Pintor and Leonardo Morlino

Rafael López-Pintor *is professor of political science at the Universidad Complutense in Madrid.* **Leonardo Morlino** *is professor of political science at the University of Florence and at Istituto di Scienze Umane, Florence.*

The democratic quality of every European polity is worthy of analysis. The fact that most European democracies are well-established does not mean that they have all achieved the same level of "quality." In recent years, there have been several meaningful assessments of several European democracies, including a study of the United Kingdom by Stuart Weir and David Beetham.[1] We chose to analyze Italy and Spain not for any strong theoretical or empirical reasons other than an inclination to focus on relatively recently established democratic polities in countries with previous authoritarian experiences, rather than older, more stable democracies. In other words, we were more interested in European democracies that may be more problematic with regard to quality because of their political traditions. Italy and Spain can be usefully compared, as the Italian democratic transition and consolidation go back to the 1940s and 1950s, whereas the Spanish experience occurred during the second half of the 1970s and the early 1980s.

From an empirical perspective, the research on Italy[2] and Spain[3] emphasizes the following flaws and problems: for both countries, territorial limits to the rule of law, ongoing corruption, and party decline and transformation; for Italy, significant control of the media by Silvio Berlusconi, the leader of Forza Italia (Go Italy) and prime minister since 2001 (and in 1994), slowness in the conduct of trials before the courts, attempts to influence unduly the judiciary, gaps in the guarantee of social rights for sectors of the population; and for Spain, the persistent challenge to the integrity of the state posed by the Basque conflict, which worsened during the past 25 years through continued separatist violence and mounting threats to civil and political rights among significant sectors of that region's citizenry.

The Rule of Law

Territorial Constraints and Limits to the Rule of Law. The main territorial limitation to the rule of law in Italy is the presence of various armed mafias. The influence and nature of the mafias have undergone many changes and new types of mafias have emerged as a result of immigration and the end of the Cold War. Unclear links between political parties and mafias have been repeatedly affirmed, even by parliamentary committees set up to investigate the phenomenon. The main charge was that mafia clans supported party leaders by mobilizing votes in their controlled territory in exchange for "assistance" in getting public-works contracts and manipulating criminal records pertaining to mafia members on trial. The newest business for mafias is money laundering, which has been facilitated by the introduction of new technologies. The struggle against the various Italian mafias has received increasing attention since the 1980s, thanks to some reform in the organization of the investigators and increasing power given to them. Anti-mafia legislation has strengthened some preventive measures. However, a side effect of globalization has been the development of new forms of organized crime. If the state has regained some control of its territory, the mafias have developed different *modi operandi* in which territorial control is less central.

Italy has also experienced the political interference of paramilitary forces operating behind the scenes, in alliance with segments of the secret services or, at least, with their connivance. The most organized attempt to create an occult form of government was the so-called Loggia P2, which operated during the 1970s.

Although the judiciary has a high level of institutional autonomy,[4] an increasing number of investigations of political corruption in recent years has resulted in growing criticism and attempts to limit such autonomy. Constitutional Law 2/99 has put the principle of a fair trial, already contained in Article 111 of the constitution, into practice. Yet several shortcomings of the judiciary system are evident. Particularly disturbing is the length of trials, which has brought several condemnations of the Italian judicial system by the European Court of Human Rights. The UN Human Rights Committee has also expressed concern about preventive detention. In addition, conditions in Italian prisons are alarming, and the UN Human Rights Committee has frequently documented human rights violations.[5]

In Spain, two main challenges to effective rule of law are the persistent Basque conflict, which threatens the territorial integrity of the Spanish state, and the shortcomings in security and justice administration demonstrated by the failure to control the numerous mafia groups operating throughout the country.

Basque nationalists from right and the left never formally proposed a legitimate integration of the Basque country into the Spanish state after the restoration of democracy. This has remained an open question since the inception of the new regime. In fact, conservative nationalists of the Basque Nationalist Party (PNV) called for abstention in the constitutional referendum of December 1978, although this did not stop them from negotiating a self-governance statute in 1979. The expectation existed—and still exists among a majority of the population both within and outside the Basque country—that self-governance demands could be accommodated within the current constitutional framework. A constitutional drafting committee in which Basque nationalists refused to participate purposely left open-ended the provisions for the possibility of self-governance. Such an expectation has become more problematic since the mid-1990s after the prodemocracy Ajuria Enea pact and coalition governments of the PNV and the Socialist Party ended. The PNV has led the government of the Basque country ever since the first elections in 1980 but has only recently openly rejected the validity of the Estatuto de Autonomía and announced its pursuit of a different status, suggesting independence by invoking the concepts of self-determination, *soberanismo,* and "free associate state." This latter formula recalls the legal status of Puerto Rico, and has recently been proposed with the promise by the Basque prime minister, known as *lehendakari,* of a referendum to be called in the near future, although this would violate current constitutional provisions.

Violent action, including terrorism, has accompanied the political process in the Basque country, with a death toll of more than eight hundred killed by the radical Basque Fatherland and Liberty (ETA) since 1969. After 11 September 2001, ETA was identified as a terrorist organization by the U.S. government and the European Union Council. In 2003, after an indictment by prosecutor Baltasar Garzón, the Spanish Supreme Court issued a ban on the political organization Herri Batasuna, an electoral coalition of extreme nationalist groups, after determining that it was a criminal organization tied to ETA. The ban was appealed by Herri Batasuna for review and then confirmed by the Constitutional Court. For the first time since the outbreak of democracy, Basque radicals were not allowed to run in the municipal elections of May 2003. Just before the elections, at the request of the Spanish government, Herri Batasuna was also classified as a terrorist organization by both the U.S. government and the EU Council.

Regarding the courts and the judiciary, these are generally considered independent and not subject to interference by the executive branch or other actors, although some prominent cases of corruption have come to light in the last decade. Among the most notable was the case of a high magistrate in Catalonia and former member of the judiciary self-governing body, Consejo General del Poder Judicial. Judge Jordi Estivill is currently in prison serving a six-year sentence for bribery and repeated obstruction of justice. A similar case of corruption was that of the judge Gómez de Liaño in Madrid, who, like Estivill, was stripped of his judicial powers.

A more serious threat to the rule of law is the existence of numerous criminal mafia groups operating in the country, most frequently with connections to Colombian, Balkan, and East European organizations. More than two hundred of these groups have been identified by the police, and the number is believed to be rising, as has been publicly affirmed by a Supreme Court prosecutor.[6] Mafia groups mainly engage in money laundering—funneling funds generated from drug trafficking and other criminal activities into real-estate operations—which often feature corruption involving local authorities and political parties. A recent case was uncovered after the May 2003 regional and municipal elections for the Madrid regional government; two members of parliament from the Socialist Party were bribed by some real-estate agents who belonged to the Popular Party in order to prevent installation of a leftist government in Madrid (see below). An international research group under the aegis of the Instituto Andaluz de Criminología has referred to this as a "corruption circuit" connecting massive flows of laundered money with a dramatic increase in the real-estate business and with an interest by criminals in controlling municipal governments all along the Mediterranean Costa del Sol.[7]

Regarding equal and secure access to justice by Spanish citizens, frequent criticism can be heard among the legal professions, including the ombudsmen, as well as from the public. Complaints center mainly on the length of trials and the duration of preventive detention. Both shortcomings are most harmful to the economically disadvantaged. Although justice is free of charge in Spain, good lawyers are expensive. Defendants indicted for minor crimes are also in a weak position because, until recently, different types of crimes were not distinguished in terms of bureaucratic red tape and deadlines. Furthermore, women are more often victimized in this respect than men.[8]

Successive legal reform has come to face some of these flaws. The self-governing body for the judiciary mentioned previously, Consejo General del Poder Judicial, was established in 1980 and further regulated in 1985 as a decisive step in enhancing the independence of the judiciary. In 1995, a jury was established for a number of types of criminal trials, signaling a move toward making justice more open to society. The same year, a revised penal code was implemented to fine-tune criminal legislation to democratic standards, which was referred to among the legal profession as the "penal code of democracy." The length of criminal trials was addressed in 1988 and 1992 by legislation containing procedures for accelerating them. The most recent reform in this area, in May 2003, aimed to accelerate judicial procedures for minor crimes by ensuring a trial within 72 hours after the indictment. The Ley de Enjuiciamiento Civil, a new procedural law for civil suits, was enacted in 2001. The ombudsman has raised objections to conditions in Spanish prisons, especially to overcrowding and inadequate arrangement of the cells, contravening prison legislation of the highest rank, the Ley Orgánica General Penitenciaria.[9]

Spaniards view justice in their country with ambivalence. On the one hand, most people are aware that in spite of all of its shortcomings, the administration of justice constitutes a guarantee of freedom and democracy. In a national survey conducted in 2000, 65 percent of respondents expressed this opinion. On the other hand, the courts are not held in high regard in terms of how they function, largely owing to their proverbial slowness, but also to the emergence of judicial-corruption cases in the last decade. In fact, public confidence in the capacity of the system to deliver justice ranks lower than in most EU member states: In a 1997 survey only 16 percent of respondents rated the functioning of the judicial system in Spain as good. This percentage was higher than that found for Italy (8 percent), Portugal (12 percent), and France (14 percent), but lower than for the other EU countries, with Finland and Denmark having the highest rates of satisfaction (60 percent and 55 percent, respectively) and the remaining countries showing intermediate results, such as the United Kingdom and Ireland, each with 32 percent.[10] Moreover, public trust in the courts has been consistently lower than that in other branches of government since 1984, when the judicial self-governing body began to collect opinion data on a regular basis. By 2000, on a numerical scale of 1 to 5, with 5 representing the most trust, the courts received a score of 2.7, compared with 3.0 for the national government, 3.5 for parliament, 3.1 for municipal governments, and 3.9 for the ombudsman and the king.[11] Finally, it is worth noting that a critical attitude toward the administration of justice in the areas of independence, impartiality, competence, accessibility, and efficiency is much more widespread among the general public than among members of the legal profession.[12]

Civilian Control of the Military and Police. In Italy, there is a tradition of civilian (political) control of the armed forces. However, police and security forces have always been viewed as the "police of the government," which defends the political order against opposition. Only in recent decades have some elements of a "citizens' police"—that is, one that protects citizens' rights— been introduced and the public's perception of the police been modified. In light of the fight against terrorism, the struggle against the mafia further legitimized the police, contributing to a more positive rapport with the population at large. The violence characterizing the 1970s led both protesters and the police forces to greater self-examination, and efforts to defuse violence on both sides considerably reduced the radicalism of protest. The image of the police-man as a "citizen in uniform" emerged, as did a growing sensitivity to "legitimization from below."

This democratization of the police forces has not yet been completed. Although the state police are demilitarized and more open to society, the Carabinieri and the Guardia di Finanza remain military and secretive bodies. Police reform was promoted from within, but it focused more on the living conditions of officers than on police accountability to society. Moreover, the police force has remained extremely centralized, under the control of the Ministry of Home Affairs, and with no deployment of powers to the regions or to the city councils. Overall, confidence in the police and the army is high and growing higher in Italy: 71 percent and 73 percent, respectively, in 2004.[13]

In Spain, civilian control of the military and police became increasingly effective as the democratic regime consolidated after the coup attempt of 23 February 1981 and the first socialist government in 1982. The military has enjoyed rather high public confidence ever since. On a numerical scale from 0 to 5, with 5 representing the highest confidence, the military received a rating of 2.9 in 1984 and 3.1 in 2000, compared with 2.5 for political parties, 2.7 for the judiciary, and 3.0 for the government.[14] The police also enjoy high public esteem, after becoming progressively demilitarized. There are two national police forces: the National Police and the National Guard, the latter being in charge of rural areas, road traffic, border security, and customs. Moreover, the regional governments of the Basque country and Catalonia have their own police forces, Ertxaintxa and Mocos de Escuadra, respectively.

Minimizing the Effects of Corruption. Among modern Western democracies, the case of Italy is unique owing to the intensity of corruption and the seriousness of its political repercussions. Since 1992, judicial investigations have uncovered a complex and widespread system of political corruption, with bribes going in part to enrich individual politicians and in part to finance the political parties. Public bureaucrats have often colluded with politicians. Although the investigations initially had disruptive effects on the political institutions, bringing about deep changes in the party structures and the political class, corruption still appears to be widespread, especially in public contracts.

The Italian experience confirms that the control of political corruption presents specific problems not found in the control of other crimes. They are linked largely to the potential limits that the executive power imposes on the judicial power, as well as to the potential collusion between the controllers and the controlled. To this we must add the specificity of corruption as a crime, for it is a crime without a victim: Neither the bribers nor the bribed have an interest in prosecuting their case, since they share the benefits of the corrupt exchange.

The control of corruption requires guarantees of political independence for both judges and prosecutors. It is necessary, however, to balance these needs with those of democratic control of decisions regarding justice policy. On these themes, the debate in Italy has been distorted by polarization of opinion among a segment of the public supporting the judges and an antijudicial one. The former sided in defense of the status quo, fearing that the political class might tame judges. However, the center-right parties, and particularly Forza Italia, launched a campaign against the judiciary, accusing it of "polluting" the democratic process by supporting one political wing over the other. This situation has jeopardized the reforms that are essential to reform the historically slow and inefficient functioning of the Italian judicial process. At the same time, it has reduced the legitimacy of the judiciary, portraying it as a body aiming to "control the righteousness" of the political class.

The cross-vetoes intrinsic to the reform of the judicial system have not resolved a series of problems related to the chronic inadequacy of the system. The problem of persistent ineffectiveness that torment the courts has been exacerbated by the probative difficulties that the new code of penal procedure has introduced. It is not surprising that the European Court of Justice has reproached Italy for the length of its judicial procedures. Obviously, the ineffectiveness of the judicial system reduces the function of punishment as a deterrent, as does the expected lightness of the sentence.

During the 1990s, the disclosure of a system of widespread, diffuse corruption clearly illustrated that public funding (introduced in the 1970s) had not discouraged illegitimate financing of elections, candidates, and elected representatives. These political scandals paved the way for a series of reforms aimed above all at ensuring transparency in finances and incentives and in the reduction of electoral costs. After the Mani Pulite ("Clean Hands") anticorruption investigation in the early 1990s, the 1974 law was partly abrogated and public funding of party expenses was repealed by the electorate by means of a referendum of 18 April 1993 that garnered 90.3 percent of all valid votes.

To date, the legislation has not succeeded in making the regulation of party activities more transparent, or in increasing the accountability of political candidates who carry out public duties and are given money by the state. Other measures that can help the fight against corruption have not yet been implemented. Nonetheless, the fight against fiscal irresponsibility has resulted in some positive feedback.

A particularly delicate question for any democracy is the potential "conflict of interests" within the administration. The overlapping roles of individuals operating in the political and economic arenas make the definition of boundaries difficult, and thus generates a dangerous "concentration" of political and economic power. In Italy, a recently approved mild attempt to regulate such conflicts does not seem to cope effectively with the fact that the media tycoon Silvio Berlusconi entered the political arena as the leader of Forza Italia, becoming prime minister first from May 1994 to December 1994 and more recently from May 2001 to the present.

On the whole, the political response to corruption in Italy appears weak. Specific measures taken to prevent bribery have been few and not very effective. In addition, the problem of corruption has not been resolved—statistics show that it is again on the rise. From 1992 to 2000, after discovering the extent of widespread corruption, the Italian political class came up with several very limited and unclear legislative and administrative measures aimed at preventing corruption. Since then, however, public interest in the topic has declined, and the theme of anticorruption policies has gradually disappeared from the political agenda. The commitments made by the Italian parliament (and government) to solve the problems of terrorism in the 1970s and the mafia in the 1980s are in stark contrast to activity in the area of corruption: no bill on the issue has been approved yet.

Transparency International identified Spain as among the least corrupt countries in 2002. Of 102 countries ranked from least to most corrupt, Spain was number 20, with a score of 7.1 on a scale of 0 to 10, with 10 indicating best practice. This rating was similar to that received by Belgium and Japan. Italy was ranked number 31, with a score of 5.2. The position of Spain had improved in the preceding few years, moving from number 23 on the list in 1999, with a score of 6.1, to number 22 in 2000, with a score of 6.6, and then to number 21 in 2001, with score of 7.0. In a Transparency International survey of businesses in 22 countries that specifically assessed the occurrence of bribery in business, Spain ranked number 11, with a score of 5.8, while Italy ranked 17, with a score of 4.1.

Some corruption cases involving the Spanish judiciary have already been mentioned. Several notable corruption cases involving high-ranking public officials were also uncovered in recent decades, mostly relating to political-party financing. While the Socialist Party was in power in the late 1980s and early 1990s, there was the Filesa case in 1989, in which a consulting firm charged fees to governmental agencies for services that were never rendered. Another case involved a brother of the then–deputy prime minister. Other cases, which may have helped bring about the Socialist electoral defeat in 1996, involved top officials of the Ministry of the Interior, some of whom are now in jail. The charges varied. One was the diversion of public funds to the Socialist Party and for the personal use of incumbents. This included the charging of commissions to private contractors and the misuse of Ministry funds that were allocated to covered activities and thus could be unreported. Other charges related to criminal activities, including murder and kidnapping engineered by public authorities in the fight against the Basque ETA.

Some corruption cases involving the conservative Popular Party also came to light in the 1990s. One, relating to public-works contracts, involved the chairman of the autonomous government of the Balearic Islands, who was forced to resign. Another case, still pending in court, has to do with misuse of EU subsidies to agricultural production of linen. Investigation by prosecutor Baltasar Garzón has identified two high-ranking officials in the Ministry of Agriculture who operated through a network of business firms. Two general directors of the Spanish managing body for EU subsidies, FEGA (Fondo Español de Garantía Agraria), and of the publicly owned MERCASA, along with 32 others, were indicted in an affair that unfolded between 1997 and 1999.

A major problem area in Spanish democracy concerns inadequate guarantees of rights to a decent home, the use of land, and the manipulation of the environment as regulated by Articles 45 and 47 of the constitution and current legislation on housing and the exploitation of bodies of water. In these areas, irregular governing practices at the regional and municipal levels are extremely common. On the one hand, there is the scandal scenario (mentioned above) of big housing and real-estate operations, corrupting regional and municipal authorities and the financing of political parties. Gigantic profits are generated by purchasing cheap arable land and later selling it at high cost for urban dwellings after obtaining a new legal classification of the land from regional and municipal authorities. In the case of alleged bribery of two Socialist Party members in May 2003, the political effect was immediately apparent, but the criminal case may not be resolved for years. By withdrawing their vote, the two legislators prevented a leftist coalition from taking over the Madrid regional government. This incident prompted a call for a new election, in which the Popular Party might have a better chance to obtain a clear majority. The real-estate business in which the builders were involved has been estimated to be worth approximately 6 billion euro in just a couple of municipalities on the outskirts of Madrid.

There are also abundant irregularities in house building and maintenance, involving such areas as official oversight of blueprints, height of buildings, quality of structures, water and sewage operations, and maintenance of historically protected housing. As in Italy, noncompliance with the law tends to be the rule rather than the exception in many municipalities, with no action taken by public authorities. An example was the collapse of a few old buildings in downtown Madrid in 2000, with the city mayor publicly acknowledging that only 10 percent of old buildings complied with regulations on periodic maintenance and repair. As recently as June 2003, a repair project conducted without an official permit at a nineteenth-century house in downtown Madrid resulted in the collapse of the building, killing one of the workers.

The rule of law also falters in environmental protection, despite increasingly frequent positive developments. On the positive side of the balance is a rising environmental awareness in Spain, along with a number of legal measures including the establishment of national plans on biodiversity, waste disposal, water treatment, renewable energy, and development research. All continental waters, superficial and underground, are legally part of the protected area called *dominio público* by administrative legislation. Still, Spain is the country most frequently sanctioned for infringement of EU environmental regulations.[15]

These and related issues have only occasionally come to the public eye, while a myriad of incumbents from all political parties may be involved directly or indirectly. The situation may more often be one of refraining from action and avoiding law enforcement than direct infliction of harm. Yet the final result is one of noncompliance with the law, trampling of certain rights with direct damage to citizens, and a breach of responsibility on the part of public administrators, who may act to maximize their own popularity and voter sympathies at the expense of the general interest. The typical situation is one of complicity between numerous but isolated individual interests and neglect of responsibility by public servants, all of them working in a short-sighted manner against the common good. A special anticorruption prosecution organization was established in the mid-1990's, Fiscalía Anticorrupción, but its effectiveness has been controversial.[16]

Political Participation

In Italy, political participation can be considered simultaneously a condition for better accountability and responsiveness and an important dimension of the quality of democracy. The political parties that developed a relationship of "protection" with social movements and various NGOs have traditionally mediated political participation. Rates of membership in Italian political parties were initially quite high, although with serious differences in the meanings of "membership."[17] If participation in various kinds of associations was low in comparison with other European countries, the number of people involved in unconventional forms of political participation was quite high. In some periods, protest became radicalized, even taking terrorist forms. Voluntary associations (such as charities) were traditionally associated with the Catholic Church and had only informal and sporadic relations with the public administration.

The pattern of political participation changed in the 1980s and the 1990s. In the 1980s, protest became much more moderate in repertoire and pragmatic in scope. In the 1990s, the breakdown of political parties that followed the exposure of pervasive political corruption beginning in 1992 dramatically affected political participation. Political-party membership dropped sharply while protest increased (but maintained mostly moderate forms). Social movement organizations multiplied but usually remained very small and loosely connected with one another. Voluntary associations grew too, and not only in number. New forms of "associational life" developed in the so-called third sector, with increasing although sometimes conflicting relations with the public administration, especially at the local level. Electoral participation declined slightly during this decade: from 87.3 percent in 1992 to 81.4 percent in 2001 in the general election for the Chamber of Deputies.

A persistent problem is the underrepresentation of women running in national and local elections. Participation of women in public life in Italy is quite low in comparison with other Western democracies. When the electoral results of the Chamber of Deputies and of the Senate are considered jointly, a slight increase in the percentage of elected women in the early 1990s (from 8.6 percent in 1992 to 12.7 percent in 1994) was followed by a decline in more recent years (to 10.3 percent in 1996 and 10.4 percent in 2001). According to the Inter-Parliamentary Union, in a list of 177 countries ranked in descending order based on the percentage of women in the lower or single chamber, Italy is number 56. The role of women in other areas as well has lagged behind constitutional precepts. In the area of family rights, it was only with the enactment of Law 151/75 that measures restricting the moral and legal equality accorded women by the constitution were finally abolished. These measures included the exercise of parental authority by the father alone, the father's sole right to extraordinary administration of children's and family assets, and the father's right to decide on place of residence. Finally, many laws have long been in conflict with provisions of Article 37 of the constitution, which states that a female worker has the same rights and must receive the same pay as her male counterpart for the same job, and that her special role in the family must be duly considered and protected. Formal equality was established only in the late 1970s (Law 903/77). Further movement in this direction is the introduction of legislation that not only forbids discrimination but also provides initiatives aimed at true equality in the workplace between men and women. Among other initiatives, a national commission and an ad hoc ministry have been established to invigorate the quest for real equality between the sexes in all its various aspects.

In Spain, electoral participation has remained basically unchanged since the 1970s, with a dual pattern in evidence. In general elections, turnout rates range from 70 to 80 percent, depending on the level of political conflict before and during the elections. Elections with 80 percent turnout usually produce a shift of the majority, while elections with 70 percent turnout usually retain the incumbent government. On the other hand, regional and municipal elections tend to have turnout rates of 65 to 68 percent. This phenomenon of political interest as a main trigger of political participation is conducive to comparative research.[18]

As in Italy and other countries, political-party and trade-union membership in Spain decreased in the late 1980s and the 1990s, but unlike in other countries, voter turnout did not decline. Moreover, social movements and voluntary associations have shown steady growth in both membership numbers and scope of activity. The phenomenon contradicts the stereotypical view of Spanish society as unarticulated and low in solidarity. The path of change has been unequivocally documented.[19] By 2003, approximately 60 percent of adults participated in some kind of voluntary organization, with the highest rates for neighborhood associations, sports groups, trade unions, and social assistance organizations, each involving over 10 percent of the citizenry. More highly principled organizations like political parties and environmental and human rights associations enjoy smaller memberships. Moreover, almost one out of every four adult Spaniards is a member of three or more associations. Since the 1980s, cultural, sports, and social assistance groups have been gaining in popularity, whereas political parties, unions, and religious organizations have been declining. Another main finding is that a large number of organizations are financially supported by contributors whose numbers are much larger than the group's actual membership. This is the case with social assistance organizations such as the Red Cross and Caritas; those that support disabled people, migrants, and ex-prisoners; and those that promote human rights and international development.[20]

In Spain, the participation of women in public life has been increasing dramatic and is more extensive than in Italy and many other EU member countries. Women's access to public office, both popularly elected and through competition in the professions, have improved markedly. This is notable not only in terms of the evolution of Spanish society itself, but also from an international perspective, with Spain ranking higher than many other well-established democracies both in and outside of Western Europe. First, quotas of at least 30 percent female candidates are regularly applied by political parties for all elective offices. Starting with the national parliament, female participation in the 350-seat Congress of Deputies has increased from 22 percent in 1996 to 28.3 percent in 2000, and finally to more than one-third of the current legislature. Women's share in the 259-seat Senate increased even more dramatically, from 14.8 percent in 1996 to 24.3 percent in 2000, and finally to more than one-third currently. In the last legislature, the speakers of both chambers were women. Female representatives at the European Parliament made up 32.8 percent of all Spanish representatives in 1995 and 34.4 percent in the current chamber, which is higher than the EU average of 29.7 percent.

In the executive branch, four women held portfolios in the former PP national cabinet of 14, and after the March 2004 elections, 50 percent of the cabinet members in the new Socialist Party government are women.

The percentage of women among undersecretaries and general directors increased from 11 percent in 1996 to 16 percent in 2000. In regional governments, the proportion of women in high executive positions nearly doubled, from 11 percent in 1996 to 20 percent in 2000. At the municipal level, approximately 10 percent of all mayors were women in 1999, a higher percentage than in 1995; the figure may have increased further after the municipal elections of May 2003. Most dramatically, women now hold a majority of the judicial offices, traditionally occupied by men. By 1995, women made up 43 percent of the prosecutors, judges, and court administrators. In 2000, the female share of the judiciary amounted to 53 percent. Overall, women account for 48 percent of public employment (national, regional, and local government combined), compared with 27 percent at the time of the democratic opening.[21]

Vertical Accountability

Democratic Role of Political Parties. In Italy, party socialization, recruitment, and campaigning for office are free and effective. Moreover, there are no obstacles to party formation. Yet the presence of parties in Italian society has declined markedly, which has affected the party organizations. Various kinds of party organizations still exist, but they are very "light" and poorly rooted in the territory.

Regarding parliamentary parties, the 1992 to 2001 legislatures saw recurrent "floor-crossing," whereby several members of parliament elected within a coalition have supported cabinets of opposite coalitions. Since 1994, the percentage of parliamentarians involved in floor-crossing has been 24 percent in the Chamber of Deputies and 22 percent in the Senate. Such behavior has been strongly criticized, and it virtually disappeared in the parliament elected in 2001, in which the ruling party has a solid majority.

The problem of party financing still exists. Many criticisms address the minimal transparency of the financing system and the superficiality of controls on the balance of payments and party expenses. Moreover, the parties are surreptitiously financed by a law that allocates public funds for their publicity, granting significant sums to any parliamentary group (even one composed of just two members) that declares a certain newspaper or magazine its press organ. Because the amounts are allocated based on the numbers of printed copies, rather than the effective circulation of the publication, it is suspected that the parties obtain much more money than they invest in their press. This is an important, undeclared source of financing.

Owing to the scarcity of controls, reliable data on the actual amount and sources of private financing of the Italian political parties are not available. According to the declarations of the parties and analysis of current values, public contributions to the parties have more than doubled during the past decade. Therefore, public financing is now the largest component of party revenues, especially after enactment of the 1999 law that allowed sums much greater than the declared electoral expenses to enter their budgets. The balances of many parties, which for a long time were in the red, have been rendered healthy.

Spain's party system has generally assisted the functioning of democracy, in spite of certain corruption in party finance, declining party membership, and a general public mood of skepticism. In fact, political parties have been able to maintain their organizational strength throughout the country as well as their negotiating capacity, both within the representative institutions and with respect to other significant social actors such as trade unions and business associations. Moreover, parties have contributed to the development of an increasingly robust public opinion. Yet public trust in political parties has been consistently low since the 1980s, with a majority of citizens suspecting corruption.[22] The current party system largely reflects that prevailing in Republican Spain in the mid-1930s prior to the civil war. It is basically a two-layer system, with the national layer accommodating the left-right cleavage dominated by the Socialist Party and the Popular Party. The other layer is that of nationalities and regional identities accommodating territorial cleavages, most notably, but not solely, in the Basque country and Catalonia. The broader pattern is a system of extreme pluralism,[23] with a dominating center, bilateral oppositions, and representation in the national Congress of Deputies usually including 11 to 13 different parties.

Parties can be easily created, and minimal requirements exist to run for elections. Nevertheless, as in Italy and other European countries, party membership has been declining in recent years. The two main national parties are widely though unevenly rooted throughout the country, with a weaker presence in those territories where regional nationalist parties have been historically strong (the Basque country, Catalonia, and Navarre).

Floor-crossing is very infrequent in the national parliament, and party discipline works reasonably well in spite of the fact that the legal foundation of the representative system is not in itself a guarantee of it (elected officials do not represent their respective parties but the citizenry as a whole). An anti–floor-crossing agreement, the Pacto Antitransfugismo, was signed by all political parties in 1998; until now, it has been applied only to municipal councils. All parties agreed to impede floor-crossers' participation in the constitution as well as their maintenance or change of government majorities in public institutions, to withhold support for any of their initiatives, and to discourage floor-crossing by economic, regulatory, or protocol measures. The 2003 case in the Madrid regional assembly prompted a public debate on whether the pact should also be extended to regional politics.[24]

Parties are financed principally with public funds, with generous subsidies allocated by law for three different purposes: the maintenance of party parliamentary groups, the normal functioning of party organizations, and electoral campaigns. Fund allocation is decided according to each party's electoral support and parliamentary representation. Private funding from member contributions is relatively insignificant.

The Media and Open Government. Ownership of the press in Italy is fairly pluralistic in spite of some groups that control a large number of newspapers, such as the R.C.S. Group, with *Il Corriere della Sera,* and *L'Espresso* Editorial Group, with *La Repubblica.* In contrast, ownership of television networks features a substantial duopoly. Silvio Berlusconi, the tycoon owner of Mediaset, challenged the RAI monopoly in the extremely murky legislative context that characterized the mid-1980s, and in a very short period managed to create a situation in which RAI and Mediaset dominated all other networks in terms of both advertising and audience.

Political choices still have a strong influence on the composition of the Board of Governors, and hence on editorial choice. Until the early 1990s, the main parties agreed to distribute all offices and positions among themselves, leading to a form of pluralism with economically inefficient patronage aspects. This process was known as *lottizzazione,* or the "parceling out" of a piece of land. This did not change when responsibility for appointing the Board of Governors passed from the hands of the chambers of parliament into those of the presidents of each chamber in 1993.

Berlusconi's entry into politics at the head of Forza Italia clearly posed a threat to pluralism in television news and programming and led to a new set of laws regulating political communications during electoral campaigns. Mediaset news programs (TG4 and Studio Aperto in particular) strongly favored Forza Italia and its leader. Suffice it to say that during the 2000 electoral campaign, Berlusconi appeared on the screen for a total of 367.8 minutes, while Massimo D'Alema (prime minister at the time, of Democratic Left) only "scored" 131.5, and Walter Veltroni (leader of Democratic Left) 112.7. A similar picture emerged during the campaign for the 2001 elections.

Investigative journalism is, unfortunately, much less common in Italy than the use of press releases, interviews, and editorial comments on news. Nor did journalists play a decisive role in unveiling corruption. Direct, albeit subtle, intimidation of journalists by political leaders is reportedly common: phone calls to the editor, reports on the behavior or "unwelcome" opinions of a journalist, and so on are actions frequently carried out by politicians. Since the beginning of Berlusconi's political career in 1994, the subject of the media has been much debated both within and outside of parliament.

In Spain, comparatively speaking, the democratic role of the mass media can be considered a fairly virtuous one. The media operate in a way that sustains democratic values, having played a crucial role at the installation of a democratic government after the death of Franco and at the successive crises of consolidation of the new regime in the late 1970s and early 1980s. At election times, fair access to the media by different parties and candidates is guaranteed by law and tends not to be an issue. State-owned television and radio are governed by a commission whose members are appointed by a qualified majority in parliament, guaranteeing a multiparty stance. However, episodes of news manipulation by the public television channels have been repeatedly exposed, with a zenith during the Iraqi war in 2003.[25] On the whole, mass media structures are highly pluralistic in terms of both ownership and cultural ideological leaning. There are two state-owned nationwide television stations— Channels 1 and 2—and a larger number of other stations owned by regional and municipal governments. Private television basically consists of three channels, each with different ownership, Antena 3, Tele 5, and Canal Plus, from largest to smallest audience. This pattern of mixed television station ownership stemmed from EU directives in the 1990s.

Radio broadcasting exhibits a similar structure, with two main publicly owned stations with national coverage and a larger number of other stations owned by regional and municipal governments. Private radio includes four main broadcasts, each of them with different ownership, including one owned by the Catholic Church. All significant newspapers are privately owned. Besides two national sports dailies, one of which ranks first in audience size among all newspapers *(Marca),* there are three main national newspapers. Ranked by audience size as well as from a liberal to a conservative slant, these are *El País, El Mundo,* and *Abc,* the last the only survivor from predemocratic times. The regional newspapers with the largest readerships and influence (even outside their own regions) are *La Vanguardia* and *El Periódico* in Catalonia, *El Correo Español* in the Basque country, and *La Voz de Galicia* in Galicia. Unlike television station ownership, a mixed pattern of public and private radio stations and newspapers was the tradition in Spain even before the democratic recovery in the 1970s.

Investigative journalism played an increasingly important role as democracy gained strength in the 1980s. Cases of military threats were then revealed, and illegal covert actions by governmental officials in the Basque country were brought to light. Serious cases of corruption and administrative negligence were exposed on various occasions, most recently the manipulation of elected officials by real-estate agents in Madrid and the negligent contracting of international air transportation by the military.

Horizontal Accountability

If there are few doubts about the government's control of important policy areas in Italy, accountability is more problematic. In order to address these problems, an attempt was made to build a party government with a multiparty but bipolar system. In support of this, but especially as a direct result of the growing shift of the power to regulate and apportion to EU authorities, there has been a large and growing conferral of legislative functions to government. Thus, over the last two decades a series of regulatory laws for both legislative chambers has profoundly modified the relationship between government and parliament. The main result has been the abandonment of the unanimity principle in the party whips' conferences to determine the chambers' agendas. Under the new rules, the agendas of both the Chamber of Deputies and the Senate are set by the government without the need for prior approval by the assembly, and the timing for parliamentary examination and debate is guaranteed by antifilibustering measures that go hand in hand with guarantees that give the opposition a preset amount of time and number of calendar periods. Furthermore, parliamentary activities are organized to give the executive branch virtual dominance of its agenda with a consequent strengthening of control on the opposition. The discipline of the vote of confidence should also not be underestimated as a means for the cabinet to constrain its majority when conflict arises within the coalition or majority groups. Moreover, the secret ballot has been abolished in the great majority of cases, and consequently the possibility of *franchi tiratori* (snipers), or members of the majority who vote against the initiatives of their parties, has declined dramatically.

It remains to be seen whether this collection of tools, and the more generalized attempt to position the executive centrally in the form of government with a stronger prime minister, has led to greater governmental efficiency in the implementation of its policy program. A first indicator of this is government lawmaking. According to the Study Service of the Chamber of Deputies, in 1999 "parliament further accelerated the previous years' trend by transferring many law-making functions to the government, making use of delegation and de-legislation. In 1999 a turning point was reached in delegation: the number of legislative decrees passed (94) was indeed higher than the numbers of laws passed by parliament (72)," decree laws excluded.[26] This is an important milestone in the timeworn model of policy-making, and it seems to place the government in a new, central position from which to conduct the planning and definition of an ever-growing list of crucial questions concerning the future of the administrative-political system and how it should interact with the market and society. A second important indicator is the increasing government-produced legislation, in addition to that delegated. Thus the relationship between government and parliament is undergoing realign ment: Parliament is no longer the source of government policies but only the "arena," where majority and opposition clash to sway decisions that have been essentially defined elsewhere.

Also significant has been the creation of the *independent administrative authorities* and a plethora of regulatory *agencies* whose surrogate, crucial function in economic and social regulation is now fairly significant. Born under the example of similar Anglo-Saxon bodies, these independent collegial bodies have been given ample powers of investigation, monitoring, and control. Composed of a president and a variable number of members, helped by a staff, they perform regulatory and adjudication tasks. All subjects (private individuals, companies, public administrations, and consumer associations) can approach these institutes of protection to bring to their attention irregularities in the various sectors of economics and public administration. Currently, there are eight independent authorities, such as the Authority on Telecommunication, the Authority on Competition and the Market, the Bank of Italy, the Committee for Controlling the Stock Market, and others.

On the scrutiny of the civil service by elected leaders and ministers, it is worth recalling that for a long time, unlike the case in some other democracies, Italian bureaucrats generally had a legal education. Moreover, there was little movement between the public and private sectors and thus minimal exposure of civil servants to the outside world. The preponderance of staff with legal training reflected the fact that bureaucratic functioning hinged on the principles of legality, to the exclusion of efficiency, efficacy, and economy. This legalistic attitude of the bureaucracy limited its capacity for initiative and change in a country that became first a major industrial power and then a postindustrial one. The public administration's limited capacity for initiative went hand in hand with a widespread use of veto power: nonimplementation of laws, delays in handling files, and removal of the more conflictual problems from the agendas at the top of the bureaucratic ladder. A set of exclusively legal checks often gave them a decisive opportunity for blocking or setting limits on the more innovative policies. Patronage relations often subordinated public bureaucrats to party politicians. Such behavior continued until the dawning of the 1990s, when a series of reforms (difficult to implement) addressed these issues.

Finally, regarding the distribution of formal powers between center and periphery, Italy is characterized by a growing decentralization of power and an incomplete turn toward a very strong regionalization in the 1990s. The Italian constitution provides for more than three levels of autonomy: regions, provinces, and municipalities, as well as others of lesser importance. They are run by elective bodies. The regional level of power was implemented only in the mid-1970s. The 1990s brought further decentralization. Overall reform of regional functioning has been set in motion by executive decrees following Law 59/97. From the standpoint of obtaining financial resources, tax reform—the so-called fiscal federalism (Decree Law 56/2000)—was approved. In the early 1990s, reform of the electoral system provided for the direct election of mayors and the president of the provinces and regions, with a potential increase in their visibility, legitimacy, and political importance. On the whole, the legislative reforms of the 1990s did not succeed in imposing new principles on the running of offices and proceedings. However, additional forms of decentralization are expected in 2005, as a constitutional law supported by the governmental majority has already been approved by one of the chambers.

Spain's executive branch is generally accountable to parliament and the public. On the one hand, the legislative agenda cannot be imposed by the government, and the timetable of the legislature must be approved by the presiding commission of representatives of the different parties. On the other hand, the no-confidence vote was used several times by parties on both left and right, although it functioned more as a means of obtaining an in-depth governmental review than to produce an actual shift in the cabinet.

There are other procedures of parliamentary control, including an annual debate on the state of the nation as well as weekly appearances by the prime minister in the Congress of Deputies. These two mechanisms arose out of parliamentary practice rather than by legal provision. Investigating commissions have sometimes operated and sometimes been hindered by the executive (for example, in the case of the military air crash over Turkey).

Regarding scrutiny of the bureaucracy by elected leaders and ministers, the reform thrust since the 1980s has been toward making civil servants more easily controllable by their political superiors. One aim of reform was simplifying the traditional corporate system of bureaucratic bodies. Although most elite corps remains unchanged, the main civil service component—the general corps—has been enlarged and made more open both to recruits and in the context of training. Another aim of reform has been enlarging the appointment and promotion capacity of political officials for civil service personnel, a sort of neo-spoils system designed to promote a more politically responsive bureaucracy.[27]

In general, limitations to accountability in Spanish government deserve deeper study, especially the lawmaking capacity of the executive branch at the expense of parliament and the concentration of power in independent administrative authorities and regulatory agencies, many of them created in the last couple of decades. There are 139 of these bodies in all, of which 72 are the traditional autonomous agencies, 16 are public enterprises, 46 are public entities with special statute (most of them related to the Ministries of Development, Economics, and Finance), and 5 are agencies for managing social security.

Regarding the power distribution between center and periphery—the decentralization/federalism dimension—democratic quality has to do with whether decisions are made at the level of government that is most appropriate for the people affected. As stated previously, democracy in Spain brought the transformation of state structures from centralized government to a kind of federal state comprising 17 territories with varying degrees of self-government. These territories range from a quasi-confederation in the Basque country to the more standard federalism in Catalonia, Galicia, and Andalusia, and lesser levels of self-government in the remaining "communities," the so-called *estado de las autonomías*. Devolution statutes were negotiated with the various regions between 1979 and 1983 according to the provisions of Chapter VIII of the constitution. A benefit of constitutional provisions in this area is the allowance for eventual reforms of any region's statute at the initiative of the regional government. Different finance laws were subsequently approved regulating the financing of the autonomous governments, including the establishment of so-called interterritorial compensatory funds to correct economic inequalities among the different regions. This goal was also pursued through the use of various EU funds.

Decentralization of state structures entailed a number of other changes that have progressively unfolded, related largely to a drastic reallocation of public expenses between national, "autonomous," and municipal governments. The situation has evolved from one in which public expenses at the disposal of the central government amounted to 90 percent of all public expenditures in 1980 to the current state of affairs, with 50 percent allocated to the central government, 30 percent to the regional governments, and 20 percent to local governments. Besides financial resources originating within the different regions and municipalities, an increasing part of the national budget is set aside for transfer to regional and local governments: around 22 percent of the national consolidated budget in 2003, versus 17 percent in 1998. The central government share of public expenditures in Spain is similar to that of other federal countries in the mid-1990s, such as the United States, Switzerland, and Australia.[28]

Other changes have to do with development of civil police forces by the governments of the Basque country and Catalonia and the composition of the civil service at the various levels of government. The evolutionary pattern of the latter shows a dramatic rise in public employment by more than half a million between 1982 and the mid-1990s while the new state structures consolidated. In the last ten years, public employment increased very little. However, a spectacular change occurred in the share of employment at the different levels of government. The total number of public employees was more than two million in both 1993 and 2002, amounting to 15 percent of the entire employed population, slightly below the EU average of 17 percent. Today, the largest proportion of public employees, slightly over 50 percent, belongs to the regional governments, versus 26.4 percent in 1993. Conversely, the national government currently employs only 24.5 percent of all public employees, a significant drop from its 1993 proportion of 57.3 percent. The remaining 23.8 percent of public employees work for local governments, an increase from 16.3 percent in 1993.[29]

In general, the territorial structuring of a new Spanish state since 1978 has been considered a success by common citizens, experts, and political actors.[30] A notable exception is the Basque country. Yet failure to accommodate the Basque conflict within the new state is a mark of historical misfortune rather than of democratic failure. Generally speaking, autonomous regional government and empowered municipal government together have allowed state power to come closer to the people and renewed community identities, bringing considerable dynamism to the political, social, and cultural life of Spaniards. At the municipal level, the continuing flow of otherwise centralized financial resources has drastically changed the shape of the physical environment as much as the political and cultural life of cities and villages. As recently as June 2003, a draft law on government for large cities was sent to parliament in which, among other things, enhanced popular participation in the city government by creating a city social council and organizing the city into several districts. Moreover, mayors are further empowered by being able to include nonelected officers as members of their city's governing executive committee.[31]

Freedom and Equality

Nationhood and Citizenship. In general, in Italy acquiring citizenship, regulated largely according to *jus sanguinis,* is quite difficult. This has become increasingly problematic as Italy has undergone a transition since the 1990s from an "emigration country" to an "immigration country." Equality between women and men is legally granted, but the UN Human Rights Committee has cited persistent discrimination against women in the job market. The UN Committee on Economic, Social and Cultural Rights has pointed out the weak legal protection for homosexuals. The Italian constitution protects linguistic minorities "by means of special provisions." However, only very recent legislation (Law N.482/99) has attempted to give juridical status to minority linguistic groups. Until the 1980s, immigrants enjoyed very little legal protection. A limited (although growing) number of human rights are now granted to noncitizen residents. With the exception of EU citizens, who have the right to vote in administrative, municipal, and council elections in their places of residence, noncitizen residents have no voting privileges.

Traditionally Italy has experienced a relatively low number of racist incidents in comparison with other European countries, but these incidents have been on the rise in recent years owing to the increasing number of immigrants. Although Italian legislation has shown an awareness of new phenomena such as racism and intolerance by introducing ad hoc provisions, the fear of "illegal immigrants" as potentially delinquent is widespread. The Council of Europe's Commission against Racism and Intolerance has identified some crucial areas on which Italy should focus, such as promoting awareness of intolerance, improving implementation of legislation against racism and intolerance, and strengthening cooperation between the state and voluntary organizations and NGOs that provide assistance to immigrants. Finally, the heavy influence of the Catholic Church in Italy has restricted or delayed the granting of some individual liberties, in particular those relating to family issues and sexual behavior, including the rights of women and homosexuals.

In Spain, the Basque conflict over national identity and territorial integration remains the main political problem with regard to nationhood and citizenship. No recent improvement in this issue can be reported; indeed, the situation has deteriorated since the coalition governments of the Basque conservative PNV and the Socialist Party came to an end in the early 1990s. Almost immediately, an agreement among all nationalist forces, both conservative and radical, to seek self-determination (the Pacto de Lizarra) replaced a former pact of democratic stability among all political parties, Spanish and Basque, except the radical nationalist Herri Batasuna (the Ajuria Enea pact).

As in Italy, Spanish citizenship is regulated according to *jus sanguinis* and is difficult to acquire even for Latin Americans from countries where dual-nationality treaties exist. Voting by foreigners is restricted to administrative and municipal elections and allowed only by EU citizens residing in Spain who had previously notified the electoral authorities in writing of their intention to vote. Among non-EU citizens, only Norwegian citizens are allowed to vote in Spanish municipal elections. This non-Spanish electorate amounts to just over ten thousand people.

With Spain becoming a country of immigration, a growing number of human rights are now granted to noncitizen residents, even those without proper legal status. These include the right to treatment in public hospitals and the right not to be deported to their countries of origin unless they are detained at the border when entering the country. Although successive legislation since the late 1990s has tried to accommodate the growing influx of immigrants and avoid the social exclusion of nonregistered residents, immigrants are associated with delinquency in the public mind, feeding xenophobia and racism, including a few serious incidents with fatalities. Police and security statistics show that such an association actually exists, which is at the root of citizens' identification of security as one of the main problems of the country since the mid-1990s.[32]

As in Italy, the strong influence of the Catholic Church has delayed the granting of some individual liberties, especially with regard to family issues and sexual behavior (for example, divorce, birth control, abortion, and the rights of women and homosexuals). At the legal level, these restrictions have been gone since the mid-1980s. As for practice, tolerance is the rule, although incidents of extreme discrimination sometimes emerge, especially in the form of domestic violence against women.

A total of seventy women were killed by their sexual or marital partners in 2003, and nearly 100 in 2004.[33]

Free and Fair Elections. Free and relatively fair elections are the rule in Italian politics today. Registration and voting procedures are accessible and inclusive of all citizens—although, as mentioned previously, noncitizen residents are excluded from national elections and only EU citizens can vote in local elections.

The issue of equal and fair access of parties to the media has been regulated by a law on *par condicio* (equal condition) that mandates impartiality in communication with voters. Furthermore, an independent monitoring project undertaken by Pavia University regularly publishes data on the amount of mass-media exposure of each political group represented in parliament, distinguishing between networks and individual programs. However, there is considerable debate on the effectiveness of these provisions. On the one hand, the law has been challenged for considering the television and radio exposure of party coalitions—large or small—with a minimum number of candidates on an equal basis, rather than on the basis of their electoral weight. Moreover, criticisms are directed against networks that overexpose some party leaders during the periods between electoral campaigns. This is particularly problematic because three national television networks (Rai 1, Rai 2, and Rai 3) are public and thus easily influenced by the government, and the other three (Canale 5, Rete 4, and Italia 1) belong to Mediaset, which is owned by Prime Minister Silvio Berlusconi.

Elections meeting high democratic standards have been the rule in Spain since 1977, when the first post-Franco general election took place under a provisional decree. Reflecting consensus among the contenders, that electoral legislation proved good enough to remain in place to the present day. Registration and voting procedures are all-inclusive. Ballots can be submitted by mail both at home and abroad. As in most EU countries, voting is not mandatory.

Election administration is managed by the Ministry of the Interior and municipal authorities under the regulatory and oversight authority of a National Electoral Council, appointed by parliament by a qualified majority. Equal and fair access by parties and candidates to the media is legally guaranteed and is not usually the subject of public controversy. General elections are held in Spain at least every four years, but an early election may be called by the prime minister. In the Spanish case, this also applies to governments in the Basque country, Catalonia, Galicia, and Andalusia, the four regions with the highest self-governing capacity.

Civil Rights. In Italy, freedom from physical and moral abuse is mainly enshrined in Article 13 of the constitution, which prohibits all forms of restriction of personal freedom "unless by motivated act of the legal authorities" and only where provided for by law. Only in cases "exceptional in necessity and urgency and absolutely indicated by law" may public-security authorities take temporary measures, and in all cases they must be approved by the judicial authorities within a very short time. The constitution guarantees a wide range of freedoms of movement, expression, association, and assembly.

Legislation on public security, which hinges on the 1931 Unified Text of the Law on Public Security (TULPS), still bears traces of its authoritarian origins that survived the impact of postwar constitutional principles and Constitutional Court jurisprudence. The authoritarian residue has given rise to debates that the Constitutional Court has not always succeeded in solving satisfactorily. In particular, some measures in TULPS significantly restrict rights guaranteed by the constitution, including the police power of obligatory accompaniment, the criminal status of refusal to reveal one's own identity on demand, and the prohibition of seditious shouting and demonstrations

Freedom of religion is affirmed by Article 8 of the constitution. Article 19 affirms that everyone has a right to profess their religious faith in any way they please, including proselytizing or practicing in public. And while Article 8 stipulates that "all religious faiths are equally free under law," the constitution places Roman Catholicism on a different plane from other faiths. A wide variety of groups operate without government restriction, investigating human rights cases and publishing their findings.[34]

In Spain, civil and political rights are in principle equally guaranteed for all citizens. In implementation, however, a major exception is the Basque country, where persistent political conflict hinders the guarantee of certain rights for large sectors of the population, especially those not aligned with the nationalist political forces, which constitute about half of the electorate. Street violence and intimidation within different social and institutional settings are routine in many Basque towns and villages. The freedoms and rights in jeopardy are essentially those of movement, association, expression, and public demonstration.

The death toll of violence by ETA had reached 857 by the end of June 2003, with most of the victims killed after the reestablishment of democracy. This group is responsible for nearly 80 percent of all fatalities from political violence in Spain since 1960. The remaining 20 percent were victims of another armed group of controversial identity, GRAPO, or the First of October Antifascist Resistance Group (81 victims), activists from the extreme right (42 victims), and armed and security forces (114 victims). In 1998, ETA declared "a definitive ceasefire," but an end to the truce was called in December 1999. Street violence is very frequent in the Basque country, usually by militants and sympathizers of Herri Batasuna. Frequent threats are issued to activists and headquarters of non-nationalist political parties, especially around election times.

Cultural and linguistic rights are constitutionally enshrined. There are four official languages, each of which are allowed in their respective territories. The Castilian language is the most common, but Euskera is co-official in the Basque country, Catalan in Catalonia, and Gallego in Galicia. In those three territories, the native language must be taught in public schools, and public servants, including the judiciary, must allow citizens to deal with them in their own language.

The Spanish constitution recognizes religious freedom, but as in Italy, it stresses the importance of the Catholic Church, giving Roman Catholicism a privileged status.

Social Rights. In Italy, the welfare state has traditionally been based on a nonuniversalistic employment model, which was partially reformed in the 1960s and 1970s, when social expenditures reached 22.6 percent of GDP (versus 10 percent in the 1950s). While developing a universalistic approach to the public health system and reducing particularism in the provision of social security, the welfare state retained its characteristics of overprotection of some groups (those employed in the public sector and in large industrial firms) and underprotection of the weak sector of the labor market (women, young people, and irregular workers). Employment policies have traditionally focused on the "passive" protection of those already employed, with a lack of "active" intervention to expand employment. A huge and growing part of public expenditure went toward the pension system, which was also characterized by overprotection of those in the "strong" labor market, with retirement pensions that were proportional to wages instead of contributions and a very young retirement age. Low disability pensions were often distributed in a clientelist way. Families and charity associations were forced to compensate for the weaknesses of this "breadwinner" model that was based on the protection of adult males with regular jobs.

Some reforms in the 1990s aimed to reduce public expenditures on the welfare state and help rectify the disequilibrium of the Italian model. In many areas, there has been a move from transfers of income to provision of services and incentives. In particular, policies on unemployment moved decisively toward active promotion of new jobs, stimulating professional training, creating part-time jobs, and generally encouraging greater flexibility in the labor market. As for the pension system, since 1992 several reforms have addressed, though not solved, the problems created by the "breadwinner" model. Moreover, areas such as health care, employment, and assistance have seen a trend toward decentralization, however the central government maintains the capacity for strong control.

In addition to recognizing the right to work, Article 4 of the constitution states that the Republic "promotes conditions that make this right effective." Access to work and social security, however, is more difficult for certain groups of people, especially immigrants from non-European countries. The overall unemployment rate in Italy is among the highest in Europe, but that of adult males was the lowest in Europe in the mid-1990s. Thus women and young people are most excluded from the labor market. Although the "underground" economy, traditionally robust in Italy, is now in decline, there has been an increase in "atypical" occupations, in which workers have low levels of protection. Moreover, irregular jobs are frequent among immigrants.

According to World Bank statistics,[35] health services and sanitation are fully accessible in Italy, though the Catholic association Caritas (Charity) has identified areas of health care where immigrants are particularly vulnerable. Environmental protection has not been on the political agenda for long. Only in the late 1990s was a national agency set up to monitor and enforce compliance with regulations on pollution and environmental protection, in coordination with the Ministry of the Environment.

The role of trade unions is recognized in basic Law 300/70 (the so-called Worker's Statute), which guarantees a wide range of rights to workplace trade unions. In the workplace, company union representation may be organized within the framework of the collective labor contract. Article 40 of the constitution recognizes workers' right to strike. The Constitutional Court has affirmed the legitimacy of "political" strikes, or those that are aimed at solving general grievances rather than aimed directly against the employer or containing demands of a redistributive or contractual nature. No data are available on current discrimination against trade unions, although this was an issue until the 1970s.

Consumer protection has traditionally been low in Italy, although it is gradually increasing, especially as the result of the adoption of market checks and quality standards of goods (often resulting from European Union directives).

The welfare state in Spain has evolved to cover the basic needs of more of the population. Social expenditures account for the largest share of the national budget, at 48.3 percent in 2003 versus 55 percent in 1998. In those two years, pensions (especially retirement pensions) consumed 32 percent and 27 percent, respectively, employment support policies approximately 3 percent and 2 percent, respectively, and unemployment subsidies, 5 percent in both cases. Thus social expenses as a whole have diminished, but the pension share has increased. The share of unemployment subsidies remained unchanged in spite of a drastic reduction in unemployment.

In the realm of industrial relations, social pacts among government, unions, and business organizations have been a tradition of Spanish democracy ever since the trade unions entered the so-called Moncloa pacts of 1977, in which the government and all political parties pledged to work closely to draft a constitution as well to curb inflation, which was then in the double digits. Successive overarching socioeconomic agreements were signed until the late 1980s, when collective bargaining involving more specific sectors was initiated.[36] In addition, an agreement on retirement pensions was signed by all political parties and unions in 1995 and subsequently became law; it was reviewed in 2000 and is currently under new review. The so-called Toledo pact regulates the criteria and amounts of pensions, and removes the issue from political debate during the election campaign. Retirement pensions are determined by contributions during the last 15 years of the employee's working life and amounts are subject to a minimum of approximately 400 euro and a maximum of approximately 2,000 euro. The pension system is considered healthy, and, unlike the case in other EU countries, no problems are envisaged before 2015.[37]

Taxation as an indicator of social equality and development of the welfare state has evolved positively during the consolidation of the democratic regime, although Spain occupies an intermediate position among the Organisation for Economic Co-operation and Development (OECD) countries in this respect. In 2001, tax revenues amounted to 35.2 percent of GDP, a percentage identical to that of Canada and higher than that of the United States (29.8 percent) but lower than in Italy (41.8 percent) and of course, northern European countries like Finland (46.3 percent) and Sweden (50.8 percent).[38] The right to work is enshrined in the constitution. In recent years, employment policies have moved toward more flexibility in hiring and firing employees, while employment opportunities have continued to grow. Unemployment has declined dramatically in the past few years, although Spain still has one of the highest unemployment rates in the EU: 11 percent in 2002, compared with 19 percent in 1997. As in many other countries, unemployment rates are consistently higher among women than among men: 28 percent versus 16 percent in 1997, and 17 percent versus 8 percent in 2002. Unemployment rates among young people are also consistently higher than among older age groups. Data from 1997 show rates of 51 percent among people aged 16 to 19, 36 percent for people aged 20 to 24, and 18 percent for those aged 25 to 54.[39]

The right to participate in the creation and management of working conditions, both in general and in the workplace through trade unions, is provided for by the constitution and by law, the Estatuto de los Trabajadores. Unions participate quite effectively in social pacts and collective bargaining at all levels. The right to strike, including general political strikes, is guaranteed by law.

The right to a decent home is also stated in the constitution. However, making this right effective has become more difficult in recent years, with the price of housing escalating by 82 percent between 1994 and 2002 while salaries grew only 30 percent in the same period. The average annual price increase between 1980 and 2000 was 10 percent, the highest among the OECD countries, with Italy rating fourth.[40] Regarding the rights and freedoms of immigrants, some positive developments can be reported. Legislation in this area has been enacted through an "organic law" or super law, that is, a law for which a special majority is required, normally a two-thirds vote, in 2000. Yet discriminatory practices have been reported in the last few years, mostly concerning access to education and housing. The 2002 ombudsman report identified a pattern of landlord resistance to renting apartments to foreigners. This was considered "very serious" and giving rise to "racist and xenophobic" attitudes. The ombudsman report was also critical of the poor living conditions at internment centers housing illegal migrants in the Spanish cities of Ceuta and Melilla in spite of repeated promises of improvement by the government. The ombudsman also reported that children of foreigners have much less access to publicly subsidized private schools than to public schools. The proportion of migrant children in public schools is double that in subsidized private schools, with the phenomenon especially pronounced in working-class neighborhoods. The ombudsman declared that the increasing number of this category of student (2.2 percent of all students in 2001) deserves more attention from the government.[41]

Responsiveness

Because good repeated surveys are lacking, only the responsiveness of the government will be analyzed here. In Italy, relationships between government representatives and representative organizations have given life to a pluralistic system of functional representation. Industrial relations have had a low institutional profile, thus trade unions sought an additional resource through a privileged relationship with parties, aligning with them on various fronts. Moreover, organizations representing entrepreneurs suffered from a high degree of fragmentation due to party and political alliances, weakening their capacity for collective action. State intervention in the relationships among social actors was initially weak. If the 1950s saw state intervention mainly in public-sector activity, in the following decade the center-left governments paved the way for company contract negotiations and institutionalized confrontation with workers' representatives. It was not until the late 1970s that *concertation* began to emerge in industrial policy. In the 1990s, both collective bargaining and social *concertation* became increasingly institutionalized, indicating a move toward a corporatist model, albeit a decentralized one. In Italian legislation, parliamentarians, like other elected officials, are not limited by the mandate of their electors. Yet access to elected representatives is granted in an informal, individualistic, and selective way, along patronage lines (especially in the South). Only very recently, at the local level, have some municipalities begun to develop Web sites offering citizens information and channels of communication with administrators.

Opinion polls reveal a long-standing dissatisfaction of Italian citizens with their administrators. Political parties have traditionally played a strong gatekeeping role, mediating between citizens' demands and the public administration. Traditionally, for lack of direct access to the public administration, recourse to judges has usually been the only (and expensive) mean of "complaint and redress." Indeed, the number of appeals to the judiciary is high and rising. Recent Italian legislation has been marked by an awareness of the need to improve the quality of public services. The trend over the past few years has been to entrust matters concerning the guarantee of the quality of services to independent administrative authorities set up for the purpose, as described previously. In the late 1990s, several laws were enacted that have enhanced citizen access to the administrative documentation that concerns them, increased avenues for opposing unpopular executive decisions, simplified the relationships between private and public administration, set in motion a process designed to simplify and reduce the number of laws, facilitated interest-group participation in public decision-making, and increased the visibility of public decisions.

Support for democracy in Spain has continually increased since the transition period. The percentage of the public agreeing with the statement that democracy is preferable to any other form of government increased from over 50 percent in 1980 to 84 percent in 1998 and 86 percent in 2000. Satisfaction with the actual functioning of democratic government has also been on the rise in recent years, with 50 percent of the population very or fairly satisfied in 1996, 61 percent in 1997, and 64 percent in both 1998 and 2000.[42]

Regarding assessment of incumbents, the ebbs and flows of the public mood since the 1980s have closely matched the evolution of opinion on two other issues: the nation's economic situation and whether a new government is in place. Any government is more positively assessed during its first term in office, especially when the economy is improving.[43] Assessment of the executive branch is consistently less positive than that of parliament, the ombudsman, or the king, but more positive than that of the judiciary, political parties, and politicians.[44]

Another indicator of government responsiveness is the number and types of claims brought before the ombudsman relating to the functioning of the various public administrations. As with the public mood, this has shifted dramatically over time, with 21,000 complaints in 2002, 12,848 in 2001, 26,625 in 2000, and 12,877 in 1995. Recently, about one-third of these complaints have come from citizens living in Madrid, apparently signaling a growing malaise in the capital related to increasing numbers of immigrants, declining security, and inefficient administration of justice. The largest numbers of claims concern immigrant issues (17 percent), tax administration (16 percent), civil servants at the national, regional, and local levels of government (13 percent), justice administration (12 percent), social security and labor (7 percent), and housing and real estate (5 percent).[45]

The International Dimension

No conclusion on the democratic quality of a country can be reached without considering that every democracy is a part of a geopolitical area and of a network of international relations. Italy and Spain are members of several international organizations, such as NATO, the Council of Europe, the Western European Union, the UN, the OECD, the Group of Seven (G7), the World Trade Organization, and, above all, the EU. Consequently, they are subject to certain constraints, as are most of the other European countries. Membership in the EU helps highlight the problems of the so-called democratic deficit within the Union. Italy is also fairly active in the Office for Democratic Institutions and Human Rights of the OECD, in charge of monitoring elections and developing national electoral and human rights institutions.

As an international dimension of governmental responsiveness, external relations should be evaluated for accordance with democratic norms and freedom from external subordination. This is especially important given the increasing presence of Italy and Spain in the international sphere, both economically and politically. For example, in recent decades Spanish investment in Latin America has become second only to that of the United States. The Maghreb and the Middle East have always been granted high priority in Spain's foreign policy, which made Spain's decision to become a third partner in the international coalition occupying Iraq in April 2003 a very risky affair. Direct support of the U.S.-U.K. initiative faced mounting opposition both in parliament and from the public in both Italy and Spain. Italian and Spanish military forces participated in peacekeeping operations starting in the early 1990s in Nicaragua, El Salvador, and Guatemala, and subsequently in Bosnia, Kosovo, Albania, Macedonia, the African Horn, Afghanistan, and Iraq.[46]

On the dark side of Italian and Spanish international relations is weapons exportation, an activity that is intrinsically contradictory to the democratic values of peace and human rights and even more problematic when the recipient countries are nondemocratic. Despite Italy's stated commitment to the promotion of democracy abroad, arms exports have increased to countries that either are involved in war or have poor human rights records, such as Eritrea, Ethiopia, India, Pakistan, Algeria,

Turkey, and Colombia.[47] The net export of weapons is also rapidly increasing in Spain, with exports growing from 8.7 thousand tons in 1994 to 14.9 in 2000.[48]

Concluding Remarks

In the 1980s, the situation in Spain was one of democratic consolidation and later of persistence, whereas in Italy the 1980s brought latent crisis and change, followed in the early 1990s by a deep crisis of the party system and other institutions after 40 years of hegemony of the Christian Democratic party. However, the significant institutional changes in Spain went in a similar direction to those occurring in Italy: movement toward regional and local self-government, reform of the public administration and especially the judiciary, and a deeper involvement in international affairs, both in the EU and in peacekeeping operations.

The analysis of Italy and Spain also demonstrates the persistence of territorial and other limits to the rule of law. They can be explained, and a few scholars who rightly point to the problems of cultural and institutional continuity have carried out this task. Yet this problem is significant in the overall assessment of the quality of Italian democracy, as the rule of law is a kind of precondition for some of the other criteria of democratic quality.

After the changes of the early 1990s related to electoral laws at the national and local levels and political parties, Italian democracy seems better in terms of vertical accountability because of the new party bipolarization, which facilitates clear choice and the alternation of power. On the other hand, the weakening of parties and the great influence on the mass media of an entrepreneur who became the prime minister are negative aspects, at least in terms of rule of law and vertical accountability. Moreover, the changes in the decision-making process with the weakening of parliament can be seen as decreasing horizontal accountability in that parliament loses its ability to effectively check the policies proposed by the cabinet as it becomes more of a "rubber stamp" body.

This last consideration brings to light a key aspect of the last decade that has been partially overlooked by empirical research. In the early 1990s, with the changes mentioned above, Italy began a long-term transition toward a more majoritarian democratic model. After more than a decade, this transition has not yet been completed. Some of the key elements of the majoritarian model are present, but the country falls short on other counterbalancing aspects. However, while institutional changes such as decentralization that could have such a counterbalancing effect have been formally decided on and even approved by a referendum in October 2001, they have been only partially implemented. This makes implementation of the rule of law, as well as the development of accountability and responsiveness, more difficult.

Democracy in Spain has been evolving since the early 1980s, when the new regime successfully resisted several coup attempts and alternation in government between right and left proved possible. The exercise of democratic rights and continuing decentralization of state structures have been progressing ever since. Other positive developments include the strengthening of the welfare state, legal reform aimed at a more open and efficient justice administration (establishment of the jury, reform of the penal code, simplification of procedures for civil suits, and acceleration of procedures for criminal trials), and a more professional military (changes of career structures, abolition of conscription in 2001, and a growing presence of Spanish military personnel in international peacekeeping operations).

The most serious democratic shortcoming in Spain remains the effectiveness of the rule of law in relation to the Basque conflict. Two basic and related issues of state-building are involved here. One is the conflict over national identity in a community in which half of the citizens are not ethnically Basque and among the other half a majority does not reject a dual Basque/Spanish identity. The persistence of a radical nationalist armed organization, with minority electoral support, further complicates a negotiated end to the conflict. A related issue is territorial integration of historically Basque lands into a Spanish state. There are different views on how to delineate the boundaries of Basque territories within today's Spain. Then, too, there are the French Basque provinces, which are being claimed as part of an eventually independent Basque state.

A second major concern about democratic quality in Spain is the effectiveness of the rule of law in controlling mafia groups that have been corrupting local authorities and political parties while funneling massive funds into real-estate and housing operations. Problems with the efficient administration of justice, mainly the length of trials and preventive detention, also limit the equal exercise of certain rights. Finally, certain discriminatory practices against women have been identified, especially domestic violence at the hands of husbands or sexual partners.

Why have the Italian and Spanish democracies evolved in the way that has been described? The democratic crisis of the early 1900s and its outcome in Italy are closely related to the model of its consolidation and subsequent changes. At the end of the 1940s, a strong bond was forged between the governmental parties, especially the Christian Democrats and later the Socialists, and interest associations, especially industrial entrepreneurs. Much later, in the early 1990s, a "window of opportunity" was opened for the expression of dissatisfaction and protest when certain constraints disappeared and other facilitating conditions emerged. The first constraining factor to fade away was the collective memory of fascism and the war. For a long time, memories of fascism prevented people from protesting against democratic institutions. Among moderate people, the perceived inefficacy of institutions in meeting basic demands was "kept on ice" by memories of worse moments in recent Italian history. During the 1970s and especially in the following decade, memories of the past faded away as the new generation succeeded the old.[49] Fascism was no longer an impending danger from any point of view. The anticommunist role of moderate parties was also slowly disappearing, most notably among the Christian Democrats. The defeat of terrorism in the early 1980s was a first step in this direction, but the integration of the communist left was more important. When a new international configuration emerged with the breakdown of East European socialist regimes, the communists, in a highly symbolic gesture, felt obliged to form a new party, the Democratic Party of the Left. The old fears among moderates disappeared as well, and moderate voters became free to express their dissatisfaction with the same parties for which they had felt compelled to vote in the past. They did this by shifting their support to new parties and movements.

Along with the secularization of society and the decrease in the ideological nature of politics—two widespread phenomena throughout Western Europe—the consequent disintegration of Catholic subcultures and the diminishing polarization of conflicts account for the weakening of the links of partisanship. As the organizational structures gradually disappeared, the foundation for the expression of dissatisfaction was laid. Yet this was not enough to transform a latent crisis into an open one. In a situation of deadlock, the emergence of various incentives was also decisive in bringing about the explosion of the crisis and the beginning of change. The incentives that emerged at the beginning of 1990 can be reduced to three: the delegitimizing effect of the Mani Pulite anticorruption inquiry, the economic crisis, and the referendum of April 1993 and the subsequent adoption of more majoritarian electoral laws for parliament. From 1992 on, the unveiling of widespread corruption in every sector of public life provoked a strong delegitimization of Christian Democrat and Italian Socialist Party leaders. Mani Pulite's impact is demonstrated in that by the end of 1996, about two thousand people had been prosecuted and about one-third of them had already been sentenced. Other inquiries were undertaken in a few other towns, including Rome, Perugia, La Spezia, Naples, Brescia, and Salerno. Briefly, the action of the judiciary gave the dissatisfied groups of citizens the additional stimulus needed to sever their ties with traditional parties.

The second incentive was the economic crisis. For decades, the traditional decisional inefficacy of Italian institutions was counterbalanced by efficiency at the local level. In the new context, the prolonged economic crisis and the impossibility of continuing with the same patronage system emphasized the intolerable costs of the protracted partisan occupation of the state. At this point, corruption, excessive partisanship, the inefficiency of the civil service, and even collusion between institutional powers and organized crime became the main targets of the conflicts between old and new political leaders and protest organizations. In fact, the regional Leagues, the Greens, the neocommunists, and a plethora of single-issue lists have all emerged since the 1990 local elections.

In Spain, the main factors contributing to the generally high quality of democracy relate to key aspects of society that began to emerge in the early 1960s. Beginning in the 1970s, that society was demographically young and economically prosperous, but culturally and politically repressed after years of reactionary authoritarianism, along with the strong repressive influence of the main agents of socialization such as the Catholic Church, schools, and the family. Pragmatism and moderation dominated reform strategies of both the younger elements of the late Franco regime and the opposition democratic elites. After the death of Franco and the installation of democracy, a realistic political strategy was assisted and moderated by persistent memories of civil war in the collective mind, and by the declining relevance and disappearance of the wartime political class.

The two main stains in the picture can also be explained. Regarding the persistent conflict in the Basque country, it must be recognized that a definite solution including full territorial integration into the Spanish state was never envisaged by Basque nationalists from either left or right. Therefore, the issue could never have been openly discussed by the Basque and Spanish elites. Current developments are actually rooted in the era of transition and constitution building 25 years ago. This is demonstrated by recollection of a few past events. First, Basque conservative nationalists refused to join the constitution-drafting committee in 1978. Furthermore, they called for abstention at the constitutional referendum in December 1978, although they were ready to negotiate a devolution statute in Madrid in 1979. Why could the core issue (independence) not be brought into public discourse—much less discussed at a negotiation table—until the late 1990s? Among other constraining factors were the following: fear of the military, whose actual powers were unknown until much later in the process; concerns about a split within the Basque conservative nationalists that always ruled in regional and most local governments; and the belief by conservative nationalists that the armed ETA could not be defeated and that the cause of independence would steadily advance through force.

It may be more difficult to explain other limitations to the effectiveness of the rule of law, such as the strength of mafia groups, corruption practices related to party finance, and impunity of individuals and local authorities who do not comply with building and environmental regulations. A few factors can be considered. First, the relative smoothness of democratic transition at a time of economic prosperity may have encouraged a sense of impunity among public authorities as well as the public at large. Second, these practices were probably more likely at a time when government budgets were growing faster than ever. There was so much public money to be spent in the short term that such spending was hard for elected or administrative auditing bodies to bring under control. Third, there is the insatiable need of political parties for financial resources.

Comparing the two countries more closely, during the last quarter of the twentieth century, the main problem in Spain—the challenge to the integrity of the Spanish state posed by the Basque conflict—was second in importance in Italy. The territorial demands of the North were supported by a declining Northern League and had been partially satisfied by the decentralization reforms. The two main problems in Italy with respect to the effectiveness of the rule of law—the uncontrolled mafia groups and Silvio Berlusconi's conflicts of interest in the communications arena—were much less relevant in Spain, where there is no leader like Berlusconi and the mafias are less developed.

The following similarities, though less important, can also be drawn:

• Reform directed toward improved administration of justice is occurring in both countries, as both publics recognize. In 1997, only 16 percent of Spaniards and 14 percent of Italians had a positive view of the judiciary. By 2004, however, public confidence in the judicial and legal system increased dramatically to 47 percent in Spain and 46 percent in Italy.[50] In addition, a special anticorruption prosecutor now exists in both countries.

• In both countries, there is discrimination against women and immigrants, but women's participation in public life is much higher in Spain. On the other hand, women in Spain suffer more domestic violence than those in Italy.

• The Catholic Church plays a central role in many aspects of public and family life in both countries. At the same time, there are areas of family morality in which current practice openly contradicts Catholic orthodoxy, such as birth control and abortion, with Italy and Spain having some of the lowest birthrates in the world.

A number of differences can also be highlighted:

• Unlike in Italy, no large concentration of media ownership exists in Spain, although the main newspaper, *El País,* and the radio station with the largest audience, Cadena SER, both belong to the same group. Moreover, no significant party press exists in Spain, whereas in Italy several party and even small-group newspapers play significant roles in debate among the political elite and, more generally, in the dynamics of the political parties.

• Political parties and the party system in Spain are in better shape than in Italy, precisely because the former are growing while the latter are declining.

• Finally, the social-security system, and especially the pension system, appears to be in better shape in Spain than in Italy, from both organizational and financial perspectives.

While the quality of democracy may be somewhat higher in Spain today, both countries face challenges that are increasingly common among highly industrialized democracies in Europe and beyond: The continuing struggles against corruption and inappropriate forms of political influence, the extension of basic human rights to growing immigrant populations, and the full incorporation of women into political life.

NOTES

1. Stuart Weir and David Beetham, *Political Power and Democratic Control in Britain* (New York: Routledge, 1999).

2. The empirical analysis of Italy draws largely on a report prepared by Leonardo Morlino and Donatella Della Porta that was sponsored by International IDEA as part of a larger international research project directed by David Beetham and Rafael López-Pintor.

3. For Spain, two main groups of sources have been used: social reports, official statistics, survey data, and some monographic studies; and democracy assessments conducted by students of economics and business administration at the Universidad Autónoma of Madrid (classes of 2002 and 2003) by following the methodology of IDEA in its simple version (International IDEA, 2002). This latter information should be considered public opinion.

4. On this topic see Carlo Guarnieri and Patrizia Pederzoli, *La democrazia giudiziaria* (Bologna: Il Mulino, 1997).

5. See for example, "Concluding Observations: Italy," report of the UN Human Rights Committee, 63rd session, 18 July 1998.

6. Antonio Vercher Noguera, "Delincuencia urbanística," *El País,* 20 June 2003, 21.

7. *El País,* 21 June 2002, 21.

8. Elisabet Almeda, *Mujeres encarceladas* (Barcelona: Ariel, 2002).

9. See the Spanish Ombudsman Report for 2003.

10. See data from Eurobarometer, cited in José Juan Toharia, *Opinión pública y justicia: La imagen de la justicia en la sociedad española* (Madrid: Consejo General del Poder Judicial, 2001), 87.

11. José Juan Toharia, *Opinión pública y justicia,* 91.

12. José Juan Toharia, *Opinión pública y justicia,* 142.

13. See Eurobarometer Survey, no. 61, 2004, available at *www.europa.eu.int/comm/public_opinion.*

14. José Juan Toharia, *Opinión pública y justicia,* 91.

15. Centro de Estudios del Cambio Social (CECS), *Informe España 2003: Una interpretación de su realidad social* (Madrid: Fundación Encuentro, 2003), 84–154.

16. Fernando Jiménez, "La financiación de los partidos es el gran agujero de la democracia," *El País,* 22 June 2003, 6–8.

17. Leonardo Morlino, *Democracy Between Consolidation and Crisis: Parties, Groups and Citizens in Southern Europe* (Oxford: Oxford University Press, 1998).

18. Rafael López-Pintor and Maria Gratschew, eds., *Voter Turnout Since 1945: A Global Report* (Stockholm: International IDEA, 2002), 75–91.

19. See José Ignacio Ruiz Olabuénaga, *El sector no lucrativo en España* (Madrid: Fundación BBVA, 2000); and Isabel De la Torre and Rafael López-Pintor, "Imagen pública del Tercer Sector en España," in José Luis García Delgado, ed., *El Tercer Sector en España: Un enfoque económico y sociológico* (Madrid: Escuela Libre Editorial, 2005).

20. Isabel De la Torre and Rafael López-Pintor, "Imagen pública del Tercer Sector en España."

21. Instituto de la Mujer, *La situación profesional de las mujeres en las administraciones públicas* (Madrid: Instituto de la Mujer, 2004), 31.

22. See FOESSA, *V informe sociológico sobre la situación social en España* (Madrid: Fundación FOESSA, 1994), 648–50; Francisco Andrés Orizo, *Sistemas de valores en la España de los 90* (Madrid: Centro de Investigaciones Sociológicas, 1996), 240–73; and José Juan Toharia, *Opinión pública y justicia*, 91.

23. Giovanni Sartori, *Parties and Party Systems* (Cambridge: Cambridge University Press, 1976).

24. *El País*, 25 June 2003, 21.

25. See for example, *www.comunica.org/chasqui/82/fernandez82.htm*.

26. The empirical analysis of Italy draws largely on a report prepared by Leonardo Morlino and Donatella Della Porta that was sponsored by IDEA as part of a larger international research project directed by David Beetham and Rafael López Pintor.

27. Miguel Beltrán Villalba, "La reorganización de la estructura del estado (1982–1993)," in FOESSA, *V informe sociológico sobre la situación social en España*, 557–76.

28. CECS, *Informe España 2003*, 317.

29. Miguel Beltrán Villalba, "La reorganización de la estructura del estado (1982–1993)," 569.

30. Joan Subirats and José Gallego, eds., *Veinte años de autonomías en España: Leyes, políticas públicas, instituciones y opinión pública* (Madrid: Centro de Investigaciones Sociológicas, 2002).

31. *El País*, 7 June 2003, 24; see also Joan Subirats and José Gallego, *Veinte años de autonomías en España*.

32. CECS, *Informe España 2003*, 4–7.

33. Ines Alberdi and Natalia Matas, *La violencia doméstica* (Barcelona: Fundación la Caixa, 2002).

34. On this topic see Paolo Caretti, *I diritti fondamentali: libertà e diritti sociali* (Turin: Giappichelli, 2002).

35. See World Bank statistics for 1997–2000, *World Development Report 1999/2000* (Washington, D.C.: World Bank, 2000).

36. Rafael López-Pintor, *Sociología industrial,* 3rd ed. (Madrid: Alianza, 1995), 500–10.

37. See Luis Matías López, "Peligran nuestras pensiones?" *El País,* 22 June 2003, 1–3; and CECS, *Informe España 2003.*

38. *El País,* 16 June 2003, 76.

39. Data from the Instituto Nacional de Estadística in Madrid, see *www.ine.es.*

40. CECS, *Informe España 2003,* 418.

41. See the annual reports of Spain's ombudsman, available at *www. defensordelpueblo.es.*

42. Data from the Centro de Investigaciones Sociológicas (CIS), cited by CECS, *Informe España 2003,* xxvii.

43. See Centro de Investigaciones Sociológicas (CIS), *Datos de opinión 30* (Madrid: Centro de Investigaciones Sociológicas, 2002).

44. José Juan Toharia, *Opinión pública y justicia,* 91.

45. See the annual reports of Spain's ombudsman, available at *www. defensordelpueblo.es.*

46. *Anuario El País 2003* (Madrid: Ediciones El País, 2003), 132.

47. According to the Osservatorio Italiano sul Commercio di Armi (Oscar), the Italian defense industry receives sizable orders from countries such as United Arab Emirates, Cyprus, Ghana, India, and Algeria, none of which are paragons of democratic virtue.

48. See Instituto Nacional de Estadística, *Anuario estadístico de España* (Madrid: Instituto Nacional de Estadística, 2003); and *Anuario El País 2003,* 387.

49. See Leonardo Morlino, *Democracy Between Consolidation and Crisis.*

50. See Eurobarometer Survey, no. 61, 2004, available at *www.europa.eu.int/ comm/public_opinion.*

8

BRAZIL AND CHILE

Frances Hagopian

Frances Hagopian *is the Michael P. Grace II Associate Professor of Latin American Studies in the Department of Political Science at the University of Notre Dame. She is the coeditor of* The Third Wave of Democratization in Latin America *(2005).*

For the past quarter-century, Latin America has experienced a wave of democratization unprecedented in the region's history in terms of depth, breadth, and endurance. Only in Cuba is it not possible to exercise a choice in voting for one's leaders, and with the exception of a "self-coup" in Peru in 1992 that was quickly reversed, there have been no major authoritarian regressions. Yet democracy today is not well supported. Most Latin Americans evince ambivalence toward democratic regimes, and amid stagnating growth rates, stubbornly high rates of unemployment, rising crime rates, and mounting allegations of corruption and malfeasance, elected presidents have been forced from office by mass protests in Ecuador, Argentina, Bolivia, and Haiti. Former dictators, military governors, coup-plotters, and torturers, moreover, have polled well in Bolivia, Ecuador, Venezuela, Guatemala, and Argentina.[1] Public enthusiasm for democracy is allegedly lacking because these democracies have not performed well and are not "good" democracies; that is, they suffer from various deficiencies in quality. They are also accused of being corrupt and unfair, favoring the rich through the imposition of neoliberal economic reforms, and failing to establish the rule of law, ameliorate inequality, or govern in response to the will of the people.

This typical, critical view of Latin American democracy is flawed both because it does not take account of differences across the region and because it is overly static. It does not distinguish among countries, let alone among different deficiencies, and short of sudden and dramatic political and economic change such as a regime transition, it offers no clear explanation for improvement or deterioration in the quality of democracy. Although the quality of democracy has eroded

Figure 1—The Dimensions of Democratic Quality

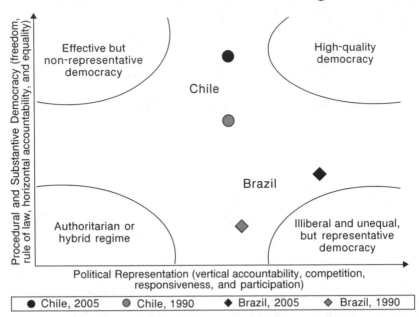

in recent years in the Andean countries—in Colombia the rule of law and the protection of political and civil rights have been severely compromised by guerrilla and paramilitary violence, and in Venezuela an enigmatic, red-bereted populist has eroded most vestiges of horizontal accountability—other Latin American countries seem to be immune from this trend. For example, democratic regimes in Costa Rica and Uruguay have been well supported by their people, even in hard times.

Most observers agree that democracies such as Costa Rica and Uruguay are highly stable because they are of high quality, but until now there has been no consensus on how the quality of democracy is to be defined, or once defined, how it can be operationalized. Recent attempts by scholars and international agencies to define and measure systematically the quality of democracy have privileged the importance of equality,[2] confused the outputs of government policy with the form and content of the regime, or placed primary value on government transparency and the establishment of the rule of law to the exclusion of democracy's normative dimensions.[3] While the protection of basic freedoms and rights, the supremacy of the rule of law, and even basic equality are crucial to the achievement of good government and a decent society, a high-quality democracy also requires a government that is accountable to other state agencies and responsive to citizens, meaningful competition for power, and satisfied citizens participating in political life (see the introduction by Diamond and Morlino to this volume).

This chapter examines these dimensions of democratic quality in Brazil and Chile. The first challenge is to compare these two countries along eight dimensions of democratic quality, thereby allowing us to describe reliably what constitutes a quality democracy and to explain what makes democracy good, what allows it to improve, and what a high-quality democracy can do that a low-quality one cannot. The alternative—to aggregate the separate dimensions of the quality of democracy into a single index that could serve as the independent variable in a study of, say, democratic stability—might enable us to answer succinctly which democracies on average provide a wider range of good governance to their citizens, but such an index would also conceal which dimensions enhance citizen support for democracy and the degree to which citizens participate in politics.

In order not only to describe and explain improvements or subversions in democratic quality across so many dimensions, but also to project and predict the impact of those values, I reduce the multiple measures of democratic quality into two dimensions: one representing the procedural and substantive dimensions of freedom, the rule of law, horizontal accountability, and equality, and the other representing the components of political representation, including vertical accountability, competition, responsiveness, and participation. The components of each dimension tend to covary—the equal protection of rights and the fair application of the law are made more difficult by socioeconomic inequality, and a government that has only limited accountability to its citizens will also be less responsive to them. These dimensions are illustrated in Figure 1.

Despite the fact that Brazil and Chile are among the most unequal countries in the world today (although in Chile the poor are better educated) and share certain institutional features such as strong presidencies, they vary along several components of the two dimensions of democratic quality. Aid agencies and human rights organizations today rank Chile especially high in the application of the rule of law, the provision of order and stability, the control of corruption, transparency of government, and the protection of civil and political rights.[4] Yet in Chile the democratic government has had to share de jure power with individuals and institutions with nondemocratic bases, support for democracy is mediocre, political participation has declined rapidly, and responsiveness and accountability have diminished. Brazil, on the other hand, is a country that has had great difficulty protecting civil rights and imposing the rule of law, and that has grappled with corruption and transparency, but in which mechanisms of political representation, responsiveness, and accountability are growing stronger. At the same time that Brazilian civil society is becoming better organized, political parties have become more programmatic and cohesive, staking out clear positions on salient issues.

This chapter makes three arguments. First, on average, the quality of democracy in both Brazil and Chile is rising. Compared against Latin America as a whole, both democracies are growing freer, stronger, and fairer over time; they are headed toward the high-quality-democracy quadrant in Figure 1, albeit from different starting points and by different routes. In Brazil, the widely heralded transfer of the presidential sash to an elected president from a radically different political party and class background in 2002 generated great enthusiasm and earned the country a Freedom House upgrade from Partly Free to Free. In Chile, former dictator Augusto Pinochet's arrest and subsequent loss of senatorial immunity has allowed the country to confront its authoritarian history and political culture. Improvements in the quality of these two democracies may prefigure a more promising democratic future for Latin America than today's reports of doom announce.

Second, I argue that Chile and Brazil differ along these dimensions of democratic quality, producing different consequences. Democracy in Chile is less violent, more effective, cleaner, and fairer than it is in Brazil, but it is also less responsive, less accountable, and less representative. This has resulted in low and even declining rates of political participation in Chile, especially when compared with Brazil. I suggest that in the long run competition, responsiveness, and accountability stimulate greater political participation and ultimately loyalty to democracy than do good government outputs. Although tradeoffs may result from the tensions between, on the one hand, effective governance and political stability and, on the other, participation, accountability, and responsiveness, I do not assume that such tradeoffs are inherently necessary. Not only are there empirical examples to the contrary, but there are theoretical reasons to believe that, in a high-quality democracy, the two can and should be complementary. Citizens cannot articulate their policy preferences if they are not guaranteed the rights and protections of citizenship, and it is difficult to see how democracy can be deepened and enriched if it is institutionally deaf to those who would push for change.

Third, I explain the trajectory of democratic quality in these countries. I attribute improvements, continuities, and subversions in democratic quality in Brazil and Chile to the strategic decisions of politicians, the capacity of civil society to mobilize, and the way in which structural economic change has shifted the incentives of politicians and the possibilities and need for civic action. I argue against those who attribute continuity to authoritarian institutional legacies and persistent inequality, improvement to the international diffusion of norms valuing human and civil rights, and subversion to a neoliberal assault on rights. I contend that whereas Chilean elites restricted the scope of competition and maintained the authoritarian era's economic reforms, institutional constraints on accountability, and citizen demobilization, Brazilian elites expanded competition, participation, and a national debate on key economic issues.

Because measures of democratic quality must be independent of highly volatile public perceptions, I draw from several datasets compiled by international agencies for comparable indicators of liberties, violence, equality, and institutional powers. Nonetheless, because no assessment of democratic quality is complete without a consideration of public satisfaction with democracy, I also draw from Latinobarómetro and national surveys for evidence of civic and political participation, trust in government, tolerance of corruption, and support for democracy. A third data source is my own set of surveys of legislative opinion, upon which I base my evidence of political competition.[5]

The first section of this chapter provides empirical measures of freedom and rights, the rule of law, horizontal accountability, and equality in Brazil and Chile. The second section conceptualizes the components of representation—vertical accountability, competition, responsiveness, and participation—and attempts to show the connection between democratic representation on the one hand and citizen satisfaction and participation on the other. The conclusion briefly reviews the explanations for the determinants of these dimensions of democratic quality and discusses their consequences.

Rights, Law, Horizontal Accountability, and Equality

Across Latin America, the project of restoring and advancing political rights has progressed to a remarkable degree, but the process of extending and enforcing constitutionally guaranteed civil rights and freedoms—of association, the press, and others—has been uneven. The class-biased application of bureaucratic procedures, racial discrimination, and other informal practices undermine the formal rules of the legal and judicial systems.[6] On average, it has been easier for organized workers to attain social rights than for the poorest and most marginalized citizens to achieve elementary civil rights.

Since democratization, Chile has consistently scored higher in political freedom and civil rights than Brazil in the annual Freedom House survey, and the divergence between the two countries for most of the 1990s was far wider in civil liberties than in political rights.[7] In the domain of the rule of law, Chile is also a high-quality democracy. Its homicide rate is comparable to that of the United States, and corruption is low by regional and global standards. In Brazil, on the other hand, state agents are often corrupt and violent, courts do not fairly apply the law, civil rights remain a privilege for the elite, ordinary people fear the police and do not seek redress from the courts, and law enforcement

often dramatically fails. Despite recent progress in disciplining state
agents, crime is rampant and the poor still lack equal access to the justice system.

Freedom and Rights

Elevating their symbolic importance, the opening paragraphs of the
1988 Brazilian constitution exalt the principles of sovereignty, citizenship, human dignity, social values, and political pluralism. Substantively, the constitution extends the traditional guarantees of individual
rights to social groups, prohibits discrimination against minorities, and
for the first time in the country's history guarantees the collective rights
of Brazil's quarter-million Indians—including the right to hold lands
necessary for production, environmental preservation, and physical and
cultural reproduction. It also grants parties, unions, and civic associations the right to take legal action against other social actors and to
challenge before the Supreme Court the constitutionality of legislation
and administrative rulings. Public employees gained the right to strike,
and all workers now enjoy an unfettered right to organize unions. Individual rights and guarantees are inviolable, along with the direct, secret, universal, and regular periodic vote and the separation of powers.
The constitution restored the freedoms of expression, press, and organization, conceded for the first time the right of *habeas data* (permitting
anyone access to information about themselves in public records), defined torture as a crime for which there could be no bail and no pardon,
and codified consumer rights and environmental protections.

While these rights exist on parchment, they are not enforced well in
practice. Even under democratic rule, the state has infringed on citizens' rights and has not guaranteed civil liberties. On the Freedom House
ratings from 1985 through 2002, whose scale runs from 1 (most free) to
7 (least free), Brazil received an average rating of 2.4 for its protection
of political rights but a less free average of 3.2 for civil liberties (see
Table 1). These ratings follow from police violence, especially against
the poor, socially marginal, and nonwhite; an imperfect penetration of
state authority throughout the national territory; and an overextended
penal system. Brazil's police routinely torture poor criminal suspects to
extract confessions, and in Brazil's major cities, police have killed thousands of civilians in confrontations that police claim are shootouts with
dangerous criminals.[8] In well-reported incidents, the police have shot
sleeping street children and *favela* residents, have been involved in
kidnapping rings, and along with penal system forces, have massacred
prison inmates. As Freedom House put it in its 2003 report, "Brazil's
police are among the world's most violent and corrupt," and "human
rights, particularly those of socially marginalized groups, are violated
with impunity on a massive scale." Understandably, ordinary people

TABLE 1—RIGHTS AND FREEDOM: CIVIL LIBERTIES AND POLITICAL RIGHTS

	BRAZIL	CHILE
Civil and Political Rights	1985–2002 average	1990–2002 average
Political rights	2.4	2.1
Civil liberties	3.2	2
Freedom of the Press		
Freedom House, 2002*	38	18.8
Reporters Without Borders, 2001–2002*	22	6.5
Journalist deaths, 1993–97	6	4
Journalist deaths, 1998–2002	0	0
Freedom of Information		
Right of access to public information	Yes	Yes, but ambiguous
Habeas data	Yes (1998)	No
Prisoners' Rights		
Imprisoned population per 100,000	137	204
Detained without trial (% prison population)	33.7	40.4
Occupancy rate as percent of official capacity	132.0	134.3

Sources: Freedom House, *Freedom in the World 2003*; Programa de las Naciones Unidas para el Desarollo, *La Democracia en América Latina* (New York: UNDP, 2004), 117–19.
*Freedom of the press ratings from Freedom House and Reporters Without Borders range from 0 to 100; lower scores indicate higher degrees of liberty. The Latin American averages were 40.4 (Freedom House, 2002), 15.2 (Reporters Without Borders, 2001–2002), and 32 journalists' deaths in 1998–2002.

fear state agents and do not understand and exercise their rights of citizenship. In a 1997 survey of metropolitan Rio de Janeiro, 57 percent of those surveyed could not mention a single right. Almost half believed it was legal to be imprisoned simply as a suspect.[9]

The Brazilian state so weakly guarantees political rights and civil liberties in part because the military police that patrol the streets (civilian police are investigators and detectives) enjoy constitutional protection from civilian authorities; since 1996, except in cases of intentional homicide against civilians, they are only subject to trial in military courts where justice is slow and impunity common.[10] In addition, politicians may sacrifice civil rights in order to broaden their electoral appeal; paradoxically, police violence against "criminals" is politically popular.[11] Recognizing Brazil's gross deficiencies in securing civil liberties, President Cardoso created a ministerial-rank secretariat charged with defending human rights, upgraded the crime of torture from a misdemeanor to a serious crime punishable by up to 16 years in prison, and proposed making all rights violations federal crimes, thereby removing their investigation from the jurisdiction of state civil and military police forces.[12] With new training in human rights and community policing, killings by police fell in the 1990s.[13] Real reform, however, depends on the state governments under whose jurisdiction the activities of the military police forces fall.

On the whole, Chile is a fairly free society today. Workers may form
unions without prior authorization as well as join existing unions (yet
only about 12 percent of Chile's 5.7 million workers belong to unions).
Throughout the 1990s, Chile received an average Freedom House score
of 2.1 for political rights and 2.0 for civil liberties (in Latin America
only Costa Rica and Uruguay received better scores). In 2002, the
Senate approved a bill eliminating film censorship. As in Brazil, prisons are antiquated and overcrowded; 40 percent are detained without
trial (Table 1).

Chile's greatest challenge in the area of restoring and guaranteeing
civil and political rights has been to settle accounts with the human
rights violations of the military regime, a task made all the more difficult by the military's insistence on an amnesty for human rights
violations as a price for exiting politics and the unwillingness of the
judicial system for many years to rule in favor of victims and their
families. During the first democratic government after the transition,
President Patricio Aylwin (1990–94) commissioned a study of human
rights violations to advance the cause of national reconciliation (the
Rettig Report), but nonetheless was unable to bring the perpetrators to
justice. Unlike in Brazil, Argentina, and Uruguay, the police in Chile
remain a branch of the armed forces, there have been no changes in
police training, and there are no new programs of civilian input. Additionally, there were no personnel purges (as there were in Argentina),
the criminal code was not reformed, and no new mechanisms of oversight over the police such as an ombudsman's office were established
to process citizen complaints. Military courts still have jurisdiction
over cases in which members of the police have been accused of abuses
against citizens, and the president does not yet fully control the head
of the police.[14]

Pinochet's 18-month household arrest in London opened space for
court actions against military human rights offenders and for members
of the judiciary to proceed with investigations and indictments concerning disappearances under Pinochet's rule. In 2003, Freedom House
upgraded Chile's civil liberties rating from 2 to 1 after the head of the
air force resigned amid accusations that he had hidden details about
human rights abuses during the dictatorship, and President Ricardo Lagos
reopened contentious constitutional issues concerning civilian primacy
over the armed forces. Lagos also created a "historical truth and new
deal commission" to consider the needs of Chile's Mapuche Indians,
who represent two-thirds of the country's 1.2 million indigenous people
(10 percent of the total population). The 1993 indigenous law recognizes the existence of cultural pluralism in Chile, but the Chilean state
has not granted constitutional recognition to the Mapuche nation nor
ratified relevant international treaties. In recent years, the Mapuches
have become increasingly vocal about their rights to ancestral lands

that the government and private industry seek to develop, and about 500,000 acres have been returned to rural Mapuche communities.[15]

Justice and the Rule of Law

Brazil has failed to eliminate lawlessness and rising violence. Since the transition to democracy in the 1980s and early 1990s, the state has failed to prevent private violence by the hired guns of landowners, especially in remote areas of the Amazonian jungle and on the agricultural frontier. Since then violence has escalated on the urban periphery of such cities as Rio de Janeiro, where drug gangs rule "in league, or in competition, with corrupt police and local politicians,"[16] as worldwide audiences learned vividly in the Brazilian film *City of God*. Since 1994, the federal government has intermittently deployed army troops to restore order to Rio's four hundred slums, including in an October 2002 attempt to protect the integrity of the electoral process that drug lords had threatened to disrupt. From 1990 through 1994, the homicide rate (a significant comparative benchmark because it is the least underreported crime) was 17 per 100,000 in Brazil, compared with 2.6 for Chile; in 1997, it was 25 per 100,000 in Brazil, nearly ten times the rate in Chile (2.8). Perhaps most dramatically, in 2002, Brazil's homicide rate for young males between the ages of 15 and 24 was 87, the highest in the world (the corresponding figure for Chile was 6.1). Also in 2002, the World Bank's Global Governance Project ranked Brazil in the fiftieth percentile worldwide in the rule of law, but Chile in the eighty-seventh percentile (by far the country with the most effective rule of law in Latin America). Ordinary Chileans also rank their state as more effective in establishing the rule of law than do Brazilians. Chileans award their state a ranking of 5.4 on a 10-point scale, whereas Brazilians assign their state only a 3.9.[17] The failure of the Brazilian state to control violence, especially when compared to Chile, stems from the ineffectiveness, poor training, and low salaries of the police (at the lower ranks, salaries start at the minimum wage of US$72 a month) and the corresponding failure of the judicial system.

In Brazil the law is also not fairly applied. The privileged notoriously manage to exempt themselves from the law, whereas the poor and the population of color suffer harsh applications of legal justice. Black defendants in cases of violent crimes tried in São Paulo courts are more likely than their white counterparts to be held in custody pending trial, to rely on public defenders, to be convicted, and to be severely punished.[18] In the mid-1980s, the prison population of color in São Paulo (52 percent) was more than double the proportion of the population of color in the state (23 percent). A similar trend was also apparent in Rio de Janeiro.[19]

Civilian and military courts in Brazil have routinely failed to impose sanctions on the offenses of the powerful, to protect citizens from abuses by the state and state agents, and to hold military police accountable for committing abuses of civil rights. In part, this is because the judicial system is overwhelmed. There are only 3.6 judges per 100,000 inhabitants, well below the Chilean ratio of 5.0 (the Latin American average is 4.9), and only 1.7 public defenders per 100,000, compared to Chile's 2.7. Yet the lack of resources cannot explain the failure of the judiciary to act in high-profile cases, or to bring to trial the perpetrators of massacres of street children or the military police and paramilitary groups implicated in the brutal intimidation of landless workers. Of the 1,730 peasants, rural workers, trade union leaders, lawyers and religious people killed in rural and labor conflicts between 1964 and 1992, only 30 cases were brought to trial, with only 18 convictions.[20] The continuing failure of the judicial system to convict those implicated in transgressions against society's powerless contributes to a sense of impunity.

Ordinary people are aware of this unequal application of the law. In an opinion survey conducted in Rio de Janeiro in the late 1990s, only about 4 percent believed that all are equal before the law. Nearly 94 percent of respondents believed that the wealthy are immune from the law, and 68 percent agree that blacks suffer more than whites.[21] More than three-quarters of Brazilians and nearly 70 percent of Chileans believe that women enjoy legal equality with men, but only about a third of respondents in both countries perceive the legal system to be fair for indigenous groups, and only a fifth believe that the system is fair to the poor. That there is so little difference between Brazil and Chile in this respect is surprising, given that the unevenness of the law in Brazil has received a great deal of negative attention, whereas Chile is referred to as a "leader in Latin America in terms of legal programs for the poor."[22]

With respect to holding state agents accountable to the law, Chile is easily the least corrupt country in Latin America. On the Transparency International (TI) 10-point "corruption perception index," with 10 being the cleanest and 1 the most corrupt, Chile's score hovered around 7.4 in 2000–2003 (in 2002 it was ranked the seventeenth least corrupt country in the world, just behind the United States),[23] and the World Bank ranked it in the ninety-first percentile worldwide in controlling corruption.[24] Brazil, which was rated the forty-fifth least corrupt country in the world by TI, has taken steps in the past decade to control corruption. In 1992 President Fernando Collor de Mello was impeached for extorting bribes from businesspersons, profiting from the privatization of state companies, and diverting public funds for his and his wife's personal entertainment. Soon thereafter, a congressional investigation of its own budget committee exposed a scandal involving committee members who had taken bribes for patronage projects, resulting in the expulsion in 1993 of seven deputies and the resignation of another five, and eventually the reform of the budget process prioritizing collective amendments (and limiting individual ones) and reducing the power of the budget committee president and subcommittee presidents.[25] Brazil's TI corruption score improved steadily from 2.7 in 1995 to hover around 4.0 since 1999. Nevertheless a congressional committee probing organized crime and drug trafficking released an explosive report in September 2000 implicating nearly two hundred officials in 17 of Brazil's 27 states.[26]

Public perceptions confirm that petty corruption is more prevalent in Brazil than in Chile. When asked whether they would describe their country as one in which there was a fair to strong likelihood that one could bribe a police officer to avoid arrest, a judge to receive a favorable sentence, or someone in a ministry to gain a favorable concession, only about a fifth of Chileans responded affirmatively to each. Yet 36 percent of Brazilians believed it likely that one could bribe a judge, 39 percent a ministry official, and 52 percent a police officer. In 2003, an extraordinary 56 percent of Brazilians but only 6 percent of Chileans reported having had a first-hand experience of corruption (the Latin American average was 21 percent).[27] Nonetheless, despite the fact that Brazil is perceived to be a more corrupt country than Chile, Brazilians cited corruption as only the sixth most important national problem in 2002.[28] Chileans are more likely to identify corruption as a serious problem that requires government attention, and they are more pessimistic about it being rooted out, most likely due to several spectacular high-level scandals in the Lagos government.[29]

Horizontal Accountability

Brazil has traveled far since the days of military rule when the executive could routinely infringe on civil liberties. Today, there are constitutional limits on the executive's prerogatives to invoke a state of siege in peacetime, impose censorship, and lift the immunity of federal deputies and senators. Nevertheless, the 1988 constitution invests the Brazilian executive with ample formal powers; in Latin America only Chile's president has more.[30] The Brazilian president now enjoys considerable legislative agenda-setting powers as well as the authority to issue decrees called "provisional measures" (medidas provisórias) that have the temporary force of law as long as the executive renews them and unless and until congress rejects them. In practice, hundreds of decree laws have been issued since 1985 and renewed, and only a small handful overturned.[31]

In the past decade, however, there have been clear improvements in horizontal accountability in Brazil, beginning with the impeachment of a corrupt president. Traditionally, Brazilian courts had the power to review legislation only on a case-by-case basis. Today, with the broader power of abstract review, courts may assume a more activist bent. The

Supreme Court, whose members are nominated by the executive but confirmed by the Senate, may review the constitutionality of legislation and try the president and members of congress for common crimes. With the power to determine the constitutionality of electoral legislation, the Superior Electoral Court constitutes another judicial check on government.

An important oversight mechanism that congress enjoys over the executive branch is the Parliamentary Investigative Committee (CPI) established by the 1988 constitution. Congress can form a CPI to investigate state agencies, its own members, or the president, although in practice it is difficult for even sincerely motivated legislators to exert effective checks on the executive.[32] Though formally part of the legislative branch of government, the Tribunal de Contas (Federal Court of Accounts) acts more like an independent agency overseeing accounts rendered by the president for the entire direct and indirect administrations of the Brazilian government, and it can even investigate congressional accounts. Its members have job tenure, and it is considered to have strong oversight powers.

Finally, the Ministério Público (Public Prosecution), which is formally independent of the executive and judicial branches of government, is responsible for defending the constitutional interests of citizens and society at large, safeguarding collective rights (such as the environmental and consumer protections) and minority rights, and monitoring public administration at both the federal and state levels. Its nearly ten thousand civil servants working in state branch offices and more than three hundred at the federal level enjoy lifetime tenure. Although prosecutors are dependent on generally inadequate police investigations and courts authorize access to private bank and tax records only 60 percent of the time (as opposed to 90 percent in the United States), between 1997 and 2002 more than two hundred mayors and former mayors charged by members of the Ministério Público were convicted for the misuse of public funds, and hundreds more faced similar charges. This institution has received high marks from the most respected newspapers in Brazil for providing a "new sense of hope that we can end public impunity."[33]

Chile emerged from authoritarian rule with what is widely regarded to be the most powerful presidency in modern Chilean history and in contemporary Latin America, and indeed one of the most powerful in the world.[34] The executive can no longer dissolve the Chamber of Deputies, force enemies into exile, and proscribe civil rights during states of siege, but the constitution confers upon the president exclusive initiative for proposing budgetary legislation and sets a high threshold (two-thirds) for overriding a presidential veto. The Chilean president can also control the legislative agenda through the use of declared executive urgencies (a prerogative that President Aylwin resorted to in 40 percent of the pieces of legislation that he sent to congress in his first two years in office).[35] The Chilean Contraloria, like the Brazilian Tribunal de Contas, has strong oversight powers, but its members, who are named by the executive, are merely ratified by the legislature, and removing any member requires the assent of both legislative chambers.[36]

The Chilean judiciary for many years did not act as an agent of horizontal accountability. Although the judiciary formally maintained its independence during the Pinochet dictatorship, it tended to uphold authoritarian laws. During the Aylwin administration, the Supreme Court unanimously upheld the constitutionality of amnesty in cases of disappearances (before investigations could take place), overturned lower-court decisions that challenged this ruling, and sanctioned the district-level and appellate court judges who attempted to break from this pattern. Aylwin, who had made judicial reform a priority, was forced to withdraw a proposal to create an office of an ombudsman *(defensor del pueblo),* but the Frei government (1995–99) did succeed in enacting fundamental structural changes to the Supreme Court, including expanding its size and instituting a new nomination system for justices.[37] The year after the reforms took effect, the Court issued rulings that modified its earlier stance on the application of the amnesty law.

Equality and Inequality

As David Beetham argues in this volume, the exercise of citizenship historically did not require economic and social equality. But does there come a point at which extreme social and economic inequality jeopardizes the exercise of citizenship and the quality of democracy? If so, which is more problematic—the spread between the wealthiest and the poorest in a society, which may threaten political equality, or an impossibly high threshold of access to the education and information needed to exercise the responsibilities of citizenship? Whereas many students of Latin America today would argue that the economic breach is most troubling, for T.H. Marshall, the level of the threshold was more significant.[38] Chile and Brazil suffer from comparable gaps in socioeconomic equality, but in Brazil the number of persons who live below the threshold of educational access is far greater.

Brazil's distribution of personal income is grossly unequal. The share of the national income captured by the richest 10 percent of the population climbed steadily from 40 percent in 1960 to 52 percent in 1989 (when the poorest 20 percent received only 2 percent) and then fell slightly to 48 percent in 1995. After peaking at .64 in 1980, Brazil's Gini coefficient also dropped to .59 in 1998, which was the third highest in the world, behind only South Africa and Malawi (see Table 2). In terms of the ratio between the average income of the wealthiest 10 percent and that of the poorest 40 percent, Brazil is the most unequal country in the world.

TABLE 2—EQUALITY AND INEQUALITY

	BRAZIL	CHILE	AVERAGE*
Income Inequality			
Gini Coefficient, 1998	.59	.56	
Share of income of top 10 percent, 1998	47.0	45.8	
Percent living below the poverty line, 2001	36.9	20.0	
Educational Opportunity and Inequality			
Primary completion rate for 20- to 25-year-olds, 1998	57	86	
Bottom decile income group	19	67	
Second decile income group	24	75	
Top decile income group	95	96	
Secondary completion rate for 20- to 25-year-olds, 1998	23	56	
Bottom decile income group	2	23	
Second decile income group	3	31	
Top decile income group	73	83	
Average years of education for 25-year-olds, 1998			
Bottom decile income group	1.98	6.24	
Second decile income group	2.49	8.88	
Adult (15+) Illiteracy, 2000	14.8	4.2	12.7
Health Care and Inequality			
Infant mortality (per one thousand births):			
1970–75	90.5	68.6	80.7
1995–2000	42.1	12.8	33.3
Percent of infants malnourished, 1996 (Brazil), 1999 (Chile)	10.5	1.9	18.9
Life Expectancy 1970–75	59.5	63.4	60.5
Life Expectancy 1995–2000	67.2	74.9	69.8
Political Inequality by Gender			
Percent seats in lower chamber won by women:			
1986–89	5.3	5.8	8.0
1994–97	7.0	10.8	9.9
2001–2002	8.6	12.5	15.5

Sources: Inter-American Development Bank, *Facing Up to Inequality in Latin America: Economic and Social Progress in Latin America, 1998–1999 Report* (Washington, D.C.: Johns Hopkins University Press for Inter-American Development Bank, 1998), 25, 27; Programa de las Naciones Unidas para el Desarrollo, *La Democracia en América Latina*, 91, 127–31, 135.
*Average in Latin America

Inequalities in income, life chances, and social rights are reproduced across regions. Northeast states contain 28 percent of Brazil's population but, in 1999, generated only 13 percent of the gross domestic product. In 2000, 47 percent of the adult population in the northeast had had fewer than three years of education, twice the rate in the south and southeast, and the northeast's infant mortality rate, which was cut in half from the very high level of 88 per thousand in 1990 to 44 in 2000, was still more than twice that of the southeast and south. Modern-day slavery exists in some parts of rural Brazil. People are "hired" to work, brought to a work site, informed that they are indebted for their transportation and food during transport, not paid wages, and threatened with death if they attempt to escape. At least 90,000 people may have been enslaved at some point during the 25-year period up to the mid-1990s.[39] Since the 1990s, rural-urban inequality has been ameliorated with land redistribution. Under pressure from the Landless Workers Movement (MST), the Cardoso government settled more than 600,000 landless peasant families on homesteads, three times as many as in the preceding 30 years.

Brazilian society is also stratified by color. Brazilians of color—according to the 2000 census, blacks represent 6 percent of the population and *pardos* (mulattoes) 39 percent—are more than twice as likely to be illiterate and to find their promotions blocked in public and private life, and they are apt to earn less than half as much as their white counterparts.[40] Racial discrimination, moreover, extends beyond the marketplace into the legal system, as discussed above. Like the black population, Brazil's Indians, too, have been seriously disadvantaged since the Portuguese first coveted Indian labor and resource-rich lands.

Dire poverty has long denied education to a large segment of the Brazilian population. In 1960, only 60 percent of the population was minimally literate. In 1998, 58 percent of all Brazilians but less than a quarter of the poorest 20 percent of the population aged 20 to 25 had completed primary school. In this age range, a mere 2 to 3 percent of the lower income groups had completed secondary school, versus 73 percent of the wealthiest 10 percent (Table 2). In the 1990s, considerable progress was made in advancing the educational achievement of Brazilians. Literacy levels rose to 85 percent in 2000, and a significant investment in education by the Cardoso government (1995–2002) increased school enrollment among primary-aged children to 97 percent in 1999. The proportion of adults who had not completed three years of schooling dropped from 41 to 31 percent between 1991 and 1999.

Because most Brazilians do not work in the formal sector of the economy, most do not enjoy such social rights as unemployment or old-age insurance. Every citizen has been entitled to medical treatment in public or contracted private facilities since 1987, but in practice access to the health-care system is uneven. Brazil's child mortality rate (the number of deaths per one thousand children under the age of five) is one of the highest in the world at 50, and its infant mortality rate (per one thousand live births), which averaged 42 from 1995 to 2000, is well above the regional average of 33. Infant mortality rates have declined markedly in the past quarter-century, but more than 10 percent of infants were still malnourished in the second half of the 1990s. Like that of other Latin American countries, Brazil's capacity to invest fresh resources in providing education, health, and other basic social rights to citizens has been constrained in the past two decades by debt service, whopping fiscal deficits in the 1980s, and state retrenchment in the

1990s. The election of Luiz Inácio Lula da Silva as president in 2002 was a dramatic statement on the part of tens of millions of Brazil's voters for a more equal society.

In Chile under the military regime, it is often charged, a select group was able to concentrate wealth while unemployment rose sharply and an estimated one-third of the population was forced to work in the informal sector with no labor rights or social protections. The privatization of health care and old-age insurance and the decentralization of public education to resource-poor local governments also made Chile a more unequal society. Since the transition to democracy, the number of Chileans living in poverty has been reduced from nearly five million in 1990 to 3.3 million in 1996 (a decline from 39 percent to 23 percent of the population), and those in extreme poverty from 13 percent to 5.8 percent.[41] Income inequality, however, has not improved. In 1998, Chile's Gini coefficient of .57 was the third highest in Latin America (only Colombia and Brazil were more unequal), principally because wealth is still concentrated in the top income group decile: If one excludes the top 10 percent, the Gini index drops to .27. Chile is also a more literate society than Brazil, with more equality of opportunity for the poor. Only 4 percent of adults were illiterate in 2000; more than half of the young-adult population had completed secondary school in 1998 (compared to less than a quarter in Brazil); and the rate of students enrolled in tertiary education in Chile was more than 2.5 times the rate in Brazil (Table 2). Similarly, Chile's rate of infant mortality in the late 1990s (13) was less than one-third that of Brazil (42), and fewer than 2 percent of infants were malnourished by the end of the decade.

Women have made more rapid gains toward social and family equality in Brazil than in Chile, and they did so earlier. The Brazilian constitution replaced the concept of *pater familiae*—which attributed greater authority to the man as the head of a married couple—with the concept of equal and shared authority. The law absolving men of the murder of their wives when done in the "legitimate defense of their honor" was abrogated in 1991, and the Brazilian congress approved a new civil code in 2001 granting men and women equal rights and obligations under the law.[42] Chile, on the other hand, remained until May 2004 one of only three countries in the world to ban divorce. Yet women have made greater gains toward political equality in Chile. The percentage of seats held by women in the Chamber of Deputies in both countries has been rising (though remaining below the Latin American average), but Chile's 13 percent is higher than Brazil's 8.6 percent (Table 2). Observers attribute these low levels to the open-list nature of both countries' proportional representation systems. The Concertación government in Chile created a cabinet-rank department for women's issues and incorporated legal equality for women and men into the Constitution. President Lagos appointed five women to his 16-member cabinet.

Finally, Brazil now also grants same-sex partners the same rights as married couples with respect to pensions, social security benefits, and taxation, but Chile does not.

Political Representation

Vertical accountability—the ability of citizens to sanction governments—is largely determined by electoral institutions and the capacity of civil society to act. Responsiveness, as G. Bingham Powell, Jr., explains it, unfolds in stages. First, parties must structure citizens' preferences into policy choices; in other words, they must be competitive. Second, governments should be formed in response to citizen preferences and should reflect the ideology and issue positions of their constituents in legislation and policy outputs. I observe responsiveness directly by matching party policies and programs with citizen preferences, and indirectly by considering both citizen satisfaction with the way democracy works (a method the introduction to this volume recommends) and rates of participation. Participation, of course, is also an independent component of democratic quality. Taken together, these four measures give us a strong sense of the quality of political representation.

In order for citizens to discern whether or not a government is representing them, governments must stand for something and citizens must know what that something is. Since in modern democracies, with few exceptions, candidates for government offices express their intentions through a party program, the party system should not disguise from citizens the true meaning of their votes. Given Brazil's history of parties with weak roots in the electorate, high levels of party switching by representatives, and politicians cultivating a personal vote, this condition is anything but guaranteed. In the 1990s, however, Brazilian parties have grown stronger and party delegations have become more stable. Rates of party switching have declined since 1990–94, when 198 deputies (out of 503) switched parties, to 169 (out of 513) between 1995 and 1998, and 92 from 1998 to 2001.[43] One measure of party cohesion in legislative voting shows improvement between 1986 and 1998,[44] and my congressional surveys show that the opinions of Brazilian legislators on a wide range of key economic and social issues cluster along party lines as much as do those of their counterparts in Chile.[45] Finally, Pederson Index rates of electoral volatility have declined from slightly over 45 for elections to the Chamber of Deputies in 1986 and 1990 to about 15 for elections in 1998 and 2002.[46] Declining electoral volatility, of course, tells us that parties are stabilizing, making it easier for voters to recognize them from one election to the next. It also tells us that voters are not rejecting parties at the polls, as we would expect if voters wanted to sanction them.

The effects of Brazil's electoral rules on vertical accountability are ambiguous. On the one hand, Brazil's system of open-list proportional representation with large districts—duly criticized for undermining strong parties by severing the lines of accountability between members of congress and party leaders[47]—allows representatives to be held accountable by their constituents. Moreover, liberal party laws ensure that almost all votes count. On average during the period 1990–2002, only 1.4 percent of votes were cast for parties that did not gain any seats in the lower chamber.[48] On the other hand, vertical accountability is limited by the malapportionment of seats in the Chamber of Deputies. The size of the delegation of each of Brazil's 26 states plus the Federal District is determined in proportion to its population—but the constitution establishes a minimum of eight and a maximum of seventy deputies for each state, resulting in the overrepresentation of the least populated states and the underrepresentation of the most densely populated ones (a deputy in the state of São Paulo may represent 35 times the number of persons as a deputy from Roraima). This distortion is an artifact of the military regime overendowing its supporters from the north and northeast regions of the country and deliberately underrepresenting opposition strongholds in the more developed southeast. On the whole, Brazil's average score from 1990 to 2002 on the index of electoral disproportionality (the difference between seats and votes obtained by the parties) was 3.8, still below the Latin American average of 5.6.[49]

Finally, Brazilian citizens have at times exercised "societal accountability," and through mass protests activated the system of checks and balances of state actors.[50] In 1992, when it appeared that the congress might fail to impeach President Fernando Collor de Mello, Brazilians in more than eight hundred unions, church groups, professional associations, and social movements took to the streets to pressure for impeachment. The media's role as an agent of accountability has also grown. Radio and television station licenses in the past were given out by the minister of communications to his political allies. More recently, the media has put an end to the terms of a number of powerful senators.[51]

As part of the Pinochet legacy, Chile's democratic regime inherited various institutions that were designed to limit the government's scope for action, insulate decision makers, and "protect" democracy from popular sovereignty. Manuel Antonio Garretón famously labeled these institutions "authoritarian enclaves."[52] The most notable of these are the "designated" senators: nine nonelected senators named by the president and the chiefs of staff of the armed forces and national police. Also significant are the National Security Council and the seven-member Constitutional Court, which must approve any change to the constitution. Both were dominated in the 1990s by military service heads and Pinochet-era appointees.

Relatively less attention has been paid to those institutional features that are democratic yet still limit vertical accountability. The congress was physically removed from the capital city of Santiago to the coastal city of Valparaíso and shrunk from 150 deputies in 1973 (when Chile's population was only about 11 million) to 120 today (for a total population of more than 15 million), while the Senate was reduced from 60 to 38 elected senators and nine appointed ones. In contrast to most of Latin America today, regional and provincial governments remain unelected. Instead, the "intendents," the chief executives of Chile's 13 administrative regions, are all appointed by the president. The 53 provinces are similarly administered by appointed governors and economic and social advisory councils. Moreover, congressional electoral districts do not correspond to these politico-administrative districts. The only subnational executive posts that are elected in Chile today are mayors of *comunas* (local government divisions of the provinces). The direct election of mayors was an important reform accomplished by the Concertación government in 1992.

The Chilean electoral system also limits vertical accountability. Prior to 1973, Chileans elected their congress in a system of proportional representation that allowed for the electoral viability of a wide range of ideological options. During the transition to democracy, the outgoing dictatorship imposed an electoral system known as the "binomial majoritarian" system. Since 1989, Chile's 120 deputies have been elected in 60 two-member districts. The ballot structure provides for open lists; voters indicate a preference for one candidate within a list of up to two candidates; all votes for candidates within each list are pooled together to determine the distribution of seats among lists; and seats are allocated to those candidates from seat-winning lists in the order of their individual vote totals. Both candidates on a list can be selected only if their list more than doubles the vote total of the second-place list— otherwise, the top candidate from each of the first two lists is elected. By design, the law overrepresents the second list, which happens to be the right, and by forcing parties to join coalitions, it has served to moderate the left. The new party system that this electoral system spawned has provided stability, but it has also constrained accountability. Nearly 9 percent of all votes cast on average from 1990 to 2002 in Chile were for parties that did not gain parliamentary representation, far above the Latin American average of 4.3 percent and the Brazilian total of 1.4 percent. Additionally, Chile received a score of 7.2 on the index of electoral disproportionality, nearly twice as high as Brazil's.[53]

Chilean civil society has been less active than its Brazilian counterpart since 1990 and, hence, has effected less societal accountability. The capacity of the Chilean media to act as an agent of accountability was restricted in the first decade of democratic rule. Formally the media operate without constraints, but Human Rights Watch in 1998 documented the cases of 25 journalists charged by the military since 1990 with defamation of a public authority under Article 6(b) of the

State Security Law, reportedly for investigating past and current military corruption.[54] As Americas Watch also reports, both the electronic and the printed media have censored themselves for fear of costly legal battles. More recently, the media have become more independent and, as one observer put it, abandoned the "almost liturgical role of representing to the masses the goodness of the institutions of law and order."[55]

Competition

The degree of competition in a democracy reveals two important insights into its quality. First, the *terms* of competition—the ease of access for new entrants as indicated by the nature of campaign finance and the degree of turnover in elections—tells us a great deal about how level the playing field is. Second, the *breadth* of competition signals the capacity of parties and politicians to respond to their constituents. Borrowing from a market model, competition should provide a powerful incentive for representative agents to tailor their programs, policies, and services to conform to the wishes of their principals—in a democracy, the voters. In this spirit, clear differences of policy and ideology, otherwise frowned upon by democratic theory for their divisive and polarizing qualities when competition becomes intense, can be beneficial for the quality of democracy.

In Chile, there are no laws governing campaign finance, and the unavailability of data in itself demonstrates the lack of transparency about the way in which electoral campaigns are financed. In Brazil, a 1993 campaign finance law made these data available, so we know that most campaign finance comes from business sources, especially banks and construction companies.[56] Leftist candidates have extremely limited access to such financing. In the presidential contests of 1994 and 1998, Fernando Henrique Cardoso raised US\$41.4 and US\$37.1 million, respectively, but Lula raised only US\$1.7 and US\$1.9 million. On average, candidates from all parties of the left raised only about 15 percent of the amount from business that candidates from non-leftist parties did in both elections, and in terms of total contributions, leftist candidates captured only about 7 percent of all corporate money.[57] Nonetheless, electoral competitiveness in Brazil has clearly been on the rise in the past two decades. Whereas in 1986, the combined parties of the left won only 52 seats in the two chambers of congress (10 percent of the total), in 2002, they garnered nearly one-third. In Chile the Concertación has governed without interruption for a decade and a half.

The range of policy alternatives is far narrower today in Chile than in Brazil, and so is the range of legislative opinion. My legislative surveys reveal that government and opposition representatives are more deeply divided over major economic and social policies in Brazil than they are in Chile.[58] Of course, these scores (reported in Table 3) represent the

TABLE 3—PARTISAN COMPETITION IN BRAZIL AND CHILE: LEGISLATORS' DISTANCE ON ECONOMIC AND POLITICAL REFORM

BRAZIL	DISTANCE BETWEEN		CHILE	DISTANCE BETWEEN
	PDSB-PFL and PT-Other Left	PSDB and PT		Concertación and Right[1]
Liberalizing measures[2]				
Liberalization of utility monopolies	.72	.80	Tax reform (1993)	.57
Temporary labor contracts	.72	.76	Elimination of designated senators	.56
Fiscal Stabilization Fund (FSE/FEF)	.70	.79	Reform of labor legislation (1991)	.55
Constitutional reform of social security (1998)	.70	.71	Association with Mercosur	.44
CVRD privatization	.68	.72	Amendments to Isapres law	.42
Financial transactions tax (CPMF)	.64	.70	Ley Docente	.37
Redefinition of enterprises of national capital	.63	.70	"Ley Aylwin"	.27
Elimination of job tenure for public servants	.63	.66	Consumer law	.25
Sanctions against states that violate Camata law	.47	.56	Native forest law	.24
Introduction of value-added tax	.36	.41	Environmental law	.22
Broad areas of reform[3]				
Liberalization of labor legislation	.63	.69	Increase in social spending	.36
Reform of social security	.62	.68	Exchange rate policy	.28
Privatization of federal state enterprises	.59	.67	Regional policy	.27
Reform of public administration	.53	.60	Policy toward foreign investment	.20
Liberalization of international trade	.49	.57	Agrarian policy	.06
			Continuation of labor policy	.02

Sources: Author's surveys

[1] Distance spread between coalitions weights scores by size of party delegations in sample.

[2] Legislators responded to the following question. "Independently of your party's position, what is or what was your personal opinion with respect to the following laws, packages, or policies proposed by the federal/national government?" Their responses, chosen from total opposition, partial opposition, neutrality, partial support, and total support, were scored -2, -1, 0, 1, and 2, respectively.

[3] Legislators responded to the question: "How would you characterize the effect of the following policies of the federal/national government on the entire country?" Their responses, chosen from very negative, negative, neutral, positive, and very positive, were scored -2, -1, 0, 1, and 2, respectively.

[4] The Sani-Sartori measure calculates the distance between the parties and then divides by the maximum spread, which is 4 (scores range from 2 for total opposition to 2 for total support). Giacomo Sani and Giovanni Sartori, "Polarization, Fragmentation and Competition in Western Democracies," in Hans Daalder and Peter Mair, eds., *Western European Party Systems* (Beverly Hills: Sage, 1983), 307–40. In order to approximate comparability in the measures of distance between the parties of the Chilean Concertación and its rightist opposition and the parties of the Brazilian left and the larger, and looser, governing coalition on the right, I calculated the difference between the combined PT and other left parties and the PSDB and the Party of the Liberal Front (PFL) (the party that held the vice-presidency, key cabinet positions, and a congressional delegation of roughly equal size to the PSDB). I also present the spread between the PSDB and the PT, as this was the choice voters essentially acted upon in the 2002 presidential election.

preferences of legislators, not actual policy, but they are nonetheless illuminating. They are also consistent with surveys of ideological distance among legislators in these two countries. In my 1998 survey, representatives of Chile's Socialist Party (the left-most party by reputation) on average located their party at 3.0 on a 10-point left-right scale (with 1 representing the extreme left and 10 the far right), and representatives of the Independent Democratic Union (the farthest right party) located themselves at 7.3, which yields a "difference score" of 0.47. In Brazil, by contrast, the self-reported spread in 1997 between the Workers' Party on the left (1.9) and the Progressive Brazilian Party on the right (7.4) was 0.61.[59] Without benchmark data we cannot know for certain whether policy and programmatic differences of the sort revealed in my legislative surveys are greater or smaller than a decade ago, but there is good reason to suspect that these differences have narrowed in Chile since the military intervened in a climate of intense polarization.

Responsiveness

Assessing responsiveness requires a two-pronged approach: We need to know whether the government is responding to citizen demands and preferences and whether citizens are satisfied with government outputs. But the connection between the preferences of citizens and the policies of parties and governments is notoriously hard to ascertain and even harder to measure. Citizen satisfaction can also mislead us when driven not by responsive policies but by results that may be shaped to a greater extent by forces beyond the control of any one administration—international financial contagion, commodity prices, acts of God, bureaucratic incompetence, and the actions of previous governments. We thus need to examine a range of public evaluations of government representatives, as well as the extent to which citizens choose to commit their time to influencing political outcomes. Most experts agree that when democracy is accountable and responsive, citizens participate more, while unresponsive governments drive citizens to reject incumbents at the polls and eventually to withdraw from politics altogether.

Matching Governments and Programs with Public Preferences. A responsive democratic regime is one that translates the preferences of citizens into the formation of governments, and a responsive government, in turn, is one that translates the preferences of citizens into public policy. In Chile, several of the institutional features that limit the accountability of democratic governments also limit responsiveness. Presidential dominance of the legislative agenda through the designation of executive-proposed legislation as "urgent," for instance, limits the legislation that individual deputies can bring to the floor of the chamber on behalf of their constituents.[60]

If government responsiveness has been limited by institutions, the limits on the responsiveness of governing parties to their voters are self-imposed by party elites. Torcal and Mainwaring contend that voters in the center-left camp believe that Chile's current income distribution is unjust and would prefer greater emphasis on redistribution, but that in order to keep the governing coalition intact and consolidate democracy, leaders of the Socialist Party and the Party for Democracy have followed a centrist line and have not politicized class and redistributive issues.[61] Also, there is a mismatch between the governing parties and the electorate in several areas of public policy. Until 2004, for example, Chile was one of only three countries in the world that did not permit divorce, despite the fact that roughly three-quarters of Chileans over time have favored a divorce law.[62]

While elites hover in the political center in Chile, among citizens opinion has become somewhat polarized. In 1991, 33 percent of survey respondents identified with the center, 7 percent with the center-right, and 14 percent with the center-left. Only 13 percent identified with the right and 9 percent with the left. (Eight percent of respondents self-identified as independents, 11 percent had no political positions, and 5 percent did not know).[63] By 2002, the percentage of Chileans that located themselves in the center had shrunk to 11 percent, to the slight benefit of the right and left extremes (16 and 10 percent, respectively), but radically adding to categories we can interpret as indifferent—35 percent said they had no political preference (three times the level in 1991).[64] Chilean public opinion, in sum, is less moderate and more ideologically dispersed than that of the political parties that represent it.

In Brazil, by contrast, salient issues such as unemployment featured prominently in the 2002 electoral campaign, and citizen preferences on key issues in economic liberalization line up with party policies and programs. On the whole, Brazilians strongly support free trade. In a 1998 survey, three-quarters approved of trade liberalization and a slight majority favored foreign investment, but respondents also more or less endorsed the role of the government in industry and clearly preferred a stronger role for the state in providing and regulating public services.[65] Reflecting public opinion, the liberalization of trade was the issue that least divided party delegations in the legislature, and the liberalization of government monopolies, including electricity and telecommunications, the most (see Table 3). In 2003, after the Workers' Party government introduced social security and tax reform legislation, more than two-thirds of mass survey respondents who had heard of the reforms approved of each piece of legislation.[66]

Citizen Satisfaction. The most commonly used comparative referent for the extent of citizen support for democracy is the level of agreement with the statement, "Democracy is preferable to any other form of government." In 1996, the first year of the Latinobarómetro surveys, support for democracy in both Chile and Brazil was far lower than in Argentina and Uruguay. Brazil's scores were generally seen as consistent with a spotty democratic history, a legacy of inequality, and checkered economic performance. Given the historic strength of Chilean democracy, however, Chile's scores were not so easily explained. The percentage of respondents that expressed themselves as "very satisfied" or "satisfied" with democracy declined from 75 percent in August 1990 to 37 percent in August 1993, and only 25 percent in October 1991 and 16 percent in October 1993 said that "democracy is fully installed."[67] Since Chileans believed that their democracy was efficacious, that government was not generally corrupt, that elections were clean, that they had access to television and a better standard of living in relation to that of their parents, and that poverty was in decline, Linz and Stepan explained the "perplexingly" low and declining levels of citizen support for democracy in Chile by the incompleteness of the Chilean transition, the place of the military in Chilean society in the mid-1990s, and the constraints under which Chilean democracy had been operating.[68] Since that time, public support for democracy in Chile has hardly recovered. A decade after the return to democracy, only slightly more than half of the population agreed that democracy was the superior form of government.

Because answers to a single survey item in a single year are not adequate to assess the responsiveness of democracy, I considered a broad range of indicators of citizen satisfaction with democracy, some averaged over more than one year. These include levels of support for democracy, satisfaction with democracy, trust in government, and trust in political parties, as well as the percentages agreeing that democracy is the best governmental system, that voting can make a difference, that politicians can recover their credibility, and that the country is moving in the right direction (Table 4). Since the first years of the Latinobarómetro surveys, citizens of Brazil have expressed as much skepticism about democracy as Latin Americans in general, but their levels of trust in government and parties are well above the average, and they agree that democracy is the best system to almost the same extent as Chileans and other Latin Americans. Moreover, in 2003 two-thirds of Brazilians were willing to concede that politicians had the opportunity to recover their credibility (the highest rate in Latin America), and 55 percent agreed or strongly agreed that the country was going in the right direction (also the highest rate in Latin America).[69] The following year, more Brazilians than Chileans agreed that "how one votes can make things different in the future" (59 percent versus 53 percent). Brazil's higher rates of satisfaction with democracy are even more impressive against the backdrop of objective measures of government performance. Chile scores much higher on the World Bank's indicators of quality of democratic governance (rule of law, control of corruption,

TABLE 4—ACCOUNTABILITY, RESPONSIVENESS, AND PARTICIPATION

	BRAZIL	CHILE	AVERAGE*
Democratic Responsiveness/Satisfaction			
Support for democracy, 2000–2004 average[1]	36	52	54
Satisfaction with democracy, 2000–2004 average[2]	23	32	30
Trust in government, 2003[3]	42	46	24
Trust in parties, 2003[3]	16	13	11
Democracy is the best governmental system, 2003–2004 avg.[4]	69	71	68
Importance of voting, 2004[5]	59	53	60
Politicians have chance to recover credibility, 2003[6]	66	39	49
Country is going in the right direction, 2003[7]	55	48	29
Index (average)	**46**	**44**	**41**
Participation			
Registered as percent of voting-age population	92.4	83.6	89.3
Voters as percent of voting-age population	75.9	74.4	62.7
Valid votes as percent of voting-age population	54.6	66.6	56.1
Democratic governance[8]	.14	7.7	
Per capita gross domestic product, 1993–2002	15	36	

Sources: Latinobarómetro, "Summary Report: Democracy and Economy (October 2003)," and "Informe-Resumen: Latinobarometro 2004, Una Decada de Mediciones (August 2004), both available at www.latinobarometro.org; Kaufmann, Kraay, and Mastruzzi, Governance Matters III, 98, 101, 104, 107, 110, 113; Scott Mainwaring and Aníbal Perez-Liñán, "Latin American Democratization since 1978: Regime Transitions, Breakdowns, and Erosions," in Frances Hagopian and Scott P. Mainwaring, eds., The Third Wave of Democratization in Latin America: Advances and Setbacks (Cambridge: Cambridge University Press, 2005).
*Average in Latin America
[1] Percent agreeing with statement, "Democracy is preferable to any other kind of government."
[2] Percent responding that they are "very satisfied" and "fairly satisfied" with the functioning of democracy.
[3] Percent expressing "a lot of confidence" and "some confidence" in government, parties.
[4] Percent agreeing with the statement, "Democracy may have problems, but it is the best system of government."
[5] Percent responding that "how one votes can make things different in the future" (and disagreeing that "independently of how one votes, things will not be better in the future").
[6] Percent responding that "politics depends on the people that are in charge and each one has the opportunity to recover that credibility" (and disagreeing with the statement "some people say politics and politicians have lost credibility and it seems they cannot recover it").
[7] Percent strongly agreeing or somewhat agreeing with the statement, "I think our country is going in the right direction."
[8] I arrived at these scores by adding the World Bank scores (on a scale from -2.5 to 2.5) for voice and accountability, political stability, government effectiveness, regulatory quality, rule of law, and control of corruption, from which the authors derive responses to multiple surveys.

political stability, the quality of state regulation, and the effectiveness of government), and in the decade of 1993–2002, Chile's per capita gross domestic product expanded by 36 percent; Brazil's grew only 15 percent.

These overall levels of satisfaction are mirrored in public evaluations of representative institutions. In a 1992 survey, whereas 22 percent of Chileans felt that the congress was doing its job "well" and 12 percent responded that it was doing it "badly," three-fifths were "not exactly sure what they were doing," and more than 85 percent felt that "there needs to be more contact between the people and the congress."[70] In Brazil, by contrast, public evaluations of congress have improved in recent years. In December 1999, at the end of the first year of the new congressional session, 15 percent of Brazilians believed that congress was doing a good job, and 40 percent that congress was doing adequately. In late 2003, also at the end of the first year of a new congress, 24 percent felt congress was doing a good job, and 46 percent an acceptable job.[71]

Participation

Some observers believe that citizens decline to vote when they are politically content and that discontent prompts citizens to vote, to join, to organize, and to protest. Other scholars contend that declining rates of participation signal disengagement and disaffection. The Brazilian and Chilean cases support the second view. Over the course of the past three decades, there has been a striking and sustained increase in citizen participation in politics in Brazil. Citizens tend to register to vote (Table 4), and when they choose to protest, they usually do so by spoiling their ballots rather than by abstaining from the process. Although the mandatory voting system's penalties are minor and rarely enforced, turnout rates are nonetheless robust in relation to other countries with mandatory voting. Brazilian citizens also participate in civic organizations. By 1993, only about one-third of Brazilians did *not* belong to a voluntary association; one-fifth belonged to three or more. While many of these associations were not formally political (most common were grassroots communities, athletic clubs, labor unions, political parties, and neighborhood associations), nearly half of Brazilians in one national survey reported dedicating sufficient time to talking about politics with other people, attending meetings or political rallies, or working for a party or candidate to earn the classification of "high political participation." Moreover, 27 percent claimed to have signed a petition or list of demands, 24 percent to have taken part in a demonstration, and 19 percent to have participated in a strike.[72]

Brazil is also home to one of the more innovative experiments in direct democracy and accountable governance that has gained a great deal of attention worldwide: participatory budgeting. What began in 1989 as an experiment in local government in the city of Porto Alegre during a Workers' Party administration has since been copied in more than 140 cities in Brazil and several others around the world. Before the legislative budget cycle begins, hundreds of thousands of citizens meet in a series of open, public assemblies to establish investment priorities, and popularly elected regional delegates and budget councilors negotiate municipal budgets with state bureaucrats, evaluate the previous year's spending, and continuously monitor investment priorities.[73] In addition to encouraging popular participation and strengthening civil society, participatory budgeting has raised public investment, rendered

FIGURE 2—CITIZEN INTEREST IN POLITICS, CHILE 1993–2003

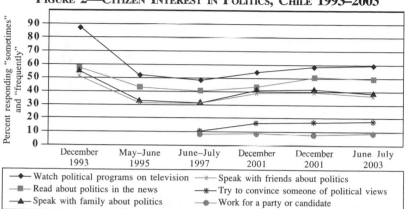

Sources: Centro de Estudios Públicos, "Estudio Social y de Opinión Pública: Noviembre–Diciembre 1993," No. 208 (December 1993); "Estudio Social y de Opinión Público Mayo–Junio 1995," No. 236 (August 1995); "Estudio Social y de Opinión Pública: Junio–Julio 1997," No. 271 (August 1997); "Estudio Social y de Opinión Pública: Diciembre 2001," (February 2002); "Estudio Social y de Opinión Pública, Diciembre 2002, Tema Especial: Mujer y Trabajo, Familia y Valores" (December 2002); and "Estudio Social y de Opinión Pública: Junio–Julio 2003," (July 2003).

municipal services nearly universal, made transparent the budgeting process, created institutions of good governance, and broken Brazil's notorious clientelistic pattern of distributing public resources.

In Chile, on the other hand, levels of participation in elections, voluntary associations, and political parties are low and declining. A 2000 survey reported that two-thirds of Chilean society participates in no social, religious, or political organizations; a 1997 poll found that only one in ten participated in some campaign act or demonstration. Overall, political party membership has declined from between 9 and 11 percent in 1961–73 to 2 percent in 1996, leading Tomás Moulián to characterize Chilean politics as "consumption-oriented" rather than participatory.[74]

Voting has been in decline in Chile since the transition to democracy. Voting is mandatory for registered voters, but registration is not automatic. Of a potential electorate of 9.5 million in 1997, around 1.5 million were not registered, more than one million abstained, and around 1.25 million voters either spoiled their ballots or left them blank. In sum, nearly 40 percent opted out in some way,[75] a dramatic increase from 12 percent in 1988.

Who has dropped out? Clearly, Chilean youth are losing interest in politics, failing to register, and deserting the electoral process in droves. Voters between the ages of 18 and 29 declined as a percentage of the electorate from 36 percent in 1989 to 20 percent in 1997.[76] In a 1997 survey, only 30 percent of youth under the age of 18 indicated that they planned to register for the 1999 presidential election. In 2002, only about

1 percent of young people belonged to a political party and 89 percent were not interested in joining one. Between 1994 and 2000, the percentage of youth who identified with neither the governing Concertación nor its parliamentary and extraparliamentary opposition rose from a third to nearly 70 percent. Two observers attribute this apathy to the failure of politicians and their parties to capture the imaginations of a generation that was too young to be a part of the struggles in the 1980s to end the dictatorship as well as to the decline in importance of university politics.[77] The generation that came of age in the 1980s, moreover, feels let down by a post-transition demobilization and the cautious governing politics of the generation that came of age in the 1960s and early 1970s.

Over the past 10 years, public opinion polls in Chile also show a general decline of citizen interest and involvement in politics (Figure 2). Between December 1993 and mid-1995, the percentage of respondents claiming to watch political programming sometimes or frequently fell from more than three-fourths to just over one-half, and the proportion claiming to read news about politics sometimes or frequently fell from 58 percent in December 1993 to 40 percent in mid-1997. Levels of interest in politics recovered somewhat in 2002.

In sum, Brazilian democracy has improved substantially in the past fifteen years in responding to citizen preferences by representing a wider range of programmatic alternatives to voters in elections. Brazil has also established new institutions and beefed up old ones to enhance horizontal accountability. Stronger parties and party identities arguably augment the capacity of citizens to sanction politicians collectively; open-list proportional representation always afforded that opportunity for them to do so on an individual basis. Chile, by contrast, has retained an electoral system designed by the outgoing dictatorship that has enhanced electoral and governing stability and general prosperity, but that has limited accountability and representativeness and has led to an impoverished public life and a disengaged citizenry. Since the transition to democracy in 1990, the strategic decision of political elites to demobilize their supporters and to narrow their differences with political opponents has also fueled a tide of citizen disinterest and disaffection.

Explaining Patterns and Levels of Democratic Quality

Why has the Chilean state been more effective at guaranteeing rights and establishing the rule of law than the Brazilian, but Brazilian democracy been more accountable and responsive to its citizens than the Chilean? Why have Brazilian democratic regimes improved the delivery of some social rights but not others and reduced corruption on the part of public officials but been slow to discipline their own police agents? Why have Chilean democratic leaders eliminated some vestiges of the protected democracy they inherited, but not others? Why, in short, do these democratic regimes experience *improvement, continuity,* or *subversion* in the various dimensions of the quality of democracy?

Improvement in democratic quality is typically explained, if at all, by the rising international cost to repressive and corrupt regimes of violating human rights. International norms protecting human rights might explain the extension of rights to indigenous groups in both countries, and international diffusion effects could conceivably explain the adoption of new institutions of horizontal accountability and even social policy reform that make educational investments more productive and effective. Yet it is hard to see how international pressure could account for growing participation, competition, and responsiveness and to explain why Chile liberalized as late as it did and why Brazil has granted greater rights to women and Indians than to Afro-Brazilians. International pressure may help to inaugurate and protect democratic regimes, but enhancing the quality of democracy is more likely a domestic affair.

Looking only at Brazil, most observers attribute the continuing failure to guarantee rights and the rule of law to a legacy of gross inequality; looking at Chile, they attribute the persistent relative weakness of democratic accountability and responsiveness to the constraints imposed by institutions designed by an authoritarian regime that was still quite powerful at the time it surrendered power. Whereas Brazil's military lost control over the presidential succession in 1984–85 and the process of constitutional revision in 1987–88, Pinochet maintained control of Chile's transition beyond the time he handed the presidential sash to his successor in March 1990. Pinochet's regime reduced the responsiveness and accountability of Chilean democracy in at least two ways: first by narrowing considerably the scope of legitimate public debate and transferring decisions about certain critical issues to nonelected government branches, and second by embedding authoritarian institutions such as designated senators in a constitution that could be changed only with great difficulty. Hite and Morlino characterize Chile as the case that "most exemplifies the impact of authoritarian legacies as potential silencers and as severe constraints on the development of a rich, deliberative, inclusive public sphere."[78]

Although a good part of the quality of democracy in Chile and Brazil can indeed be explained by the nature of the transitions to democracy and the institutions that were created during the transitions by outgoing authoritarian regimes or by the democrats who stared them down, other factors are also important. The mode of transition to democracy was obviously crucial in subverting democratic quality, but it is insufficient to explain both the increasing political detachment of Chileans from their democracy and the growing attachment of Brazilians to theirs. Brazil's transition, too, began with a powerful, successful military that retained certain veto powers over the political system, yet Brazil was able to overcome this and other authoritarian legacies.[79] Institutions can be sticky and formal institutional constraints very real, but we have seen time and again that formal powers can be underutilized, laws can go unenforced, and when politicians strategize and citizens mobilize, the walls of Jericho can indeed come tumbling down.

Finally, the possibility of democratic subversion is most often traced to a deliberate assault on rights and responsiveness in order to serve a neoliberal project. The Chilean version of neoliberalism went far beyond divesting the state of productive enterprises and deregulating commerce and prices, and instead completely disengaged the state from politics. Proceeding from the premise that Chile had become ungovernable because citizens that belonged to organizations controlled by political parties had overloaded the state with material demands, Pinochet and his advisers reordered society along traditional hierarchical and patriarchal lines, atomized it, and disengaged it from politics, thus undermining the basis for collective action. Yet Brazil's transition to economic liberalism has weakened neither accountability nor responsiveness. Scholars have left undertheorized such important topics as when legacies and institutions can be overcome and even compensate for structural inequalities and when they can do neither, and when paradigmatic economic change subverts democracy and when it does not.

I argue that when legacies survive and when they are discarded is dependent on the strategic decisions of democratic political elites, the mobilizational capacity of civil society, and the way in which both have responded to democratic opportunities and structural economic change. I begin with the strategies of politicians. Initially, fears of hypermobilization led Chilean party elites to demobilize their followers,[80] and at least part of the initial democratic coalition has been cautious about reforming institutions that confer on them "governing advantages."[81] While the Concertación did on two occasions unsuccessfully try to repeal the designated senators, and partially succeeded once, it did not push for the reform of an electoral system that "virtually guaranteed that the composition of the congress would have a minimal relation to the will of the electorate."[82] Two observers have persuasively argued that the cleavages of the new party system did not arise organically from new social cleavages, but rather were shaped from above by party elites.[83] Party leaders accepted responsibility for the democratic breakdown in 1973 and made a strategic decision to offer good government rather than big ideas. Catholic Church leaders who were inclined to turn to the right in line with the policy shift of the Roman Catholic Church were also more comfortable in a world in which there were strict controls on television programming and in which divorce and abortion were outlawed.

Brazil is different in this respect. During the transition to democracy and the deliberations of the constituent assembly, the military prioritized the preservation of certain political institutions (especially the presidential system of government), military prerogatives, and the corporatist labor system that restricted the right to strike. It did not, however, attempt to devise a political system that would repress political creativity and possibilities for change. Neither the military nor any party elites attacked the basis for civic associations or attempted deliberately to demobilize civil society. Although the frenetic level of civic activity ebbed after the transition to democracy, it could be resurrected when needed. A foundation for civic and political association was laid during and after the political transition.

Because party leaders and other political elites in Brazil have become more responsive to their constituents, contrary to predictions of gloom and doom, democracy has not been irreparably weakened by neoliberal economic reform. Rather, economic liberalization in Brazil, which has otherwise exacerbated economic inequality and undermined social solidarity, has also prompted parties to reconsider their programs and positions with respect to how to liberalize, privatize, and reregulate; to cohere internally and widen their policy differences with one another; and to become identified in the public mind with new issue cleavages. These changes have enhanced the capacity of these parties to respond to citizen preferences.

In Chile, where economic liberalization took place during the dictatorship, the two principal coalitions have narrowed their differences over economic policy. Many scholars welcomed this moderation, and particularly a more pragmatic Christian Democratic Party, as the corrective for political instability born of excessive polarization and uncompromising behavior,[84] but political stability based on pragmatism and the narrowing of public debate has had its costs. The electorate has not been enthusiastic about the pragmatic turn of a party that once inspired voters with the promise of a noncommunist route to a more just society based on Catholic social doctrine. Citizens are rewarding parties of the right that espouse clear programs and maintain representative-constituent linkages at a time when the opportunities to distribute pork, fill patronage jobs, and practice clientelism have been reduced in both countries by economic reform and by statute. In short, political elites and religious and secular civil leaders can offer bold choices or opt for cautious ones, compete outright or circumscribe their competition, and embrace democratizing social change or seek to thwart it. Citizens can mobilize or retreat to their private lives and private pursuits. The strategies and capacities of political actors, in short, can expand or restrict democracy, and the possibilities of doing so are not forfeited at any point in time.

The Rising Quality of Democracy in Brazil and Chile

By now, it should be clear that democracy is a multidimensional concept, that the nature of democracies can vary considerably, and that there can be different routes to a high-quality democracy. Fifteen years ago, given the role of the military in Brazilian politics, egregious levels of inequality, and incoherent parties on the right and tiny parties on the left, many distinguished scholars were pessimistic about democracy's prospects in Brazil. Similarly, the omnipresence of the former dictator Augusto Pinochet on the Chilean political scene augured poorly for the rapid elimination of the vestiges of one of the continent's most repressive authoritarian regimes. Yet the quality of democracy in Brazil and Chile is rising. Brazil's democracy is more participatory, competitive, responsive, and accountable today than 15 years ago, and in Chile there are fewer checks on popular sovereignty and more on executive power.

In these times when electoral democracies in Latin America appear to be highly vulnerable to the deep disaffection of ordinary citizens, this chapter also asked which dimensions of democratic quality matter for public support and in what ways. My second key conclusion is that effective government performance, the protection of civil and political rights, the rule of law, and the control of corruption may not compensate for weak democratic accountability and responsiveness. Chile's democracy has deservedly been praised for having the least corrupt government in Latin America, a fairly well-functioning justice system, balanced budgets, and reasonable growth rates, as well as for lifting more than 1.5 million people out of poverty. These are not small accomplishments. Yet reasonable progress in guaranteeing some rights and removing the military as a veto player has also been accompanied by slow advances in removing the veto of the designated senators and reforming an electoral and party system that distorts the relationship between government formation and the preferences of citizens, and by a near suspension of programmatic competition on big questions of the day. Political participation in Chile is low and declining. Brazilian democracy, by contrast, is messy; it struggles with corruption, the rule of law is highly uneven, its courts are not fair, and inequality is egregious. Yet it has grown more competitive, accountable, and responsive in the past 15 years. Political competition is intensifying among increasingly cohesive political parties for the entire range of political offices; political participation, responsiveness, instruments of accountability, and representation, once so weak, are improving; and Brazilians engage with their democracy to a greater degree than do their counterparts in most Latin American countries.

A cursory examination of the Latin American political landscape suggests that this framework for understanding democratic quality travels well to other cases. At the high end, not only is Uruguay a more equal society than most, and one in which the civil, political, *and* social rights of citizenship have long been honored and in which the rule of law prevails, but its democracy is competitive, responsive, and accountable. The left has improved its vote totals from bare double-digits in the years before the 1973 military coup to a solid third of the vote and, most recently, to winning the presidential election. It is also a highly participatory society; voting rates are the highest in Latin America. At the other extreme, in Venezuela political parties long ago suspended programmatic competition, and in Bolivia, although levels of political participation have remained high, citizens no longer feel connected to, and do not feel represented by, democratic political agents.[85]

It is always a challenge, when talking about democracy in Latin America, to avoid, on the one hand, being overly critical of democracy and denying upward trends and, on the other, giving a pass to democracies that are such in name only. Although neither Chile nor Brazil has achieved greater equality in the past 15 years, both nonetheless today have improved the quality of their democracies. Brazil has become more democratic over the course of the past quarter-century as its politicians have become more competitive and responsive, its civil society better organized and engaged, and its citizens better educated and more politically experienced. Looking ahead, the quality of Chilean democracy can be predicted to rise as well. Since General Augusto Pinochet's October 1998 arrest in London and his subsequent loss of senatorial immunity, society in Chile has begun to mobilize, the courts have become an effective arena of democratization, presidential elections have become more competitive, public debate on previously taboo subjects has broadened, and Chile has begun to confront its authoritarian past and political culture. Soon after his arrest, the Chilean right that had benefited from Pinochet's electoral system and other institutional and cultural legacies of his authoritarian regime began to shed its association with the discredited dictator. The incumbent center-left coalition, which to date has benefited from an insulated position in government, may now have to stake out stronger positions on the issues of the day and reach out to new political generations and constituents that will not restrain their demands. Both coalitions may yet be willing to reform institutions and allow for more political expression.

High-quality democracies generate satisfaction, support, and perhaps even better governance. They also produce more socially cohesive and decent societies. And if they do not guarantee political stability or insulate their political systems from crises, high-quality democracies surely help their countries to survive them.

NOTES

Earlier versions of this article were presented at the conference on "The Quality of Democracy: Improvement or Subversion," at Stanford University's Center on Democracy, Development, and the Rule of Law, 10–11 October 2003 and at the annual meeting of the American Political Science Association, Chicago, 2–5 September 2004. It was improved immeasurably by comments from Scott Mainwaring, Leonardo Morlino, and especially Larry Diamond.

1. The list includes Hugo Banzer, the dictator of Bolivia from 1971 to 1978, who was elected president in 1997; the former coup-plotters Lucio Gutiérrez, who won the 2002 presidential election in Ecuador, and Hugo Chávez, who was elected president of Venezuela in 1998; Colonel Efraín Rios Montt, the former dictator of Guatemala, who was elected president of the legislature in 1993 and 1999; and three former military governors (Antonio Bussi, José David Ruiz Palacios, and Roberto Ulloa), a leader of two military rebellions (Aldo Rico), and a former police officer accused of torture during the dictatorship (Luis Patti), who were elected to gubernatorial and mayoral positions in Argentina. Amber Seligson and Joshua A. Tucker, "Feeding the Hand that Bit You: Voting for Ex-Authoritarian Rulers in Bolivia and Russia," unpubl. ms., September 2004, 2, available at *www.wws.princeton.edu/jtucker.*

2. The conventional wisdom is well summarized by the United Nations Development Programme, which recently claimed that "in many cases, the growing frustration with the lack of opportunities and with high levels of inequality, poverty, and social exclusion is expressed in unrest, loss of confidence in the political system, radicalism, and a crisis of governability, which puts the stability of the democratic system itself at risk." Programa de las Naciones Unidas para el Desarrollo, *La Democracia en América Latina: Hacia una democracia de ciudadanas y ciudadanos* (New York: UNDP, 2004), 23.

3. The Global Governance Project of the World Bank, for instance, has disaggregated the quality of democratic governance into six dimensions, which include government effectiveness and regulatory quality (along with rule of law, control of corruption, voice and accountability, and political stability). Daniel Kaufmann, Aart Kraay, and Massimo Mastruzzi, *Governance Matters III: Governance Indicators for 1996–2002,* World Bank Policy Research Working Paper 3106 (2003), available at *www.worldbank.org/wbi/governance/govdata2002.*

4. Daniel Kaufmann, Aart Kraay, and Massimo Mastruzzi, *Governance Matters III;* Freedom House, *Freedom in the World 2003,* available at *www.freedomhouse.org.*

5. I surveyed the Chilean legislature in 1998 and the Brazilian congress in 1999–2000. Members were invited to participate through a cover letter as well as personal visits by graduate student assistants who delivered an original 16-page questionnaire to the office of every member of congress. This procedure yielded a response rate of 31 percent in Chile (51/165). In Brazil, students from the University of Brasília followed up with personal interviews. The response rate in Brazil—25 percent (151/594)—was lower than in Chile, but the sample is fairly representative of the legislature by party and region.

6. One of the earliest, and most persuasive, works to advance this argument was Guillermo O'Donnell, "Illusions About Consolidation," *Journal of Democracy* 7 (April 1996): 34–51.

7. Scores from earlier years of *Freedom in the World* are available at *www. freedomhouse.org.*

8. For the documentation of the use of torture against criminal suspects, see Anthony Pereira, "An Ugly Democracy? State Democracy and the Rule of Law in Postauthoritarian Brazil," in Peter R. Kingstone and Timothy J. Power, eds., *Democratic Brazil: Actors, Institutions, and Processes* (Pittsburgh: University of Pittsburgh Press, 2000), 217–35; Paulo Sérgio Pinheiro, "Popular Responses to State-Sponsored Violence in Brazil," in Douglas A. Chalmers, Carlos M. Vilas, Katherine Hite, Scott B. Martin, Kerianne Piester, and Monique Segarra, eds., *The New Politics of Inequality in Latin America* (New York: Oxford University Press, 1997), 261–80; and Freedom House, *Freedom in the World 2003.* For treatments of extrajudicial

killings, see Daniel Brinks, "Legal Barriers and Illusory Rights: The Rule of Law in Argentina, Brazil, and Uruguay" (Ph.D. dissertation, department of political science, University of Notre Dame, 2004); and James Holston and Teresa P.R. Caldeira, "Democracy, Law and Violence: Disjunctions of Brazilian Citizenship," in Felipe Agüero and Jeffrey Stark, eds., *Fault Lines of Democracy in Post-Transition Latin America* (Miami: North-South Center, 1998), 270–71.

9. José Murillo de Carvalho, *Cidadania no Brasil: O Longo Caminho* (Rio de Janeiro: Civilização Brasiliera, 2001), 210.

10. Anthony Pereira, "An Ugly Democracy," 232.

11. James Holston and Teresa P.R. Caldeira, "Democracy, Law, and Violence," 272, 276.

12. Anthony Pereira and Mark Ungar, "The Persistence of the *Mano Dura*: Authoritarian Legacies and Policing in Brazil and the Southern Cone," in Katherine Hite and Paola Cesarini, eds., *Authoritarian Legacies and Democracy in Latin America and Southern Europe* (Notre Dame: University of Notre Dame Press, 2004), 263–304.

13. Anthony Pereira, "An Ugly Democracy," 234.

14. Anthony Pereira and Mark Ungar, "The Persistence of the *Mano Dura*," 270, 285.

15. Guillaume Boccara, "The Struggle of the Mapuche Peoples: Deepening Democracy in Chile," *ReVista: Harvard Review of Latin America* 3 (Spring 2004): 31.

16. Freedom House, *Freedom in the World 2003*.

17. Daniel Kaufmann, Aart Kraay, and Massimo Mastruzzi, *Governance Matters III*, 110. The authors use an unobserved components model to construct aggregate indicators, and they present the point estimates of the dimensions of government (a scale of -2.5 to 2.5) as well as the margins of error (which range from .13 to .15 for the rule of law). On this scale, Brazil earned a score of .30, and Chile, 1.3.

18. Sérgio Adorno, "Discriminação Racial e Justiça Criminal en São Paulo," *Novos Estudos* 43 (November 1995), 54–55, 62–63.

19. Peter Fry, "Color and the Rule of Law in Brazil," in Juan E. Méndez, Guillermo O'Donnell, and Paulo Sérgio Pinheiro, eds., *The (Un)Rule of Law and the Underprivileged in Latin America* (Notre Dame: University of Notre Dame Press, 1999), 189.

20. Paulo Sérgio Pinheiro, "Popular Responses to State-Sponsored Violence," 272.

21. Peter Fry, "Color and the Rule of Law," 188.

22. Alejandro M. Garro, "Access to Justice for the Poor in Latin America," in Juan E. Méndez, Guillermo O'Donnell, and Paulo Sérgio Pinheiro, eds., *The (Un)Rule of Law and the Underprivileged in Latin America*, 283.

23. Transparency International, *Corruption Perceptions Index 2002*. Available at *www.transparency.org/pressreleases_archive/2003/2003.10.07.cpi.en.htm*. The corruption perception index is a poll of polls, reflecting the perceptions of both resident and nonresident businesspeople and country analysts.

24. Daniel Kaufmann, Aart Kraay, and Massimo Mastruzzi, *Governance Mat-*

ters III, 113. On the scale of -2.5 to 2.5, Chile earned a score of 1.55 for control of corruption, whereas Brazil scored a -0.05, which placed it in the fifty-seventh percentile worldwide. Brazil ranked fourth in the region in control of corruption after Chile, Costa Rica, and Uruguay.

25. David Samuels, *Ambition, Federalism, and Legislative Politics in Brazil* (Cambridge: Cambridge University Press, 2003), 141–42.

26. Freedom House, *Freedom in the World 2003.*

27. Latinobarómetro, "Informe—Resumen: Una Década de Mediciones," August 2004, 30, 51, 54, available at *www.latinobarometro.org.*

28. IBOPE, OPP 570/December 2002 (n=2,000), available at *www.ibope.com.br.*

29. Cited in Alfredo Rehren, "Politics and Corruption: The Underside of Chilean Democracy," *ReVista: Harvard Review of Latin America* 3 (Spring 2004): 15.

30. According to the UNDP index that averages measures of legislative and non-legislative powers (the capacity of the legislature to censure the cabinet and the capacity of the executive to dissolve congress). Programa de las Naciones Unidas para el Desarrollo, *La Democracia en América Latina,* 93.

31. During the administrations of José Sarney (1985–90) and Fernando Collor de Mello (1990–92), only 18 of 307, or 6 percent, were expressly rejected by the congress. Timothy J. Power, "The Pen Is Mightier than the Congress: Presidential Decree Power in Brazil," in John M. Carey and Matthew Soberg Shugart, eds., *Executive Decree Authority* (Cambridge: Cambridge University Press, 1998), 215.

32. Argelina Cheibub Figueiredo, "The Role of Congress as an Agency of Horizontal Accountability: Lessons from the Brazilian Experience," in Scott Mainwaring and Christopher Welna, eds., *Democratic Accountability in Latin America* (Oxford: Oxford University Press, 2003), 190–91.

33. Maria Tereza Sadek and Rosângela Batista Cavalcanti, "The New Brazilian Public Prosecution: An Agent of Accountability," in Scott Mainwaring and Christopher Welna, eds., *Democratic Accountability in Latin America,* 209–11, 213–15, 225.

34. Scott Mainwaring and Matthew Soberg Shugart, "Presidentialism and Democracy in Latin America: Rethinking the Terms of the Debate," in Scott Mainwaring and Matthew Soberg Shugart, eds., *Presidentialism and Democracy in Latin America* (Cambridge: Cambridge University Press, 1997), 49; Peter Siavelis, "Executive-Legislative Relations in Post-Pinochet Chile: A Preliminary Assessment," in Scott Mainwaring and Matthew Soberg Shugart, eds., *Presidentialism and Democracy in Latin America,* 322–24.

35. Peter Siavelis, "Executive-Legislative Relations in Post-Pinochet Chile," 325–28.

36. Programa de las Naciones Unidas para el Desarrollo, *La Democracia en América Latina,* 96.
37. Lisa Hiblink, "An Exception to Chilean Exceptionalism? The Historical Role of Chile's Judiciary," in Susan Eva Eckstein and Timothy P. Wickham-Crowley, eds., *What Justice? Whose Justice? Fighting for Fairness in Latin America* (Berkeley: University of California Press, 2003), 80–84.

38. T.H. Marshall, "Citizenship and Social Class," in *Citizenship and Social Class and other essays* (Cambridge: Cambridge University Press, 1950), 1–85.

39. Paulo Sérgio Pinheiro, "Popular Responses to State-Sponsored Violence," 270.

40. Sergei Suarez Dillon Soares, "O Perfil da Discriminação no Mercado de Trabalho— Homens Negros, Mulheres Brancas e Mulheres Negras," IPEA (Instituto de Pesquisa Econômica Aplicada), Texto para Discussão No. 769, Brasília (November 2000).

41. Patricio Meller, "Pobrez y distribución del ingreso en Chile (Década de la noventa)," in Paul Drake and Iván Jaksic, eds., *El Modelo Chileno: Democracia y desarrollo en los noventa* (Santiago: LOM, 1999), 47.

42. Mala Htun, *Sex and the State: Abortion, Divorce, and the Family Under Latin American Dictatorships and Democracies* (Cambridge: Cambridge University Press, 2003), 113, 157.

43. Figures are from personal communication with Scott Desposato and my own calculations.

44. The Rice Index represents the difference between the percentage of party members voting yes and the percentage of party members voting no averaged over the votes in a particular congress. The scores for Brazil were 68 in the period from 1986 to 1990 and 80 from 1995 to 1998. Party discipline scores are reported in Argelina Cheibub Figueiredo and Fernando Limongi, *Executivo e Legislativo na nova ordem constitucional* (Rio de Janeiro, Brazil: FGV, 1999), 112.

45. Party cohesion on major economic policy issues was measured by calculating standard deviation, averaged across areas. Party scores were 0.70 for the Chilean Concertación, 0.73 for the Brazilian Workers' Party, 0.87 for the Brazilian Party of Social Democracy, 1.02 for the coalition of parties of the Chilean right, and 1.17 and 1.18, respectively, for the Brazilian Party of the Brazilian Democratic Movement and the Party of the Liberal Front.

46. The Pederson Index of electoral volatility is calculated by adding the net change in percentage of votes (or seats) gained or lost by each party from one election to the next, then dividing by two. Figures for 1986 and 1990 are from Scott Mainwaring, *Rethinking Party Systems in the Third Wave of Democratization: The Case of Brazil* (Stanford: Stanford University Press, 1999), 128, 108. Figures for 1994, 1998, and 2002 are based on my own calculations.

47. This system is alleged to undermine legislative cohesion, although two Brazilian scholars have argued that the internal rules of the Brazilian congress create competing incentives for party delegations to fall into line behind party leaders in floor voting. See Argelina Cheibub Figueiredo and Fernando Limongi, *Executivo e Legislativo na nova ordem constitucional*.

48. Programa de las Naciones Unidas para el Desarrollo, *La Democracia en América Latina*, 92.

49. Programa de las Naciones Unidas para el Desarrollo, *La Democracia en América Latina*, 92. Electoral disproportionality is calculated by squaring the sum of the differences between votes and seats obtained by each party for the lower chamber, dividing by two, and then taking the square root of this result. A high score indicates that the relationship between seats and votes is disproportional.

50. Catalina Smulovitz and Enrique Peruzzotti, "Societal Accountability in Latin America," *Journal of Democracy* 11 (October 2000): 147–58.

51. Fernando Lattman-Weltman, "Medios y Transición Demmocrática: La (Des)Institucionalización del Panóptico en Brasil," in Vicente Palermo, ed., *Política Brasileña Contemporánea: De Collor a Lula en Años de Transformación* (Buenos Aires: Instituto de Tella/Siglo XXI, 2003), 546–47.

52. Manuel Antonio Garretón, "Redemocratization in Chile," *Journal of Democracy* 6 (January 1995): 146–58.

53. Programa de las Naciones Unidas para el Desarrollo, *La Democracia en América Latina*, 92.

54. Cited in Katherine Hite and Leonardo Morlino, "Problematizing the Links between Authoritarian Legacies and 'Good' Democracy," in Katherine Hite and Paola Cesarini, eds., *Authoritarian Legacies and Democracy in Latin America and Southern Europe*, 57.

55. Pedro E. Güell, "Chile Has Changed . . . but in what ways has it changed?" *ReVista: Harvard Review of Latin America* 3 (Spring 2004): 7.

56. In 1994 and 1998, respectively, corporate contributions amounted to 97 and 94 percent of the total in the presidential races, 85 and 69 percent in the gubernatorial races, 9 and 43 percent in the senate races, and 62 and 57 percent in the federal deputy elections. David Samuels, "Money, Elections, and Democracy in Brazil," *Latin American Politics and Society* 43 (Summer 2001): 27–48. Samuels contends not that these entities exercise undue influence over policy, but that public officials "extort" firms to donate to their campaigns, or effectively punish them through denial of contracts or business.

57. David Samuels, "Money, Elections, and Democracy in Brazil," 31, 39.

58. This was done using the Sani and Sartori measure developed to gauge the ideological distance between parties to calculate the distance in the mean positions of party representatives in government and opposition, with respect to the merits of more than two-dozen market reforms including labor legislation, social security reform, the privatization of state-owned enterprises, and the treatment of national and foreign capital.

59. In the case of the standard left-right scale, the Sani-Sartori measure is calculated by dividing the (absolute) difference between the mean self-classification of the extreme parties by the theoretical maximum of 9. The scores of Brazilian legislators are from Scott Mainwaring, Rachel Meneguello, and Timothy J. Power, "Conservative Parties, Democracy, and Economic Reform in Contemporary Brazil," in Kevin J. Middlebrook, ed., *Conservative Parties, the Right, and Democracy in Latin America* (Baltimore: Johns Hopkins University Press, 2000), 184–85.

60. Peter Siavelis, "Executive-Legislative Relations in Post-Pinochet Chile," 325–26.

61. Mariano Torcal and Scott Mainwaring, "The Political Recrafting of Social Bases of Party Competition: Chile, 1973–95," *British Journal of Political Science* 33 (January 2003): 80.

62. Centro de Estudios Públicos, "Estudio Social y de Opinión Pública: Mayo–Junio 1995. Tema Especial: La Mujer Chilena Hoy: Trabajo, Familia y Valores." Documento de Trabajo No. 237 (August 1995), 9.

63. Centro de Estudios Públicos, "Estudio Social y de Opinión Pública: Marzo 1991," Documento de Trabajo No. 156 (June 1991), 5.

64. Centro de Estudios Públicos, "Estudio Social y de Opinión Pública: Diciembre 2002. Tema Especial: Mujer y Trabajo, Familia y Valores," (December 2002), 4.

65. As evidenced by MORI data reported in Beatriz Magaloni and Vidal Romero, "Support for Globalization and State Retrenchment in Latin America: Economic Performance and Partisanship," paper prepared for delivery at the Workshop on the Analysis of Political Cleavages and Party Competition, Duke University, April 2004, 34–36.

66. Public opinion data from 2003 IBOPE survey, available at *www.ibope.com.br*.

67. Juan J. Linz and Alfred Stepan, *Problems of Democratic Transition and Consolidation: Southern Europe, South America, and Post-Communist Europe* (Baltimore: Johns Hopkins University Press, 1996), 217–18.

68. Juan J. Linz and Alfred Stepan, *Problems of Democratic Transition and Consolidation*, 222–23.

69. Latinobarómetro, "Summary Report 2003," 22, 48.

70. Peter Siavelis, "Executive-Legislative Relations in Post-Pinochet Chile," 332–33.

71. Datafolha, "Opinião Pública: Brasileiros consideram desempenho do Congresso Nacional regular," São Paulo, 1 February 2004, available at *www1.folha.uol.com.br/folha/datafolha/po/aval_congresso_02012004.shtml.*

72. Peter McDonough, Doh C. Shin, and José Álvaro Moisés, "Democratization and Participation: Comparing Spain, Brazil, and Korea," *Journal of Politics* 60 (November 1998): 924, 944, 946.

73. Gianpaolo Baiocchi, "Participation, Activism, and Politics: The Porto Alegre Experiment and Deliberative Democratic Theory," *Politics and Society* 29 (March 2001): 43–72.

74. Katherine Hite and Leonardo Morlino, "Problematizing the Links between Authoritarian Legacies and 'Good' Democracy," 55.

75. Alfredo Riquelme Segovia, "Quiénes y por qué 'no están ni ahí'? Marginación y/o automarginación en la democracia transicional. Chile. 1988–1997," in Paul Drake and Iván Jaksić, eds., *El modelo chileno: Democracia y desarollo en los noventa* (Santiago: LOM, 1999), 261.

76. Alfredo Riquelme Segovia, "¿Quienes y por qué 'no están ni ahi'?" 267.

77. Katherine Hite and Sarah Shanley, "Bridging the Political Generation Gap? Left Youth Activism and Memory in Chile," unpubl. ms., Vassar College, 8.

78. Katherine Hite and Leonardo Morlino, "Problematizing the Links between Authoritarian Legacies and 'Good' Democracy," 51.

79. For an account of the way in which democratic politicians were able to overcome military influence over Brazilian democracy, see Wendy Hunter, *Eroding Military Influence in Brazil: Politicians Against Soldiers* (Chapel Hill: University of North Carolina Press, 1997).

80. Philip D. Oxhorn, *Organizing Civil Society: The Popular Sectors and the Struggle for Democracy in Chile* (University Park: Pennsylvania State University Press, 1995).

81. Juan J. Linz and Alfred Stepan, *Problems of Democratic Transition and Consolidation*, 212.

82. The expression was coined by Marc Ensalaco, "In with the New, Out with the Old? The Democratising Impact of Constitutional Reform in Chile," *Journal of Latin American Studies* 26 (May 1994): 418. The vote to repeal the designated senators was finally passed (unanimously) in the senate in October 2004, but even in the most optimistic scenario will not take effect until the terms of the current designated senators expire in March 2006. "Untying the knot," *The Economist,* 21 October 2004.

83. Mariano Torcal and Scott Mainwaring, "The Political Recrafting of Social Bases of Party Competition," 54–84.

84. See, for example, Timothy R. Scully, *Rethinking the Center: Cleavages, Critical Junctures, and Party Evolution in Chile* (Stanford: Stanford University Press, 1992).

85. For arguments about the centrality of party decline and especially the severing of representative links between parties and citizens in the erosion of Venezuelan and Bolivian democracy, see Michael Coppedge, "Explaining Democratic Deterioration through Nested Inference" and Rene Mayorga, "Bolivia's Democracy at the Crossroads," in Frances Hagopian and Scott Mainwaring, eds., *The Third Wave of Democratization in Latin America* (Cambridge: Cambridge University Press, 2005).

9

BANGLADESH AND INDIA

Sumit Ganguly

Sumit Ganguly is the Rabindranath Tagore Professor of Indian Cultures and Civilizations in the department of political science at Indiana University, Bloomington. He is the author of India Since 1980 *(forthcoming) and the founding editor of* India Review, *a social-science journal dedicated to the study of contemporary India.*

This paper will assess the "quality of democracy" in India and Bangladesh. It argues that the democratic successes and failures in these two countries are in large measure a function of the sociopolitical milieu within which the democratic transitions took place in both states. It will also argue that despite a range of striking shortcomings India has made significant progress in a number of arenas toward enhancing the quality of its democracy. Bangladesh, on the other hand, has failed to make similar progress. Instead, there is much evidence that suggests that the quality of democracy in Bangladesh is actually declining.

The proposition that the emergence of democracy in India is a legacy of British colonialism has considerable scholarly as well as popular appeal.[1] Perhaps the fact that India reigns as the world's largest democracy contributes to this impression. Yet despite its wide appeal, that proposition is largely devoid of merit; indeed it is deeply flawed, as even a quick survey of other British colonial bequests reveals. From a historical standpoint, ample evidence can be adduced to show that British colonial administrators did much to stultify the growth of democratic political forces and institutions in British India (which included much of what today is Pakistan and Bangladesh). For example, during much of the independence movement, the British authorities in India enforced a series of draconian laws limiting press freedom, restricted the right of free assembly, and most egregiously, sought to suppress the explicitly liberal and democratic elements of the nationalist movement.

Furthermore, a comparison with other legatees of British colonialism, whether in Africa, in other parts of Asia, elsewhere in South Asia, should lead one to scoff at suggestions of a benign contribution by British imperialism to the growth of democracy. In South Asia, outside of India democracy has failed to take deep root in any of the other states emergent from the detritus of the British Indian empire. In Pakistan, for example, it has been brittle at best and nonexistent at worst.[2] In Sri Lanka, it has involved institutionalized ethnic discrimination and contributed to a seemingly unending ethnic civil war.[3]

In Bangladesh, democracy remains at best procedural. Bangladesh's failure to consolidate and deepen democracy requires some explanation. Once again, historical legacies are of extraordinary importance. Bangladesh emerged as an independent state only in 1971 with the break-up of Pakistan. From 1947 to 1971, what is today Bangladesh was the noncontiguous eastern wing of Pakistan. During this period it was not only subject to the vagaries of Pakistan's turbulent politics and long bouts of authoritarian and military rule, but was also treated mostly as an internal colony. These years, which constituted the formative phase of Bangladesh, shaped a number of its critical institutions, most notably the army. Unlike India, Pakistan and subsequently Bangladesh failed to establish firm civilian control over the military.[4] Long years of authoritarian military rule in Pakistan also contributed to an antidemocratic political culture in Bangladesh. Any attempts at democratic consolidation and deepening have had to contend with these adverse historical legacies. This comparison is interesting and useful for a number of compelling reasons. It gives a glimpse of the underlying structural factors that contributed to the markedly divergent political trajectories of India and Bangladesh even though they emerged from the common detritus of the same imperial entity.

India: The Rule of Law

The success of democracy in India must be traced instead to individuals within the Indian nationalist movement who seized upon certain British liberal ideas and principles and then sought to transplant them in Indian soil over a span of several decades.[5] It is also closely related to the emergence of a "catch-all party," the Indian National Congress, that, at least in principle, sought to represent all Indians regardless of their regional, caste, class, or ethnic affiliations. The participation of this unrelentingly anticolonial party in slowly expanding forms of self-government prepared it to seize the reins of democratic governance in the postindependence era.

India, which made its transition to democracy with a remarkable absence of violence (once the extraordinarily bloody process of partition by the British was over), saw a high degree of adherence to the rule of law in the early years of its independence.[6] The country's first prime minister, Jawaharlal Nehru, a key member of the nationalist movement, was committed to the highest standards of probity in public life. Many of the members of his cabinet were equally committed to similar norms of conduct.[7] The exigencies of politics did, of course, lead Nehru to make minor concessions. On occasion, for example, he chose not to investigate allegations of illegal activities on the part of some of his ministers.[8] Nevertheless, for the most part during the initial years after independence, especially in comparison with most other postcolonial states, the adherence to the rule of law in India was exemplary.

Yet this outstanding start has not carried through to the present. The decline in the rule of law, ironically, started under Nehru's daughter and India's third prime minister, Indira Gandhi. In the 1970s, in an attempt to bolster the sagging popularity of the Congress Party, she promoted a series of populist slogans and measures. One of her key electoral promises was *garibi hatao* or (literally "drive out poverty"). This slogan, not surprisingly, won many adherents, and shortly after her sweeping electoral victory in 1970 she embarked on a series of populist measures including the nationalization of banks and key industries such as iron and steel. She also did away with the "privy purses," the annual government subsidies to the former princely rulers of India. Few of these measures made any dent in India's endemic poverty, however. Economic growth rates continued to hover around 3 to 4 percent annually, and India's rural and urban poor saw few improvements in the quality of their daily existence.[9] What her slogans and policies did do, was create a climate of increased expectations among India's impoverished electorate.

When confronted with these dramatic and expanding expectations, Indira Gandhi quickly realized that the country lacked the institutional and material capacities to address them adequately. Soon she saw these newly enfranchised voters turn to regional political parties in pursuit of their goals. In a crude attempt to bolster the declining electoral prospects of the Congress Party, she resorted to two techniques that dramatically undermined the rule of law. The first was her rampant abuse of Article 356 of the Indian constitution, a clause that allows the national government to dismiss a state government if it has lost the confidence of the local electorate or if it cannot maintain a modicum of civil order. On the most dubious pretexts she dismissed state governments, thereby making a mockery of India's constitutional provisions.[10] The second set of moves was even more egregious. She and her elder son, Sanjay Gandhi, brought large numbers of callow youth into the Congress Party to be used as enforcers. These prospectless young men had little regard for democratic procedures or legal norms. Their principal purpose was to serve as a private army in closely contested elections to intimidate voters, cow political opponents, and, on occasion, to attempt the subversion of other electoral processes. The political protection and patronage that these men enjoyed frequently demoralized local police and other administrative authorities, creating a climate in which the rule of law could be flouted with impunity. Worse still, civil servants who refused to knuckle under to the demands of politicians were frequently transferred to less desirable postings; in a short time the political independence of the bureaucracy was thoroughly compromised. Inevitably, the norms of professional conduct within the previously highly regarded Indian Administrative Service (IAS) started to decline, as political interference became rampant. As these norms frayed, politicians increasingly came to rely on local kingpins to threaten and harass political opponents with little fear of police and other authorities.

In the 1990s, the blatant involvement of politicians with known criminals became so widespread that the government felt compelled to create a one-man commission to investigate and report on the politician-criminal nexus. The commission, created in 1995, was headed by N.N. Vohra, a former senior IAS officer known for his impeccable professional record. Vohra's report, which was submitted within a year, provided a damning indictment of the politician-criminal nexus. Though excerpts from the report were leaked to prominent Indian newsmagazines, the full contents of the report were never made public. The underlying problem that Vohra identified in his report continues to plague Indian politics. According to one reliable source, as many as seven hundred state legislators and forty members of parliament have criminal backgrounds.[11] In some states, the ties between politicians and criminals are quite tight.[12] Since Vohra submitted his famous report, there have been few improvements in this arena. In the parliament that was convened in June 2004, at least a hundred of the 542 members had criminal cases pending against them.[13] Though the Election Commission has long recommended that individuals under indictment should not be allowed to contest elections, no political party has found it desirable or expedient to implement this injunction. Given the composition of the many state legislatures, not to mention the national parliament, it is highly unlikely that this critical issue will receive legislative attention anytime soon.

Another key problem with the rule of law in India is the enormous caseload confronting Indian courts at local, state and national levels. According to one estimate it takes an average of twenty years to resolve a civil lawsuit in India.[14] Despite periodic calls for judicial reform, little effort has been expended to address this severe backlog. Ironically, the advent of a new form of judicial activism, public-interest litigation, which is designed to provide access to the indigent and the dispossessed, may increase this extraordinary burden on the courts.[15]

Accountability

The quality of governmental accountability in India varies widely. At the most basic level of accountability—reasonably free and fair elections at local, state and national levels—India no longer fares badly. The existence of the politician-criminal nexus notwithstanding, three factors have played a vital role in preventing the corruption of the electoral process. First, the extraordinary level of political mobilization that has taken place over the last two decades has made hitherto disenfranchised voters far more conscious of their political rights and privileges. All Indian national electoral surveys reveal that citizens from the "lower" castes are becoming increasingly assertive in state and national politics and are playing a vital role in ensuring electoral alternations. Second, since the 1976–77 "emergency," when civil liberties and press freedoms were dramatically curtailed, the Indian press has assumed an important watchdog role. Politicians still resort to the use of local *condottieri* to try and alter electoral outcomes. Press vigilance, however, frequently exposes these dubious schemes. When such malfeasances are brought under public scrutiny, the revitalized Election Commission routinely countermands the election outcome and arranges a revote. Third, and in a related vein, some institutions have shown renewed signs of vigor. In this context, the Indian Election Commission, long a somnolent body, has in recent years evinced an increasing willingness and ability to ensure the fairness of electoral outcomes.[16] The success of the Election Commission has even attracted the attention of more mature democracies. Ironically enough, the British Election Commission, established in 2000, has sought to study the successful practices of its Indian counterpart.[17]

At another level, however, governmental accountability leaves much to be desired. A tradition has long existed in India, hailing back to British colonial practices, to appoint commissions of inquiry. More often than not, retired judges, drawn from the higher realms of the judiciary, are called upon to head these commissions. Commissions may examine such matters as the excessive use of force by local police, the failure of a state government to prevent a riot, or, most recently, a significant intelligence failure.[18] The commissions usually have the power to subpoena key individuals, to hold public hearings and to make recommendations based upon their findings. The commissions frequently produce thoughtful, candid, and honest accounts of the issue that they were asked to address. Unfortunately, since the findings of the commissions have no binding legal features, governments are free to disregard their recommendations. For example the Shah Commission headed by retired Justice Shah was asked to investigate the causes of the pogrom against the Sikh community in New Delhi in the aftermath of the assassination of Prime Minister Indira Gandhi in 1984. The commission, to its credit, correctly and courageously identified certain members of the ruling Congress Party and significant segments of the New Delhi police force as the principal perpetrators of heinous crimes against the hapless Sikh population. Yet in the intervening two decades, apart from a few

low-level police personnel, none of the principals involved in organizing, directing, and implementing the pogrom have been produced in
court, let alone faced criminal prosecution.[19] What explains this abject
failure to act on the recommendations of a commission of inquiry? The
answers are complex. In the case of the New Delhi pogrom, the ruling
Congress Party was simply loath to move against many of its powerful
notables. Subsequent governments have been either too short-lived or
too willing to engage in political logrolling to bring criminal charges
against the perpetrators. Compounding this problem, of course, is the
enormous backlog of cases facing courts at local, state, and national
levels. Finally, with the passage of time, evidence once collected is lost,
memories of the victims tend to fade, and other, more immediate issues
crowd the political agenda of national parties and governments.

Is accountability, then, simply absent from Indian political life? Such
an assertion is unsustainable. One of the more novel methods of ensuring accountability is the previously mentioned development of public-
interest litigation. This revolution can be traced to the pioneering work
of Justice P.N. Bhagwati, a former chief justice of the Indian Supreme
Court. Bhagwati cogently argued that in a vast country with widespread
poverty one way of rendering the courts accessible to ordinary citizens
seeking legal redress was through the development of public-interest
litigation. Accordingly, any citizen of India who believes that a particular set of laws is not being implemented, or that the government
stands in violation of an existing set of laws, need only send a postcard
to the Supreme Court seeking action. If the case is deemed to be justi-
ciable, the Court will respond accordingly. In the wake of Bhagwati's
decision, the Court has been bombarded with such requests. Some, of
course, have been frivolous and the Court has accordingly tossed them
out. But in a range of cases brought to its attention the Court has acted,
to much salutary effect.[20] It has shut down polluting industries, ordered
major metropolitan governments to conform to auto-emission rules, and
provided redress to unconvicted prisoners incarcerated for extended
periods of time.

One possible misgiving about this form of judicial activism may be
the overextension of the judiciary's powers. This is a legitimate concern
in a democratic state where balance has to be maintained between the
various branches of government. In the Indian case, however, the judiciary has evinced a willingness not to encroach on the authority of the
other branches of government.[21]

One key mechanism for vertical accountability in India remains the
free press. In the years following independence, it was both professional
and diligent. Sadly, it did not display these qualities during the state of
emergency that Indira Gandhi declared largely to ensure her political
survival, when most of the rights that are guaranteed under the Indian
constitution were in abeyance.[22] The Indian press, for the most part,

acted in a fairly supine fashion under the state of emergency. With minor exceptions, most newspaper editors all too readily submitted to censorship. In the aftermath of the emergency, however, the press, perhaps because of the chagrin about its role during that period, took on a markedly different orientation. Indeed it can be argued that the press assumed a remarkably feisty character and focused on investigative journalism with considerable vigor and efficacy. Since that time, the Indian press has performed a yeoman watchdog role, exposing governmental corruption, taking recalcitrant civil servants to task, revealing governmental indifference to violence against minorities and lower-caste groups, and reporting on failures of governance in all parts of the country. Among other matters, in recent years the press has been responsible for bringing to light the Rajiv Gandhi government's payment of kickbacks for the purchase of the Swedish Bofors field gun; for revealing the financial malfeasances of a minister of communications, Sukh Ram, in the allotment of wireless-telephone licenses; for uncovering Prime Minister Narasimha Rao's offer of financial inducements to members of an opposition party to support the ruling regime on a crucial vote in parliament; and for drawing attention to the financial irregularities of the then–chief minister of Bihar, Laloo Prasad Yadav, in the purchase of animal fodder using state funds. The results of the revelations have been mixed. At the time of this writing, despite extensive investigations carried out by the Central Bureau of Investigation (CBI), India's apex investigative body, no convictions have been obtained in the Bofors case. Rao, indicted but never brought to trial, left office in disgrace. Ram and Yadav, however, were both charged and indicted, losing their respective offices.[23] Subsequently, however, despite various cases pending against him, Yadav was elected to national office in June 2004 even though a number of his associates, including members of the Indian Administrative Service, have received prison terms for their involvement in the animal fodder scam.

Responsiveness

The responsiveness of Indian democracy to the expectations of its citizens also varies enormously depending on the area under discussion. Despite a fairly consistent history of procedural democracy since independence (barring Indira Gandhi's 1976–77 state of emergency), poverty and hunger remain endemic in India. Yet it would be inaccurate to suggest that the Indian state is utterly unresponsive to the needs of its citizens. One of the most dramatic and least heralded successes of Indian democracy has been the avoidance of mass death from famine or famine-like conditions. It appears that one of the critical institutions whose presence helps to guard against the tragedy of mass starvation is the Indian media. Amartya Sen, the Indian Nobel laureate in economics, has deftly argued that India's free press has prevented mass death in times of drought and famine. The logic of his argument is deceptively simple. A free press ensures the prompt flow of information about the prospects of mass deaths from hunger. Politicians fearful of an electoral backlash in the face of mass starvation ensure that the machinery of the state acts with alacrity to prevent such an occurrence.[24] Sen contrasts postindependence India's avoidance of mass death during famines with that of China under the totalitarian regime of Mao Zedong during the Cultural Revolution as well as India under authoritarian British rule as late as the 1940s.[25] Although Indian democracy has not made sufficient progress toward the eradication of mass poverty and hunger in fifty-odd years of independence, it has managed to ensure that mass death from hunger no longer stalks the land when the country is confronted with a crop failure.

In the realm of primary education, however, Indian democracy has proven to be singularly unresponsive to existing needs. Even though India can justifiably boast an extraordinary degree of success in promoting higher education, its record in providing universal primary schooling is abysmal. Myron Weiner's harsh 1991 indictment of India's failure to address this issue is worth quoting:

> Primary education in India is not compulsory, nor is child labor illegal. The result is that less than half of India's children between ages six and fourteen—82.2 million—are not in school. They stay at home to care for the cattle, tend to younger children, collect firewood, and work in the fields. They find employment in cottage industries, tea stalls, restaurants, or as household workers in middle-class homes. They become prostitutes or live as street children, begging or picking rags and bottles from trash for resale. Many are bonded laborers, tending cattle and working as agricultural laborers for local landowners.[26]

Conditions have not significantly improved in India since the publication of Weiner's important study. In 2003, India spent a mere 1.7 percent of its Gross Domestic Product (GDP) on primary education and a total of 3.4 percent of its GDP for education overall.[27] The results of such low spending are apparent. According to World Bank statistics, in 2003–2004, 39 percent of the population over the age of 15 was illiterate.[28] The reasons for this neglect of primary education are complex. Part of the explanation is sociological. It can be traced to the elitist class background of India's first generation of political leaders, who emphasized higher education over universal primary education. Another component of the explanation involves path dependence.[29] Critical elite choices made through India's extensive and labyrinthine economic-planning process locked in certain developmental priorities that are not easy to modify. In the wake of the June 2004 electoral defeat of the coalition government led by the Bharatiya Janata Party (BJP), the new ruling coalition led by the Congress party has chosen to allocate significantly greater resources to primary education. How well this new developmental priority will be implemented remains an open question.[30]

Freedom and Rights

The Indian constitution provides a range of guarantees in terms of personal rights and civil liberties. The vast majority of these rights are procedural, and include the freedoms of expression and assembly, the prohibition against arbitrary detention and trial, and the right to profess the religion of one's choice. A preamble to the constitution, the "Directive Principles of State Policy," also exhorts the state to provide citizens with a range of substantive, albeit nonjusticiable, socioeconomic rights.[31] It should be underscored that these rights are entirely hortatory: The state is not legally obligated to guarantee these rights to its citizens.

The actual implementation of many of these most laudable rights can be a highly uncertain affair. To begin with, one's social class profoundly influences one's ability to secure many of these procedural rights. The indigent, minorities, and members of lower castes often receive arbitrary treatment at the hands of those who wield coercive power. Police frequently resort to extort, harass, and intimidate individuals whose social class affords them little or no protection from such illegal behavior. It needs to be underscored, however, that the degree of police misbehavior varies considerably from state to state within India. Certain states are more likely to curb police malfeasance than others. For example, in poorly governed northern states such as Uttar Pradesh, Bihar, and Madhya Pradesh, atrocities committed against lower castes are routine. Worse still, local police and judicial authorities rarely aggressively pursue the perpetrators of these acts. On the other hand, systematic caste violence is mostly absent in southern India and much of eastern India. Furthermore, state governments in these areas are far more likely to take cognizance of such outbreaks of caste violence and seek to put a quick end to them.[32]

The explanation for these geographic variations lies in a complex congeries of factors. In the 1950s and 1960s, Southern India underwent a virtual nonviolent revolution that transformed the social importance of caste.[33] A similar process is now under way in northern India. However, as lower castes and minorities (who are more numerous in northern India) seek to assert their rights, the wielders of political power, who are disproportionately high-caste Hindus, are resorting to both legal and illegal means to preserve the old social order. This contest has contributed to much violence and political turmoil throughout northern India over the past decade. The realization of the rights of the poor, the dispossessed, and minorities, however, is simply a matter of time as long as India can maintain some facets of its democratic institutions and practices.

The initial verdict of some of the ablest social scientists working on the subject of lower-caste empowerment reinforces this optimistic conclusion. As the Congress party, the dominant postindependence political organization, failed to address the felt grievances of citizens from the historically lower castes, other forces stepped into the breach. Congress's empty populism may never have delivered on its promises, but it did raise lower-caste expectations. Not surprisingly, other regional political parties, often caste-based, successfully capitalized on Congress's shortcomings. As lower-caste voters and groups have come more thoroughly to grasp the logic and power of electoral politics, they have over the last two decades shifted their allegiances away from Congress and toward a number of caste-based political parties. This growing political sophistication of voters in northern India is now fueling what one social scientist has dubbed "India's silent revolution."[34]

This discussion of freedom and rights would be incomplete without some attention to whether and how rights have been upheld in places and at times when normal politics are in abeyance. The suspension of normal politics in India has taken place on a nationwide basis only once during a half-century and more of independence. This occurred during the "state of emergency" that Prime Minister Indira Gandhi declared in 1976. It is well known that most constitutional safeguards protecting the freedom of expression as well as personal rights and civil liberties were flagrantly violated during this time. The experience of the emergency, however, is widely regarded as little more than an anomaly, albeit an important one, in India's democratic career.

The abuse of constitutionally guaranteed rights, however, has been widespread in India when the Indian state has sought to quell insurgent movements.[35] Such abuses have occurred in the state's response to secessionist movements in the northeast, in the Punjab, and most recently in Kashmir. The abuses have included, but have not been limited to, the use of torture to extract information from suspected terrorists, extrajudicial killings, and arbitrary detention without trial.[36] In the Punjab, in particular, the police and paramilitary forces developed the practice of "encounter killings," in which suspected terrorists, once captured, were frequently summarily executed without trial. When questioned about these deaths, the police would routinely and vaguely reply that the suspects had been killed in an "encounter."[37]

The success of this extrajudicial method of dealing with suspected terrorists and criminal gangs within the context of an insurgency had a sweeping demonstration effect in India. There is some evidence that police in particular metropolitan areas—tired of dealing with judicial sloth, the resort to dilatory tactics on the part of deft defense lawyers, and the prospect of intimidation of key witnesses to violent crimes—have now adopted "encounter killings" when dealing with the most violent elements of the organized criminal underworld.[38] Understandable but particularly distressing is the substantial public support for these methods in the absence of other legal means to bring hardened criminals to the dock. The routinization of these methods of police work threatens to undermine the bedrock of a fundamental right in a democracy, namely adherence to the due process of law even when dealing with the most egregious of suspected criminals.

The rights of religious minorities, most notably Muslims, have been under systematic attack since the late 1980s. On a number of occasions, various state governments in India have at best been complicit, and at worst actively implicated in attacks on India's Muslim minority. The worst of these events occurred in February 2003 in the town of Godhra, in the northwestern state of Gujarat. After some Muslim miscreants allegedly set fire to a train carrying Hindu pilgrims, killing some fifty individuals, Hindu mobs, either in concert with or with the passive connivance of local police and politicians, attacked Muslims in Godhra and other parts of the state. Before public order was finally restored a week later, several thousand Muslims had lost their lives at the hands of these rampaging mobs.[39] Police cases have been lodged against a number of individuals believed to have been involved in orchestrating the pogrom. Yet it is far from clear that Gujarat's state government, which did little in the first place to stop the anti-Muslim mayhem, will prosecute the perpetrators with any vigor. More recently, forensic evidence has come to light which suggests that the attack against the Hindu pilgrims by putative Muslim miscreants may not have taken place at all.[40] The only hope for some redress lies in the continued willingness and ability of India's Supreme Court to intervene on behalf of a petition that the National Human Rights Commission submitted to move the cases from Gujarat to the neighboring state of Maharashtra to ensure a fair trail.[41] The statement of Chief Justice Khare of the Indian Supreme Court that there was "complete collusion" between the prosecutors and the accused in the rioting cases in Gujarat underscores the utterly compromised features of the judicial process in Gujarat under a viciously partisan and anti-Muslim state government.[42]

The challenge that violently antisecular sentiments and actions pose to the quality of Indian democratic life cannot be overstated. Should Indian democracy be stripped of its secular orientation, the quality of that democracy will be severely compromised. Indeed, India may head toward becoming what Fareed Zakaria has aptly termed an "illiberal democracy," wherein the rights of religious and ethnic minorities are at risk even though electoral alternations take place routinely and in a moderately free and fair fashion.

Equality

According to the World Bank's estimate for 2003 and 2004, 29 percent of India's population of more than one billion people remain at an income level below the national poverty line. Nearly half (47 percent) of all children under five are thought to be malnourished. Other statistics also suggest significant and persistent gaps in wealth and income. Indeed according to some measures, the pattern of inequality that pervaded Indian society at independence persists. One important indicator thereof, the Gini coefficient of per-capita expenditure, has remained largely constant over this extended time span. However, as thoughtful analysts have argued, this measure may not adequately capture profound social changes that have taken place since independence.[43] Upper-caste dominance is steadily on the decline, progress has been made toward universal elementary education, absentee landlordism has been legally abolished, and the right of universal adult franchise constitutionally enshrined. Consequently, even fitful attempts to promote equality through public policies have had significant ameliorative effects that cannot be adequately measured through conventional statistical techniques. Even one of the most eminent and staunchest critics of social stratification in India concedes that Indian democracy is "a secular miracle in the modern world" while acknowledging that "the quality of our democracy is poor."[44]

Since 1991 India has embarked upon a fitful but significant effort at economic liberalization.[45] There is little question that economic growth has improved dramatically as a result. The Indian economy, having shed a labyrinthine set of economic controls, production quotas, and internal and external tariffs, has managed to transcend what the economist Raj Krishna once posited as "the Hindu rate of growth"—meaning 3 percent or less per annum during the long years of pseudosocialist economic planning. Over the last decade, India's annual rate of economic growth has hovered between 5 and 7 percent, and this despite exogenous shocks. Some Indian economists believe that with even more of the right policies in place, India can achieve double-digit annual economic growth. A vigorous debate has now emerged about the contribution of rapid economic growth to poverty alleviation. It is beyond the scope of this paper to discuss in any detail this debate, but unsurprisingly, the devotees of liberalization contend that rapid growth has contributed to poverty alleviation. Those opposed to the dismantling of the structure of economic planning argue otherwise.[46]

Bangladesh

Bangladesh fares poorly on most indicators of the "quality of democracy." Much of its difficulty in consolidating and enhancing democracy can be traced to its semicolonial past. Until 1971, overwhelmingly Muslim Bangladesh was the eastern province of the Pakistani state that had come into being as a result of the 1947 partition of British India. During this time, West Pakistan treated East Pakistan— from which it was widely separated by the vast expanse of northern

India—as a virtual internal colony.[47] West Pakistan absorbed most of the foreign aid and investment while also dominating the ranks of the powerful Pakistani civil service and armed forces. Most galling to East Pakistanis, however, was the denial of national status for their own language (Bengali) and the imposition instead of Urdu, the dominant language of West Pakistan. Ultimately, the accumulated grievances drove the growth of Bengali subnationalism, which in turn led to civil war. Indian intervention in this civil war ultimately contributed to the creation of Bangladesh.

Sadly, the nascent state started its political existence with a number of important institutional handicaps. The first postindependence leader of Bangladesh, Sheikh Mujibur Rehman, was a remarkably charismatic populist. Notionally, he was committed to the creation of a democratic, egalitarian, and secular polity. In practice, however, Sheikh Mujib, as he was popularly known, did little or nothing to foster an institutional legacy to promote those ends. The Awami League, the party to which he belonged, was mostly woven around his political personality. Additionally, soon after assuming power following Bangladesh's independence from Pakistan, Mujib proved singularly inept at addressing the vast tasks of social and economic reconstruction. Moreover, his administration was riddled with corruption, nepotism, and inefficiency. As political instability mounted and the government's ability to maintain public order declined, Mujib increasingly resorted to authoritarian measures. He declared a state of emergency in 1975 and dispensed with the parliamentary form of government, declaring himself to be the president of Bangladesh.[48]

In fairness to Mujib, it should be noted that the tasks which he confronted were daunting. To begin with he had to contend with creating a state out of a breakaway province. Additionally, he had to deal with a segment of the Bangladeshi military that remained unreconciled to the breakup of Pakistan and still harbored pro-Pakistani sentiments. He faced the intransigence of the radical Islamist Jamaat-i-Islami, a political party fundamentally opposed to the creation of a separate, independent state of Bangladesh. Finally, his administration had to contend with the simple but compelling matter of curbing the powers of local *condottieri* who had emerged in the wake of the civil war. All these factors undermined the stability of his regime, and he was assassinated along with most members of his immediate family in a sanguinary military coup later in 1975.

The military regime led by General Zia-ur-Rehman justified its takeover on the usual grounds: the previous government had failed to curb growing lawlessness, had been involved in corruption, and had failed to address a number of pressing social and economic needs. Zia's regime promised to address these myriad ills. To some small degree he did deliver on his promises: as economic development did take place, some of the cronyism of the Mujib years was curbed, and efforts to limit problematically rapid population growth were put into place. Yet civil liberties and personal rights were squelched and the Zia regime displayed scant regard for the rights of the substantial Hindu minority. The formal commitment to a secular state that promised equality before the law for all citizens, regardless of religious affiliation, evaporated under Zia's military dictatorship.

Zia's regime, in turn, was overthrown in yet another military coup in May 1981. The democratic interregnum that ensued proved to be short-lived. In March 1982, Lieutenant General Husain Mohammed Ershad overthrew the faltering and inefficacious regime of President Abdus Sattar. Ershad's regime, in turn, lasted until 1991. Since then Bangladesh has made a rocky transition to democracy. Yet the fundamental norms that should undergird a democratic polity have yet to take hold. Even though routine alternations of government take place through the electoral process, none of the major political parties has accepted the principle of an honest and loyal opposition. The aftermath of every national election follows a predictable, desultory pattern: The victorious party exults while the defeated party promptly contends that the electoral process was flawed and refuses to abide by the results of the election.[49] Both the Awami League and the Bangladesh National Party (BNP) have shown scant regard for the other when in opposition. They have routinely resorted to extraparliamentary tactics including demonstrations, strikes, and chicanery in order to undermine each other's ability to govern.[50] Unsurprisingly, Bangladesh fares poorly in assessments of democratic quality.

The Rule of Law

In Bangladesh, the rule of law is decidedly brittle. The state has a nominally independent judiciary that follows the canons of British common law. In practice, however, the judiciary is quite pliant and subject to political intervention and direction. The police are underpaid, poorly trained, ineffective, and venal. The inadequate training and skills of the police lead them to use uncalibrated force, frequently resulting in the deaths of innocent bystanders. Most importantly, they are acutely subject to blatant political interference. Particular governments regularly use the police to harass political opponents rather than as neutral instruments for the maintenance of public order. Furthermore, oversight of police conduct is exceedingly weak. Individuals are frequently arrested without adequate cause under the terms of the sweeping Special Powers Act, and deaths in police custody are disturbingly common.[51]

A recent example illustrates the problem of rampant, state-sanctioned police misconduct. In late 2002, in an ostensible effort to enhance the quality of law and order across the country, the BNP regime of Prime

Minister Begum Khaleda Zia launched "Operation Clean Heart." This operation involved some 40,000 military personnel and was putatively designed to arrest "listed criminals," to recover illegal firearms, and to improve the deteriorating law-and-order situation across the country. Contrary to these stated aims, however, much of this police and military operation was turned into a vendetta against political opponents.

Such state-sanctioned police misconduct further undermines the professional mores of an already overburdened, underequipped, and poorly trained police force. Consequently, the police forces are not nearly as good as they need to be at upholding the law and solving common crimes, but are dismayingly energetic at corrupt activities such as extortion and bribe-taking. To compound all these problems, rampant political interference in the day-to-day functioning of the police further erodes their professionalism, effectiveness, and credibility.

Accountability

At one level, the forms of behavior recounted above can be traced to the bureaucratic-authoritarian political culture that pervaded East Pakistan. Bureaucrats wield significant amounts of political and coercive power and can exercise it with considerable impunity. Furthermore, the country's shaky transition to democracy has done little to instill a culture of accountability into its bureaucracy. Since the nation's parliament functions fitfully and in a blatantly partisan fashion, little effort is expended in ensuring systematic oversight of the bureaucracy. The norms of parliamentary democracy, so well embedded in India, are acutely lacking in Bangladesh. Consequently, while political meddling with the bureaucracy is common, responsible oversight by elected officials is rare. The meddling is often manifest in the manipulation of official appointments, promotions, and transfers, and also in the blatantly partisan ways in which state funds are diverted to or from various public projects.[52]

One instrument of accountability in a democracy is a free press. Bangladesh does have feisty media outlets with little fear of criticizing the government of the day. And yet journalists who especially annoy the powerful can become victims of harassment tactics ranging from physical assault to outright death threats. Matters have worsened significantly under the coalition government of Begum Khaleda Zia.[53] The Zia government has been especially sensitive about its record on minority rights, the behavior of some of its radical Islamist coalition partners, and the possible ties of some Bangladeshi political organizations to Islamic radicals in Indonesia and Pakistan.[54]

A relative bright spot in the area of accountability has been the conduct of national elections. While losers still regularly hurl charges of skullduggery, deceit, and perfidy, pressure from the international donor community has led the Bangladeshi state to make significant progress toward conducting moderately free and fair national elections.

An independent Election Commission monitors the conduct of elections, which are held under the aegis of a "caretaker government." This innovation, which came about with the Thirteenth Amendment to the Bangladeshi constitution, proved necessary because of the lack of faith that the opposition typically felt toward the party or parties in power at any given moment. Under the terms of this system, the most recently retired chief justice of Bangladesh heads up the caretaker regime and is responsible for the neutral conduct of elections in conjunction with the Election Commission. Despite the existence of this institutional arrangement, political parties of all coloration have questioned the neutrality of the caretaker government when they have fared poorly at the polls.[55]

Systematic and statistical evidence on vertical accountability is unavailable in Bangladesh. Though the Bangladeshi press is mostly free, it cannot provide effective vertical accountability. The reasons are complex. To begin with, the level of professionalism in Bangladeshi journalism has always been extremely low. Again, the legacy of authoritarianism is a major cause. During the long years of Pakistani rule, the press both in both East and the West faced severe restrictions. After the establishment of Bangladesh as an independent state, a free press did emerge. However, as Jack Snyder has cogently argued, a free press does not amount to one that is necessarily professional and norm-bound.[56] The press in Bangladesh—lacking adequate training, bereft of independent professional organizations that engage in self-policing, and subject to the demands of powerful owners—cannot be deemed autonomous. Instead, it is so bias-ridden, and so frequently publishes articles based upon rumor and innuendo, that it cannot serve a useful and reliable watchdog role. In recent years, particularly under BNP-led regimes, it has even faced a degree of government harassment especially when it has sought to highlight the plight of hapless minorities.

Responsiveness

State responsiveness to felt needs and grievances is extremely weak in Bangladesh. Ironically, the state is more responsive to the demands and expectations of the international donor communities than to the hopes of much of its own populace. The responsiveness to the donor community stems from Bangladesh's acute dependence upon foreign aid. As one of the poorest nations in the world, it can ill afford to incur the wrath of its global donors.[57] Consequently, certain governmental programs in Bangladesh have been remarkably successful. These include efforts to reduce the endemic incidence of cholera and to curb runaway population growth. Both of these matters were important priorities of major international donors and, not surprisingly, have received sustained attention from various Bangladeshi governments.

One area where the state has shown some promise in the arena of responsiveness without the benefit of external pressure is that of judicial reform. As in India, the Bangladeshi judiciary is hopelessly swamped by an overdue caseload. In an effort to address this million-case backlog, the Bangladeshi Ministry of Law set up a pilot program of Alternative Dispute Resolution in 2001 in the city of Comilla. This pilot program allows people to bring their grievances first to citizen mediators who have some familiarity with the law before going to court. Initial citizen response has been mostly positive. It remains to be seen if the government will now extend the reach of this program nationwide.[58]

Freedom and Rights

The constitution of Bangladesh formally guarantees a range of civil and political rights. Their realization, however, is another matter entirely. Weak judicial institutions, partial and unprofessional police, and an unresponsive bureaucracy blight the prospects that most Bangladeshis will in practice be able to call on these rights when they need them.

For example, in the area of civil rights, the constitution formally bans the use of torture as well as cruel, inhumane, and degrading forms of punishment. Yet police routinely use torture as an instrument of policy and those responsible for these acts are rarely, if ever, punished. Bangladesh's record in protecting the rights of its religious and ethnic minorities is even worse. Created as a secular state, Bangladesh abandoned this constitutional commitment within the first decade of its existence and made Islam its state religion. Its substantial Hindu minority, which includes somewhere between 11 and 16 percent of the populace, has faced routine harassment and even physical intimidation in recent years.[59] Other ethnic minorities, most notably the Buddhist Chakmas, have seen the steady erosion of their rights since Bangladesh came into being in 1971.[60] The state has sought to deny them their linguistic rights, has alienated their land, and has sought to forcibly assimilate them into the majority culture.

The rights of religious minorities deserve some discussion. Their rights, though long formally guaranteed under the constitution, have been under assault since the inception of the Bangladeshi state and have eroded dramatically since the late 1990s. Members of non-Muslim communities face routine employment discrimination, especially when seeking government jobs. Their property rights have also been severely undermined, with state consent, by the now-repealed Vested Property Act. Though this law was overturned in 2001, the state has made only feeble efforts to return property seized from the Hindu minority under the act's aegis.[61]

The rights of women have also come under increasing assault despite the presence of women at the head of each of the two main political parties. Outside the highly educated uppermost precincts of Bangladeshi society, women face severe discrimination. Their plight has worsened in recent years with the rise of Islamic zealotry,[62] especially since 2001 when the radical the Jamaat-i-Islami joined the ruling coalition. As the principal member of the coalition, the BNP remains dependent upon the Jamaat-i-Islami for parliamentary support and thus the BNP's leader, Begum Zia, has been loath to contain the activities of the Islamic zealots.[63]

Equality

Any notion of human equality confronts almost insuperable barriers in Bangladesh, a desperately poor country with an annual per capita income of about US$375.[64] According to the World Bank, in 2003–2004, 50 percent of the population remained below the national poverty line and 48 percent of children under five were malnourished.[65] The bulk of the country's wealth and productive resources remains concentrated in the hands of a tiny and rapacious elite. This elite resides mostly in Dhaka, the capital, and is noted for taking much interest in conspicuous consumption and little in Bangladesh's overall development. In the foreseeable future there is little prospect for the growth of a substantial middle class.

Though Bangladesh boasts a large number of nongovernmental organizations (NGOs) dedicated to the alleviation of both rural and urban poverty, their actual impact appears slight. One of the better-known indigenous NGOs, which pioneered the provision of microcredit, is the Grameen Bank. Founded in 1976 and formally converted into a bank in 1983, Grameen lends primarily to poor women and claims a 98 percent repayment rate. (A figure that some critics question.) Since its inception, the bank has disbursed as much as $4.2 billion through some 1,200 branches. It is now seeking to help beggars start businesses under a new and innovative program.[66] These efforts, though well meaning, appear extremely limited when compared to the vast, endemic, and pervasive problems of poverty and inequality that confront Bangladesh today.

As in India, the social rights that the Bangladeshi constitution lists are merely hortatory. The Bangladeshi state has no formal or legal commitment to the preservation or enhancement of the social rights of its citizens. Consequently, any attempt to provide social rights to the vast majority of Bangladeshi citizens stems from the activities of a range of nongovernmental organizations. When it comes to providing effectual social rights to citizens, the Bangladeshi state is more hindrance than help.

Conclusions

What explains the uneven quality of democracy in India and the very poor quality of democracy in Bangladesh? In both cases, their historical legacies explain a great deal. In the Indian case, the long period of British colonial rule reinforced existing social and economic hierarchies and crystallized certain social mores that are inimical to democracy. For example, the social artifacts of caste and religious community were significantly bolstered and strengthened under British rule. The colonial census played a significant role in sharply delineating both religious boundaries and caste distinctions. Consequently, social identities that had once been fluid now became firm and fixed. The defining of these identities provided the basis of much social conflict as political entrepreneurs sought to exploit religious differences and accentuate existing caste conflicts. Such ethnoreligious cleavages could hardly be conducive to the development of democratic politics.

At another level, the reinforcement of existing social and economic hierarchies proved a barrier to democratic politics. India had many leaders who were notionally committed to egalitarian principles, but who at the same time had imbibed influential British cultural ideas about the putative need for class stratification and social hierarchy. Happily, however, the persistent efforts of social activists and the continued working of democratic institutions (especially free and fair elections) kept salutary challenges to the existing social order alive and effectively propelled the cause of fuller democratization.

All these problems, of course, manifested themselves even more intensely in Bangladesh, which during its first 24 years as East Pakistan had access to none of the benefits of open, democratic politics. As a virtual internal colony of its western wing it had a double burden to bear. Its elites had inherited many of the same social prejudices as their Indian counterparts, and still worse, were not forced to make any meaningful accommodations even after the creation of Pakistan. Instead, as Pakistan quickly fell victim to authoritarian rule, many of these norms of hierarchy and deference, far from coming under challenge, met instead with nothing but reinforcement. Moreover, since the state of Pakistan had done little to foster democratic institutions and practices, the key inheritance of the Bangladeshi nationalists were an elitist bureaucracy and an army unused to serving civilian authority. Neither of these two features of the polity was conducive to the growth of democracy, let alone its deepening or consolidation.

As far as the quality of democracy is concerned, both countries still face substantial challenges. India has a long way to go, but at least it will be building on a record of significant achievement over the last six decades. Despite Indian democracy's myriad shortcomings, its prospects of further democratic consolidation and enhancement are substantial. As argued earlier, the dramatic political mobilization that has taken place over the past several decades makes Indian politics volatile, unpredictable, and sometimes even violent. And yet these are merely the symptoms of a moribund sociopolitical order sliding toward rigor mortis. The demise of this social order, though turbulent, promises to leave India more egalitarian, open, and democratic. The hitherto dispossessed of India are now using the power of the ballot to bring about fundamental social changes and breach longstanding socioeconomic barriers.

At another level, the decline of the Congress party and the absence of a truly nationwide alternative created opportunities for the rise of regional political parties. These parties now wield considerable political clout across India, even at the national level. As a consequence, India is now becoming a truly federated polity in which all regions actively seek the representation of their various interests at the national level. The logic of Indian economic liberalization will bolster these federating propensities. States and, more importantly, entrepreneurs no longer have to look to New Delhi for a plethora of industrial licenses, quotas, and permits. This is contributing to a form of economic devolution across India, granting states far greater autonomy in terms of making economic and investment choices. The days of central planning are numbered.

These positive trends in Indian democracy are heartening. Two issues, however, continue to dog Indian public life. The first involves India's flagging commitment to secularism. In recent decades, the antisecular movement in India has gathered considerable force. This trend, if it continues to grow, can ring the death knell of Indian democracy. India's cultural, religious, and ethnic heterogeneity necessitates a secular political order. A democracy that failed to respect some variant of secularism would consign India's substantial religious minorities to second-class status or worse. India would then become nothing more than a majoritarian democracy in which the rights of ethnic and religious minorities would receive little if any respect. Of course, secularism does not face an imminent end. A substantial and growing intellectual class remains committed to the secular enterprise. The Indian judiciary and much of the Indian press also see the need to maintain a secular political dispensation. Nevertheless, the ability of unscrupulous political entrepreneurs to scapegoat minorities, especially Muslims, for India's varied social and economic problems remains a profoundly worrisome trend.

The other threat to the quality of Indian democracy stems from the willingness of both politicians and citizens to flout the rule of law when it appears politically and socially expedient to do so. These breaches range from the lack of tolerance for slow, awkward, and cumbersome legal procedures when dealing with the rights of suspected criminals to the rampant violation of human rights when counterinsurgency operations are afoot. The disregard for both moral norms and established legal procedures is highly corrosive of the basic expectations upon which liberal democracy itself must always rest. Whether or not countervailing civic institutions and a free press can limit and ultimately end these practices remains an open question.

As serious as India's two key barriers to enhanced democratic quality may be, they appear paltry next to those that confront Bangladesh. The Bangladeshi political class has yet to internalize the most basic precepts of a democratic polity. The principal political parties have not accepted the necessity of a loyal opposition. They continue to question electoral outcomes even when there is little doubt about their fairness. The Bangladeshi military refrains from open intervention in politics, but is nevertheless subject to political interference. It has allowed itself to be used as a political instrument rather than acting as a neutral force primarily responsible for the defense of the nation's borders. Bangladesh's inability to protect the rights of women and minorities, and worse still, state complicity in acts of repression against these groups further undermines its nascent democracy. Consequently, enhancing the quality of democracy in Bangladesh will take considerable effort. Bangladeshi democracy remains to be improved beyond a superficial state, and to be consolidated.

NOTES

1. For a popular statement of this position, see Niall Ferguson, *Empire: The Rise and Demise of the British World Order and Lessons for Global Power* (New York: Basic, 2003); the academic argument is made in Myron Weiner, "Introduction," in Samuel Huntington and Myron Weiner, eds., *Understanding Political Development* (Boston: Little Brown, 1987).

2. Allen McGrath, *The Destruction of Pakistan's Democracy* (Karachi: Oxford University Press, 1996).

3. The literature on this subject is vast. One important contribution is James Manor, ed., *Sri Lanka in Change and Crisis* (New York: St. Martin's, 1984).

4. See the excellent treatment of this subject in Veena Kukreja, *Civil-Military Relations in South Asia: Pakistan, Bangladesh and India* (New Delhi: Sage, 1991).

5. For a discussion of this subject see Sumit Ganguly, "Explaining India's Transition to Democracy," in Lisa Anderson, ed., *Transitions to Democracy* (New York: Columbia University Press, 1999).

6. Close to a million individuals perished in the process of partition. However, this violence was largely a consequence of hasty British colonial withdrawal and

not part and parcel of the nationalist movement. On the haste and the lack of preparation for the partition of the British India, see Sir Penderel Moon, *Divide and Quit* (New Delhi: Oxford University Press, 1998).

7. James Manor, "Nehru's Legacy and the Condition of Indian Democracy," *World Policy Journal* 13 (Winter 1996–97): 89–95.

8. For a particularly critical account of these infractions see Christophe Jaffrelot, "Indian Democracy: The Rule of Law on Trial," *India Review* 1 (January 2002): 1.

9. For a detailed description of these policies see Francine Frankel, *India's Political Economy, 1947–2004: The Gradual Revolution* (New York: Oxford University Press, 2005).

10. Pradeep K. Chibber, *Democracy Without Associations: Transformation of the Party System and Social Cleavages in India* (Ann Arbor: University of Michigan Press, 2001), 97–98.

11. Prafulla Ketkar, "Organized Criminal Networks: A Challenge to Indian Democracy," Institute of Peace and Conflict Studies, 7 March 2003, available at *www.ipcs.org.*

12. Garima Singh, "Extortion, Governance and Bihar," Institute of Peace and Conflict Studies, 8 February 2003, available at *www.ipcs.org.*

13. Bahvdeep Kang, Poornima Joshi, and Rajesh Sinha, "The Law vs. the Legislator," *Outlook,* 21 June 2004, 32–42.

14. Tavleen Singh, "Law Long Arm, Late Embrace," 21 September 2003, available at *www.expressindia.com.*

15. For a discussion of some of these concerns see Arvind Verma, "Taking Justice Outside the Courts: Judicial Activism in India," *Howard Journal* 40 (May 2001): 148–65.

16. M.S. Gill, "India: Running the World's Biggest Elections," *Journal of Democracy* 9 (January 1998): 164–68.

17. Sanjay Suri, "Vote for Curry," *Outlook,* 10 May 2004, 24.

18. See, for example, *The Kargil Commission Report* (New Delhi: Sage, 2000). The head of this commission was not a retired judge but a highly respected, retired senior civil servant, K. Subrahmanyam.

19. Uma Chakravarti and Nandita Haksar, *The Delhi Riots: Three Days in the Life of a Nation* (New Delhi: Lancer International, 1987).

20. Lloyd I. Rudolph and Susanne Hoeber Rudolph, "Redoing the Constitutional Design," in Atul Kohli, ed., *The Success of India's Democracy* (Cambridge: Cambridge University Press, 2001).

21. For an extremely careful assessment see P.P. Craig and S.L. Deshpande, "Rights, Autonomy and Process: Public Interest Litigation in India," *Oxford Journal of Legal Studies* 9 (Autumn 1989): 356–73.

22. For a useful discussion of the factors that led to the declaration of the "state of emergency" and its consequences for the Indian polity see Henry Hart, ed., *Indira Gandhi's India: A Political System Re-Appraised* (Boulder, Colo.: Westview, 1976).

23. See Lloyd Rudolph and Susanne Rudolph, "Redoing the Constitutional Design."

24. For an elaboration of Sen's argument see N. Ram, "An Independent Press and Anti-Hunger Strategies: The Indian Experience," in Jean Dreze, Amartya Sen, and Athar Hussain, eds., *The Political Economy of Hunger: Selected Essays* (Oxford: Clarendon, 1995).

25. On the horrors of the Great Leap Forward, see Jasper Becker, *Hungry Ghosts: Mao's Secret Famine* (New York: Henry Holt, 1996).

26. Myron Weiner, *The Child and the State in India* (Princeton: Princeton University Press, 1991), 3.

27. Amy Waldman, "India's Poor Bet Precious Sums on Private Schools," *New York Times,* 15 November 2003, A5.

28. "India Data Profile," World Development Indicators Database, World Bank, August 2004, available at *www.worldbank.org/data/countrydata/countrydata.html.*

` 29. For a discussion of the concept of path dependence see, Steffan Hulten, "The Construction of Path Dependence Theory: Influences from Science and Literature," available at: *www.schumpeter2004.uni-bocconi.it.*

30. Jay Solomon, "Finding the Balance," *Far Eastern Economic Review,* 22 July 2004, 48–49.

31. Granville Austin, *Working a Democratic Constitution: The Indian Experience* (New Delhi: Oxford University Press, 2000).

32. Omar Khalidi, *Khaki and the Ethnic Violence in India* (New Delhi: Three Essays Collective, 2003).

33. For a pioneering study of this process see Robert L. Hardgrave, Jr., *The Nadars of Tamilnad* (Berkeley: University of California Press, 1969).

34. Christophe Jaffrelot, *India's Silent Revolution: The Rise of the Low Castes in North Indian Politics* (Delhi: Permanent Black, 2002); see also Myron Weiner, "The Struggle for Equality: Caste in Indian Politics," in Atul Kohli, *The Success of India's Democracy.*

35. On this point see Kuldeep Mathur, "The State and the Use and Abuse of Coercive Power in India," *Asian Survey* 32 (April 1992): 337–49.

36. See for example on the northeast, Luingam Luithui and Nandita Haksar, *Nagaland File. A Question of Human Rights* (New Delhi: Lancer International, 1984).

37. See Human Rights Watch/Asia report, "India: Arms and Abuses in Indian Punjab and Kashmir," September 1994.

38. Rama Lakshmi, "Gun-Slinging Police Battle Bombay's Mob: Feared Officers Earning Celebrity Status," *Washington Post,* 25 August 2003.

39. For a discussion of the Godhra incident and the growing tide of intolerance against Muslims and other minorities see Sumit Ganguly, "The Crisis of Indian Secularism," *Journal of Democracy* 14 (October 2003): 11–25; see also Siddharth Varadarajan, *Gujarat: The Making of a Tragedy* (New Delhi: Penguin, 2002).

40. Darshan Desai, "The Bogey Fires," *Outlook,* 12 July 2004, 36.

41. Dionne Bunsha, "Justice, Against All the Odds," *The Hindu* (Chennai), 4 December 2003.

42. Press Trust of India, "I'm Pained over Gujarat: Chief Justice of India," *Indian Express* (New Delhi), 2 May 2004.

43. Jean Dreze and Amartya Sen, "Democratic Practice and Social Inequality in India," *Journal of Asian and African Affairs* 37 (March 2002): 6–27.

44. M.N. Srinivas, "The Pangs of Change," *Frontline,* 9–22 August 1997.

45. Jagdish Bhagwati, *India in Transition* (Oxford: Clarendon, 1993).

46. The debate is discussed in the following sources: Gaurav Dutt and Martin Ravallion, "Is India's Economic Growth Leaving the Poor Behind," *Journal of Economic Perspectives* 16 (Summer 2002): 89–108; Angus Deaton, "Adjusted Indian Poverty Estimates," Research Program in Development Studies, Princeton University, 2000.

47. One of the best treatments remains Raonaq Jahan, *Pakistan: Failure in National Integration* (New York: Columbia University Press, 1972).

48. Tazeen M. Murshid, "Democracy in Bangladesh: Illusion or Reality?" *Contemporary South Asia* 4 (July 1995): 193–214.

49. Howard B. Schaffer, "South Asia Faces the Future: Back and Forth in Bangladesh," *Journal of Democracy* 13 (January 2002): 76–83.

50. M. Rashiduzzaman, "Political Unrest and Democracy in Bangladesh," *Asian Survey* 27 (March 1997): 254–68.

51. "Suman Dies from RAB Torture: BSEHR Probe Finds," *New Nation* (Dhaka), 18 July 2004, 1.

52. Howard Schaffer, "South Asia Faces the Future."

53. "Twenty-two Journalists Receive Death Threats from Islamist Zealots," *Daily Star* (Dhaka), 11 July 2004, 1.

54. Bertil Lintner, paper presented at an international workshop on Religion and Security in South Asia, Asia Pacific Center for Security Studies, Honolulu, Hawaii, 19–22 August 2002.

55. M. Rashiduzzaman, "Political Unrest and Democracy in Bangladesh."

56. Jack Snyder, *From Voting to Violence* (New York: W.W. Norton, 2000).

57. For Bangladesh's aid dependence see World Bank, *Global Development Finance: Striving for Stability in Development Finance* (Washington, D.C.: World Bank, 2002).

58. U.S. Department of State, "2002 Country Reports on Human Rights Practices: Bangladesh," Washington, D.C., 2003. Available at *www.state.gov.*

59. For recent examples of the widespread use of torture by the Bangladeshi police and the maltreatment of religious minorities, see the U.S. State Department "2002 Country Reports on Human Rights Practices: Bangladesh."

60. For a discussion of the plight of the Chakmas, a tribal community, primarily located in the Chittagong Hill Tracts, see Amena Mohsin, "Bangladesh" in Michael E.

Brown and Sumit Ganguly, eds., *Fighting Words: Language Policies and Conflict in Asia* (Cambridge: MIT Press, 2003).

61. "Decades-Old Land law Marginalizes Hindus," *OneWorld South Asia,* 14 June 2004; also see the extended and thoughtful discussion of the Vested Property Act in Ali Riaz, *God Willing: The Politics of Islamism in Bangladesh* (Lanham, Md.: Rowman & Littlefield, 2004).

62. Elora Shehabudin, "Beware the Bed of Fire: Gender, Democracy, and the Jama'at-I-Islami in Bangladesh," *Journal of Women's History* 10 (Winter 1999).

63. For a recent discussion of the rise of Islamic zealotry and the seeming unwillingness and inability of the BNP-led regime to curb this trend, see Eliza Griswold, "The Next Islamist Revolution?" *New York Times Magazine,* 23 January 2005, 35–39.

64. See *World Development Indicators* 2002 (Washington, D.C.: World Bank, 2002).

65. "Bangladesh Data Profile," World Development Indicators Database, World Bank, August 2004, available at *www.worldbank.org/data/countrydata/countrydata.html.*

66. Sayed Kamuluddin, "Not Just Alms," *Far Eastern Economic Review,* 20 May 2004.

10

SOUTH KOREA AND TAIWAN

Yun-han Chu and Doh Chull Shin

Yun-han Chu *is Distinguished Research Fellow of the Institute of Political Science at Academia Sinica and professor of political science at National Taiwan University. His recent publications in English include* Consolidating the Third-Wave Democracies *(1997),* China Under Jiang Zemin *(2000), and* The New Chinese Leadership *(2004). He has directed the East Asia Barometer since 2000.* **Doh Chull Shin** *is professor of political science at the University of Missouri at Columbia and the author of* Mass Politics and Culture in Democratizing Korea *(1999). Professor Shin has directed the Korea Democracy Barometer Program since 1988, and is one of the founding members of the East Asia Barometer.*

The Republic of Korea (South Korea) and Taiwan are widely recognized as the two most successful third-wave democracies in Asia.[1] For more than a decade, these two new democracies have regularly held free and competitive elections at all levels of their respective governments. Both nationally and locally, citizens have chosen the heads of the executive branches and the members of the legislatures through regularly scheduled electoral contests. Unlike many countries in the region, moreover, the two countries have peacefully transferred power to opposition parties, the Millennium Democratic Party in Korea and the Democratic Progressive Party in Taiwan. Accordingly, there is little doubt that the political regimes of Korea and Taiwan fully realize the democratic principle of popular sovereignty featuring free and fair elections, universal adult suffrage, and multiparty competition. Less well-established, however, is how well their current regimes realize other important principles of liberal democracy and uphold its basic values, such as freedom, equality, and justice.

   This chapter assesses the progress Korea and Taiwan have made in becoming well-functioning liberal democracies. Conceptually, it focuses on the notion of *liberal democracy*. Substantively, freedom and equality are considered the basic values of liberal democracy. In addition, we examine the accountability of popularly elected leaders to the electorate, the rule of law, and the responsiveness of political leaders and governmental officials to the citizenry as the most fundamental procedural norms of liberal democratic rule. Democratic quality, like beauty, is assumed to lie in the eye of the beholder. Thus the citizenry is assumed to be the best judge of democratic political life. Data from the first wave of the East Asia Barometer (EAB) surveys conducted in Korea and Taiwan enables us to evaluate the quality of democracy from the perspectives of ordinary citizens who experience it on a daily basis.[2]

This chapter is organized into four sections. The first briefly explicates the notion of liberal democracy and identifies its distinct properties, or qualities. The second section reports how well citizens believe their respective regimes perform as liberal democracies. To what extent do the Koreans and the Taiwanese think their current regimes embody all the essential properties of liberal democracy? What particular properties do they perceive to be most or least lacking in the regimes? The third section explores the problems of liberal democratic development from the perspective of popular demand. Finally, the fourth section highlights the dimensions that are most important to the quality of democracy in Korea and Taiwan and identifies the cultural and institutional sources for their democratic underperformance.

Conceptualization and Measurement

The quality of democracy has recently become a subject of increasing and widespread concern in policy circles and the scholarly community.[3] How well do democracies perform as examples of government by the people and for the people? What democratic qualities are most lacking in new democracies? These questions have been raised in response to a growing sense of public discontent with the democratic political process in both old and new democracies.[4]

Universal adult suffrage, free and fair elections, multiparty competition, and party alternation in power are fundamental characteristics of all electoral democracies. In addition to these elements, what constitutes liberal democracy? A liberal democracy is a political system that, substantively, allows for political freedom and equal rights and, procedurally, limits the arbitrary use of governmental authority and power for the benefit of individual citizens.[5]

The norm of individual freedom demands that citizens be free to think, talk, and act in order to formulate and express, individually and collectively, their views in the political process. Furthermore, the norm of political rights demands that individual citizens be treated equally before the law and that their views be weighed equally in the policy-making process. The norm of limited government, on the other hand, requires that democratically elected political leaders as well as state officials observe the rules prescribed in the constitution and other laws and that they serve the interests of the citizenry rather than their own. The same procedural norm also requires that democratically elected government officials be accountable to the legislature and ultimately to voters by making their actions transparent. In short, freedom, equality, the rule of law, accountability, and responsiveness are considered the essential properties or qualities of liberal democracy (see "Introduction" in this volume).

In the Korean 2003 EAB survey, five pairs of questions were asked to determine the extent to which ordinary citizens perceive that their political system has achieved each of the five properties of liberal democracy. Most of these questions, or functional equivalents of them, were also found in Taiwan's 2001 EAB survey and in a more recent island-wide survey.[6]

The Quality of Liberal Democracy

How much progress have Korea and Taiwan made in moving from electoral democracy to liberal democracy? To address this question systematically, we examine the extent to which the current regimes exhibit each of the five essential properties of liberal democracy discussed earlier: freedom, equality, the rule of law, accountability, and responsiveness.

Political Freedom. Both Korea and Taiwan have made giant strides in safeguarding political freedom since the two embarked on democratic transitions in late 1980s. Yet the persistence of some residual elements of the authoritarian era continues to qualify their rating as Free by Freedom House. Korea has been recognized as a Free nation since 1988, and Taiwan achieved that status in 1996 after its first popular election for president. While both countries have come close to getting the best possible score in both political rights and civil liberties by 2005, there are still lingering deficiencies in their respective political systems. For instance, neither Taiwan nor Korea scores very high on Freedom House's press-freedom ratings. In its 2004 freedom-of-the-press survey, which gives results on a 0 (most free) to 100 (least free) scale, Taiwan received 23 and Korea 29, indicating some deficiency in this important domain of political freedom.[7]

Freedoms of the press and of expression in South Korea are generally respected, although provisions in the National Security Law are sometimes used to restrict the propagation of ideas that authorities consider communist or pro–North Korea. In recent years, several journalists have been prosecuted under criminal libel laws for critical or aggressive reporting.[8] All leading newspapers are controlled by or associated with substantial business interests, and some journalists are also susceptible to bribery. Two of the three Korean television networks are publicly owned.[9] Because the government maintains a strong influence in the

appointment of the presidents of those television networks, their neutrality and independence remain controversial.[10]

In Taiwan, the press in general enjoys a much higher degree of freedom than in most of its Asian neighbors. Formal censorship is a thing of
the past. The media sector has been fiercely competitive, especially
since the late 1990s with the mushrooming of cable television news
services, which have substantially reduced the viewership of the three
government-controlled television networks. Many media watchers had
high hopes for the eventual removal of governmental control over the
electronic media after the historic power rotation in 2000, because Chen
Shui-bian made a campaign pledge to turn two government channels
into public television stations. The government stations are owned and
operated by the government, and converting them into public stations
would have allowed them to continue receiving government funding
support, but be independent of the government's direct control. Yet the
new Democratic Progressive Party (DPP) president reneged on his campaign pledge, as people with controversial partisan background were
appointed to head these government-controlled media. Moreover, the
DPP government has subtly muffled critical media through a ginger
allocation of government-controlled advertising funds and the provision of soft loans through government-controlled banks.

In both countries, during the authoritarian years the presence of an
elaborate and ubiquitous security apparatus posed the most serious threat
to political freedom. During Taiwan's democratization, some elements
in the abolished Temporary Articles (the hallmark of the old authoritarian rule), including the emergency powers of the president and the
creation of a National Security Agency under the president, were trans-
planted into the new system. As a result, Taiwan's elaborate intelligence
and security apparatus has preserved most of its status and prerogatives.
Its operations remain opaque to members of parliament. Both Lee Teng-
hui and Chen Shui-bian, when they came to office, chose to retain top
officials of the intelligence and security apparatus to smooth the transition. While these decisions may have been politically savvy, they
blocked the possibility of probing into the security apparatus's history
of unlawful actions against dissidents and illegal surveillance of political figures and opposition parties.[11] Even more disappointing is Chen
Shui-bian's apparent failure to stop the security apparatus, in particular
the National Security Agency and the Investigation Bureau, from continuing their practice of unlawful political surveillance.

After Korea's democratization, on the other hand, the power of the
National Intelligence Service, which had been a major state apparatus of
surveillance and investigation of opposition parties, was much curtailed,
and the agency was kept out of domestic politics. In addition, the National Human Rights Commission Act was legislated in 2001 to monitor
human rights issues. Furthermore, human rights activists, such as Ko Young

Koo and Kang Kum Sil, were appointed to important government positions in the office of the director of the National Intelligence Service and
in the Ministry of Justice, respectively. However, Amnesty International
reports that Korea retains the National Security Law allowing arbitrary
restriction of such political rights as the freedom of expression and association.

In both countries, democratization brought about a notable relax-
ation of governmental control over the organized sector of civil society.
For example, the Korean Federation of Trade Unions and the Korean
Teachers Union obtained legal status in 1999. Yet some mass organizations are not allowed to engage freely in political activities. *Han Chong
Ryun,* the largest university-student association, is banned because of
its antisystemic program, and *Chun Kong Ro,* a nationwide trade union
of low-ranking civil servants, is suppressed and its political activities
are forbidden by law.[12] Discrimination against women and foreign workers still exists, and many trade unionists were harassed and arrested for
strikes and demonstrations they organized against the government's
economic policies, according to Amnesty International. In addition,
most foreign migrant workers who moved to Korea illegally through the
"side-door" are not protected from human rights violations due to their
illegal status.[13]

In Taiwan, democratization triggered a meltdown of existing corporatist arrangements, which had chained many organized sectors to the state as
well as to the ruling party. Even before its defeat in the 2000 presidential
election, the Kuomintang (KMT) had lost control of some of the state-
sanctioned peak interest organizations. After the election, the Labor Union
Law was amended and the provision for singular representation was removed. Since then, the Taiwan Confederation of Trade Unions, the organizational fixture of the independent labor movement, has been legally
recognized. The reelection of the leadership of the Chinese National Federation of Industry in July 2000 spelled the end of the KMT's stranglehold
on peak business organizations. Given the dependency of most trade associations on government subsidies, however, the state bureaucracy still
retains considerable influence over the organized sector of civil society.

How much freedom do ordinary people in Korea and Taiwan experience when they want to talk about politics, form groups or associations
for their personal or communal interests, or take part in demonstrations
and protests?

On freedom of expression, the Korean 2003 EAB asked, "To what
extent do you think people like you are free to express their political
opinions?" One-fifth replied "very free," and an additional three-fifths
replied "somewhat free." On freedom of association, the EAB asked,
"To what extent do you think people like you are free to join the group
they would like to join?" Once again, about one-fifth replied "very
free," while three-fifths replied "somewhat free." As in the case of free-

TABLE 1—INDICES MEASURING THE SPECIFIC QUALITIES OF
LIBERAL DEMOCRACY IN KOREA

QUALITIES	INDEX VALUES (%)										
	1	2	3	4	5	6	7	<4	>4	DIF*	MEAN
FREEDOM	0.4	0.6	8.2	16.9	46.7	17.5	9.7	9.2	73.8	+64.6	(5.0)
EQUALITY	3.0	11.5	36.4	35.6	11.3	2.0	0.3	50.9	13.6	-37.8	(3.5)
RULE OF LAW	6.3	18.9	29.3	33.1	9.8	2.4	0.3	54.5	12.5	-42.0	(3.3)
ACCOUNTABILITY	4.9	6.6	28.7	41.8	14.5	2.7	0.7	40.2	17.9	-22.3	(3.7)
RESPONSIVENESS	5.0	10.3	29.8	27.5	13.6	11.7	2.1	45.1	27.4	-17.7	(3.8)

Source: 2003 East Asia Barometer survey conducted in Korea
Note: Index values are the percentages of the public rating the dimension of democratic quality
of a particular point on the 7-point-scale
*Difference refers to the percentage difference between those scoring higher than the scale
midpoint of 4 and those scoring lower than it.

TABLE 2—INDICES MEASURING THE SPECIFIC QUALITIES OF
LIBERAL DEMOCRACY IN TAIWAN

QUALITIES	INDEX VALUES (%)										
	1	2	3	4	5	6	7	<4	>4	DIF*	MEAN
FREEDOM	0.6	1.2	29.9	21.9	38.9	4.1	3.4	31.7	46.3	+14.6	(4.2)
EQUALITY	6.4	8.8	33.4	24.4	21.3	3.6	2.2	48.5	27.0	-21.5	(3.6)
RULE OF LAW	4.3	14.1	46.1	28.1	6.8	0.5	0.1	64.5	7.4	-57.1	(3.2)
ACCOUNTABILITY	0.4	4.3	21.7	49.1	22.6	1.6	0.4	26.4	24.6	-1.8	(3.9)
RESPONSIVENESS	2.9	3.8	30.8	35.5	25.8	1.2	0.1	37.5	27.0	-10.5	(3.8)

Source: The TEDS 2003 Survey
* For explanation see Table 1.

dom of expression, it is a small minority who feels fully free to form an
organization, although four out of every five Koreans feel at least somewhat free to do so.

In the 2003 Taiwan Election and Democratization Survey (TEDS),
respondents were asked if they agreed or disagreed with the following
statement: "Nowadays everyone can freely criticize the government
without worrying about getting into trouble." Only 6 percent of respondents "strongly agreed," while 51 percent "agreed." About a third of the
respondents worried that criticizing the government might get one into
trouble. On freedom of assembly, the survey asked the respondents if
they agreed or disagreed that "nowadays everyone can freely take part
in protests and demonstrations without worrying about getting into
trouble." The portion of Taiwanese citizens who feel free to protest and
demonstrate is depressingly low. Only 3.3 percent of respondents answered "strongly agree," and 40 percent responded "agree." Forty percent
also worried that doing so might get one into trouble.

To measure the overall level of political freedom experienced by the
people, in each country we combined the responses to the two available
questions and constructed a 7-point index ranging from a low of 1 to a
high of 7. On this index, a score of 1 indicates a perceived absence of
freedom and a score of 7 indicates that people feel fully free. Table 1

reports the mean score on this index and the percentages placed in each of its seven values for the Korean case; Table 2 does the same for Taiwan. The mean in Korea was 5, a score only one step above the midpoint (4) of the scale but two steps below the score indicating full freedom. According to the percentages reported in the table, nearly half (47 percent) of the Korean population scored 5, which indicates being much less than fully free. Only a tenth registered the highest score of 7 on the index. In Taiwan, the mean is 4.2, a score barely above the midpoint. Also, very few people scored above 6. From these findings, it appears that both Koreans and Taiwanese see their respective countries as less than fully free. Two possible reasons might explain why more people in Taiwan feel that the system is not free. First, Taiwan's one-party dominance persisted much longer than Korea's, after their respective founding elections. Second, the increased polarization of the Taiwanese populace over the national identity issue has made people much less tolerant toward others holding opposing political views. As a result, more people experience an intimidating political atmosphere.

Political Equality. In both Korea and Taiwan, in some important respects political equality remains an unfulfilled promise of the new democracies. The ruling party often denies the opposition a level playing field, including equal access to the mass media. Political discrimination against people with particular regional or subethnic backgrounds has been a perennial issue in both countries and remains serious. Gender inequality in politics has long roots in East Asian soil, and the room for improvement remains vast.

As Leonardo Morlino's chapter in this volume indicates, the enforcement of the law has the potential to be used as a weapon against political adversaries and opposition parties. In Taiwan, politically motivated selective prosecution and tax auditing has always been wielded by the ruling party as a potent weapon to intimidate and harass recalcitrant business groups, hostile media, and political enemies. Corruption within the judicial system also exacerbates the problem of unfair enforcement of the law.

In Korea, the government's monopoly on the power to prosecute and the existence of highly politicized prosecutors exacerbate the problem of unfair law enforcement. Ruling parties exploit this situation and threaten opposition parties by prosecuting specifically targeted corrupt members of parliaments (MPs). The partial and uneven law enforcement is deeply rooted in the limited autonomy of the Prosecutors' Office from the influence of the ruling party and the president and in the collusion between politicians and conglomerates in Korea.

The recent disclosure of business conglomerates' illegal financial support, totaling more than US$80 million, for the presidential candidates of two major parties (the ruling *Uri* party and the largest opposition party, the Grand National Party [GNP]) shows the limits of law enforcement in Korea. Although the resulting investigation of suspects including supporters of President Roh Moo Hyun is evidence of some progress in equal law enforcement, the investigation focused excessively on the GNP's acceptance of bribes, and the two major candidates and most of the owners of the conglomerates were suspected but not prosecuted.[14]

Historically, discrimination based on regional or subethnic origin has constituted the most serious barrier to political equality in both countries. In Korea, people from the Honam region (in the southwest) were underrepresented in the nation's elite structure, which was dominated by people from the Youngnam region. In Taiwan, the native Taiwanese were long denied full access to national politics, which was monopolized by the mainlander elite. Although democratization creates opportunities to redress these past injustices and grievances, it also opens up the possibility of reverse discrimination against the formerly dominant groups.

In Korea, the existence of political parties based on regional loyalty led to strong discrimination in the appointment of high-ranking civil servants. Under the authoritarian regime, the Youngnam region was highly overrepresented in the allocation of politically appointed civil servants, whereas the Honam region, the main political base of opposition leader Kim Dae Jung, was significantly underrepresented.[15]

A recent government report about the regional distribution of 120 high-ranking civil servants in the last few decades also confirms the presence of strong regional discrimination.[16] Under the authoritarian Chun Doo Hwan government (1980–88), personnel from the Youngnam region held 41 percent of high-ranking positions while people from Honam occupied only 14 percent. The strong discrimination against Honam personnel did not change until Kim Dae Jung won the 1997 presidential election. Under the Kim Dae Jung government (1997–2002) the portion of Youngnam personnel decreased to 35 percent, whereas that of Honam personnel rapidly increased to 29 percent. Under President Roh Moo Hyun, who succeeded Kim Dae Jung in 2002, Youngnam personnel in the highest government positions decreased to 32 percent, while the proportion of Honam personnel increased slightly. These changes show an improvement in balancing the regional allocation of high-ranking positions in the government. Yet it should also be emphasized that the rapid increase in the number of high-ranking civil servants from the Honam region has intensified the public suspicion that the Honam region is becoming overly represented since the inauguration of Kim Dae Jung.[17]

In Taiwan, democratization has been entangled with the issue of power redistribution away from the mainlander elite (about 15 percent of the population) to the native Taiwanese majority, whose rights of political participation and access to political power were systematically suppressed during the long rule of the mainlander-dominated KMT. Toward the end of his presidency (1978–88), Chiang Ching-kuo adopted a policy of indigenization to salvage the dwindling legitimacy of the KMT, culminating in the decision to nominate Lee Teng-hui, a native Taiwanese, as his official successor in 1984. After the passing of Chiang, the pace of both democratization and indigenization quickened. During his 11-year tenure (1989–2000), Lee brought an end to mainlander dominance in national politics. KMT old-timers were pushed out of the center of power and substantially marginalized. For instance, in 1988, native Taiwanese accounted for only about 34 percent of the 180-member Central Committee of the KMT and only 25 percent of the 316-member parliament, the Legislative Yuan, which had been dominated by life-long mainlander members.[18] By the end of Lee's tenure, native Taiwanese accounted for about two-thirds of the KMT Central Committee. Furthermore, after the first full reelection of the legislature in 1992, the proportion of MPs of Taiwanese native background surged to 85 percent as all the life-long members were forced to retire. Thus, toward the end of Lee's tenure, the leadership stratum of the KMT and the state bureaucracy were thoroughly indigenized in both personnel and ideology, although mainlanders are still overrepresented in the civil service and the professional military corps.

The DPP, which came to power in 2000, built up its electoral support by highlighting the shared sense of suffering and deprivation among the native Taiwanese. Its leadership is overwhelmingly dominated by Fujianese-speaking native Taiwanese, who constitute about 70 percent of the population. As a result, the Hakka-speaking native Taiwanese (about 12 percent), the mainlanders, and the aboriginal minorities have become more sensitive about their minority status and worry about reverse discrimination under DPP rule.

Another source of political inequality is rooted in the sociocultural structure of the two societies. Both Taiwan and Korea inherited a cultural legacy sanctioning a male-dominated social hierarchy. Even though in both countries women were fully enfranchised from the very beginning, the participation of women in politics is a relatively recent phenomenon. The average percentage of female MPs before Korea's democratization in 1988 was only 2.2 percent. Even after its democratization, the figure remained below 3 percent in two consecutive legislative elections. In the 1988 legislative election, the six female MPs accounted for only 2 percent of the total. Then the figure marginally increased to 2.7 percent in the 1992, 4.0 percent in 1996, and 5.9 percent in 2000. Thus the political representation of women remains only a "rhetoric of rights," even though legal discrimination against women has almost been eradicated in Korea.[19]

Women also remain severely underrepresented among high-ranking civil servants.[20] Furthermore, most female civil servants are in only a few departments, such as the Ministry of Women's Equality (61 percent women), the Commission of Youth Protection (32 percent), the National

Police Agency (29 percent), the Food and Drug Administration (27 percent), and the Health and Social Security Department (27 percent).

In the Korean national legislative election of 2004, the proportion of female MPs sharply increased to 13 percent.[21] Furthermore, the Korean government claims that it will increase the proportion of women among high-ranking civil servants to 10 percent.[22] However, the level of political representation of women in Korea is still far from that of some Western democracies such as Canada, Great Britain, Denmark, Norway, and Sweden. Furthermore, even though the ratio of female high-ranking civil servants is increasing, it is still unclear whether politically important positions will ever be open to women. Yet a woman, Park Geun-hye, daughter of the late dictator Park Chung Hee, has recently assumed the leadership of the principal opposition party, the GNP, and may be a serious candidate for president in 2007.

The level of women's participation in politics in Taiwan has been consistently higher than in Korea. The share of female MPs was 14 percent in 1994 and increased to 22 percent in the December 2001 parliamentary elections. In addition, by 2001 women accounted for almost 17 percent of senior civil servants and 43 percent of middle-rank bureaucrats.[23] One of the reasons for Taiwan's higher level of women's participation in politics has been the introduction of various legal means of affirmative action. For example, there is a minimum quota of female members in national and local representative bodies.

From the viewpoint of ordinary citizens, the concept of political equality is represented by equal treatment by the government and before the law. The Korean EAB survey asked a pair of questions addressing this equality. First, "How fairly or unfairly do you think laws are enforced on someone like you these days?" To this question, about three-fifths said they had been treated either "not very fairly" (52 percent) or "not at all fairly" (7 percent). Only 2 percent replied "very fairly." The same survey also asked, "To what extent was the Kim Dae Jung government regionally biased in treating people?" Nearly three-quarters said either "a great deal" (18 percent) or "somewhat" (55 percent).

A similar, but not identical, pair of questions was asked in Taiwan's 2003 TEDS survey. First, respondents were asked, "How likely do you think common people are to get fair treatment when they deal with government agencies?" More than half of the respondents answered either "somewhat unlikely" (43 percent) or "very unlikely" (11 percent). When they were asked the likelihood of "'common people' getting a fair trial from the court when they are involved in litigation," considerably more respondents gave an unfavorable answer than a favorable one (48 percent versus 35 percent).

Again we combined these two items into a 7-point index. For Korea, the combined ratings average 3.5, a score below the midpoint of the scale (see Table 1). For Taiwan, the mean score is 3.6 (see Table 2). The two scores, and the distributions of responses, indicate that ordinary citizens in Korea and Taiwan perceive their systems to be somewhat unfair and unequal. Such common perceptions of political inequality contrast sharply with those of political freedom. Fewer than 6 percent in either country perceive a high level of political equality (as indicated by a score of 6 or 7 on the index).

The Rule of Law. Korea and Taiwan have an advantage over most third-wave democracies in that both acquired modern, rational-legal, competent bureaucracies before they were democratized. Thus from the start the two democracies had one of the minimum requirements for establishing the rule of law. Yet a daunting challenge remains for both countries, as the rule of law also requires establishing civilian control over the military. Korea's new democracy has to clean up a legacy of direct military intervention into political and civil affairs and entrenched factionalism within the officer corps. Genuine civilian control was not achieved until the presidency of Kim Young Sam (1994–99).[24]

On the eve of Taiwan's democratic transition in 1986, the military played an active role in domestic politics and enjoyed considerable prerogatives by virtue of its role implementing martial law. During the 1990s, the armed forces have largely withdrawn from the domestic political sphere, as active military officers no longer serve in the civilian government, the military no longer oversees internal security, and the organizational links between the military and the KMT have steadily dissolved. The passage of the National Defense Law in 2000 and the growing oversight role of the Legislative Yuan have strengthened the institutions of democratic control.[25] The military was finally forced to eliminate its remaining ties with the KMT after the historic power turnover of 2000.

In Taiwan, a unique hurdle to the rule of law is the slow growth of constitutionalism. The credibility, legitimacy, and integrity of the existing constitutional order have been under severe strain. In the past, KMT-initiated constitutional changes carried too many elements of unilateral imposition and short-term partisan calculation to give the new democratic institutions the kind of broadly based legitimacy that a constitution in a consolidated democracy normally enjoys. There is an acute lack of consensus among the contending political forces over both the nature and logic of the emerging constitutional order.[26] During democratization, the opposition fundamentally challenged the legitimacy of the existing constitutional order. The DPP had long vowed to abolish the existing constitution, which it viewed as the quintessential legal embodiment of the one-China principle. (The current constitution was originally adopted in 1947 when the Nationalist government still exercised effective governance over most of mainland China.) Instead, the DPP has persistently favored the adoption of a new constitution reflecting the general will of the Taiwanese people.

Another major task in fulfilling the basic requirements of the rule of law is to develop an independent judicial system. In both countries, allegations of politically motivated selective prosecution against recalcitrant business groups, hostile media, and political enemies abound. Also, corruption within the judicial system continues to erode popular confidence in the impartiality of the courts.

In both countries, an even more serious corrosive factor is corruption among politicians, senior government officials, and rank-and-file civil servants at both national and local levels. The Korean EAB survey used a pair of questions concerning the extent of corrupt practices by local and national government officials. When asked about the extent of corruption among those officials at the national level of government, nearly one-half perceived corruption in either "almost all" (9 percent) or "most" (38 percent) of the people working on that level, and similar proportions perceived all or most local officials to be corrupt. Considering responses to the two questions together, more than one-third (35 percent) perceived corruption by most or almost all national and local government officials. Yet a substantial minority (44 percent) did not perceive widespread corruption among local or national government officials.

Perceptions of corruption are even higher in Taiwan. When Taiwanese were asked in 2001 about the extent of corruption among officials at the national level of government, 8 percent of the respondents perceived corruption in "almost everyone," and 58 percent of them perceived that "most" officials are corrupt. Concerning local government officials, about 7 percent of respondents perceived that "almost everyone" is corrupt and close to two-thirds (63 percent) considered "most" to be corrupt. When the two responses are combined, close to three-fifths perceived most or almost all national and local government officials to be corrupt.

In both countries, one of the structural sources of widespread corruption is the high expenses of electoral campaigns. Elected politicians are constantly looking for opportunities to replenish their campaign coffers. In Korea, MPs are easily seduced into corrupt schemes or become dependent on financial support from party leaders who systemically collect and distribute "dirty money" to their members.[27] In Taiwan, elected representatives feel compelled to find ways to pay back the local factions and fat-cat donors that sponsored their political careers. Both countries have also experienced recurring scandals involving collusion between big business and elected politicians. Korean presidents under both authoritarian and democratic regimes were imprisoned on charges of accepting bribes and kickbacks from large conglomerates, in sums up to as high as US$900 million.[28] Also in Korea, democratically elected president Kim Dae Jung was suspected of illegally spending US$100 million of taxpayers' money in pursuit of a Nobel Peace Prize (through payments to North Korean dictator Kim Jong Il), and his sons were arrested for taking bribes.[29] In Taiwan, it is no secret that in every presidential election millions of dollars in unreported contributions are handed over by big-business donors to candidates.

Widespread corruption is intimately linked to the practice among high-ranking officials of breaking rules and ignoring legal procedures. In Korea, under the "imperial" presidential system, legal decision-making procedures for governmental policy have been ignored frequently. As the case of financial payments to North Korea under the Kim Dae Jung government shows, presidents often resort to illegal methods to achieve their policy goals, especially in the area of national security. Furthermore, the abuse of presidential power has often led to corruption scandals involving presidents' relatives. Both Kim Young Sam and Kim Dae Jung witnessed their sons' imprisonment during their presidencies. In Taiwan, one of President Lee Teng-hui's closest aids was charged with a series of criminal offenses for allegedly soliciting kickbacks for arranging soft loans from state-controlled banks. The wife of President Chen Shui-bian was also recently implicated in insider trading.

To examine the popular perception of the extent to which laws are observed in the policy-making process, two questions were selected from the eight about the rule of law on the Korean 2003 EAB survey. The first question concerns the extent to which the office of the president abides by the laws. The second question addresses the extent to which the National Assembly does. Less than half the Korean population (49 percent) replied that the presidential office tends to follow rather than to break laws. About the National Assembly, less than one-fifth (17 percent) replied that it tends to follow rather than to break laws. Strikingly, less than 1 percent (only four out of 1,500 respondents) rated both institutions as fully law-abiding.

When Taiwanese were asked in 2003 if they agreed or disagreed that "generally speaking, the officials of the national government are abiding by the law and are not doing illegal things," only 1.3 percent of the respondents answered "strongly agree" and 30 percent answered "agree." When asked if they agreed or disagreed that "nowadays politicians will do anything to grab power and positions," only 0.9 percent of the respondents "strongly disagreed" and 9 percent of them "disagreed." Most Taiwanese gave their democracy a very low rating on conformity to the rule of law in the political process.

Again we combined the two responses for each country into a 7-point index (see Tables 1 and 2). In Korea, ratings of the two democratically elected institutions averaged 3.3, significantly lower than the midpoint of the scale. Those reporting scores below the midpoint number are more than four times more numerous than those reporting scores above it (55 percent versus 13 percent). Although different questions were used, the results from Taiwan are strikingly similar. The mean score is 3.2. More than eight times as many scores are below the midpoint than are above it (64 percent versus 7 percent). These mean scores and percentages make it clear that citizens in the two countries perceive significant deficiencies in the rule of law.

Accountability. Regular popular elections provide the citizens with only a limited mechanism for holding political leaders accountable. There are many ways government leaders can avoid accountability.[30] In a poor-quality democracy, the citizen casts his or her vote and is subsequently ignored until the next election. Unless there are other mechanisms and institutions that are capable of enforcing transparency and horizontal accountability, citizens are left with no effective means of controlling corruption and bad government.

In both Taiwan and Korea, the mechanisms of horizontal accountability are not well-developed. The parliament typically lacks adequate institutional power to check the president and oversee the operation of the executive branch. In Taiwan, the constitutional amendment of 1997 took away the parliament's power to confirm the appointment of the premier by the president. While the new amendment empowered the parliament to unseat the sitting cabinet with a vote of no confidence, it also gave the president the option of dissolving parliament in that circumstance. In practical terms, the competitiveness and high campaign cost of Taiwan's electoral system make members of the parliament very reluctant to use the no-confidence vote, rendering this institutional tool almost useless.[31] In the end, the premier, who is formally the head of the government and constitutionally accountable to the parliament, is reduced to nothing more than the president's dispensable political shield.[32]

Furthermore, under the five-branch constitutional design, the budgetary power of Taiwan's parliament (the Legislative Yuan) is reduced by its lack of auditing authority. The auditing power belongs to the Control Yuan, which is functionally equivalent to an independent ombudsman. The Legislative Yuan's power to supervise the Executive Yuan is hampered by its lack of powers of investigation, which are also the prerogative of the Control Yuan.[33]

In Korea, the parliament has made various attempts to legislate the provision of information about governing procedures to the public. The legislation of the investigation hearing in 1988, the revised laws of Civil Servants Ethics in 1993, the Information Disclosure Act in 1997, and the confirmation hearing in 2000 have improved democratic accountability in Korea. As the case of Kim Dae Jung's financial support for North Korea shows, however, the information provided to the public is very limited and the process of policy making remains a murky area for citizens.[34] The legacy of the authoritarian regime leads to secret patterns of policy-making.[35]

Parliamentary hearings are held for the confirmation of very few positions in Korea, including the prime minister, justices of the Supreme Court, the director of the Office of National Tax Administration, and the chief of the prosecutor's office. Many high-ranking civil-servant appointments are made as rewards for contributions during presidential campaigns.[36] In addition, the short term of regular parliamentary sessions makes it hard for MPs to examine and discuss thoroughly draft legislation before voting. The lack of a roll-call voting system, which would allow more accurate information on MPs, and the small number of standing committees exacerbate the shortcomings of democratic accountability in Korea. Furthermore, the lack of television networks like C-SPAN in the United States limits people's information on the performance of their MPs.[37]

While the effectiveness of horizontal accountability is usually beyond the comprehension of ordinary citizens, the extent to which politicians are (vertically) held accountable to the voters is much closer to their experiences.

Only in democracies can citizens vote against incumbents and throw the rascals out. This practice enables the voters to hold elected officials accountable for their actions.[38] To hold officials accountable, however, voters must be informed about what officials do. To what extent do the Korean people think that their political leaders are accountable to ordinary voters like themselves through voter awareness of leaders' actions? To estimate the level of such vertical accountability, the 2003 Korean EAB survey asked a pair of questions, one on governmental efforts to cover up illegal and corrupt practices and the other on the extent to which the government allows the public to see what its various agencies do.

When asked about the government covering up illegal and corrupt practices, a majority replied that the government does so "always" (12 percent) or "very often" (42 percent). A plurality (43 percent) said "sometimes," and a negligible minority (4 percent) said "rarely." In Korean political circles, covering up bad practices appears to be commonplace and not a rare phenomenon. When asked about the openness of government agencies to the public, only about one-third of Koreans perceived "a lot" (2 percent) or "some" (30 percent) openness. More than two-thirds, on the other hand, said that government agencies were not very open to the public (60 percent) or not at all open to it (8 percent). Political leaders of the ruling party attempt to cover up their illegal actions, and government agencies try to keep the public from seeing what goes on within them. Given these practices, one can conclude that elected officials seek to avoid accountability to the electorate.

In Taiwan's 2003 TEDS survey, a different pair of questions was used to measure citizens' evaluations of the effectiveness of vertical accountability and the transparency of decision making. In response to the statement, "The holding of regular elections compels the government leaders not to defy what the majority wishes when making decisions," 5 percent of the respondents answered "strongly agree" and 57 percent of them "agree." In response to the statement, "Nowadays government leaders try to put all important matters out of the sight of the public," 5.8 percent of our respondents answered "strongly agree" and 57 percent of them answered "agree." This suggests that while a majority of Taiwan's citizens do feel that regular elections are effective in compelling government leaders to respect public opinion, they lament the rather low transparency of the decision-making process.

When the responses to the two questions are considered together, Korean democracy appears to suffer from weak accountability. On a 7-point index ranging from a low of 1 to a high of 7, the Korean people as a whole reported a very low average score of 3.7. Those who scored accountability lower than the midpoint exceed those who scored it higher by a margin of more than two to one (40 percent versus 18 percent). Taiwan's democracy fares slightly better on the accountability dimension, although it is measured by a different pair of questions. The mean score is close to 4.0. The responses to the second questions on both surveys, which were comparable, demonstrated that citizens in the two countries gave their respective system rather low marks on openness and transparency.

Responsiveness. From the demand side, in both Korea and Taiwan emerging civil societies and the development of Internet media promote democratic responsiveness by organizing public demand for good governance. Also, the prevalence of public-opinion polls provides benchmarks against which the popularity of leaders and their policies can be gauged on a regular basis. From the supply side, however, the state's overall capacity in the provision of a stable and enabling environment is severely constrained by the forces of globalization, as was made clear in the 1997 regional financial crisis. Limited financial resources and the absence of sufficient public support for the ruling parties have made it difficult to reduce higher unemployment rates and widened income inequality since the 1997 crisis. The situation is more acute in Taiwan where the accumulated public-sector debt is fast approaching an unsustainable level.[39]

Furthermore, in both countries, an "imperial" (semi)presidential system makes it difficult to improve democratic responsiveness by promoting the personalization of politics. The underdevelopment of disciplined political parties in Korea and the arcane single nontransferable vote (SNTV) system for parliamentary elections in Taiwan each in its own way makes it difficult to mediate political supply and demand.

In the eyes of ordinary citizens, to what extent is the democratically elected government in Korea responsive to its citizens? To address this general question, the 2003 survey asked the extent to which respondents agreed or disagreed with two specific statements regarding the government's responsiveness to the mass citizenry. Presented with the statement, "The nation is run by a powerful few and ordinary citizens cannot do much about it," three-fifths rated their government as unresponsive to the people by agreeing with the statement either "strongly"

(12 percent) or "somewhat" (48 percent). In response to the statement, "People like me don't have any influence over what the government does," three-fifths also rated Korean democracy as unresponsive, agreeing with the statement "strongly" (12 percent) or "somewhat" (47 percent).

In the 2003 Taiwan survey, a slightly different pair of questions was used. The first asked people if they agreed that "government officials don't really care what people like me think." Next, our respondents were asked if they agreed that "the officials of the national government don't know what the people at the grassroots really need." On the first question, a majority (54 percent) rated Taiwan's democracy as responsive, answering either "disagree" (52 percent) or "strongly disagree" (2 percent). On the second question, however, only about 29 percent of Taiwanese rated the system as responsive, by "agreeing" (28 percent) or "strongly agreeing" (1 percent) with the statement.[40]

To measure the overall level of governmental responsiveness, we combined responses to the two questions into our standard 7-point index. Both Korea and Taiwan fall just below the midpoint, with mean scores of 3.8. For Korea, the proportion above the midpoint constitutes 27 percent, while almost half (45 percent) fall below it. In Taiwan, 27 percent are above the midpoint and 38 percent below it (Tables 1 and 2). Thus, in strikingly similar fashion, majorities in Korea and Taiwan believe that their democracies fall well short of being responsive systems.[41]

What properties of liberal democracy are most and least apparent in the two new democracies today? The means and summary percentages reported in Tables 1 and 2 can be compared to address this question. For Korean democracy, of the five mean ratings reported in Table 1, political freedom, which scored 5.0, is the only property of liberal democracy that scored higher than the midpoint. Of the four properties with average ratings below the midpoint, responsiveness ranks best with 3.8. This property is followed by accountability (3.7), equality (3.5), and the rule of law (3.3). For Taiwanese democracy, political freedom (which scored 4.2) is also the only property of liberal democracy to score higher than the midpoint. Of the four properties with average ratings below the midpoint, accountability ranks best with 3.9, followed by responsiveness (3.8), equality (3.6), and the rule of law (3.2). Thus, in both countries, citizens tend to perceive a low-quality liberal democracy that is deficient in most dimensions of democratic quality. Except in terms of political freedom, both Korea and Taiwan have failed to make significant progress toward liberal democracy in the eyes of their people.

Popular Demand for Liberal Democracy

For years, Korea and Taiwan have been known as two of the most successful democratic transitions in the current wave of global democratization. Why have these two new democracies failed to transform their electoral democracies into high-quality liberal democracies? One answer to this question assigns sole responsibility to political leaders and institutions, which have failed to supply the key properties of liberal democracy. After all, as discussed above, political leaders and government agencies in Korea all too often engaged in illegal and corrupt practices that they later attempted to cover up. According to the people, leaders and agencies are neither accountable for their actions nor responsive to what their voters demand.

Taiwan's citizens are also very cynical toward similar conduct of elected leaders. A great majority of them see widespread corruption at both national and local levels of government and consider their new democracy to be far from responsive. Undoubtedly, such undemocratic behavior by those who supply leadership in the democratic political marketplace has hindered progress in the two countries' march toward liberal democracy.[42] In both countries, however, the failure to become a high-quality liberal democracy involves much more than an inadequate supply provided by political leaders and institutions. It also has a great deal to do with what the people demand from those leaders and institutions.[43] As Amartya Sen notes, "In a democracy, people tend to get what they demand, and more crucially, do not typically get what they do not demand."[44] For a satisfactory account of democratization in Korea and Taiwan, therefore, we need to consider the contours and dynamics of demand for liberal democracy from the mass public.

How strongly do the Korean and Taiwanese people demand the creation of liberal democracy in their countries? To find out, we consider whether and how much they prefer liberal democratic methods to authoritarian ones. We assume that a preference for the former indicates a demand for liberal democracy. How strongly do the Korean and Taiwanese people endorse the principles of liberal democracy over those of an authoritarian government? To address these questions, the EAB asked three pairs of questions in each country, dealing with different aspects of liberal democratic governance. One pair deals with the rule of law, one with the separation of powers, and one with the values of political freedom and rights.

In Korea, more than three-quarters (77 percent) of respondents expressed opposition to the arbitrary use of power by the government, disagreeing with the statement, "When the country is facing a difficult situation, it is alright for the government to disregard the law in order to deal with the situation." An equally large majority (77 percent) also expressed opposition to the age-old illiberal practice of justifying illegal means by favorable ends. They disagreed with the statement, "The most important thing for a political leader is to accomplish his goals even if he has to ignore established procedures." The results from Taiwan are quite similar. More than two-thirds (68 percent) of Taiwanese respondents expressed disagreement with the first statement, and an overwhelming majority (86 percent) disagreed with the second statement. Considering these responses together reveals that in both countries a substantial majority (63 percent in Korea and 62 percent in Taiwan) is fully committed to the liberal constitutionalism of a *Rechtsstaat,* a law-bound state.[45]

By sharp contrast, in both countries a substantial majority (61 percent in Korea and 78 percent in Taiwan) is not fully committed to the liberal principle of separating executive and nonexecutive powers and maintaining checks and balances among them. In Korea, about two-thirds (69 percent) endorsed the separation of powers by disagreeing with the statement, "When judges decide important cases, they should accept the view of the executive branch." A significantly smaller majority (54 percent) endorsed legislative checks on the executive branch by disagreeing with the statement, "If the government is constantly checked by the legislature, it cannot possibly accomplish great things." Yet those who voiced liberal responses to both of these questions constitute less than two-fifths (38 percent) of the Korean electorate.

Taiwan's data show a similar pattern but with an even wider gap between the two measures. A much greater share of Taiwanese respondents endorsed the principle of an independent judiciary (70 percent) than approved of the principle of parliamentary oversight (30 percent). This dramatic contrast is consistent with previous findings that Taiwan's citizens register a depressingly low level of institutional trust in the parliament while upholding a moderate level of trust in the courts.[46] Considering the two measures together, less than a quarter (22 percent) of Taiwanese gave pro-liberal responses to both of these questions. Obviously, in both countries many citizens who accept the liberal principle of constitutional rule nevertheless favor a powerful executive instead of the separation of powers.

When it comes to popular commitment to the liberal-democratic values of political freedom and respect for minority rights, about 52 percent of Taiwanese respondents show a full commitment. In Korea, however, a much smaller proportion of just one-quarter (25 percent) embrace these two liberal-democratic values. In Korea, more than three-fifths (62 percent) endorse political freedom, agreeing with the statement, "A political leader should tolerate the views of those who challenge his political ideals." One-half (50 percent) embrace the value of minority rights, disagreeing with the statement, "As long as a political leader enjoys majority support, he should implement his own agenda and disregard the view of the minority." Overall, three-quarters (75 percent) fail to endorse both political freedom and minority rights. In Taiwan, about 81 percent of the people embrace the value of political freedom, while less than two-thirds (57 percent) are committed to minority rights. The Taiwanese who are not committed to both political freedom and minority rights constitute a substantial minority of 48 percent.

In both countries, the proportion of citizens who are fully in favor of liberal-democratic governance varies considerably across the three dimensions that we included on the surveys. In Korea, a substantial majority of more than three-fifths (63 percent) fully favors the rule of law. In sharp contrast, a minority of less than two-fifths (38 percent) favors limited government by embracing both the principle of independent judiciary and the principle of checks and balances. An even smaller minority of one-quarter (25 percent) fully endorses the values of political freedom and minority rights.

In Taiwan, a substantial majority of more than three-fifths (62 percent) is fully in favor of the rule of law. More than half (52 percent) fully endorses the values of political freedom and minority rights. In sharp contrast, a minority of less than one-quarter (22 percent) embraces both the separation of powers and checks and balances. Neither the Korean people nor the Taiwanese people have fully internalized the important values and norms of liberal democracy. In Korea, beyond the rule of law, citizens remain more uncommitted than committed to liberal democracy. In Taiwan, people are divided over the values of political freedom and minority rights while showing a low level of commitment to the separation of powers.

In the figure below, we explore the overall commitment of the people to liberal democracy by counting their pro-liberal responses to the six separate questions discussed above for both countries. In Korea, those who voiced pro-liberal responses to all six questions constitute less than one-tenth (9 percent). Three times as many (27 percent) expressed pro-liberal responses to five of the six questions. Thus less than two-fifths (36 percent) are fully or nearly fully committed to liberal democracy. Slightly less than one-half (47 percent) are moderately committed to liberal democracy, with pro-liberal responses to three or four of the six questions. Those who are completely uncommitted or barely committed to it, on the other hand, make up less than one-fifth (16 percent). According to the mean score reported in the figure, the average Korean endorsed slightly less than four (3.9) out of six essential norms of liberal democracy, rejecting two of them.

Analysis of the Taiwanese EAB reveals a similar distribution. Among the Taiwanese electorate, people who gave pro-liberal responses to all six questions constitute slightly more than one-tenth (11 percent). About a quarter of our respondents (26 percent) expressed pro-liberal responses to five of the six questions. Thus, in Taiwan the percentage of people who are fully or nearly fully committed to liberal democracy (36 percent) is identical to that of Korea. The percentage of Taiwanese citizens who are moderately committed to liberal democracy with pro-liberal responses to three or four of the six questions is also highly comparable with the Korean figure (50 percent versus 48 percent). In Taiwan, those who are completely uncommitted or barely committed to it, on the other hand, make up less than one-sixth (13 percent). According to the mean score

FIGURE—LEVELS OF SUPPORT FOR LIBERAL DEMOCRACY IN
KOREA AND TAIWAN

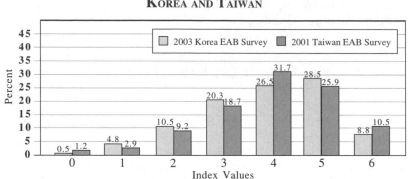

reported in the figure, the average Taiwanese endorsed exactly four of the six essential norms of liberal democracy. On the basis of these findings, we can reasonably conclude that in both Korea and Taiwan liberal democracy is not in high demand among a large majority of the citizens. The insufficiency of such demand must be considered a powerful force working against liberal democratic development in the two new democracies.

Summary and Conclusions

This study has focused on the question of how well a democratic regime performs as a liberal democracy. The essential properties of a liberal democracy are political freedom, citizen equality, the accountability of popularly elected leaders to the electorate, the rule of law, and the responsiveness of political leaders and governmental officials to the citizenry. We propose that a democracy becomes a high-quality liberal democracy when ordinary citizens perceive all of these properties. Analysis of the first wave of the EAB survey conducted in Korea and Taiwan reveals that the perceived quality of democracy is a multi-dimensional subjective phenomenon. Moreover, collective perceptions of quality vary a great deal from one dimension to another, and from one domain to another even within the same dimension. We found that the quality of a democratic regime, especially in terms of liberal democracy, depends on both a popular demand for and an elite supply of these essential properties. That combination of high supply and high demand may constitute the most intractable task of democratization.

The answer to the question of why people in South Korea and Taiwan have not yet fully embraced the principles of liberal democracy over those of authoritarianism lies in the two countries' rather similar authoritarian legacies. People in South Korea and Taiwan experienced a variant of soft authoritarianism that seemed less corrupt and more efficacious in delivering national security, social stability, and economic prosperity. Facing this historical legacy, democracy will have a more difficult time winning over the hearts of a great majority of the mass public.[47] This common historical legacy also explains the relatively low level of popular satisfaction with overall democratic performance. In this sense, both South Korea and Taiwan are burdened with authoritarian nostalgia, generating unreasonably high expectations about the performance of the new democratic regimes.[48]

Last but not least, deficiency in the existing institutional arrangements is also partially responsible for the undersupply of many essential properties of liberal democracy in the two countries. In both countries, the constitutions are weak on horizontal accountability, leaving the legislative branches without the necessary institutional power to check the imperial presidency and oversee the operation of the executive branch. In both countries, the term of the parliament and that of the presidency are not harmonized, which inevitably increases the frequency of divided government and the resultant political gridlock, while making the issue of political accountability much more complicated. In both countries, presidential electoral systems without thresholds or runoffs (which would guarantee the election of a president with a majority mandate) have produced two predictable outcomes: the fragmentation of major political parties and the election of minority presidents. Both countries desperately need more serious attempts to strengthen the legal deterrents against corruption by elected politicians. Both need more rigorous regulations on campaign finance and financial disclosures to arrest the encroachment of money into politics. At the same time, it is imperative to strengthen the independence and integrity of the judicial branch to make it less susceptible to political influence. Without this, a systematic crackdown on the unethical conduct of elected politicians will remain an elusive goal.

NOTES

1. Yun-han Chu, Larry Diamond, and Doh Chull Shin, "Halting Progress in Korea and Taiwan," *Journal of Democracy* 12 (January 2001): 122–36; Larry Diamond and Marc F. Plattner, eds., *Democracy in East Asia* (Baltimore: Johns Hopkins University Press, 1998); and Doh Chull Shin and Junhan Lee, "Comparing Democratization in the East and the West," *Asia Pacific* 3 (May 2003): 40–49.

2. In Taiwan, the first round of the East Asia Barometer was administered in July and August 2001. In Korea, it was administered during February 2003. In both instances, face-to-face surveys were conducted by trained interviewers and based on a stratified probability sampling in accordance with the probability proportional to size (PPS) principle. More technical details are available at *www. eastasiabarometer.org*.

3. Larry Diamond, *Developing Democracy: Toward Consolidation* (Baltimore: Johns Hopkins University Press, 1999); The United Nations Development Programme, *Human Development Reports* (New York: Oxford University Press, 2002); and Leonardo Morlino, *South European Society & Politics* 8 (Winter 2003): 1–32.

4. Pippa Norris, ed., *Critical Citizens* (Oxford: Oxford University Press, 1999); Susan J. Pharr and Robert D. Putnam, eds., *Disaffected Democracies* (Princeton: Princeton University Press, 2000); Richard Rose and Doh Chull Shin, "Democratization Backwards: The Problem of Third Wave Democracies," *British Journal of Political Science* 31 (April 2001): 331–54; and Michael Bratton, Robert Mattes, and E. Gyimah-Boadi, *Learning About Reform: People, Democracy, and Markets in Africa* (New York: Cambridge University Press, 2003).

5. Larry Diamond, *Developing Democracy*; C.B. Macpherson, *The Life and Times of Liberal Democracy* (New York: Oxford University Press, 1977); Fareed Zakaria, *The Future of Freedom: Illiberal Democracy at Home and Abroad* (New York: W.W. Norton & Company, 2003).

6. The last survey was conducted in the summer of 2003 under the auspices of the Taiwan Election and Democratization Survey (TEDS) Committee, sponsored by the Center for Social Science of the National Science Council.

7. In freedom-of-the-press rankings the scores from 0 to 30 denote Free; 31–60, Partly Free; and 61–100, Not Free. See *www.freedomhouse.org*.

8. Aili Piano and Arch Puddington, eds., *Freedom in the World 2004* (New York: Rowman & Littlefield, 2005), 169–70.

9. Heung Kil Koh, "Broadcast: 'Public' or 'Governmental'?" (in Korean), *Kwanhoon Journal* (2003).

10. Kuen Hwang, "Reforming the Press" (in Korean), in Dae Hwa Jung et al., eds., *The Analysis of Reforms under Kim Dae Jung's Government* (Seoul: Geejung, 1998), 277.

11. Yun-han Chu and Larry Diamond, "Anatomy of Taiwan's Political Earthquake," *Journal of East Asian Studies* 1 (February 2001).

12. Mingahyup, "Let off Political Prisoners" (in Korean), *Soshikji* 5 (June 2004), 152.

13. Dong-Hoon Seol and Geon-Soo Han, "Foreign Migrant Workers and Social Discrimination in Korea," *Harvard Asia Quarterly* 8 (Winter 2004): 45–50.

14. For the corruption scandal, a total of 13 MPs and two conglomerate entrepreneurs were imprisoned. *Moonhwa Ilbo,* (Seoul), 21 May 2004; *Hankyurae Shinmoon,* (Seoul), 12 April 2004.

15. Man Soek Jung, "Politically Appointed Civil Servants in Korea" (in Korean), *Insahaengjung* 7 (2001). Available at *www.csc.go.kr*.

16. Republic of Korea Civil Service Commission, 2003.

17. Hyuck Jae Son, "Reforming the Assembly" (in Korean), in Dae Hwa Jung et al., *The Analysis of Reforms under Kim Dae Jung's Government*.

18. Tef-fu Huang, "Elections and the Evolution of Kuomintang," in Hung-mao Tien, ed., *Taiwan's Politics and Democratic Transition* (Armonk, N.Y.: M.E. Sharpe, 1996).

19. Hyun Hee Kim, "Women, an Alternative Political Force" (in Korean), *Economy and Society* 52 (2001), 230.

20. Women made up only 6.4 percent in 2003, according to figures from the Republic of Korea Civil Service Commission, 2004.

21. *Jungang Ilbo* (Seoul), 27 April 2004.

22. Republic of Korea Civil Service Commission, 2004.

23. Cheong-lin Chang, "The State of Women's Participation in Politics and its Outlook" (in Chinese), NPF Research Report No. 17 (Taipei: National Policy Foundation, 2003).

24. Kie-Duck Park, "Civil-Military Relations in Korea," paper delivered at Regional Seminar on Civil-Military Relations in Asia, organized by the Partnership of Democratic Governance and Security, Manila, 22–24 March 1999.

25. Tayler Fravel, "Civil-Military Relation and the Consolidation of Taiwan's Democracy," paper presented at the International Workshop on Challenges to Taiwan's Democracy in the Post-Hegemonic Era, sponsored by the Institute for National Policy Research, Taipei, 7–8 June 2002.

26. Yun-han Chu, "Consolidating Democracy in Taiwan: From *Guoshi* to *Guofa* Conference," in Hung-mao Tien and Steve Yui-sang Tsang, eds., *Democratization in Taiwan: Implications for China* (New York: St. Martin's, 1998).

27. Dae Hwa Jung, "Distorted Political Reform, Delayed Party Reform" (in Korean), in Dae Hwa Jung et al., *The Analysis of Reforms under Kim Dae Jung's Government*, 137.

28. Doh Chull Shin, *Mass Politics and Culture in Democratizing Korea* (New York: Cambridge University Press, 1999), 208.

29. Sung-Su Bang, "More Allegations Backs HMN's W400 Billion Scandal," *Digital Chosunilbo* (Seoul, English edition), 7 December 2002; "DJ Reviewed and Ordered the Transfer of $100 Million to North Korea," *Donga Ilbo* (Seoul), 20 August 2003; and "The President Apologises," *The Economist*, 11 May 2002.

30. J.A. Maravall, "Surviving Accountability," Jean Monnet Chair Paper, (Florence: European University Institute, 1997).

31. Under the single non-transferable vote (SNTV) system, a system that is unique to Taiwan now that Japan has abandoned it, voters are allowed to vote for only a single candidate in multi-seat district, and the excess votes of popular candidates cannot be transferred to other candidates on the same party ticket in the district.

32. Jih-wen Lin, "Institutionalized Uncertainty and Governing Crises in the post-Hegemonic Taiwan," *Journal of East Asian Studies* 3 (September 2003).

33. Shiow-duan Hawang, "The New Parameters of Legislative Politics," paper presented at the International Workshop on Challenges to Taiwan's Democracy in the Post-Hegemonic Era, Institute for National Policy Research, Taipei, 7–8 June 2002.

34. The special prosecutor for the secret financial support for North Korea disclosed that the Kim Dae Jung government illegally provided US$100 million to North Korea just before the summit between Kim Dae Jung and Kim Jung Il in 2000. *Donga Ilbo*, 26 June 2003.

35. Kuen Hwang, "Reforming the Press," 291.

36. Pan Soek Kim, "Appointment" (in Korean), in Sae Il Park, ed., *The Presidency in Korea: Role, Power, and Accountability* (Seoul: East Asia Institute, 2003), 296.

37. Hyuck Jae Son, "Reforming the Assembly" (in Korean), in Dae Hwa Jung et al., *The Analysis of Reforms under Kim Dae Jung's Government*, 173.

38. G. Bingham Powell, Jr., *Elections as Instrument of Democracy* (New Haven: Yale University Press, 2000), 47.

39. The official estimate of the accumulated public-sector debt of governments of all levels was around 40 percent of the GNP at the end of 2003. But most experts put the figure around NT$11 trillion, roughly 107 percent of the GNP, when all the unaccounted as well as unfunded liabilities of various sources are taken into account. See *Commercial Times* (Taipei), 30 September 2003, 4.

40. In the 2001 Taiwan EAB survey, we did employ two identical questions that were used in Korea. The results are strikingly similar to what we found in Korea. Almost the same percentage (60 percent) of the respondents agreed with the statement, "The nation is run by a powerful few and ordinary citizens cannot do much about it," with 7.5 percent agreeing with the statement "strongly" and 52.9 percent "somewhat." When asked about the statement, "People like me don't have any influence over what the government does," even more (69 percent) rated Taiwanese democracy as unresponsive, agreeing with the statement "strongly" (8.9 percent) or "somewhat" (60.1 percent).

41. The results from the 2001 Taiwan EAB survey are very similar. After converting the two items (which are identical to what the Korean survey used) to 7-point index, the mean rating in Taiwan is 3.6.

42. Fu Hu and Yun-han Chu, "Neo-authoritarianism, Polarized Conflict and Populism in a Newly Democratizing Regime: Taiwan's Emerging Mass Politics," *Journal of Contemporary China* 5 (Spring 1996).

43. Richard Rose, William Mishler, and Christian Haerpfer, *Democracy and Its Alternatives: Understanding Post-Communist Societies* (Baltimore: Johns Hopkins University Press, 1998); and Richard Rose and Doh Chull Shin, "Democratization Backwards."

44. Amartya Sen, *Development as Freedom* (New York: Anchor, 1999), 156.

45. Guillermo O'Donnell, "Illusions about Consolidation," *Journal of Democracy* 7 (April 1996): 34–51; and Guillermo O'Donnell, "Polyarchies and the (Un)Rule of Law," in Juan E. Mendez, Guillermo O'Donnell, and Paulo Sergio Pinherio, eds., *The (Un)Rule of Law and the Underprivileged in Latin America* (Notre Dame: University of Notre Dame Press, 1999).

46. In the 2001 Taiwan EAB survey, when asked about how much trust they have in public institutions, 68 percent of the respondents expressed that they have "not very much" or "none at all" in parliament, while only 42 percent of them expressed distrust toward the courts.

47. Yun-han Chu, Larry Diamond, and Doh Chull Shin, "Halting Progress in Korea and Taiwan."

48. Yun-han Chu, "Lessons from East Asian Struggling Democracies," paper presented at the 19th World Congress of the International Political Science Association, Durban, South Africa, 3 July 2003.

11

POLAND AND ROMANIA

Alina Mungiu-Pippidi

Alina Mungiu-Pippidi is director of the Romanian Academic Society, a think tank in Bucharest, and a consultant for the World Bank and the United Nations Development Programme in the Balkans and the former Soviet Union. She has been a Harvard University Shorenstein Fellow, a Fulbright Fellow, and a Jean Monnet Fellow at the European University Institute, as well as director in charge of the reform of Romanian Public Television. She is coeditor, with Ivan Krastev, of Nationalism After Communism: Lessons Learned *(2003).*

The notion of quality is evasive and at the same time inseparable from a comparative perspective. If, as many utopists dreamed, the world were united in only one political unit, where political office were accessed via some form of competition, the meaning of quality would slide completely beyond our reach or become a simple equivalent of satisfaction with government (see "Introduction" in this volume). When Europeans speak of a specific model of "European" democracy, they implicitly define it by comparison with the United States. If the European model were generalized to the rest of the world, therefore missing any comparison benchmarks, we would live in a "brave new world," in a world of "dystopia." From all this relativism, one certainty emerges: Only in consolidated democracies can we discuss democratic "quality."

Postcommunist Central and Eastern Europe provides a more straightforward case than any other region of the world. Due to their proximity to Western Europe, countries of this region could aspire to become members of the European Union (EU), the economic and political body that unites some of the most advanced democracies of the world. After a few initial years of exploring all possible models of democracy, the standards set by the EU became the only points of reference for postcommunist Europe. At the 1993 Copenhagen Summit, confronted with the pressure from newly liberated European countries to accede to the Union, the EU was compelled to put into words this model of European democracy. The result was a variant of a definition of democratic consolidation. Aspiring new members must have achieved, in order to be considered for membership, "stability of institutions guaranteeing democracy, the rule of law, human rights and respect for and protection of minorities."[1]

Combined with other EU requirements, such as the Social Charter, the definition comes close to what Larry Diamond and Leonardo Morlino call a "good" democracy—"one that provides its citizens a high degree of freedom, political equality, and popular control over public policies and policy makers through the legitimate and lawful functioning of stable institutions."[2] The democratic criteria agreed upon in Copenhagen created a yardstick that was applied rigorously to the transitional democracies of Eastern Europe, despite occasional deteriorations within the EU proper. Between 1994 and 2004, such deteriorations included the election in Austria of populist xenophobic leader Jörg Haider; the assassination of populist leader Pim Fortuyn in the Netherlands, a country which ranks highly in quality among EU democracies; the growth in popularity of right-wing parties nearly everywhere; and contestations of the central state by regions with a distinct cultural identity, such as Spain's Basque country and France's Corsica, which spilled from a handful of terrorists into mainstream political life. Nonetheless, as the proverbial parent tells the child, "do what I say, not what I do." Thus, throughout the accession years postcommunist countries struggled to meet the EU democracy criteria, attempting to endow their democracies with quality of the highest European standards.

Postcommunist Europe provides favorable grounds for comparing democratic quality, as we expect countries with close historical backgrounds, comparable social structures, and similar political objectives (accession to the EU) to develop similar political regimes. Roughly, this is the case for Poland and Romania, the countries that are the focus of this chapter. Throughout their transitions, these countries have often been cited as the prodigy (Poland) and the foot-dragger (Romania) of the EU-accession class. This chapter aims to establish the similarities and differences between Romania and Poland on both formal and substantial indicators of the quality of democracy.

Similarities and Differences

After 2000, the similarities between Poland and Romania seem to have surpassed the differences. Poland managed only with great difficulty and tremendous political support from the West to complete its EU accession in 2004, with the understanding that many of the accession criteria would have to be completed later. Romania will follow Poland's suit and join the EU in 2007. Beginning in 2000, the political section of the European Commission's (EC) regular reports—the main instrument to evaluate the yearly performance of EU candidates—was very similar for the two countries. It stated that both Poland and Romania fulfilled the Copenhagen political criteria, and criticism and recommendations focused on reform of the justice and prison systems, the fight against corruption, and other postcommunist "legacies."

Other sources, such as Freedom House's Nations in Transit (NIT) reports are usually more critical, especially towards Romania. The difference is that the EC reports focus on the adoption of legislation compatible with or similar to that of EU democracies, and to a lesser extent the implementation and impact of this legislation. The EC reports are usually positive because they rate the success of the *imitation process* of the European Union model; nobody expects the adopted legislation of the *acquis communautaire*, EU's common legislation, immediately to change the candidate countries.

On the contrary, Freedom House reports mostly focus on events that infringe on democracy, so the differences from one year to another emerge mostly from the history of that particular year. In the NIT reports, Poland seems to do on average three times better than Romania on all the democratic-quality indicators utilized, such as the rule and law and constitutionalism, governance, the media, and political process, with a closer performance only on corruption. But the ratings developed by Freedom House and Transparency International are based on perceptions of experts and businesspeople, and are therefore subjective. They are useful in monitoring a trend over time, but their use in cross-country comparisons remains very limited, as country and regional experts assign national ratings mostly on the basis of previous years, not by using a comparative method across the panel of postcommunist countries.

Discussing the quality of democracy in these two countries has a twofold advantage. On one hand, differences in the recent histories of Poland and Romania, especially in their transition modes, are sufficient to provide variation; on the other, similarities between the two provide enough grounds to make inferences valid for the postcommunist region more generally. By 2001, both countries had held at least three rounds of elections qualified as free and fair and experienced changes in government between the anticommunists and the postcommunists; both also received invitations to start negotiations with the EU at the December 1999 Helsinki summit. Their publics have also come to have comparable democratic attitudes, considering democracy the best system of government despite its shortcomings, and giving less support to authoritarian alternatives. At the beginning of the transition, both Romania and Poland showed in the first *Times Mirror* polls some preference for strong leaders; a decade-and-a-half later, they displayed attitudes comparable with countries of the previous European wave of democratization.

Poland is mainly Catholic and Romania is largely Christian Ortho-

TABLE 1—QUALITATIVE DIFFERENCES BETWEEN POLAND AND
ROMANIA'S DEMOCRACIES*

YEAR		ELECTORAL PROCESS	MEDIA	GOVERNANCE	CORRUPTION	JUSTICE
1997	Poland	1.50	1.50	1.75	—	1.50
	Romania	3.25	4.25	4.25	—	4.25
1998	Poland	1.25	1.50	1.75	—	1.50
	Romania	3.25	4.00	4.00	—	4.25
1999–	Poland	1.25	1.50	1.75	2.25	1.50
2000	Romania	3.25	3.50	3.50	4.25	4.25
2001	Poland	1.25	1.50	1.75	2.25	1.50
	Romania	3.25	3.50	3.75	4.50	4.25
2004	Poland	1.25	1.75	2.00	2.50	1.50
	Romania	3.25	3.75	3.75	4.40	4.25

Source: Freedom House, Nations in Transit survey, 2004, available at *www.freedomhouse.com.*
* Scores on a 1-to-7 scale on which a score of 1 represents most free.

dox. This cultural difference is the only noteworthy one, as otherwise
they have comparable histories: partial autonomy and foreign occupation for many centuries, formation of national states and limited
modernization after World War I, and Soviet-imposed communism after
World War II. They also have similar social structures (agrarian or rural
societies with political rights traditionally confined for the most part to
landowning elites), similar cultures of peripheral European societies
endlessly discussing their position between the West and the East, and
the tendency to blame their relative underdevelopment (when compared
to Western Europe) on the heroic, sacrificial history of defending "the
gate of Europe" from the infidel Turk.[3]

In 1937, Romania's average annual income was US$81 and Poland's
was $100; it was only later that economic differences started to arise.
Poland's main territorial problem was with Germany, while Romania's
was with the Soviet Union: This led to Germany's occupation of Poland,
and to the invasion of the Soviet Union by Romania alongside Germany. These territorial disputes were remnants of World War I, and
mattered enormously for the trajectory of the two countries in World
War II and the fate assigned to them at the peace conference ending the
latter war. Although both countries fell behind the Iron Curtain, Western interest in Poland was greater than in Romania, which had fought on
the wrong side of the war, changed sides too late, and which had fewer
exiles and an unfortunate strategic position surrounded by communist
states.

By the end of the communist era, however, the social structure was
remarkably similar in the two countries. The middle class, traditionally
considered a prerequisite for democracy, had been completely destroyed
under communist rule and had been replaced by a technocratic class

created in communist universities. In the early 1990s, surveys showed that in both countries, nearly all social stratification had been annihilated. Poland was regarded a consolidated democracy by 1993; for Romania it took until 1996, when anticommunists came peacefully into office by means of democratic elections.

Procedural Criteria: Rule of Law and Accountability

Despite these similar patterns, subjective ratings of rule of law and accountability in both countries show Romania at a great disadvantage compared to Poland. Transparency International's corruption index, on which 0 is the most corrupt and 10 the least, Romania's rating is 2.6 and Poland's is 4. Likewise, NIT scores find Romania doing much worse on governance, judiciary, and accountability (see Table 1).

The history of reinstating the rule of law after the fall of communism is similar in both countries. The newly formed democratic governments had to rule on the basis of communist legislation, because they were unable to replace it all overnight. That legislation could have been cancelled, but the understanding at the time was that "the umbrella principle of upholding the law meant that however bad or inappropriate communist laws should continue to apply until revoked or amended."[4] In both countries, legislators focused primarily on regulating political competition, and only then did they move on to other areas. That meant that the corpus of law in force remained internally contradictory and that laws were not always consistent with one another.

Newly elected legislators also often proved to be incompetent and over-opinionated. The inexperience and high turnover of parliamentary deputies obstructed the process of legal change. Much of the legislative process was ad hoc, and changes of government often meant shifts and reversals in the underlying principles of certain pieces of legislation.[5] The burden on the judiciary was particularly high in the contexts of "legal transition" and of the extensive adoption of EU legislation. Statistics for both countries show an increase in lawsuits of all kinds, while the judiciary remained inadequately paid and court infrastructure remained poor. By 2005, lawsuits still took years to complete in both countries.

The international community has been critical of Romanian courts. Similarly in Poland, three successive judicial ombudsmen criticized "the abysmal state of the courts."[6] This highlights, however, one of Poland's successes—the creation of a strong ombudsman, who has proven to be an independent and authoritative voice. In contrast, although Romania's 1991 constitution provided for an ombudsman office, the office was created only after the anticommunists came to power in 1996. The Romanian ombudsman's legal powers are modest, however, and every holder of the position has done even less than the law allows so as not to upset the government. This difference in status of the Polish and the Romanian ombudsmen stems from the difference between the governments that passed the legislation creating the offices. In Poland, it was a government with strong roots in civil society and dissent; in Romania, it was the government of a communist successor party, which was merely paying lip service to civil society's demands, while in reality it did not want the ombudsman office to challenge its own authority.

A crucial feature of *horizontal* accountability refers therefore to the political neutrality of the courts and the judiciary. For democracy, it matters even more that the courts are able to deliver justice in a fair and nonpartisan style than if they work promptly and effectively. A nonpartisan justice system, even if underdeveloped, can evolve through capacity building. It is much harder to change a vicious justice system, such as the one communism planted, which is designed to side with the government against the citizen. In this respect, the story of the Romanian ombudsman and higher courts show marked differences compared to Poland, Hungary, or even Bulgaria; in no important matter did the Romanian ombudsman or constitutional court defy the government, unlike in the other countries.

The Romanian Supreme Court of Justice (SCJ) tried for years to become independent, but unlike in Poland, its members were not granted tenure until 2004. Nevertheless, the SCJ endorsed lower-court decisions to restitute property confiscated without papers by the communist government, thus going against the policy of President Ion Iliescu (a former communist official). After 1994, Iliescu was an outspoken critic of the SCJ. The general prosecutor he appointed attacked the final sentences of the SCJ with extraordinary appeals. Initially, an exception in the procedural codes allowed the general prosecutor to challenge final judicial rulings favoring the owners of nationalized real estate and condemning clients of Iliescu and his party. In practice, this meant that a new panel of SCJ judges was appointed and asked to try the case again until they ruled in favor of the government.

One could hardly expect accountability to work properly in a postcommunist environment. Voters, as well as governmental and nongovernmental agencies, are new at the game. People who are resocialized and learn the basics of democracy cannot become sophisticated voters overnight.[7] Two-thirds of Romanian voters claim that they do not even consider the left-right spectrum when voting for a candidate, and indeed many cannot tell the essential elements of the political left from those of the right.[8]

Nevertheless, in most Central European countries there is some rough form of *vertical* accountability—which becomes evident when governments are not reelected, even those who perform reasonably well by Western standards. Poland is a clear case of this: Neither the government that managed to bring Poland into NATO nor the one that completed its EU accession were rewarded with reelection. Romania has hardly been different since its more peculiar transition from democracy was completed. In 1996, voters ousted President Ion Iliescu, despite his large popularity in rural areas, manipulation of state-owned media, and subjugation of the secret services. The anticommunist coalition elected in 1996 performed poorly, mainly due to frequent bickering among member parties and decision deadlocks of the government, and was duly voted out of office four years later. It returned to power in the 2004 elections, albeit in a smaller format (just three of the original four main parties), by taking advantage of the popular discontent with corruption of the 2000–2004 postcommunist government.

The media played an important role in both countries as an agent of accountability during and after transition. In Romania, the free media was largely responsible for the erosion of Iliescu's popularity, as well as that of his anticommunist opponents. The electronic media is equally developed in Romania and Poland, with hundreds of local radio and television networks. The independence of state broadcasting remains a source of concern: The sacking of top executives has become a common practice, and corruption scandals have plagued both countries surveyed. As parliamentary majorities reflect the same political interests as governments, passing the authority over state broadcasting from the executive to the legislature does not change much. The Italian model of *lottizzazione* (dividing influence over TV networks among political parties) dominates the formal and informal arrangements in both countries; with broadcasting boards reflecting the composition of the parliament, there is no room for civil society or the public interest as such. Nonetheless, both countries have a large private media that should theoretically provide good opportunities to criticize the government.

By 2005, the Freedom House Freedom of the Press survey captured a mixed picture of the broader postcommunist region. Fourteen years after the fall of the Berlin wall, just one-third of the former communist countries was rated as Free (the new EU members), with another third rated Partly Free, and the rest Not Free. In 2004–2005, the Romanian media actually became less free, while the media in Poland and the Baltic states have become closer to EU standards as regards the legal context, political influences, and economic environment. Some structural features of the media explain part of the difference. The overall newspaper readership is far higher in Poland, and broadsheets dominate the print media. In contrast, the most popular Romanian dailies are tabloids, and have a much lower circulation (controlling for population size). Limited readership is a factor of weakness. Only 18 percent of Romanians read daily political news or columns in newspapers, and the 45 percent of the population living in the rural areas do not even have access to newspapers due to poor distribution.[9] As the Polish economy is larger and has done better in the last decade, the media in that country is far wealthier than it is in Romania, where hidden debts and manipulation of advertising make the media far more vulnerable to political pressure. By mid-2004, the debts of private television channels to the state budget were so high that editors themselves censored any criticism of the government. In other words, the Romanian media is far more captured by vested interest than is its Polish counterpart.

Poland has not been exempt of media-related corruption—as revealed in the 2003–2004 Rywingate scandal, which involved numerous high-level public characters.[10] In Poland, however, the attempt to bribe a publisher, as was the case with this affair, ended in a public scandal; in Romania, such cases are wrapped in silence. Also, a striking difference between the countries remains that Romanian media is dominated by former communists while the Polish media is dominated by former anti-communist dissidents and intellectuals. In both countries, partisan or corrupt journalists often abuse freedom of expression, and no solid media unions or associations exist to defend the rights of the individual journalist and to self-regulate the media. Quite to the contrary, the Romanian publishers formed an association with the purpose of curbing the freedom of their employees. One of the main (informal) rules of this Romanian Press Club stipulates that if a conflict between a journalist and a publisher leads to the resignation or firing of the journalist, no other member of the Club would hire him or her.

This has contributed greatly to the environment of self-censorship in the Romanian media. It has also helped the government, because instead of facing hundreds of free journalists, it only has to deal with a handful of publishers, ready to be corrupted with government advertising or pardon of tax arrears. Government intervention in the media therefore operates through informal channels.

Horizontal accountability faces the same difficulties as the rule of law. The agencies that are supposed to enforce it are themselves in the process of construction. Both petty and grand corruption is hard to tackle by a police force that is poorly trained and paid based on ever-changing legislation. Poland and Romania have struggled to adopt legislation against corruption, money laundering, and cross-border crime, as well as national anticorruption strategies under pressure from the European Union. Nevertheless, the European Commission's regular reports have criticized the two countries' corruption-fighting institutions for being weak and themselves easily corrupted.

Substantive Criteria: Freedom and Equality

In terms of freedoms and rights, two different patterns emerged in post-1989 Poland and Romania, grounded in their specific transitions. In Poland, a pact among elites swiftly produced an elected and legitimate government, leaving the legislative developments behind. Poland's democratic consolidation was accompanied only by mere amendments to the communist constitution of 1952. Therefore, the "Small Constitution" of 1992 focused exclusively on the state's power structure. Provisions of the 1952 constitution (as amended) respecting civil and religious rights were left intact.

In November 1992, President Lech Wałęsa introduced in parliament a Charter on Rights and Freedoms, intended to become part of the Small Constitution. It contained 22 "basic civil and religious rights common to all liberal democracies," including freedom of religion, the right to privacy, and freedom from government censorship. In the end, it took postcommunist Poland eight years, three different parliaments, and six different governments to adopt a new constitution in 1997. It was bitterly fought over by anticommunists and postcommunists.

By that time, however, Freedom House had already qualified Poland as a consolidated democracy, and the Council of Europe was satisfied with the status of human rights in the country—thus, this symbolic battle had little practical consequence for the country. In other words, informal institutions, due to the consensus among elites and civil society on broad fundamental values, produced a democracy respectful of human rights before its legal enactment and the establishment of formal (constitutional) institutions. So small was the threat to basic freedoms in postcommunist Poland from the part of the old regime and its authoritarian structures that the main scare in the early 1990s—as it turned out, quite exaggerated—was that of a Wałęsa dictatorship.

A completely different pattern emerged in Romania. The spectacular fall of communist dictator Nicolae Ceauşescu in 1989 left an unfinished power struggle between elements of the former communist establishment led by Ion Iliescu and the unorganized street rioters who had contributed decisively to the end of the regime. There had been practically no opposition to Ceauşescu prior to 1989, and political parties started forming from scratch only in January 1990. At that time, a master coup of Ion Iliescu, self-appointed interim president after Ceauşescu's flight, turned the ad hoc committees of the Romanian revolution into one mega-party, the National Salvation Front (NSF).

In the 1990 parliamentary elections, the NSF won nearly two-thirds of the vote. Supported from the beginning by the army and the secret services, the party was initially a mix of spontaneous elements and former apparatchiks: After the elections, however, three former *nomenklatura* members managed to secure the country's top three political posts: the presidency and the chairs of the Senate and the Deputies' Assembly. The small anticommunist parties, which were mostly based on interwar historical parties, took many years to become organized, and as a result, Romania had the most belated political swing in the region, which came in 1996. To control the urban opposition fearful of a communist restoration, President Ion Iliescu more than once resorted to vigilante groups, such as coal miners, who in June 1990 destroyed the University of Bucharest—headquarters of opposition parties and the opposition press—with the quiet endorsement of the police, creating hundreds of casualties.

During its first years after the fall of the Ceauşescu regime, Romania was the textbook example of an illiberal "electoral democracy." All resources were concentrated in the hands of the NSF, which was strongly supported by the army and the secret services. Praise for both Ceauşescu and Ion Antonescu, Romania's wartime fascist dictator, was often heard in the Constitutional Assembly. In 1991, the country adopted a liberal constitution, which even carried an article stating that international law was supposed to override domestic law with regard to human rights. But a law on national security, which sealed for fifty years the archives of the Communist Party, had been rushed through the Constitutional Assembly prior to the constitution's adoption to ensure that the de facto political order would not be affected. Freedom of the press took effect immediately with Ceauşescu's downfall as students, intellectuals, and print-press workers launched newspapers without waiting for any regulations or approvals.

On the first day of the Romanian revolution, the provisional government also granted freedom of association, so that hundreds of political parties and thousands of NGOs surged by the end of 1990. Throughout years of political unrest and the uneven competition between old and new elites, Romania's democratization progressed steadily: Mass media and civil society groups gained ground, and three rounds of elections qualified as free and fair in 1992, 1996, and 2000. Even in 2004, when election irregularities were reported, problems were sorted out peacefully between domestic watchdogs and the government.[11] During Romania's long and disputed transition, the state oscillated between being the main defender and the main violator of human rights. Despite its formal constitutional arrangements guaranteeing extensive rights (failing to do justice only to two minorities, homosexuals and monarchists), Romania was trailing in terms of actual behavior. Rallying around the NSF, out of the fear of having communism—and themselves—placed on trial, senior judges, police officers, and generals invested more in defending the authoritarian past than in bringing the informal institutions to the level of the formal democratic ones.

If progress was nevertheless made in the end, this was due to a combination of foreign and domestic pressures, which played a large role in the Romanian transition. Pushed by the Council of Europe, charters and treaties regulating everything from the treatment of prisoners to the use of minority languages were gradually adopted; domestic civil society, especially the well-organized Hungarian minority, also pushed from within. After 1996, the anticommunists who won office allied themselves with the Hungarian-minority party, which thereby secured a share of government positions on both the central and local level. The former communists maintained this original Romanian attempt at consociational power-sharing after they returned to power in 2000.

The anticommunist government also initiated prison reforms and affirmative-action programs for the poorest Roma (Gypsy), and Iliescu's government maintained and extended these reforms after his return to power in 2000. The rights of children became a special issue in Romania, as Ceauşescu's demographic policies had left thousands orphaned. Under communist rule, children had been given up for adoption and trafficked by parents, authorities, and NGOs. In fact, in the 1999 report on Romania's EU application stating that the country generally satisfied the political criteria, the European Commission expressly mentioned the rights of children as a negative exception. Regulations and practices with regard to children's rights have only recently caught up with the requirements of the EU.

Thus, Poland and Romania had distinctly different patterns of democratic emergence. In Poland, informal institutions came first and the formal institutions and regulations came after, while in Romania it was the other way around. Nevertheless, there were also significant similarities, the most important of which was the underdevelopment of organizations dedicated to ensuring the implementation of rights. Such a lack of capacity frequently causes problems more frequently than the conscious will to infringe on somebody's rights; this applies to all rights, from those of prisoners to those of the Roma—the poorest minority in both countries. Restitution of property to those dispossessed during communism was late and incomplete due to the lack of political will among successor communist parties and the lack of resources to compensate former owners.

Freedom of expression, taken for granted even in 1990, has gradually come under attack. The extreme competition between media outlets (far more newspapers are published in Bucharest or Warsaw than in New York) has cleared the way for economic pressures on publishers and journalists. Freedom of expression in state broadcasting, especially in television, remains inferior to that of privately owned media, and its legal regulation has proved a disappointment, as it did not manage to discontinue political intervention. Throughout these countries' democratic transitions, journalists had to fight against the general lack of transparency of postcommunist administrations, and against absurd legislation inherited from communism (such as laws against the defamation of the nation or an official in office).

In both countries, the treatment of people arrested or imprisoned long remained closer to communist standards than Western European ones, and is still a source of concern. After the fall of communism, Romania experienced a religious revival, which brought it even closer to Poland—always the most religious country in the region. Because the church and the religious NGOs occasionally display illiberal attitudes, this revival has complicated the democratic evolutions of both countries and fed the conservative policies of the administrations.

Equality

The way postcommunist societies handle equality is utterly specific. "Transition" is understood in a postcommunist context to be the evolution from a collectivist society to an individualist one, from the ideal of equality of income to the equality of opportunity. The liberal discourse— in fact, the libertarian one—is nearly the only legitimate intellectual discourse. Postcommunist countries are the only transitional countries where intellectuals praise capitalism and poets dedicate hymns to the consumption society. Of course, trade unions, workers, and pensioners have other ideas, and that is why there is an important collectivist base in the countries of East Central Europe—but their voices are heard only in elections and strikes. In the media, everybody who is not a former communist shies away from being even a moderate leftist. There is a consensus among all parties at least on equality of opportunity, but as in the case of human rights, there are both formal and informal obstacles to its enactment. The legislation is missing, and it takes time and EU coaching to start adopting it; the informal institutions are clearly opposed to it, as they are rooted in communist habits. Except for in limited sectors—all of them new and related to high skills, such as computers— the culture of postcommunist society is deeply against offering opportunities equally and randomly.

Inequality should not have been a problem in postcommunist societies. When they embarked on their transitions, the Gini coefficients showed remarkable equality across Eastern Europe, in particular compared to Latin American countries. The economic transition was supposed to break with this social uniformity and initiate a capitalist regime where incomes would be different according to entrepreneurship and skills. The economic reforms, however, with their insider dealings and fraudulent privatization, created first and foremost a class of "new rich," whose members rose partly by merit and chance—but also in part by abusing power and violating the law, conflicts of interest notwithstanding.

Resentment against the newly enriched class is high in both countries, as sales of luxury goods, especially such extravagant cars as Mercedes and Hummers, boomed during the transition to democracy. A survey item, phrased as: "The same people enjoy privileges regardless of the regime" evokes widespread agreement in both countries, which indicates a lack of social trust. The cleavage between the new rich and the rest of the population is a source of concern, especially as it is a reminder of the particularism of communism. In particularistic societies, individuals are treated unequally, and their treatment depends strongly on their position in society or their status—which in this context means their distance from the groups or networks holding power. The closer an individual is to the source of power, be it a charismatic leader or a privileged group (such as the *nomenklatura* or secret service during the communist era), the better positioned he or she is to enjoy a superior status.

As other resources or forms of social stratification had been de facto annihilated by communist regimes, status (deriving from proximity to power) became the main determinant of social hierarchy, and a high status gave disproportionate access to scarce public goods.[12] Communism created special "politocracies" as power was the main instrument of allocating social rewards and political office was closely intertwined with social status, generating what Andrew Janos called a "modern version of the old tables of rank."[13] Influence was therefore the main currency during communism, and during the transition that influence was easily converted into cash. This uneven distribution is accepted by a large part of society because status groups are not as closed as they were during communism—some degree of social mobility based on connections or exceptional merit is possible. Therefore, many individuals strive to become part of such status groups rather than trying to change the rules of the game: this is the culture of privilege underpinning status societies. These arrangements naturally subvert the rule of law.

Max Weber originally defined status societies as societies dominated by certain groups that monopolize resources and ruled by convention rather than law; the term applies well to many postcommunist societies, especially Romania and Russia but also to a degree Poland.[14] Examples of status holders during communism range from *apparatchiki,* directors, and secret-service officers, to civil servants or state salespersons in charge of distributing resources to members of officially acknowledged groups, such as the Union of Writers and Journalists and sports clubs. Those high up in these old status-based networks had ample opportunity to convert their influence into wealth during the transition to democracy. That such conversions succeeded to some degree nearly everywhere is perhaps the saddest story of postcommunist transitions in Eastern Europe.[15] As one needs to be part of a network to succeed in business or to get a share of the state assets available through privatization, these transitions have been rife with opportunities for the privileged minority that possesses more knowledge, skills, and resources. Barrington Moore called such groups "predatory elites"—people who in the process of generating prosperity for themselves produce social poverty on a scale otherwise unwarranted in that society.[16] The networks cut across political cleavages and by means of opportunistic strategies, they control much of the country's resources regardless of what party is in power.[17]

Particularism becomes, therefore, the main provider of inequality

TABLE 2—MECHANISMS TO RECEIVE PUBLIC SERVICES IN ROMANIA

STRATEGY AND RESOURCES	PERCENTAGE OF POPULATION	MECHANISM	SATISFACTION WITH SERVICE
Connections	20–25	Personalize service	Very good
Bribery	10–20	Increase efficiency of service	Fair
Occasional bribery or abstention	> 50	To get some service	Low or none

Source: Romanian Academic Society 2004

and subverts the rule of law and social trust. Data from both Romania and Poland show that bribing is only a minor complement of widespread particularism. In both countries, the groups of privileged individuals that have the right connections report the maximum satisfaction from public services (see Table 2). This is not surprising, as the state works for them. Second in satisfaction come those who lack good connections, but summon enough resources to bribe when they need a public service.[18] Their satisfaction is mixed, despite the attempt to make public service more efficient. Finally, the large majority is unable to use status or bribes, and they are quite unsatisfied with what public services they get. Clearly, the administration and many public services still operate within the communist mindset of "short supply," as if there were not enough public goods for everybody.

It is difficult to compare quantitatively Poland and Romania in this respect. NGOs in both countries would argue that their country is the most corrupt, and they sometimes seem to compete in producing reports on corruption. Identical stories surface in the media, and privatization horror stories seem to be carbon copies from one country to another. Transparency International, Freedom House, and the European Commission usually rate Romania as more corrupt, but because Romania is less developed than Poland, this is only to be expected. The case of Greece shows, however, that European integration is compatible with some degree of particularism, which only gradually recedes as universal institutions become stronger.

The landscape of social rights is otherwise similar in both countries, due to their common trajectory from communism to EU membership. For most of the transition, a slightly amended version of the old communist labor code has continued to function and strikes have been an integral feature of economic reform in both countries. Although Poland and Romania were early to adopt the European Social Rights Chapter, which is part of the *acquis communautaire* (the common EU legislation), both countries asked for more time to implement it during negotiations with the EU. The social *acquis* had never been adopted by more liberal EU member states, such as Britain, and the East European countries clearly do not have the resources to implement it fully. Nonetheless, EU law is

TABLE 3—CITIZEN TRUST IN STATE AND GOVERNMENT
(PERCENTAGE OF POPULATION)

COUNTRY	PARLIAMENT	PARTIES	COURTS	POLICE
Bulgaria	26	25	24	31
Czech Republic	20	21	34	40
Poland	20	8	15	21
Hungary	16	14	36	29
Romania	13	9	19	36
Slovenia	10	8	26	24
Estonia	10	8	26	30
Lithuania	9	8	16	19
Latvia	8	7	24	27
Slovakia	8	9	15	26
New Europe mean	14	12	25	28
Russia	7	7	23	13

Source: The Center for the Study of Public Policy's New Europe Barometer (2001) and New Russia Barometer (2001).
Note: Trust indicates persons giving an institution a rating of at least 4 on a 7-point scale with 7 indicating very high trust and 1 very low trust.

merging the two sets of practices that have coexisted during the democratic transition: the old communist ones in the shrinking public sector—still quite large in Romania in 2004—and new liberal ones in the private sector, where employees often found themselves unprotected.

Subjective Criteria of Quality: Responsiveness

The regular use of the right to punish the government does not seem to ease dissatisfaction with the way the political system operates in these two countries, or more generally in East Central Europe. Their parliaments continue to enjoy little trust compared to those of Western democracies. Voters do not think that they have the power to hold governments accountable. Quite the contrary, common to the whole region is the perception that regardless of whether there is party alternation in government, the same unpopular political elite will hold on to power. Trust in government is a scarce resource throughout the postcommunist world. Although in surveys majorities have declared a strong commitment to democracy, few people express trust in political parties and politicians (see Table 3 above).[19]

The level of trust is also low for law and order agencies, whose reform is difficult and takes years to produce sizable results. Both NGOs and ordinary citizens believe that corruption is widespread among civil servants and top politicians, despite the frequent lack of serious evidence to prove this. Explanatory models of trust in the state indicate that discontent with particularistic behavior by the administration and top political figures undermines public confidence. Put simply, citizens of postcommunist countries are critical and not yet convinced that the state and the government are there to grant universal access to public goods, not to provide advantages to the same old profiteers.[20]

According to the New Democracies Barometer,[21] however, in both countries most people consider that government fairness improved (Romania) or stayed the same (Poland) compared to communist times, with only a minority perceiving deterioration on this score. While Poles believe there has been little improvement since the end of communism, Romanians are in general less skeptical—they think that people can influence the government more during the transitional period than during communism. Nevertheless, while most Poles believe that the level of corruption in their country has remained the same, Romanians perceive an increase in corrupt practices since the onset of the democratic transition.

The way the new regimes dealt with the crimes of communism did little to help them gain legitimacy. In September 1994, two Polish generals were found not guilty for masterminding the murder of Father Jerzy Popieluszko, a Warsaw priest whose sermons criticized the Soviet-controlled government. A Wrocław court freed the militiamen who repressed the Lublin demonstrations in August 1982. In Romania, the extraordinary appeals of the general prosecutor attempted to save generals who had ordered the shooting of anti-Ceauşescu protesters, as well as the banker who bankrupted the most important Romanian state bank to bail out President Iliescu and his cronies. During the transition Ceauşescu's court poets, the founders of the ideology of national communism, ended up in parliament and even in government while Romanian dissidents remained mostly in opposition. The Romanian Academy, modeled after the French Academy as Romania's highest academic and cultural forum, had during communism restricted access to members of the Communist Party. After 1989, the Academy notoriously gave up only two of its members—namely the Ceauşescu couple, who were shot. The rest of its membership remained intact, and members retained their ability to select their peers throughout the transition, which ensured a continuation of the communist academic establishment.

One can hardly blame the skepticism of East European citizens when it comes to their governments. Most people supported the economic reforms despite the considerable hardship they suffered as a result. In the first part of the transition, purchasing power fell dramatically, and still the reforms progressed with only limited opposition from certain groups (such as coal miners). Most people say in regular opinion surveys that they support market economy and even the closure of unprofitable state enterprises, although in Romania it took until 1995 to reach this point.[22] What makes the economic suffering unbearable is the feeling that it is not equally distributed, that some pay and others profit. This may have been the case more in Romania, where we now find a smaller middle class and more new rich with political connections, but it was felt strongly in both countries. Governments did not manage to disperse this general perception of injustice, so each and every government, regardless of whether they governed better or worse, paid the bill in its turn.

Explaining Similarities and Differences

Although the public perception of democratic quality is similar in the two countries, external observers argue that Poland's democracy is of a higher quality than Romania's. The challenge is then to explain why there is a difference in quality between Polish and Romanian democracy, despite the fact that both countries are consolidated democracies inhabited by unsatisfied and to some extent inconsistent democrats. Explanations of the difference in the democratic performance of regimes, in general as well as for postcommunist Europe, can be grouped in two broad categories of factors: path-dependent factors and institutional factors. We would expect path-dependent factors to matter more in determining if a certain country is a democracy in the first place, and institutional factors to explain that democracy's quality. As Douglass North has put it, however, the choice of institutions is often grounded in the past, so the separation of these two sets of factors is not complete.[23] Three determinants seem more important in explaining quality of democracy in postcommunist countries: modernization legacies, authoritarian legacies, and current institutions. Those refer to the peasant population, the degree of communization of society under communism, and the quality of communist successor parties and political elites more generally. I will discuss them in this temporal sequence.

Peasants. Romania and Poland have always been rural societies, and they still have some of the highest percentages of peasant population among the former Warsaw Pact countries, with the proportion in Romania more than double that of Poland (see Table 4 below). The strong correlation between democracy and peasantry rests with the historian Barrington Moore, who saw the nonrepressive commercialization of agriculture—the creation of farmer agriculture—as a foundation of democratic development.[24] In postcommunist Europe, large-scale mechanized but collectivized landholding, and the uncertain transformation of property relations since the fall of the old regime, have produced specific rural social structures, which have as their essential common trait the persistence of subsistence farming.

In Romania, decollectivization meant a return to family plots and subsistence farming, a "peasantization" of urbanites who became unemployed and resorted to agriculture on their recuperated lots,[25] and a drastic fall of production as household consumption, not commerce, became the main use for crops. Even in Poland, where the average size of agricultural lots is largest and where communist collectivization failed, there are few commercial farmers and many "peasants." In both

TABLE 4—MODERNIZATION LEGACY

	CZ	ES	HU	PL	SL	BU	LV	LI	RO	SK
Percentage of workforce in agriculture	5	7	6	19	10	27	15	27	44	6
Percentage of EU average GDP per capita adjusted by purchase power parity	57	41	51	40	69	28	29	38	25	48

Source: Eurostat (2001)

countries, peasants are generally against the liberalization of the economy; they vote for the former communist party, demand high subsidies, and fear the competition from the European Union.

The differences among such countries as Poland and Romania may then be explained by the different number of subsistence farmers, which is a legacy of precommunist times. There is a veritable black hole of accountability in subsistence-farming areas, where rules from the more modern urban areas do not apply. In addition to peasants' traditionally conservative outlook, there are also informal arrangements that contribute to their voting behavior. There is considerable local "state capture" in subsistence-farming areas, meaning that ex-communist rural elites control state resources and fight to maintain that arrangement (for instance, by opposing restitution of forests to the peasants in Romania). This allows them to act as "gatekeepers" who seek to conserve their own privileges by controlling and trading resources and votes. Thus, villages vote fully for the party or person that rural elites decide to support in exchange for preserving their privileges, as peasants are completely dependent on these "gatekeepers" for everything—from authorizations to cut firewood, to receiving the small cash subsidies the government disburses as social aid. In Romania's 2004 local elections, the impoverished Roma villages, which are wholly dependent on social aid, had their allowances cut for months and received them only on the eve of the election after promising to vote for their local mayor.[26] The model does not hold in richer, more developed areas where peasants are de facto farmers able to produce in large quantities and commercialize their products. It also does not apply to urban residents, who are influenced by electoral campaigns and divide their votes among parties.

Degree of communization. Romanian and Polish communism differed greatly, despite the two countries having nearly identical societies at the end of World War II. The usual explanation points to the higher Western interest in Poland; that interest prevented Soviet influence from being as all-encompassing as in other countries in the region. For instance, there was a formal presence of puppet opposition parties in parliament throughout communist rule, and within the Polish Communist Party itself there were different factions. Collectivization in Poland was stalled soon after its start, and about 80 percent of arable land remained the private property of farmers. Dissent, both within the Communist Party and outside it, remained a permanent feature of Polish society. In Romania, on the other hand, factions were not possible even within the Communist Party, and all dissent had been completely liquidated by 1960—later it resurfaced only in sporadic and isolated outbursts. The collectivization of Romania's countryside was nearly total and it destroyed the peasant class, the majority of the population.

In the early 1950s, Romania's nationalist communists, the Lucretiu Patrascanu group, were physically eliminated—not sidelined for a while as Władysław Gomułka and his group were in Poland. In the 1970s, comparative-politics scholars were already noting that while dissent was relatively tolerated in Hungary, Czechoslovakia, and Poland, it was brutally and completely suppressed in Romania and Bulgaria.[27] This created very different conditions for the emancipation of these countries from communism and their transitions to democracy. The end of Stalinism in Poland in 1956 meant a compromise formula between the Soviet model and Polish society—a form of liberal communism. This had its ups and downs, but clearly, as Juan J. Linz and Alfred Stepan have acknowledged, the imposition of a totalitarian regime never succeeded in Poland.[28]

In contrast, when Stalinism ended in Romania in 1963 it had already established the Soviet totalitarian model in its entirety: full collectivization, full liquidation of political opponents, a monolithic party, and a society so repressed and terrorized that a dictator like Ceauşescu could successfully emerge and rule unchallenged for more than two decades. Prior to asking ourselves if democratization has been a success or a failure in the countries of East Central Europe, we should first discuss if communism succeeded or failed in these societies.

At the time when Polish director Andrzej Wajda was filming his masterpiece *Marble Man,* which criticized Stalinism in particular and the hypocrisy of communism in general, Ceauşescu was destroying the historical center of the capital, Bucharest, to raise his formidable "House of the People." A few years before the fall of the regime in Poland, martial law was decreed as an open acknowledgement that the Communist Party could no longer control society, and the army had to step in to prevent Soviet intervention. At that time in Romania, totalitarianism went further and deeper: a new mass organization, the Democratic United Front, was created to include all those not included elsewhere (such as pensioners and non-members of Communist Party), and censorship reached new heights, with such words as "abstract" and "neurosis" being forbidden to print even in the cultural media.

By that time, the Romanian Communist Party had 4 million members, the highest in East Central Europe per capita (three times more than in

TABLE 5—COMMUNIST LEGACIES COMPARED

DIMENSIONS	POLAND	ROMANIA
Destruction of economic autonomy		
• nationalization of industry	Total	Total
• nationalization of services	Partial	Total
• collectivization	Failed	Total
Destruction and replacement of elites	Partial	Total
Manipulation of social conflict	Yes, but limited autonomy	Yes, unlimited
Manipulation of lifestyle	Limited to Stalinist years	Considerable (throughout communist era)
Mobilization and cooptation	Limited (party membership around 6 percent)	Significant (party membership around 18 percent)

Poland), a figure reflecting Ceauşescu's mobilization ambitions. Generally, recruitment took place among the most educated, another explanation for the post-1989 difference in quality between the Romanian and Polish political elites. A comparison of the extent to which the communist states were able to modify their societies shows that while Poland suffered the repression and nationalization common to all communist states, the Party failed to control society (see Table 5 above). In Romania, however, it succeeded, through higher mobilization and cooptation, complete destruction of economic autonomy, ruthless manipulation of social conflict (for instance, land from opponents were redistributed to submissive peasants), and even a radical attempt to change life styles of people through "systematization" (the replacement of villages and older urban neighborhoods with communist-designed concrete apartment blocks).

The quality of communist successor parties. There are few "pure" differences between Poland's and Romania's political institutions. Both are semipresidential regimes, have proportional-representation electoral systems, and have similar judiciaries. Constituencies are also very similar in size and attitudes, and the party systems are nearly identical, with low institutionalization of parties but good institutionalization of the party system, fractious center-right parties, and frequent reshuffles and changes of prime ministers.[29]

As their current institutions are nearly identical, we need to look for differences elsewhere. The main difference between Romania and Poland is the domination of the Romanian transition by Ion Iliescu and his party of former communists, who ruled for 10 of the first 14 years of democracy. This domination originated in Romania's difficult and disputed parting with communism. Iliescu came to power in 1990 by tactical

Figure—The Performance of Communist Successor Parties in Poland and Romania (Percent of Vote in Post-1989 Elections)

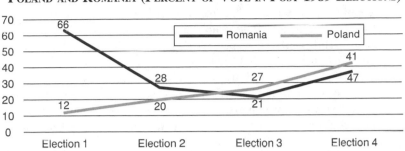

means ranging from conspiracy and revolutionary decrees to the summoning of vigilante miners to fight his democratic opponents. The Romanian revolution had more in common with the Bolshevik Revolution than with the smooth, legal, and friendly pacts in made Poland and Hungary. Once Iliescu's power was secured, he started to resuscitate the conservative elements of the former Communist Party, especially from the nationalist circles, and by 1991 he had already pushed out the reformers.

In contrast, the Polish communists started by giving away power during the 1989 roundtable, through a compromise formula suggested by the young bright *nomenklatura* member Aleksander Kwaśniewski, who later became a popular president. Solidarity crushed the postcommunists in the 1989 elections, but their reserved seats allowed them to maintain a presence in parliament until the next round of elections in 1991. Meanwhile, Poland's former Communist Party proceeded to undertake substantial internal reform, turning into a social-democratic party, and cutting with the past by every means. When they returned to government for the first time in 1993, it became obvious that there were few policy differences between them and the opposition. After a new electoral switch brought a fractious and unstable anticommunist alliance to power in 1997, the former communists won by a landslide in the fourth set of elections in 2001, and have since performed excellently in the EU-membership negotiations.

The best indicator of the degree of transformation of the postcommunist party is the degree to which the *nomenklatura* had convertible skills for the new environment of electoral competition and technocratic government.[30] Clearly the Polish communist leaders, with a tradition of internal party pluralism and patriotism, were far better prepared to build a modern social-democratic party than the ruthless Romanian leaders who shot Ceauşescu and sealed the Communist Party's archives. In both Poland and Hungary, postcommunist parties embarked on market reforms as convincingly as the anticommunists, while in Romania, Iliescu's party campaigned with antimarket and xenophobic messages, turning more market-friendly only in the late 1990s.

The policy distance between incumbent and challenger elites was therefore smaller in Poland, and more generally in Central Europe, than in Romania, Bulgaria, and the post-Soviet states. The more elites agreed on essential issues, such as privatization, the smoother and faster the transition. In East Central Europe, there was a consensus in favor of democracy when communism fell in 1989, because the communist parties there had already exhausted the possibilities of reforming the socialist economy. Where they had not, as in Romania, they tried an in-between approach in the first years of the transition and failed.

To explain the achievements of the new democratic regimes, the behavior of postcommunist parties in transition is far more important than the behavior of the opposition anticommunists, as the latter group behaved similarly in all postcommunist countries. The imbalance of power among parties in the first part of the Romanian transition is the most reasonable explanation of why Ion Iliescu could afford to be so authoritarian, and why the Romanian state eventually became more "captured" by one party, which thrived on making administrative and privatization resources largely its own. Once the political system saw more of a balance of political forces in Romania, policy distance decreased, important democratic reforms could finally be enacted, and Romania grew more like Poland.

Conclusion

The key factor in explaining how Poland and Romania reached similar endpoints despite the extremely different starts of their transitions is the incentive of EU membership. Both countries' decisions to apply to join the EU were strongly related to their geographic positions and histories. The countries of postcommunist Europe provide the grounds for a remarkable institutional experiment. As they adopt identical institutions, they are expected to end up quite similar; however, as their histories and especially their exit paths from communism were not identical, the main indicator of their success became the distance between the formal institutions adopted—which were the same everywhere—and the informal practices in politics and society.[31] As Douglass C. North noticed aptly, in times of sudden change institutions in a given society reflect more the former formal institutions than the current ones, as people are bound by habit.[32] The change of regime was more abrupt in Romania than in Poland, which explains the differences in the quality of democracy that we have noted. The greater the difference between the past and the present formal institutions, the larger the distance between current formal and informal institutions.

This greatly affects the perception of responsiveness. People are impatient and they tend to attribute this distance between written rules and current practices to the hypocrisy of rulers, rather than understanding all its complex determinants. Their anger over what they perceive to be the injustice of postcommunism is not directed against democracy itself, which constantly rates higher than communism in surveys, but rather against those in power. Does this tell us something about the quality of democracy, or rather about the quality of society? Regardless of whether they are democracies or not, some societies have always been better to live in than others at any given moment in time, even if the reference point for this evaluation has been constantly shifting. Postcommunism, with its uncertainties and institutional upheaval, cannot provide the environment for great quality of life, despite the enjoyment of freedom at a scale inconceivable during communism. To borrow the language of Czech novelist Milan Kundera, there is an "unbearable lightness" to democracy: Only after you have it do you realize how many other things are needed for a government to be able to provide quality of life to its citizens.

NOTES

1. These principles are now embodied in the Treaty of Nice (signed on 26 February 2001 and entered into force on 1 February 2003) as well as in the draft constitution of the European Union. For reports on these two countries see *europa.eu.int/comm/enlargement.*

2. Larry Diamond and Leonardo Morlino, "Introduction," in this volume, xi.

3. See Andrei Pippidi, "La croisade au Bas-Danube: les 'remparts' des chretiente," in Antoine Mares, ed., *Histoire des idees politiques de l'Europe centrale* (Paris: L'Harmattan, 1998).

4. Frances Millard, *Polish Politics and Society* (London: Routledge, 1999), 58, 89–90. For information on Romania, see the UNDP Early Warning Report 2001, "legal" section, available at *www.undp.ro,* and the Freedom House audit of Romania's judiciary, available at *www.just.rortrv_mc.php?param=audit _freedom_house.*

5. Frances Millard, *Polish Politics and Society,* 63.

6. Frances Millard, *Polish Politics and Society,* 69.

7. For resocialization, see the conclusions of Stephen White, Richard Rose, and Ian McAllister, *How Russia Votes* (Chatham, N.J.: Chatham House, 1997).

8. Alina Mungiu-Pippidi, "Enlightened Participation? Political Learning in a Post-Communist Environment: Lessons from the Fall 2000 Romanian Campaign," working paper no. 19 (Bucharest: Romanian Academic Society, 2000), available at *www.sar.org.ro.*

9. Data from the Center for Regional and Urban Sociology (CURS), available at *www.curs.ro.*

10. On the opportunity of privatizing a TV channel, an intermediate allegedly

acting on behalf of the government offered to change antitrust legislation to allow the main bidder participate in the tender, in exchange for material rewards.

11. Romania has a small but committed monarchist minority, which claims that Romania is still legally a monarchy, since a referendum has never been organized on the issue and King Michael was forced out in 1948 by the Soviets. The 1991 Constitution rules out the organization of such a popular consultation even for the future.

12. See Ken Jowitt, *New World Disorder: The Leninist Extinction* (Berkeley: University of California Press, 1992), ch. 1; Ken Jowitt, *Social Change in Romania: 1860–1940* (Cambridge: University of Cambridge Press, 1993).

13. Andrew C. Janos, *East Central Europe in the Modern World: The Politics of the Borderlands from Pre- to Postcommunism* (Stanford, Calif.: Stanford University Press, 2000), 357.

14. Max Weber, *On Charisma and Institution Building*, S.N. Eisenstadt ed., (Chicago: University of Chicago Press, 1968), 177–80.

15. Gil Eyal, Ivan Szelenyi, and Eleanor Townsley, *Making Capitalism without Capitalists: Class Formation and Elite Struggles in Post-Communist Central Europe* (London: Verso, 1998); Gil Eyal, *The Origins of Post-Communist Elites: From the Prague Spring to the Break-up of Czechoslovakia* (Minneapolis: University of Minnesota Press, 2003).

16. Barrington Moore, Jr., *Injustice: The Social Bases of Obedience and Revolt* (White Plains, N.Y.: M.E. Sharpe, 1978).

17. Iain McMenamin, "Parties, Promiscuity and Politicisation: Business-Political Networks in Poland," *European Journal of Political Research* 43 (2004): 657–76.

18. World Bank report, "Corruption in Poland: Review of Priority Areas and Proposals for Action" (the study was conducted at the Polish government's request and publicly issued in March 2000); on Romania, see Alina Mungiu-Pippidi, "Deconstructing Balkan Particularism: The Ambiguous Social Capital of South-Eastern Europe," working paper no. 18 (Athens: Hellenic Foundation for European and Foreign Policy, 2004).

19. See the New Democracy Barometer surveys, Center for Policy Studies, University of Strathclyde, available at *www.cspp.strath.ac.uk/index.html?catalog13_0.html*.

20. See Alina Mungiu-Pippidi, "Deconstructing Balkan particularism: the ambiguous social capital of Southeastern Europe," *Journal of South East European and Black Sea Studies* 5 (January 2005): 49–68.

21. The New Democracies Barometer is administered by the Centre for the Study of Public Policy at the University of Strathclyde, United Kingdom. For more information, see *www.cspp.strath.ac.uk*.

22. See the New Democracies Barometer, at *www.cspp.strath.ac.uk*.

23. Douglass C. North, *Institutions, Institutional Change and Economic Performance* (New York: Cambridge University Press, 1990).

24. Barrington Moore, Jr., *Social Origins of Dictatorship and Democracy: Lord and Peasant in the Making of the Modern World* (Boston: Beacon, 1966).

25. Pamela Leonard and Deema Kaneff, eds., *Post-Socialist Peasant? Rural and Urban Constructions of Identity in Eastern Europe, East Asia, and the Former Soviet Union* (New York: Palgrave, 2002).

26. "The 2004 Local Elections and the Reform of Local Governments: analysis, forecasts and recommendations," Policy Warning Report series (Bucharest: Romanian Academic Society, June 2004).

27. Ghita Ionescu, *The Politics of the European Communist States* (London: Weidenfeld Nicolson, 1967); and H. Gordon Skilling, *Czechoslovakia's Interrupted Revolution* (Princeton: Princeton University Press, 1976).

28. Juan J. Linz and Alfred Stepan, *Problems of Democratic Transition and Consolidation* (Baltimore: John Hopkins University Press, 1996), 435–55.

29. Radosław Markowski, "Party-System Institutionalization in New Democracies: Poland; A Trend Setter with No Followers," paper presented at the conference "Rethinking Democracy in the New Millennium," organized by the University of Houston, 16 19 February 2000, Houston, Texas.

30. Anna M. Grzymala-Busse, *Redeeming the Communist Past: The Regeneration of Communist Parties in East Central Europe* (Cambridge: Cambridge University Press, 2002).

31. Guillermo O'Donnell, "Horizontal Accountability in New Democracies," in Larry Diamond, Marc F. Plattner, and Andreas Schedler, eds., *The Self-restraining State: Power and Accountability in New Democracies* (Boulder, Colo.: Lynne Rienner, 1999), 29–52.

32. World Bank, "Corruption in Poland."

12

GHANA AND SOUTH AFRICA

Robert Mattes and E. Gyimah-Boadi

Robert Mattes *is associate professor of political studies and director of the Democracy in Africa Research Unit in the Centre for Social Science Research at the University of Cape Town.* **E. Gyimah-Boadi** *is executive director of the Centre for Democratic Development (CDD-Ghana) and professor of political science at the University of Ghana, Legon. The authors are cofounders and codirectors of the Afrobarometer.*

While the "third wave" of democracy rolled unevenly across sub-Saharan Africa in the 1990s, South Africa and Ghana stand out as two of the continent's political success stories.[1] Beginning in the late 1980s, South Africa's leaders steered the country out of the shadow of what appeared to be irreconcilable conflict and unavoidable racial or ethnic civil war to create a common nation. Since 1994, they negotiated two democratic constitutions and held five successful nationwide elections for national and local government. South Africa's constitution has become the darling of liberals and social democrats around the world because it includes an extensive set of political and socioeconomic rights. Since 1993, Ghana has enjoyed 11 years of democratic, constitutional rule and held three successful multiparty elections. It is now one of the few African countries ever to change leaders peacefully through the polls.

Both South Africa and Ghana have received plaudits from international observers of democracy and governance. Both are rated as Free by Freedom House: They are two of only ten African countries to be so labeled.[2] And since both are functioning multiparty democracies, by Larry Diamond's definition they also qualify as "liberal democracies."[3] Yet a review of available evidence—recent events, data produced by professional rating indices, and the results of mass-based opinion surveys—suggests that neither country can claim to have a high-quality democracy.

While Ghana recently joined the even more exclusive club of African countries to turn a ruling party out of power peacefully at the ballot box, a range of professional expert ratings award South Africa significantly higher scores than Ghana. The 2003 Freedom House survey gave South Africa a higher "status of political freedom" than Ghana (1.5 and 2.5, respectively, on a 1–7 scale on which 1 represents most free).[4] Similarly, the 2003 Bertelsmann Transformation Index (BTI) awarded South Africa a Democracy Status of 4.2 (out of 5), reflecting a country with "good prospects for consolidation of a market-based democracy," while Ghana received a 3.2 rating, placing it in a group of countries that have "deficiencies in terms of a market-based democracy."[5]

As we shall see, South Africa has also consistently received higher or better scores than Ghana in various other governance indices produced by Freedom House, the Bertelsmann Foundation, the World Bank Institute (WBI), and Transparency International. When we look at public-opinion surveys, however, we find that ordinary Ghanaians generally judge their country to have a higher quality of democracy than do South Africans. In late 2002, just one-half of the South African public (52 percent) told Afrobarometer interviewers that their country was either a "full democracy" (14 percent) or a "democracy with minor problems" (38 percent). In contrast, three in four Ghanaians (76 percent) felt their country was completely (30 percent) or largely democratic (47 percent). Roughly half of the South African respondents (47 percent) were "very" or "fairly" satisfied "with the way democracy works" in their country, compared to about three-quarters of their Ghanaian counterparts (72 percent).[6]

Are these popular responses accurate reflections of the relative quality of democracy in the two countries?[7] Do the South African responses prove what South African writers widely refer to as the "whinge factor," a supposedly prominent feature of their political culture? Conversely, do the Ghanaian responses evince a post-turnover euphoria? We cross-examine these overall popular judgments of the quality of democracy by looking at its constituent dimensions: rule of law, competitiveness, participation, accountability, responsiveness, equality, and freedom. Across each dimension, we review recent elite behavior, take note of "expert" assessments, and compare these with the judgments of ordinary citizens as measured by the 2002 Afrobarometer surveys (and other surveys where available).

In doing so, we assume that citizen opinions—regardless of what professional evaluators think, of what constitutions say, or of what elected leaders actually do—are ultimately what matters most in terms of the feasibility of the democratic project.[8] But a completely "user-based" approach focusing only on citizen perceptions faces significant limitations: In the great majority of instances, to paraphrase John Stuart Mill, citizens are indeed most likely to know where the democratic shoe pinches; however, demanding citizens may be overly critical of the quality of democracy while uncritical and uninformed citizens may be overly generous. Thus, the most complete academic assessment of the state of democracy must take into account both subjective and objective indicators, both by professionals and by citizens.

Assessing the Rule of Law

South Africa and Ghana have confronted quite different challenges in developing the rule of law. While apartheid South Africa never experimented with military rule (though the political influence of the military grew significantly during successive states of emergency in the 1980s), Ghana's postcolonial experience had been characterized by a steady alternation between attempts at multiparty civilian government and reversions to military rule. Its current experiment with civilian rule, which started in January 1993, has been marked by a serious attempt to reestablish the rule of law and create a rule-bound state and government, following 11 years of official arbitrariness and impunity under the quasi-military Provisional National Defence Council led by dictator Jerry Rawlings. Since 1993, military personnel have been steadily withdrawn from ordinary policing and the police have gradually become the main guarantor of internal security, especially since Rawlings's electoral defeat in 2001. Yet this road has been far from smooth. The military was brought under full democratic control only in 2001; until then, the elite 64 Infantry Battalion operated largely outside of the regular military command. As recently as 1999, military personnel and municipal authorities, acting upon instructions from superiors, razed a brand new privately owned hotel without a court order.[9]

In contrast to the arbitrary rule of Ghana's recent predemocratic past, apartheid South Africa was nothing if not rule-based; virtually every act of separation, removal, oppression, and repression carried out by the state could be located in or derived from an Act of Parliament.[10] Instead, South Africa's task was to introduce a rule of *just* law that respected human rights and was applicable to all citizens regardless of race. Thus, the concept of a Rechsstaat and constitutional supremacy replaced the British heritage of parliamentary sovereignty (which prevented judges from ruling on the legality or morality of apartheid legislation) and placed a significant check on the majoritarian concept of mass "people's power" that had long fueled the antiapartheid movement.

South Africa's rule of law has been strengthened by the virtual disappearance of politically motivated violence, which had marked the armed resistance to apartheid and the 1990–94 transition.[11] Part of this decline, however, may simply owe to the electoral dominance of the ruling African National Congress (ANC), because whatever political violence has reemerged since 1994 has tended to occur in areas where the ANC has faced strong electoral challenges.[12] Since 1994, however, the country's rule of law has been simultaneously weakened by an increase in criminally motivated violence, especially rape, armed robbery, and murder. Not only do the police lack training and resources, they also confront a society awash in illegal arms. Moreover, significant proportions of police are annually charged for committing crimes themselves.[13] As crime increased, limited skills in collecting evidence that can withstand new criteria of admissibility in court and an over-stretched prosecutorial system resulted in a decline in the number of prosecutions and convictions over the same period.[14]

South Africa now has one of the largest private-security industries in the world. The country also experiences high levels of white-collar crime. A recent survey by PricewaterhouseCoopers found that South African companies are subject to exceptionally high levels of theft, product piracy, and counterfeiting.[15] In contrast, Ghanaians enjoy a relatively low rate of crime. Yet popular frustration with an ineffective and inadequate police force (approximately 17,000 officers for a population of around 20 million) and an inefficient judiciary have resulted in persistent vigilantism by private militias and mob lynching.

Accordingly, in 2002 just one-half of the South Africans polled (49 percent) told Afrobarometer interviewers that they felt secure in their home, as opposed to seven in ten Ghanaians (71 percent). While Ghanaians and South Africans were roughly similar in their security against home break-ins (25 and 31 percent, respectively, said something had been stolen from their house), almost as twice as many South Africans (16 percent) as Ghanaians (9 percent) reported being physically attacked in the preceding year. Of greater concern is the possibility that lawlessness may become indelibly linked in the public mind with the democratic transition. While 52 percent of Ghanaians said that safety from crime and violence was better or much better in 2002 than under the military junta, six in ten South Africans (60 percent) said that safety was worse than under apartheid.

Ghana's and South Africa's evolving constitutional and legal frameworks guarantee a rule of law that extends to all geographic regions and to all groups of the population. In neither case is the authority of the state absent in any identifiable geographic area. Yet the prevalence of large informal economies that operate free of taxation or regulation speaks volumes about the limited reach of the state in both countries. The South African government has made headway in expanding the tax and regulatory net in some areas, such as household and farm labor, while it has met stubborn resistance in other areas, such as the taxi industry.

This has led to declining confidence in the government's willingness to enforce the law. In the 2002 Afrobarometer survey, one in ten South Africans (13 percent) said that the authorities are "not very" or "not at all" likely to enforce the law if a person like themselves committed a serious crime. One in five (19 percent) said the same thing with regards to tax evasion or obtaining household services (like water and electricity) without paying (22 percent). In contrast, the relevant pro-

TABLE 1—PERCEIVED RULE OF LAW IN GHANA AND SOUTH AFRICA

	GHANA	SOUTH AFRICA	AFROBAROMETER MEAN
Over the past year, how often (if ever) have you or anyone in your family?	*Percent answered at least "once or twice"*		
Feared crime in your own home	30	51	35
Had something stolen from home	23	31	29
Been physically attacked	9	16	12
How likely is it that the authorities would enforce the law if a person like yourself?	*Percent answered "likely" or "very likely"*		
Committed a serious crime	92	78	87
Did not pay a tax on some of the income they earned	88	69	76
Obtained household services (like water and electricity) without paying	82	66	73
Is the current government more or less able to enforce law than the old regime *(percent answered "more" or "much more")*	59	39	56
In our country:	*Percent answered "I agree"*		
The constitution expresses the values and aspiration of the people	55	61	60
How often:	*Percent answered "never" or "rarely"*		
President ignores the constitution	61	57	55
Party competition leads to conflict	49	36	40
People are treated unequally	55	45	42
How many of the following people do you think are involved in corruption, or haven't you heard enough about them to say?	*Percent answered "most of them" or "all of them"*		
President	68	69	56
Elected leaders	65	66	55
Government officials	56	63	51
Police	36	56	43
Border officials	34	47	37
Judges/magistrates	46	65	51
Teachers/school administrators	74	70	67
Is the current government more or less corrupt than the old regime *(percent answered "less" or "much less")*	47	24	36
In the past year, how often (if ever) have you had to pay a bribe, give a gift, or do a favor to government officials in order to:	*Percent answered at least "once or twice"*		
Get a document or a permit	82	94	86
Get a child into school	88	95	91
Get a household service	81	94	91
Cross a border	81	95	85
Avoid problem with the police	84	93	88

Source: Afrobarometer Round 2 (2002)

portions of Ghanaians were 4, 7, and 10 percent, respectively. While most Ghanaians (59 percent) felt that state's law-enforcement capacity had *increased* since the advent of multiparty democracy, a plurality of South Africans (41 percent) said it had *decreased.*

What the Experts Say

In contrast to popular evaluations, professional raters give both countries relatively similar scores. On Bertelsmann's dimension of "stateness"—which captures, among other things, the state's monopoly on violence over the entire territory and its workable administrative structures—both countries received a score of 4 out of 5 in 2003, meaning that the criteria has been met with reservations.[16] On the dimension of "political stability/absence of violence," the WBI is more critical, awarding scores that in 2004 placed Ghana in the 46th percentile and South Africa in the 38th, putting both countries in the second quartile of all countries.[17]

Both countries, however, have taken important steps to strengthen the rule of law. South Africa's drawn-out process of constitutional negotiations has been marked by a fascination with institutional design and experimentation, establishing new institutions such as the National Directorate for Public Prosecutions (NDPP)—which has its own high-profile elite unit with powers of investigation and arrest (called the Scorpions)—and a range of independent constitutional bodies such as the Independent Electoral Commission, Public Protector, Auditor General, Human Rights Commission, Gender Commission, Land Commission, and Youth Commission. South Africa's already well-developed court system has been complemented by a respected and interventionist Constitutional Court. Ghana has created a constitutionally independent Electoral Commission and a Commission on Human Rights and Administrative Justice (CHRAJ).

Many of these are in the process of becoming real, predictable political institutions. None of them, however, is as important as the ability to hold regular free and fair elections. In contrast to South Africa's hectic 1994 election—which had no voter registration, 165 "no go" areas out of bounds for various political party campaigns, and 35 percent of polling stations under-equipped[18]—the country's 2004 elections came and went with little drama and few "hot spots" of partisan conflict.[19] Key international monitoring organizations declined to send observer delegations.[20]

Ghana's Electoral Commission is also becoming increasingly effective and independent. Ghana's courts and the CHRAJ have asserted their political independence by delivering several important decisions against the government and the ruling party, for example overturning the public holiday that marked the anniversary of Rawlings's second coup, and ruling that the government must return unlawfully confiscated private assets. In South Africa, a variety of law-enforcement institutions such as the Special Investigating Unit, the Assets Forfeiture Unit, and the NDPP/ Scorpions have developed real prowess. The South African Revenue Service has steadily increased capacity to monitor tax compliance and financial movements, consistently collecting more than anticipated. The courts have handed down stiff fines and jail sentences to high-profile ANC figures, such as Allan Boesak, Tony Yengeni, and Winnie Mandela.

The Constitutional Court has told the government that it must honor constitutional rights to housing, and that public hospitals and clinics must begin to administer antiretroviral drugs to AIDS sufferers. Yet its recent failure to find any contradiction between the constitution's requirement that the electoral system produce proportionality and a constitutional amendment allowing "floor-crossing" in parliament (which can severely disturb such proportionality) has cast doubt on the Court's willingness to challenge the government on politically strategic issues.

In both countries, the government has tended to subject itself to the constitution and decisions of courts and other independent bodies. Yet Ghana's underdeveloped regulatory framework and administrative law offers public officials wide discretionary powers, which allows them to circumvent the law or evade sanction. The administrations of the National Democratic Congress (NDC) and the New Patriotic Party (NPP) have failed to pass legislation implementing the constitutional requirement of gender equality in marriage.[21] In South Africa, the government has dragged its feet complying with the landmark case on antiretroviral AIDS drugs, passing constitutionally required legislation enabling parliament to amend spending bills, and replacing expiring electoral legislation. Moreover, the final recommendations of the Truth and Reconciliation Commission regarding victims' compensation are still unfulfilled.

More seriously, the ruling ANC has shown itself quite capable of simply dissolving or discrediting independent institutions, even those of its own creation, that are seen to counteract the interests of the ruling party. For instance, the Special Investigative Unit (SIU) was originally created by the Mandela government to investigate and prosecute official corruption and recover stolen state funds in the Eastern Cape province. The SIU's popularity increased as the scope of its work broadened across the country; nonetheless, it became involved in successive conflicts with the government. Once it decided to begin investigating charges related to the government's R30 billion (US$5 billion) arms deal in 1999, its director was relieved (based on the logic that his appointment violated the separation of powers because he still retained his judgeship) and the Unit itself was disbanded. The ANC government has also moved to discredit and suppress a report by its own Medical Research Council that directly contradicted President Thabo Mbeki's attempts to minimize the impact of AIDS.[22]

South Africa's constitutional order faces perhaps its most difficult test in the NDPP indictment of former ANC guerilla Shabir Schaik on corruption charges. The charges involve personal payments to Deputy President Jacob Zuma as well as the facilitation of a bribe for Zuma from a French arms company in connection with the 1999 arms deal. On the positive side, the ANC has not interfered with the indictment; on the negative side, even though the NDPP claimed it had prima facie evidence that Zuma had accepted the bribe, they never charged him nor called him as a witness in the Schaik case, even though his name appeared throughout the charge sheet.[23]

The ANC government has also amended the constitution with worrying frequency and speed. Since the document's adoption in 1996, it has been amended by 11 separate pieces of legislation; these amendments resulted in at least 31 separate substantive changes to the document, several of which have contained important reordering of constitutional powers. Not only have such rapid and often far-reaching changes had grave implications for the integrity of the constitution, but the omnibus nature of the amendments often denies opposition parties the opportunity to take separate positions on each provision.[24] Even more seriously, the government's 2003 constitutional amendment was motivated by pure partisan gain: The ANC suddenly dropped its steadfast opposition to floor-crossing in order to enable an alliance with the New National Party (the direct heirs of the architects of apartheid), divide the opposition Democratic Alliance, and gain control of the Western Cape and KwaZulu-Natal provinces along with the Cape Town and Durban city councils (giving it control of the only two provinces and two cities it did not already dominate).

The incomplete application of the rule of law in both countries can be seen in the far-from-consensual sense of public attachment to the constitution. In the 2002 Afrobarometer surveys, just six in ten Ghanaians (65 percent) and South Africans (61 percent) agreed that "our constitution expresses the values and hopes" of the citizenry. Less than half of Ghanaians (46 percent) and one-third of South Africans (37 percent) thought that the president "never . . . ignores the constitution." In fact, 14 percent of Ghanaians and 20 percent of South Africans said that it happens "often" or "always." Consistent with these observations, the WBI gave Ghana and South Africa relatively mediocre rule-of-law ratings—Ghana ranked in the 49th percentile and South Africa in the 61st percentile internationally—which measure the extent to which agents have confidence in and abide by the rules of society, perceptions of the incidence of crime, and the effectiveness and predictability of the judiciary.[25]

In both countries, rule of law has faced sharp challenges from corrupt elite behavior. In Ghana, the government's inability to pay lower-level civil servants a living wage has created fertile ground for petty corruption. Moreover, Ghana's leaders have failed to elaborate and promulgate a credible code of conduct for public officials, or to reform the weak asset-declaration regulations for public officials. At present, public officials must declare their assets only once every four years, out of public sight, and do so to an agency with limited independence from the president.

Official corruption has been a major political issue in South Africa since 1994. Scholars and policy makers have debated, however, whether the actual frequency of corrupt behavior has really increased or whether it is simply more visible due to a more activist news media and civil society, and a more open government. Major scandals have emerged involving abuses of donor funding by cleric Alan Boesak; illegal gifts and bribes to Defense Minister Joe Modise, Majority Whip Tony Yengeni, and Deputy President Jacob Zuma related to the government arms deal; and most recently a travel voucher scam involving at least two dozen members of parliament. Government defenders point out that some of the highest-profile cases are known simply because of sustained state action to root out corruption through institutions like the SIU, the Public Protector, the Auditor General, and NDPP.

According to Transparency International's Corruption Perception Index (CPI), neither South Africa nor Ghana rate among the world's cleanest governments. Since its inclusion in the CPI, Ghana has received steadily negative ratings placing it between 50th and 70th of ranked countries. South Africa has fared only slightly better: In 1995, it was placed 21st internationally, but since 1997, it has dropped to between 32nd and 48th place. Consistent with South Africa's investment in anti-corruption institutions, the WBI awarded South Africa relatively higher scores in terms of official efforts to control corruption, placing it in the 71st percentile internationally in 2004. Nonetheless, this score marks a decline since 1996 when it placed in the 78th percentile. Again, Ghana fared considerably worse, being placed in the 52nd percentile internationally. Bertelsmann also ranks South Africa higher on its so-called rule of law indicator—which measures the independence and interdependence of branches of government, the independence of the judiciary, and the extent to which abuse of office is prosecuted—in 2003 giving it a score of 4 of 5, while Ghana only received a score of 3.

In contrast to professional ratings, ordinary South Africans are more likely to see corruption among elected and government leaders than Ghanaians. In the 2002 Afrobarometer survey, one in five South Africans (23 percent) said that "all" or "most" elected leaders are involved in corruption, and one in four (29 percent) said the same thing about government officials. The corresponding proportions of Ghanaians are 13 and 23 percent, respectively. It should be noted, however, that consistently higher proportions of Ghanaians also said that they "don't know" or "haven't heard enough about them to say." The situation was also different when it came to officials and institutions that are closer to the people: One-half of Ghanaian respondents said that most or all police (53 percent) and border officials (48 percent) were corrupt, and one-third said so about judges and magistrates (35 percent), compared to 38, 28, and 15 percent, respectively, in South Africa.

Ghanaians were also more likely to report being a victim of corruption than are South Africans: About one in ten said they had to pay a bribe, give a gift, or do a favor for a government official in order to cross a border (13 percent); get a service like water, electricity, or phones (13 percent); obtain a document or permit (13 percent); avoid a problem with the police (8 percent); or get their child into school (9 percent). The corresponding figures for South Africans are 3, 5, 6, 7, and 4 percent. On the whole, 63 percent of Ghanaians approved of government efforts in fighting corruption, compared to just 29 percent in South Africans (where 63 percent said the government was doing fairly or very badly). Slightly less than one-half of Ghanaians said that multiparty democracy had resulted in *less* corruption, while only one-quarter of South Africans thought so.

Competitiveness

In contrast to the rule of law, these two countries differ sharply when we turn to democratic competitiveness. South Africa's party system is dominated by one party and has thus become less competitive; by contrast, Ghana has one of the most competitive party systems in Africa. The differences are rooted in the two countries' dissimilar electoral systems, opposition parties, and historical legacies shaping the development of political parties.

Under South Africa's electoral system of closed-list proportional representation, the ANC has won increasing proportions of the vote, while the opposition has splintered and become weaker. The ANC won 63 percent of the vote in 1994, 66 percent in 1999, and 70 percent in 2004. In 1994, its vote tally gave it a three-to-one advantage over the National Party (NP), which came in second with 21 percent, and a two-to-one advantage over the combined 32 percent of the vote garnered by the NP and the third-place Inkatha Freedom Party (IFP). By 2000, its margin increased to a five-to-one advantage over the 12 percent of the first runner-up, the Democratic Alliance (DA), and roughly a three-to-one advantage over the combined 20 percent won by the DA and the IFP. While South Africa's weak federal arrangement initially provided for increased competitiveness at the provincial level, the ANC now controls each of the country's nine provinces; it is the majority party in seven and enjoys overwhelming dominance in at least five. As a result of the constitutional amendment allowing legislators to switch parties while keeping their seats and salaries, it now also has decisive control of the country's six largest city governments.

Part of this dominance is due to the numerically imbalanced social cleavage created by the struggle against apartheid. The ANC managed to fashion itself as the prime champion of the formerly oppressed black South Africans, while opposition parties receive their support from racial minorities or ethnoregional enclaves. At the same time, the ANC has managed to deliver the goods in a wide range of relevant issue areas, thereby earning strong performance evaluations. Yet part of the ANC's dominance is also due to the substantial numbers of dissatisfied voters, especially blacks, who hold thoroughly negative views of virtually all other parties.[26]

The ANC also receives considerable assistance from a set of structural advantages. First, executive and legislative elections are fused, and national and provincial elections are held concurrently: This "presidentializes" the elections and forces voters to make package decisions about an entire government, allowing the ANC to capitalize on the advantage of incumbency. It also focuses attention on national rather than regional dynamics where opposition parties might enjoy a relative advantage. Second, as the largest and governing party, the ANC attracts a disproportionate share of media coverage.[27] The country's ban on television campaign advertising means that small parties are unable to use what would be the most effective way to make up wide gaps in voter awareness.

Third, free two-minute public-election broadcasts on national radio stations are allocated to parties based on their share of national and provincial assembly seats and the number of candidates they have fielded for the campaign, disadvantaging smaller parties. Fourth, while there is public funding for political parties, the lion's share is given out proportionally, based on current legislative seats and the number of candidates on party lists. Only a very small share of public funding is distributed equally to all legislative parties. Fifth, there is no regulation on private financial donations to political parties, yet private donors have a strong incentive to contribute to the party that controls the legislative and regulatory framework. In 2004, the ANC spent at least R20.5 million (US$3 million) on various forms of advertising compared to approximately R12.2 million ($1.8 million) spent by all other parties combined.[28] Finally, the recent constitutional amendment allows legislative floor-crossing *only* if at least 10 percent of their party defects, making it much easier for dissidents to leave small opposition parties rather than from the ANC. All of this conspires to create a "home-field advantage" for the largest party, helping it to maintain its electoral dominance.

Under Ghana's first-past-the-post constituency-based system, elections to the 200-seat legislature have become increasingly competitive. While the 1992 parliamentary election—the first under Ghana's Fourth Republic—produced a virtual one-party legislature, with all but two members affiliated with the NDC, the 1996 and 2000 elections gave 67 and 99 seats, respectively, to members from the opposition NPP. Subsequent by-election victories have now given the NPP majority control. In the 2000 presidential election, NPP leader John Kufuor won 57 per-

TABLE 2A—GHANAIAN PRESIDENTIAL AND LEGISLATIVE ELECTION RESULTS 1992–2004 (PERCENT OF VOTE)

ELECTION	NDC	NPP	OTHER
1992 presidential	58.4	30.3	11.3
1992 legislative	94.5	–	5.5
1996 presidential	54.4	39.6	6.0
1996 legislative	66.5	30.5	3.0
2000 presidential	44.5	48.1	7.4
2000 presidential runoff	43.1	56.9	–
2000 legislative	46.0	50.0	4.0
2004 presidential	44.6	52.5	2.9
2004 legislative	40.9	55.7	3.4

Source: Electoral Commission of Ghana

TABLE 2B—SOUTH AFRICAN NATIONAL ELECTION RESULTS 1994–2004 (PERCENT OF VOTE)

PARTY	1994	1999	2004
African National Congress	62.6	66.4	69.7
Democratic Party/Democratic Alliance	1.7	9.6	12.4
Inkatha Freedom Party	10.5	8.6	7.0
National Party/New National Party	20.4	6.9	1.7
Other	4.8	8.5	9.2

Source: Independent Electoral Commission

cent of the vote, defeating John Atta Mills of the NDC. Yet as competitive as Ghana's elections have become, serious problems remain with electoral competitiveness. The ruling party and president enjoy unequal access to both state and private-sector funds (via political extortion) and other crucial election resources such as radio and television exposure and advertising.

Participation

At first glance, South Africans appear to possess far higher levels of the skills and resources on which to build an active and critical citizenry than do Ghanaians. Almost one-third of Ghanaians (31 percent) have no formal education, and just one-fifth (21 percent) have any form of secondary education—compared to 7 and 57 percent, respectively, in South Africa. South Africans are also far more likely to get news from radio (91 percent), television (79 percent), and newspapers (53 percent) on a regular basis. Not only are Ghanaians far less likely to receive news than South Africans, but they actually fall below the Afrobarometer average.

Yet these sharp differences in skills and resources fail to account for patterns in citizen awareness and engagement in politics. In the 1999–2000 Afrobarometer surveys, substantial portions of both Ghanaians (74 percent) and South Africans (80 percent) said they were "somewhat" or "very" interested in politics, though a relatively lower portion of Ghanaians (49 percent) said they took part in political discussion with friends and neighbors (compared to 62 percent in South Africa). Looking at a key indicator of political knowledge—the awareness of incumbents— Ghanaians were about as likely as South Africans correctly to identify their vice president (60 percent versus 57 percent) and minister of finance (32 percent versus 38 percent). Reflecting the impact of different electoral systems, Ghanaians are far more likely than South Africans to know who is their member of parliament (49 percent versus less than 1 percent) and local government councilor (59 percent versus 1 percent). Moreover, Ghanaians exhibit higher levels of economic awareness: In Ghana, 41 percent of respondents had heard of their government's structural-adjustment reform program, compared to the 13 percent of South Africans who had heard of the ANC's highly controversial and widely debated Growth Employment and Redistribution (GEAR) program.

Differences in access to formal education and news media also fail to account for differences in voter turnout. In South Africa, voter turnout has fallen from an estimated 86 percent in 1994, to 72 percent in 1999 and 58 percent in 2004. This is not coincidentally almost exactly the cross-national average turnout in one-party–dominant systems.[29] In sharp contrast, turnout in all of Ghana's first three general elections was around 70 percent. The declining turnout of South African voters is a result of increasing apathy amongst opposition voters, and the tendency of dissatisfied ANC supporters who see no legitimate alternative among the opposition to abstain rather than shift their vote. Thus in 2004, just 39 percent of all eligible voters actually cast a ballot for the ANC. This might not be so problematic in a mature democracy, or in a country where there are frequent elections or other ways for people to influence the government. But hardly any of these conditions apply to South Africa. If left unchecked, the trend of declining voter turnout raises the specter of a ruling party that sees itself as politically omnipotent yet in reality rests on an increasingly narrow electoral base.

Neither country stands out in terms of popular affiliation with civil society groups: Both are at or below the Afrobarometer average for membership in trade unions or religious, business, and community. They also exhibit low levels of participation in collective behaviors like community meetings, issue groups, or demonstrations—with the one exception of political protest in South Africa. Larger differences emerge in terms of contact between citizens and their elected representatives: In 2002, a mere 4 percent of South Africans had contacted a member of parliament "for help to solve a problem or to give them your views," compared to 12 percent in Ghana and an average of 25 percent across Africa. Only 4 percent had made contact with a government or ministry official, compared to 12 percent in Ghana and 14 percent on average across the continent. Interestingly, the difference in contact rates disappears when we turn to local government, where

TABLE 3—CITIZEN PARTICIPATION IN GHANA AND SOUTH AFRICA (PERCENT)

	GHANA	SOUTH AFRICA	AFROBAROMETER MEAN
How interested are you in public affairs *(percent answered"somewhat" or "very")*	74	81	80
How often do you get news from the following sources?			
Radio	77	91	81
Television	25	79	38
Newspapers	21	53	28
Are you an official leader, an active member, or an inactive member of:			
Religious group	83	73	73
Business/professional association	11	17	26
Community development association	22	17	26
Trade union/farmers association	21	12	22
Have you done any of these things during the past year?	*Percent answered at least "once or twice"*		
Discussed politics with friends/neighbors	49	62	59
Attended community meeting	57	58	65
Joined with others to raise an issue	39	43	50
Attended a protest or demonstration march	8	21	14
Contacted local government councilor	15	16	25
Contacted a member of parliament	11	4	12
Contacted government/ministry official	12	4	14
Contacted political-party official	17	13	18

Source: Afrobarometer Round 2 (2002)

South Africans directly elect ward representatives as part of a mixed-member electoral system.

Accountability

Vertical accountability. Ghanaians vote directly in single-member constituencies for national-level legislators every four years, and directly for the president every four years. Given the increasing competitiveness of Ghanaian elections, politicians must ensure that their actions give as little reason as possible for the voters to turn against them in the next election. In contrast, South Africans cast one ballot each for a party list for national and provincial assemblies every five years; the president is then selected by the National Assembly. Thus, no single individual in national or provincial government is elected on a direct basis, and no single representative is personally accountable to the voters. Because representatives at both levels lose their seats (and hence their salaries and privileges) if they cease to be a member of a party, South Africa's elected representatives must worry about pleasing party bosses rather than voters. In the 2004 election, the ANC did not even see fit to name its candidates for premier, which meant that voters did not know who would run their province if the party won. Moreover, the recent constitutional amendment allowing legislative floor-crossing (at all levels) violates the one thing South African voters *can* determine: the partisan proportionality of the legislature.

Some degree of indirect accountability might be created if the ruling party had to worry about pleasing voters to retain or increase their political strength at the next election, but the ANC has little reason to fear its electoral support dropping under 50 percent any time soon. Another possible form of indirect accountability might be offered by South Africa's relatively extensive organized civil society. South Africa does have over 100,000 non-profit organizations, but there is a large gap between the vast majority of community-based groups and the few, relatively well-resourced civil society organizations who try to influence government policy.[30] Moreover, the largest and best organized section of civil society, the trade unions, still remains loyal to the ANC even as its leaders oppose the government's economic reforms. The umbrella Congress of South African Trade Unions (COSATU) remains involved in an electoral alliance with the ANC: COSATU leaders (along with those of the South African Communist Party) receive parliamentary seats in return for electoral support. Notably, labor leaders take up these seats as members of the ANC. When COSATU and its allied organizations have publicly criticized ANC policy, the party has simply condemned them as "ultra left," rather than justified its own economic policy.

Yet there is evidence that well-organized groups can influence the ruling party on at least some issues. For instance, the nongovernmental Treatment Action Campaign has used criticism, advocacy, publicity, protest, and court challenges to force the government to change its policies on providing anti-AIDS drugs. Other organizations have found points of access in certain receptive parliamentary committees and managed to influence legislation on parliamentary ethics, access to official information, and protection of whistleblowers.

South Africa has a significant range of private news media that are quite vocal and critical of government policy. The once white-owned newspaper industry is rapidly diversifying in terms of racial ownership, with important titles now controlled by Zimbabweans and Nigerians. The government has sold six radio stations, and a vibrant privately owned community radio network has developed. There is now also a private television channel.[31] Although the South African Broadcasting Corporation (SABC) is generally free of heavy-handed government intervention, news reporting often suffers from self-censorship, and a number of recent news directors have come and gone after reported conflicts with government. Most recently, controversy flared after the SABC decided to cover the launch of the ANC's 2004 election campaign (but no one else's), yet fired a popular talk radio host when she was placed as a candidate on the list of the main opposition party.[32]

While Ghanaian civil society enthusiastically demands public accountability, it remains weak, divided, and vulnerable to government manipulation and cooptation. Civil society organizations, including ones that preach good governance and anti-corruption, do not always practice the virtues of transparency, accountability and anticorruption: Few groups adhere to any credible code of conduct or basic rules of corporate governance, and many are personal empires with no succession plans or any meaningful degree of internal accountability. All of this compromises their ability to demand official accountability.

The combination of relaxed censorship, libel laws, and broadcast liberalization has led to the emergence of an increasingly vibrant news media which has helped to increase accountability through the risk of exposure. Where Ghana had absolutely no private daily newspapers or radio and television stations in the early 1990s, there are now approximately one dozen newspapers (ten independently owned), seventy radio stations (68 are state-owned), and four television stations (three independently owned). Yet the ability of the news media to promote accountability is limited by huge gaps in levels of professionalism and integrity. There have been disturbing but credible reports of emerging practices of shake-downs, blackmail, and "pocket-book journalism."

Horizontal Accountability. Ghana's constitution limits government powers and provides for checks and balances as well as at least a formal separation of powers. In addition, the creation of the CHRAJ as an independent constitutional body with a mandate to support human rights, administrative justice, and anticorruption has provided a focal point for the promotion of public accountability and fighting corruption. This has been complemented by the emergence of a reasonably strong opposition in parliament. Ministers are now more vigorously questioned, and executive appointees to key public offices are vetted. The process of reviewing the annual budget has become more rigorous as the Public Accounts Committee and the Committee on Government Assurances actively scrutinize the Auditor General's Report and follow up on government promises. The Audit Service has also been revived and its annual report somewhat more timely (only about three years in arrears); moreover, parliamentary review of the report has become more serious and thorough.

Severe limitations and challenges confront the institutionalization of horizontal accountability, however—especially legislative oversight of the executive. First, the constitution fosters a "hegemonic" presidency by requiring that the president select 50 percent of the cabinet from parliamentary ranks, but placing no absolute ceiling on the size of the cabinet or on the number of Supreme Court justices the president can appoint. The president also has direct or indirect control over the appointments of district chief executives as well as of heads and board members of parastatal companies. The constitution also grants the president a near-monopoly over the public purse, as all spending bills must emanate from the executive rather than the legislature. And, as noted above, the parliamentary Public Account Committee has a backlog of audit reports to review, with the 2000 report scheduled for review only in 2004.

Second, enduring neopatrimonial authority relations and its accompanying patronage and corruption remain entrenched.[33] Members of parliament are highly susceptible to executive cooptation through appointments to lucrative ministerial positions and public boards. The speaker of parliament in the NDC administration was part of the president's "kitchen cabinet" and the present speaker is the immediate past national chairman of the ruling NPP; both have frequently benefited from state-sponsored medical treatment overseas. Ruling-party backbenchers are appointed as ministers or to other prestigious and profitable positions in the ever-expanding presidential retinue.

President Kufuor, who originally came to power on the back of the parliamentary caucus, has now tamed it through extensive ministerial and deputy-ministerial appointments. The self-confidence and independence of important official watchdogs and investigative agencies such as the Serious Fraud Office and the Auditor General have been effectively undermined by the practice of keeping heads of key oversight agencies in "acting" positions without confirmation to serve in perpetuity. Such agencies suffer from a chronic lack of resources, and are too weak to offer meaningful oversight over the executive. Finally, Ghana's courts remain financially and operationally dependent on the executive, leaving them weak and short of resources. The absence of a constitutional or statutory ceiling on the maximum number of judges that can be appointed to the Supreme Court enables the president to pack the Court with political allies, which fuels public perceptions of the judiciary's corruption and lack of independence.

South Africa's 1996 constitution contains at least a formal separation of powers between the president (who, elected by the majority party in parliament, is actually a "hybrid" prime minister), the popularly elected parliament, and the court system. Members of the cabinet, including the president, are formally accountable collectively and individually to parliament for the exercise of their powers and performance of their functions. They can be removed by motions of no confidence, as can the president. Parliamentary committees have considerable powers to summon and compel witnesses to provide testimony or reports. Accountability is putatively enhanced by the presence of elected provincial governments and local municipal councils. There is also a range of independent watchdog agencies and commissions.

Yet virtually all of this is compromised by three factors. First, the separation of powers in South Africa is actually a separation of functions—in reality, executive and legislative powers are fused—and other than a formal vote of no confidence, the legislature has few formal mechanisms with which to check executive action. Second, the country's system of closed-list PR combined with the ability to eject members from parliament increases the power of party leaders—and for the ANC this means the president and his ministers—over individual legislators. This removes any incentive for members of parliament to represent public opinions running counter to the party line. Any rigorous parliamentary oversight by majority-party MPs places them in the difficult position of criticizing senior party leaders, who could eject them from the party for disloyalty and hence from parliament. Thus, parliamentary committees have made substantive changes to government legislation in only a tiny fraction of cases.

The president rarely appears before parliament to answer questions. And despite attempts to provide the ANC with the lion's share of question time, the vast majority of questions are asked by opposition members.[34] In fact, the antidefection clause, which remains in effect outside of the relatively infrequent windows for floor-crossing, gives the ANC the potential to preclude any vote of no confidence by sniffing out disloyal MPs and replacing them with loyal ones. Any doubts that the governing party would resort to such measures were removed in 1997 when it jettisoned one of its most popular figures, Bantu Holomisa, because he publicly accused a sitting cabinet minister and former Bantustan ruler of apartheid-era corruption.

Indeed, imposing party discipline has become an increasing preoccupation. At a 2000 national ANC meeting, Secretary General Kgalema Motlanthe reminded members that, "the principles of democratic centralism still guided party structures," and that new ANC members must promise to combat "any tendency toward disruption or factionalism."[35] It appears that the ANC (along with the IFP) have also engaged in "purging" potentially disloyal local councilors in KwaZulu-Natal province in the run up to the first scheduled floor-crossing in 2004.[36]

The ANC has invoked party loyalty to prevent its MPs from vigorously questioning the health minister about unauthorized expenditure of R14 million (US$2 million) for a dubious HIV/AIDS educational musical.[37] And President Mbeki reportedly blocked internal party demands that the majority whip appear before the parliament's Ethics Committee to explain why he did not report a discounted luxury car he received from a European defense company that was bidding for an arms subcontract. The ANC caucus ultimately allowed the party to decide on his fate rather than parliament.[38] But the most profound crisis in executive-legislative relations occurred in relation to the government's 1999 arms deal. Backed by a unanimous parliamentary resolution, the Standing Committee on Public Accounts (SCOPA), which traditionally operates along nonpartisan lines and is headed by an opposition member of parliament, launched an inquiry including a Special Investigating Unit (SIU). Senior government leaders subsequently attacked the investigation, replaced the leader of the ANC delegation in SCOPA, and pressured committee members into distancing themselves from the inclusion of the SIU.[39]

Moreover, a trend toward centralism within the ANC has limited the ability of ordinary rank-and-file members to hold their party to account. National party structures have increasingly extended their powers at the provincial and local levels. Candidates for provincial premierships and local mayoralties are now nominated by a central "redeployment" committee rather than by provincial or local ANC branches. Several provincial party structures have simply been dissolved and reformed by the national party, ostensibly because of "disunity" or "ill discipline," but critics have viewed these actions as attempts to head off grassroots movements critical of the president. The national party machinery has also deposed several provincial premiers, some of whom have been popular leaders widely seen as future challengers for party leadership. Finally, the interval between party conferences has been extended from three years to five, thereby limiting opportunities for the rank-and-file to elect senior party organs.

Yet in contrast to the narrative set out above, in 2004 the WBI placed South Africa among the top third of all countries in terms of what it calls "voice and accountability" (which taps the public's ability to participate in the selection of government and the independence of the media) placing it in the 71st percentile across the world.[40] Nonetheless, the WBI appears to have detected a sharp drop off in accountability since it placed South Africa in the 80th percentile in 2000. Again, Ghana scores substantially lower (58th percentile), though this is a substantial gain over where it was in 1996 (41st percentile).

In contrast to the professional ratings, however, Ghanaians are more likely to think that they can hold their elected leaders to account than are South Africans. In 2002, six in ten Ghanaians (63 percent) compared to one-half of South Africans (51 percent) agreed that they would be able to get together with others and make elected officials listen to them. Given the major transformations in political power embodied in the transition from white-minority rule to an open democracy, it is surprising that just one-half of South Africans (50 percent) say that "the ability of ordinary people to influence what government does" is better or much better now than it was during apartheid. Almost six in ten Ghanaians (58 percent) think that they are better able to influence government now than under Rawlings's military regime.

Responsiveness

While many citizens in both countries feel they have the potential to hold elected officials accountable, they do not perceive a high level of actual responsiveness. When the Afrobarometer asked whether "elected leaders, like parliamentarians, or local councilors, try their

TABLE 4A—APPROVAL OF INCUMBENT LEADERS AND STATE
RESPONSIVENESS IN GHANA AND SOUTH AFRICA

	GHANA	SOUTH AFRICA	AFROBAROMETER MEAN
Do you approve or disapprove of the way that the following people have performed their jobs over the past year?	*Percent answered "strongly approve" or "approve"*		
President	74	51	70
Members of parliament	57	45	54
Regional government	54	43	44*
Local government	43	33	48
Based on your experience, how easy or hard is it to obtain the below services?	*Percent answered "very easy" or "easy"*		
Voter registration card	81	86	80
Place in school for your child	64	78	73
Identity document	26	70	41
Help from the police	17	41	32
Household services (water, electricity)	14	54	12
Government loan or payment	5	23	10

Source: Afrobarometer Round 2 (2002)
* Not asked in Botswana, Mali, and Cape Verde

best to listen to what people like you have to say," just 22 percent of
Ghanaians and 11 percent of South Africans answered "always" or
"most of the time." Almost identical results were gathered by a question that asked how often elected leaders "look after the interests of
people like you."

Another way to measure responsiveness is to examine people's evaluations of government performance on the issues which they prioritize.
In 2002, Ghanaians emphasized issues of job creation (51 percent), education (36 percent), poverty and destitution (24 percent), the water supply
(27 percent), health care (24 percent), and economic management (24
percent) as the most important issues facing the country that government should address (they were able to offer up to three issues). The
Afrobarometer measured public evaluations of government performance
in five of these areas; in all of them, more than 45 percent said that the
government was handling the matter "very well" or "well." When asked
to give an overall assessment, three-quarters (74 percent) approved of
President Kufuor's performance in 2002, and a majority approved of the
performance of the parliament (57 percent).

This mirrors the frequent praise that the government receives from the
local media as a "listening government," especially after it backed away
from a controversial attempt to acquire a US$1 billion loan from a dubi-
ous overseas source and decided not to privatize the Ghana Commercial
Bank. Political leaders and state officials are increasingly accessible to
the news media through occasional presidential and regular ministerial
interviews and press conferences. Government spokespersons and public officials are often readily available to answer questions on radio and

TABLE 4B—PRIORITY ISSUE AREAS AND GOVERNMENT PERFORMANCE
IN GHANA AND SOUTH AFRICA

In your opinion, what are the most important responsibilities of your parliamentary representative? How well or badly would you say the current government is handling the following matters, or haven't you heard enough about them to say?

Issue	GHANA		SOUTH AFRICA	
	% Listing Issue as Priority	Satisfied with Performance	% Listing Issue as Priority	Satisfied with Performance
Create jobs	51	45	84	9
Address educational needs	36	64	15	61
Deliver household needs	27	56	9	60
Improve basic health services	24	63	10	54
Manage the economy	24	64	7	38
Keep prices stable	9	57	7	17
Ensure enough food	7	55	9	21
Reduce crime	6	65	34	23
Resolve intercommunity conflict	3	70	2	38
Combat HIV/AIDS	3	77	28	46
Fight government corruption	2	63	13	29
Narrow income gap	1	36	3	19

Source: Afrobarometer Round 2 (2002)

television talk shows. Slightly over half of Ghanaians also approve of local and regional government (just above the Afrobarometer mean).

South Africans focused far more singlemindedly on jobs (84 percent), but also on crime (34 percent), poverty and destitution (28 percent), AIDS (26 percent), education (15 percent), corruption (13 percent), and health care (10 percent) as government-priority issues. The Afrobarometer measured public evaluations of six of these issues; the South African government received majority approval on only two of them—education (61 percent) and health care (54 percent). On the two most frequently cited issues, jobs and crime, the government received abysmal ratings, with only 9 and 23 percent, respectively, saying the government handled these issues "well" or "very well."

When respondents were pressed for an overall assessment, President Mbeki received slight majority approval (51 percent), while parliament received the approval of 45 percent; regional government, 43 percent; and local government, 33 percent. Across a range of other fundamental issues, survey research has demonstrated wide gaps between ANC policies and a public that favors capital punishment, opposes abortion, has little use for traditional leaders, and wants a strong constituency element in the electoral system.[41]

Yet another method of capturing responsiveness focuses on the ability of the state to anticipate and meet citizens' needs for basic services and opportunities.[42] Examined in this way, South Africa has a much more responsive state. Large majorities in both Ghana (81 percent) and South Africa (86 percent) say it is easy to obtain a voter registration card in their country, but gradually larger differences emerge when we turn to other issues. In Ghana, 64 percent say it is easy or very easy to find a place in school for their children (compared to 78 percent of South Africans). But just one-quarter or less of Ghanaians say that they can easily obtain an identity document (26 percent), help from the police (17 percent), household services like water and electricity (14 percent), or a government loan or payment (5 percent). While not overwhelmingly positive, the figures for South Africa are substantially and consistently higher. Yet Ghanaians (47 percent) are more likely than South Africans (41 percent) to say that the new democratic regime is more or much more effective in the delivery of services than the old regime; in fact, over one-third of South Africans (35 percent) think it is *less* effective than the apartheid government.

Freedoms and Rights

Both the South African and Ghanaian constitutions guarantee a wide range of civil and political rights and liberties that the majority of black South Africans were denied during apartheid, and that were limited in Ghana by repeated military governments—especially the brutal and oppressive Rawlings junta. South Africa's constitution goes on to guarantee a range of cultural (linguistic and cultural choice and practice) and socioeconomic rights, such as the right to fair labor practices, environmental protection, access to adequate housing, health care services, sufficient food and water, social security, basic and adult education, and access to information held by the state.

In practice, there are very few limitations to South Africans' ability to enjoy their newfound civil and political rights. The country is marked by an impressive degree of debate in the news media, vibrant associational life, and religious and cultural diversity. Yet the state broadcaster often suffers from self-censorship, and the ANC government has still not abandoned the apartheid government's practice of wielding lawsuits against those critical of government performance or those who publicize corruption. Moreover, the increasing fear of crime and violence detailed above significantly limits the personal freedoms of South Africans. Rights are also compromised by the country's criminal-justice system, with lengthy pretrial detention, poor prison conditions, and abuse, torture, and death in police custody.

The South African government also faces severe obstacles to realizing the constitution's socioeconomic promises. Massive unemployment, a narrow tax base, strict fiscal discipline, low wages, and an undereducated and underskilled workforce mean that many people are unable to pay for water and electricity, to receive a decent education, or to buy a new home. In 2002, between one-quarter and one-third of Afrobarometer survey respondents said they went without clean water or cooking fuel

TABLE 5—PERCEIVED FREEDOMS AND RIGHTS IN
GHANA AND SOUTH AFRICA

	GHANA	SOUTH AFRICA	AFROBAROMETER MEAN
Are the following things worse or better now than under the previous system of government?	Percent answered "much better" or "better"		
Freedom to say what you want	69	76	76
Freedom to join any organization	68	80	76
Freedom from arrest when innocent	69	59	62
Freedom to vote without pressure	68	77	48
Citizen's ability to influence government	58	50	55
Safety from crime and violence	52	22	46
In this country how often:	Percent answered "never" or "rarely"		
Must people self-censor political speech	56	60	49
Over the past year, how often have you or your family gone without:	Percent answered at least "once or twice"		
Enough food to eat	40	37	53
Enough clean water for home use	43	27	45
Medicine or medical treatment	54	33	58
Enough fuel to cook food	27	27	42
A cash income	69	48	75

Source: Afrobarometer Round 2 (2002)

(27 percent), medicine (33 percent), food (37 percent), or cash (48 percent) at least once in the previous year.

Ghana's return to democratic constitutional rule has brought steady improvements in the enjoyment of freedoms and rights, especially under Kufuor's NPP government. The principle of *habeas corpus* is now consistently applied and the prison cells of the notorious internal-security agency, the Bureau of National Investigations, have been empty since 1994. Extrajudicial public tribunals have been curtailed and brought under the jurisdiction of the appellate courts. After initial hesitation and obstruction, freedom of assembly has been fully restored: The Supreme Court has interpreted the legal requirement to notify the police prior to a public demonstration as one of merely serving notice, placing the burden on the police to provide reasonable grounds to prevent it. Religious freedom, a significant civil society, and a lively print media prevail. Religious and voluntary civil society organizations continue to proliferate. Women have benefited from the outlawing of such longstanding practices as female genital mutilation and slavery of vestal virgins *(trokosi),* and the CHRAJ and other civil society groups wage sustained campaigns against such practices.

Yet the advance of freedom and liberty was slowed by the reluctant democrats that dominated the Rawlings government; they often attempted to intimidate the courts whenever they lost a case, or delayed the implementation of constitutional provisions they saw as inconvenient or inexpedient. On several occasions, the government failed to comply with *habeas corpus,* especially in matters affecting Rawlings himself, his family, or close associates. This shallow commitment to human rights partly reflected the persistence of traditional cultural values, which are not necessarily liberal and often do not foster popular sensitivity to human rights.

Moreover, severe resource constraints and political intimidation hobble those institutions established to monitor abuses and foster adherence to rights legislation—such as the courts, the CHRAJ, and the Legal Aid Board. In Ghana, those accused of crimes face very long periods of pretrial detention, and prison conditions remain atrociously inhumane—this despite campaigns by the CHRAJ and others on behalf of prisoners and against mandatory custodial sentences for frivolous offences. Inadequate access to justice in rural areas compels citizens to seek justice in the traditional realm of the chief's palace, where liberal values are far less likely to apply. Mob lynching and vigilante justice still exist in poorer areas and urban centers.

As mentioned at the beginning of this chapter, both South Africa and Ghana are rated as Free by Freedom House (South Africa since 1995 and Ghana since 2002). Since 1996, South Africa have been rated as having the highest level of political rights possible (a score of 1 on the 1-to-7 scale), but a score of 2 on civil liberties. Ghana received a 2 for both political rights and civil liberties. Both countries are now rated as Free in terms of press freedom.

Nonetheless, the 2002 Afrobarometer surveys found that more than one-third of citizens in both countries (34 percent in South Africa and 37 percent in Ghana) perceive significant limitations on their own freedom of speech, saying that people "often" or "always" "have to be careful of what they say about politics." Other surveys have found high levels of attitudinal intolerance, which may prevent disliked minorities from exercising their rights.[43] At the same time, 69 percent in Ghana and 76 percent in South Africa said their "freedom to say what you think" is "better" or "much better" than it was under the old regime. Three-quarters of Ghanaians said that they are now freer to "join any political organization you want" (69 percent), "to choose whom to vote for without feeling pressured" (68 percent), and "freedom from being arrested when you are innocent" (69 percent). Even larger majorities of South Africans noted that since the end of apartheid, there have been improvements in freedom of speech (76 percent), freedom of association (80 percent), and voting (77 percent). Only when it comes to freedom from unjust arrest are South Africans less positive: Only 59 percent said things have improved since the end of apartheid.

Political Equality

Ghanaians and South Africans both enjoy generous formal constitutional guarantees of equality before the law and the right to equal protection under the law. The adoption of such formal protections ended decades of legally sanctioned inequality in South Africa and removed an eleven-year ban on political parties in Ghana, allowing exiled politicians to return home. Both governments have also taken positive steps to ensure equality through independent state institutions specifically intended to protect or promote political equality.

Somewhat ironically, seeking to promote equality through legislation on matters such as affirmative action or the empowerment of blacks, the South African constitution even allows certain types of discrimination and unequal treatment—if it can be shown that the discrimination is not "unfair."[44] Meanwhile, the South African parliament has passed a host of legislation to prevent racist hate speech and discrimination in the workplace on the basis of race, ethnicity, or gender, and to enable affirmative action favoring "designated groups." Some lower courts have now become designated as "equality courts" to review accusations of discrimination.[45] Ghana has created a separate Ministry for Women and Children's Affairs and appointed a minister of state for girl-child education in the Ministry of Education. The new government has also recently announced that it would reserve fifty percent of appointments to district assemblies for women.

Nevertheless, neither legal guarantees of equality nor positive government redress immediately erase deeply entrenched patterns of discrimination and inequality. In South Africa, the overall level of income inequality, as measured by the Gini coefficient, remains one of the highest in the world. Yet that inequality has changed over the past decade. The change has been attributed to the government's targeted use of massive government-investment and relief programs in combination with its 1996 decision to move away from its redistributionist economic policy (the so-called redistribution and development program) toward a fiscally conservative set of policies (growth, employment, and redistribution).

In many ways, the conditions of the poorest South Africans have improved substantially since 1994. The government has facilitated the construction of 1.6 million low-cost houses and built 56,000 new classrooms; it has launched massive infrastructure projects, which have given 9 million people access to clean water, provided sanitation to 6.4 million, and electricity to 2 million. It now provides various forms of social grants to 7.4 million people, and more than 700 new clinics provide the poor with free medical care. Over 5 million needy children now get between one-fifth and one-quarter of their daily nutritional needs through school feeding programs. And finally, 1.8 million hectares of land have been transferred to some 140,000 households.[46]

Over the same period, however, the country's sluggish economy has actually shed half a million formal jobs and deprived hundreds of thousands of households of the income needed to make ends meet. Broadly

TABLE 6—PERCEIVED POLITICAL INEQUALITY IN
GHANA AND SOUTH AFRICA

	GHANA	SOUTH AFRICA	AFROBAROMETER MEAN
In general, how would you describe:	*Percent answered "worse" or "much worse"*		
Your living conditions compared to other people in your country	39	24	36
Economic conditions of your group compared to other groups in your country	30	39	29
Equal and fair treatment for all people by government compared to previous regime	36	47	45
How often:	*Percent answered "often" or "always"*		
Are people treated unequally under the law	28	45	42
Are [self-defined identity group] treated unfairly by the government	40	37	53

Source: Afrobarometer Round 2 (2002)

defined, unemployment now stands at almost 40 percent.[47] The bottom two-fifths of black households are now earning less in real terms than they were in 1995.[48] At the same time, public and private affirmative-action initiatives in education, business ownership, and hiring have created a sizeable black middle class.[49] The incomes of the top one-fifth of black households have made impressive strides.[50] Thus, while inter-racial inequalities have been reduced as a result of increasing black incomes and the redistributive effects of government spending, inequality *within* all race groups has increased.[51] Massive increases in HIV infection in the teenage and adult populations threaten to create a new line of inequality between the healthy and the infected or sick and their families, who face substantially increased financial burdens, stigmas, discrimination, and intolerance.

Ghanaians face enduring class inequalities and significant income gaps. Disproportionate numbers of those living in the countryside, the savannah, and the northern regions of the country continue to live in poverty, as does a large proportion of women. Women also face significant social discrimination, especially in rural areas, and many face domestic violence. In certain regions, traditional practices—such as the slavery of vestal virgins and penal villages for young girls accused of practicing witchcraft—continue to limit women's rights.[52] Poor women lack access to basic state services, and widows face persistent discrimination in terms of inheritance and widowhood rituals. On the whole, poor and rural Ghanaians are far more likely to be victims of police extortion and brutality.

To what extent do these social and economic inequalities translate into political inequalities, real or perceived? Women are poorly represented in public life and elective positions in both countries, although South Africa's electoral system allows parties to appoint an unusually high number of female parliamentarians. Ghana's 200-seat parliament

TABLE 7—THE POLITICAL IMPACTS OF SOCIAL, ECONOMIC, AND POLITICAL EQUALITY (ETA COEFFICIENT)

	GHANA				SOUTH AFRICA			
	Ethnic Group	Gender	Urban/Rural	Lived Poverty	Race	Gender Group	Urban/Rural	Lived Poverty
Empowerment and Agency								
Politics is too complicated	.142***	.027	.059*	.005	.141***	.066*	.093**	.036
People do not listen to me	.121*	.007	.010	.033	.080	.010	.040	.027
Able to make elected leaders listen	.058	.012	.037	.112	.184***	.018	.036	.070*
Elected leaders listen to people like me	.158***	.034	.048	.027	.117***	.012	.050	.081*a
Participation								
Contacted councilor	.073	.001	.104***	.007	.126***	.036	.096***	.076**
Contacted member of parliament	.061	.040	.041	.028	.062	.060*	.012	.003
Contacted government official	.073	.023	.020	.028	.069	.036	.016	.011
Obtained government document with ease	.071	.011	.199***	.070*	.082*	.055	.042	.060*
Obtained school placement with ease	.111*	.012	.012	.029	.145***	.038	.042	.089
Registered to vote with ease	.116*	.051	.054	.068*	.071	.016	.003	.045
Obtained household services with ease	.177***	.001	.347***	.062	.088*	.019	.069*	.058*
Obtained government payment with ease	.085	.045	.111***	.049	.107**	.020	.043	.058*
Obtained help from policy with ease	.147***	.023	.086***	.035	.063	.030	.020	.031
Equal Treatment								
People are treated unequally	.183***	.006	.060	.033	.166***	.007	.038	.116***
My group is treated unequally	.230***	.009	.010	.101***	.097*	.039	.057	.082***

Source: Afrobarometer Round 2 (2002)
Note: For ease of comparability, all correlations are computed using Eta.
* p < .05
** p < .01
*** p < .001

currently has no more than twenty women members. In both countries, a lack of regulation on party funding and campaign donations means that the wealthy can "buy" extraordinary amounts of influence over the governing party. Inadequate state legal aid means that many poor people still appear in court without representation, or even without proper translation so that they can follow the case in their own language. The gaps between a few well-heeled NGOs and the rest of civil society mean that groups representing the poor or the rural dwellers are rarely heard in the halls of parliament.

Significant proportions of Ghanaians (28 percent) and South Africans (45 percent) said that people are "often" or "always" "treated unequally under the law." When asked more directly about their self-defined identity group, 27 percent of South Africans said their group is "often" or "always" "treated unfairly by the government," compared to 15 percent of Ghanaians. When asked to compare political equality under multiparty democracy with the former regime, a scant majority of Ghanaians (54 percent) saw an improvement in "equal and fair treatment of all people by government, " 24 percent saw no change, and 12 percent felt things had become worse under the democratic system. In South Africa, the balance of opinion is significantly more negative: 48 percent said equality has increased, 19 percent saw no change, and 29 percent said that it had become worse.

Even deeper analysis demonstrates that perceptions of inequality cut *across* both societies and are not concentrated disproportionately among the poor, women, rural, or other historically deprived groups. There are few substantively important differences between the poor and the nonpoor, between rural and urban dwellers, and between men and women in terms of their perceptions of empowerment, influence, and unfair treatment. These differences also influence the extent to which they participate in the political process or make use of the state. This suggests that even though both these societies exhibit high levels of economic and social inequality, the major lines of perceived inequality may run between the "state class" and everyone else.

The Quality of Democracy Revisited

No credible analyst would dispute that either South Africa or Ghana is a democracy. Both hold regular free and fair elections and there are few limitations on political rights or civil liberties. People are formally more free and more equal than they were under the former authoritarian regimes, as a result of the formal constitutional and legal recognition of rights and liberties and the legislation and political institutions designed to give effect to these formalities. Real and important steps have been taken to ensure that governments conform to the rules of the new democratic game. Nevertheless, in comparison to the other members of the global family of democracies, neither can yet be said to provide its citizens with high-quality democracy.

South Africans live in one of the most minimal democracies imaginable. They have very little influence over their elected representatives, and the legislature has very little influence over the executive. There are few incentives to participate in the political process between elections, and even participation in national elections has plummeted dramatically over the first decade of democracy. Opposition voters see less reason to vote because the electoral outcomes are not in doubt, while dissatisfied former ANC supporters see no real alternative among the opposition.

Ghanaians belong to the exclusive club of Africans that have brought about a turnover in power by means of the ballot box. Their new electoral environment offers exciting opportunities for public influence over government. Yet the features of executive dominance contained in Ghana's 1992 constitution largely negate the checks and balances contained in the very same document. The president's vast appointive and patronage powers undermine the institution of parliamentary oversight, and the corruption spawned by the president's neopatrimonial practices undermines government effectiveness. All of this leads to low popular expectations of democratic performance and high tolerance of official wrongdoing. Fueled by chronically weak economic performance, constitutionally independent bodies—the parliament, the judiciary, the electoral commission, the CHRAJ, and the National Commission on Civic Education—remain financially and operationally dependent on the executive branch.

The signs of democratic quality that we do see in Ghana and South Africa exist because of several factors. First, the groups of citizens and civil society organizations that organized and sustained the initial protests and opposition against the apartheid government and Rawlings junta still constitute an important core of democracy advocates in both countries. Second, both countries have ruling parties which, while not necessarily deeply committed to democratic practice and pluralism, are at least open to and generally tolerant of these concepts. In South Africa's case, while it clearly has negative impacts on interparty competition, the very size of the ANC's "broad church" encapsulates a wide range of social, economic, and ideological variation that restrains the party leaderships' impulse to conformity. Finally, international democratic norms limit authoritarian tendencies, as both South Africa and Ghana value the roles they play on the regional and global stage. Ghana, in particular, is dependent on substantial external inflows, and international approval of its democratic achievements enables it to better access donor assistance and international debt relief.

Limitations on the quality of South Africa's and Ghana's democracies can be traced to five factors. First, many of these limitations are legacies of the authoritarian past. In Ghana, the culture of neopatrimonialism and tolerance of official corruption are remnants from years of military rule. The culture of South Africa's ruling ANC still contains several important strands from the struggle against apartheid, such as the tendency to see itself as the only legitimate representative of the people, an emphasis on public unanimity, and a discomfort with public dissent, open competition, and pluralism.

A second limitation on the quality of democracy stems from constitutional-design flaws, many of which were related to the nature of the democratic transition. Ghana's constitutional fusion of executive and legislative powers enabling presidential dominance resulted from a fervent desire for "strong" government to avoid the types of government crises which led to the first Rawlings coup, as well as a desire to preserve most of the authoritarian powers that Rawlings had enjoyed as a military ruler. South Africa's constitution fails to enable accountability of the executive to parliament, of individual members of parliaments to parliament itself, or of the overall political system to the voters. It also encourages elected representatives to neglect citizen opinions and provides few incentives for citizen participation between elections. These problems stem from the environment in which the constitution was designed: The constitution emerged from two decades of trying to find processes and institutional arrangements able to contain a looming violent conflagration by accommodating its political elite. But such arrangements are often antithetical to the requirements of a democratic system accountable and responsive to ordinary voters. Moreover, the country's constitutional designers assumed that people participate out of inherent interest or a sense of civic duty: The constitution and resulting legislation are filled with requirements for a range of mechanisms and forums of public participation, but few of them contain any incentive for people to do so.[53]

A third limitation on the quality of democracy in both countries, and particularly in Ghana, is the lack of resources for political institutions. While South Africa is relatively privileged in its ability to support infrastructure and good salaries for parliament and a wide range of watchdog agencies, unequal funding formulas put opposition parties at a significant disadvantage in both finances and skills. In Ghana, difficult economic circumstances, the absence of constitutional limits on presidential profligacy, and the lack of rational formulas for the funding of institutions leaves key democratic institutions chronically starved of resources, undermotivated, and susceptible to executive cooptation.

A fourth limitation on democratic quality is the "personalization" of politics. Given the youth of these democracies, it is not surprising that both countries' transitions have been highly dependent on personality. It is likely that Ghana's democracy would have progressed much further if Oxford-trained lawyer and patrician John Kufuor had been in power during the first eight years of Ghana's Fourth Republic instead of Jerry Rawlings, an ex-military dictator turned democrat who once assaulted his vice-president in full view of his ministers at a cabinet meeting. Conversely, it is unlikely that South Africa would have reached its first election or gone through such a successful first five years of democracy without the presence of Nelson Mandela. But just as Ghana's democratic progression has picked up speed under Kufuor, South Africa's has slowed under Thabo Mbeki. He has presided over the closing, rather than the opening, of avenues of pluralism and competition within the ANC. Moreover, Mbeki has in the face of one of the most extensive HIV infection rates in the world chosen to waste the considerable domestic and international symbolic authority of his office by questioning the link between HIV and AIDS.

Deepening the Quality of Democracy

Deepening the quality of democracy in Ghana and South Africa will require constitutional and economic reform, as well as changes in elite political culture and institutional skills and infrastructure. Sustained economic growth is needed to allow the state to provide an effective security net, meet basic socioeconomic needs, and create jobs. Governments and ruling parties need to cease their tolerance of corruption and patronage, while becoming more tolerant of dissidence and pluralism and developing more respect for other institutions of democratic government. Yet this advise is a counsel of perfection, as value structures change slowly and economic trends are notoriously unpredictable and difficult to control.

A more practical avenue to improve the quality of democracy appears to lie in constitutional and legal reform. But curbing neopatrimonialism, corruption, and the arrogance of power requires prodemocratic reforms based on a new set of assumptions: Rather than putting the emphasis on harnessing power to enable "good men" to govern in the public interest, reforms need to counteract the universal predisposition of elected and appointed leaders to use state power for their own narrow interests instead of for the public good. Rather than creating official mechanisms that allow motivated and dutiful citizens to participate, reforms need to provide incentives for interested voters to contact leaders or join action groups that attempt to influence legislative bodies at the national, regional, and local levels.

With this in mind, the quality of South African democracy could substantially increase if the electoral system were changed to include at least some element of constituency representation and direct election of a large proportion of parliamentarians. This would immediately create a significant number of national leaders directly accountable to identifiable sections of the electorate. It would also make the executive more accountable to the legislature, as such personal mandates would make members of parliament less vulnerable to internal party discipline and thus freer to question ministers and scrutinize legislation, budgets, and spending. They would also be freer to vote against the party whip on legislative bills opposed by constituents, which would enhance participation and responsiveness by giving citizens and groups an incentive to contact their representatives and lobby the legislature. In Ghana, the quality of democracy would substantially increase if constitutional changes reigned in the powers of the executive by limiting the numbers of cabinet and Supreme Court appointments the president can make, by narrowing the number of appointed offices, or by increasing the role of the legislature in the appointment process.

Constitutional reforms to limit the powers of executives and ruling parties are problematic, however, since it is the government and the ruling parties that ultimately need to make those reforms. Thus, deepening the quality of democracy requires democrats to focus on the institutional development of existing constitutional bodies, such as parliament and watchdog agencies. Institutional development would include such basic things as salaries: Well-paid members of parliament are more likely to resist side payments or executive inducements like offers of employment in better-paying executive positions. Institutional development would also include greater resources for parliament, key committees (such as Public Accounts), political parties, and other watchdogs (such as the Public Auditor). Resources should be targeted to enable these institutions to conduct research and budgetary and policy analysis, service constituents, and develop policy alternatives.

Again, however, increases in resources for these institutions are often dependent on the goodwill of the governments and finance ministries. Thus democrats need to seek out these assets from other sources, such as domestic civil society organizations and universities who can work with parliamentary committees, political parties, or public auditors to train officials or offer research and support. Democrats should also develop alliances with foreign donors who can provide scarce financial resources for salaries and institutional development. By taking advantage of their governments' desire for international respect and status, democrats can encourage both governments to continue increasing the quality of democracy in their countries.

NOTES

1. Mauritius and Botswana would be the other candidates.

2. Aili Piano and Arch Puddington, eds., *Freedom in the World 2004* (New York: Freedom House, 2004). Ratings are also available at *www.freedomhouse.org/research/freeword/2004/countryratings*.

3. Larry Diamond, "Introduction," in Larry Diamond and Marc F. Plattner, eds., *Democratization in Africa* (Baltimore: Johns Hopkins University Press, 1999), ix–xxvi.

4. Adrian Karatnycky, "The 2003 Freedom House Survey: National Income and Liberty," *Journal of Democracy* 15 (January 2004): 82–93.

5. *Bertelsmann Tranfromation Index 2003: Political Managagment in International Comparison* (Gütersloh, Germany: Bertelsmann Foundation, 2003).

6. 2002 Afrobarometer Survey, available at *www.afrobarometer.org*. These results *exclude* those who said that they "don't know" or did not understand the question. In the 1999 first round of Afrobarometer surveys, national research partners decided whether to use the English word "democracy," a slighly indigenized version of the word (for example, "edemocracy" in Xhosa), or a wholly indigenous translation. Botswana and Ghana were the only countries where national researchers decided that a wholly indigenous version would be better received. In the 2002 second round, however, it was decided that for the sake of consistency, the word "democracy" would always be put in English. This has resulted in only slightly higher levels of "don't know" in most countries, but far higher levels of Ghana and Botswana: In Ghana, 24 percent said they did not understand the question about how democratic their country is, and another 17 percent said they did not know; 36 percent said they did not know how satisfied they were with democracy.

7. Across 12 countries in Afrobarometer Round 1 (1999), popular perceptions of the extent of democracy in respondents' own countries were highly correlated with Freedom House ratings. The two major exceptions were South Africans, who were far more pessimistic than the experts, and Zambians, who were more optimistic. See Michael Bratton, Robert Mattes, and E. Gyimah-Boadi, *Public Opinion, Democracy and Market Reform in Africa* (Cambridge: Cambridge University Press, 2005).

8. See Michael Bratton, Robert Mattes, and E. Gyimah-Boadi, *Public Opinion, Democracy and Market Reform in Africa*.

9. See Eboe Hutchful, "Pulling Back from the Brink: Ghana's Experience" in Gavin Cawthra and Robin Luckham, eds., *Governing Insecurity: Democratic Control of Military and Security Establishments in New Democracies* (London: Zed, 2003), 78–101; and Baffour Agyeman-Duah, *Civil-Military Relations in Ghana's Fourth Republic* (Accra: Ghana Center for Democratic Development, 2002).

10. James L. Gibson and Amanda Gouws, "Support for the Rule of Law in the Emerging South African Democracy," *International Social Science Journal* 152 (June 1997).

11. According to the South African Institute of Race Relations, 5,539 people died between 1984 and 1989 as a result of political violence, and an additional 16,022 died during the transition years of 1990 to 1994. 2,255 died between 1995 and 1998. For yearly comparsions, 3,794 died in 1993, 325 in 1999, and just 57 in 2002. Cited in Pierre du Toit, *South Africa's Brittle Peace: The Problem of Post-Settlement Violence* (New York: Palgrave, 2001), 34; Pierre du Toit, *Affirmative Action and the Politics of Transfromation: A Survey of Public Opinion* (F.W. de Klerk Foundation, 2004), 5. In the six months preceding the 1994 election, 300 people died each month in KwaZulu-Natal; less than 300 died in the five-month period before the 1999 election. By 2004, the number of politically related deaths was minimal. See Jessica Piombo, "The Results of Election '04: Looking Back, Stepping Forward," in Lia Nijzink and Jessica Piombo, eds., *Electoral Politics in South Africa: Assessing the First Democratic Decade* (New York: Palgrave Macmillan, forthcoming).

12. Jessica Piombo, "The Results of Election '04."

13. Pierre du Toit, *South Africa's Brittle Peace*, 50.

14. David Bruce, "Suspect Crime Statistics Cannot Obscure Grim Truth," *Sunday Independent* (Johannesburg), 10 June 2001, 9; Michael Dynes, "South Africa's Huge Steps on Long Walk to Prosperity," *Sunday Independent*, 26 August 2001, 4; S. Pedrag, "Crime out of Control in South Africa," MSNBC News, 29 May 2000; *Economist*, 24 February 2001. A recent study by the South African Law Commisson indicates found that only one in twenty reported crimes are eventually successfully prosecuted.

15. Shirley Kemp, "South Africa's Crime Culprits," Moneyweb, 9 July 2003. Available at *http://ml.mnw.co.za*.

16. Bertelsmann Tranformation Index, "On the Way to Democracy and Market Economy—International Ranking of Transformation and Developing Countries: Questionnaire for Evaluation Development and Transformation Processes," n.d.

17. World Bank Institute, "Governance Research Indicator Country Snapshot." Available at *http://info.worldbank.org/governance*.

18. Pierre du Toit, *South Africa's Brittle Peace*, 66.

19. Jessica Piombo, "The Results of Election '04."

20. Jessica Piombo, "The Results of Election '04."

21. "Legislative and Policy Inertia?" Center for the Study of Democracy and Development, June 2003, 5. Available at *www.cddghana.org/documents/jun_03_vol4_No.2.pdf*.

22. Nicoli Nattrass, "Ethics, Economics and AIDS Policy in South Africa," Center for Social Science Research working paper, University of Cape Town, August 2001; Howard Barrell and Jaspreet Kandra, "Shocking Aids Report Leaked," *Weekly Mail & Guardian* (Johannesburg), 5–11 October 2001, 2. For a detailed review of Mbeki's statements on the disease, see Drew Forrest, "Behind the Smokescreen," *Weekly Mail & Guardian*, 26 October–1 November 2001, 25.

23. Sam Sole, "Politics of Patronage," *Weekly Mail & Guardian*, 8–14 October 2004, 4; and Rapula Tabane and Ferial Haffajee, "We've Got the Balls of Elephants," *Weekly Mail & Guardian*, 8–14 October 2004, 2.

24. Patrick Laurence, "Debate These Changes One at a Time," *Focus* 23 (September 2001): 13–15.

25. Daniel Kaufmann, Aart Kraay, and Massimo Mastruzzi, *Governance Matters III: Governance Indicators for 1996–2002* (Washington, D.C.: World Bank, 2004), 4.

26. Robert Mattes and Jessica Piombo, "Opposition Parties and the Voters in South Africa's 1999 General Election," *Democratization* 8 (Autumn 2001): 101–28.

27. Gavin Davis, "Media Coverage and the Election: Were Some Parties More Equal Than Others?" Center for Social Science Research working paper, University of Cape Town, June 2004.

28. Gavin Davis, "Media Coverage and the Elections," 13–18.

29. The avarage turnout of voting age population in countries in which the winning party wins over 60 percent of the vote is 56 percent. See Pippa Norris, *The Democratic Phoenix* (Oxford: Oxford University Press, 2003).

30. Cathi Albertyn, "Protecting Citizens Equality and Their Ability to Control Decision-Makers," in Paul Graham & Alice Coetzee, eds., *In the Balance: Debating the State of Democracy in South Africa* (Cape Town: IDASA, 2002), 54.

31. Gavin Davis, "Media Coverage and the Elections," 1–2, 9.

32. "South Africa" in *Freedom in the World 2004*; Gavin Davis, "Media Coverage and the Elections," 9.

33. Richard Sandbrook and Jay Oelbaum, *Reforming the Political Kingdom: Governance and Development in Ghana's Fourth Republic* (Accra: CDD-Ghana, 1999); Staffan Lindberg, "'It Is Our Time Chop:' Do Elections Feed Neo-Patrimonilasm Rather Than Counteract It?" *Democratization* 1 (Summer 2003): 121–140.

34. Adam Habib and Collette Schultz-Herzenberg, "Servants of the People: Accountability and Democracy; Is the Ruling Elite Responsive to the Citizenry?" in Richard Calland and Paul Graham, eds., *Democracy in the Time of Mbeki: IDASA's Democracy Index* (Cape Town: IDASA, 2005), 167–188.

35. Cited in Tom Lodge, "Romantic Aspiration," *Weekly Mail & Guardian,* 10–16 August 2001, 17.

36. IDASA Political Information and Monitoring Service, "Local Government Floor Crossing, 2004," *ePoliticsSA,* 31 August 2004.

37. Richard Calland, ed., *The First Five Years: A Review of South Africa's Democratic Parliament* (Cape Town: IDASA, 1999), 36.

38. Lia Nijzink and Jessica Piombo, "The Institutions of Representative Democracy," Center for Social Science Research working paper, University of Cape Town, November 2004.

39. Sam Sole, "Politics of Patronage," *Weekly Mail & Guardian*, 8–14 October 2004, 4.

40. Daniel Kaufmann, Aart Kraay, and Massimo Mastruzzi, *Governance Matters III,* 3.

41. Public Opinion Service (South Africa), "Public Opinion and the New Constitution," POS Reports 4, March 1996.

42. Afrobarometer Network, "Afrobarometer Round 2: Compendium of Comparative Results from a 15 Country Survey," Afrobarometer working paper, 2004, 40.

43. James Gibson and Amanda Gouws, *Overcomoming Intolerance in South Africa* (Cambridge: Cambridge University Press, 2003).

44. The South African constitution, Chapter 2, Section 9.2 says that "to promote the achievement of equality, legislative and other measures designed to protect or advance persons, or categories of persons, disadvantaged by unfair discrimination may be taken." Sections 9.3 and 9.4 bar "unfair discrimination" on the basis of race, gender, sec, pregnancy, marital status, ethnic or social origin, colour, sexual orientation, age, disability, religion, conscience, belief, cultural, language or birth." But 9.5 notes, "Discrimination on one or more of the grounds listed in subsection (3) is unfair unless it is established that the discrimination is fair."

45. "South Africa" in *Freedom in the World 2004.*

46. Reg Rumney, "A Question of Perceptions," *Weekly Mail & Guardian,* 3–9

August 2001, 15; Howard Barrell, "Back to the Future: Renaissance and South African Domestic Policy," *African Security Review* 9 (2000): 87; "Housing: A Good News Story," *RDP Monitor* (May 2001), 2; "Electricity: Seeing Clearly Now," *RDP Monitor* 6/7 (July 2000), 2; Josey Ballenger, "Troubled School Feeding Plan Is Still Essential," *Reconstruct* 11 (October 1998): 1; and Judith February, "Political Debates Lack Substance," Business Day, 5 April 2004, 7.

47. John Daniel, "Discussion Paper on Socio-Economic Issues," presented at a seminar entitled "South Africa: Future of Democratization" organized by the U.S. Department of State's Bureau of Intelligence and Research, Washington, D.C., 5 April 2001; Jonathan Katzenellenbogen, "Jobless Figures Remain Over 25%," *Business Day* (Johannesburg), 27 January 2001, 3.

48. Andrew Whiteford and Dirk Van Deventer, *Winners and Losers: South Africa's Changing Income Distribution In the 1990s* (Johannesburg: WEFA, 1999), 11–19; Debbie Budlender, "Earnings Inequality in South Africa, 1995–1998," in *Measuring Poverty In South Africa* (Pretoria: Statistics South Africa, 2000), available at *www.statssa.gov.za*.

49. Andrew Whiteford and Dirk Van Deventer, *Winners and Losers*, 25–26; Jeremy Seekings, "Inequality, Mobility and Politics in South Africa," paper presented to the World Congress of the International Political Science Association, Durban, South Africa, 30 June 2003; and Jeremy Seekings and Nicoli Nattrass, "The Post-Apartheid Distributional Regime," Centre for Social Science working paper, University of Cape Town, 2004.

50. Andrew Whiteford and Dirk Van Deventer, *Winners and Losers*, 11–19; Debbie Budlender, "Earnings Inequality in South Africa, 1995–1998."

51. Murray Leibbrandt, Laura Poswell, Pranushka Naidoo, Matthew Welch, and Ingrid Woolard, "Measruing Recent Changes in South African Inequality and Poverty Using 1996 and 2001 Census Data," Centre for Social Science working paper, University of Cape Town, 2004.

52. "Ghana" in *Freedom In the World 2004*.

53. Cathi Albertyn, "Protecting Citizens Equality and Their Ability to Control Decision-Makers," in Paul Graham and Alice Coetzee, eds., *In the Balance: Debating the State of Democracy in South Africa*, 53.

INDEX